Credit Repair Kit For Dummies®

Cheat Sheet

The Big Three Credit Bureaus

✓ **Equifax,** P.O. Box 740241, Atlanta, GA 30374; phone 800-685-1

✓ **Experian,** P.O. Box 2104, Allen, TX 75013-2104; phone 888-397-3

✓ **TransUnion,** TransUnion Consumer Solutions, P.O. Box 2000, C
800-888-4213; Web site www.transunion.com

How to Handle an Overdue Mortgage

When your mortgage is late, you need to take immediate action. What follows is my list of essential advice:

✓ **Call your lender or servicer immediately if you're going to be late**. The worst thing you can do is nothing. More programs are available to help today than ever before.

✓ **Contact a HUD-certified counseling agency for more options.** (Go to www.hud.gov or call Project HOPE at 888-995-HOPE). A HUD-certified counselor can advise you on options and refer you to local resources that you may not know about.

✓ **Don't allow your mortgage to become 90 days past due.** Partial payments may not be accepted after 90 days. After you're late, your grace period disappears, so a foreclosure action may be two weeks closer than you think.

✓ **Beware of companies who contact you to offer help.** Some companies will try to take advantage of your problem by charging high fees for themselves.

✓ **Find out your alternatives to foreclosure.** Find options at www.ftc.gov/bcp/edu/pubs/consumer/homes/rea04.shtm.

If your mortgage is in jeopardy, contact someone for help fast. The earlier you act, the more options you'll have. The Mortgage Forgiveness Debt Relief Act of 2007 has conditions, and not everyone is eligible. See the CD for details.

Questions to Ask a Credit Counselor

Finding a good credit counselor is all a matter of knowing which questions to ask. Here's a list of the most important ones:

✓ **Is your organization not-for-profit?** You definitely don't want an agency that's *not* nonprofit. But that said, some nonprofits are shams.

✓ **Are your agency and counselors certified? Who provides the certification?** Both the Council on Accreditation (COA) and the International Standards Organization (ISO) accredit nonprofit credit-counseling agencies. The National Foundation for Credit Counseling (NFCC) and the Institute for Personal Finance (part of the Association for Financial Counseling and Planning Education [AFCPE]) certify credit counselors.

continued

For Dummies: Bestselling Book Series for Beginners

Credit Repair Kit For Dummies®

Questions to Ask a Credit Counselor (continued)

- **What fees will I be charged?** Do not, under any circumstances, work with an agency that charges a large upfront fee. The best agencies will work with you for free. If the agency recommends a debt-management plan, you may pay a low monthly fee (no more than $50 to $75 per month), and the agency may charge a one-time setup fee (which should not exceed $75 to $100).

- **How long will the counseling take?** Anything less than 30 to 45 minutes will just deal with surface issues and won't help you to set new goals, understand how you got into debt in the first place, or figure out how to stay out of debt in the future.

- **What lifestyle changes will I need to make to be successful?** To be successful in getting out of debt, you'll probably have to make changes in your spending habits. The agency should help you learn to budget, set financial goals, and begin a savings program.

Quick Tips for a Better Credit Score

Building good credit takes time. Follow these tips to get a great credit score the first time around or, if you've made some mistakes in the past, to recover in the shortest time possible.

- **Review your free credit report every year.** You can get it for free!

- **Keep balances below 50 percent of your credit limits.** This is the second biggest factor affecting your score. High balances mean high risk and maybe higher interest rates for you.

- **Dispute any errors or out-of-date information.** Up to 25 percent of credit reports have errors; yours may too. Disputing negative errors can boost your score.

- **Pay your bills on time.** The largest part of your credit score is based on your payment history. Get a system in place that suits your style to make sure you don't forget any due dates.

- **Keep your accounts open longer.** Length of credit history is another important factor. Don't close your older accounts if possible. Add new accounts if you like, but don't automatically close your older ones when you do. Doing so can cause you to lose points for having new inquiries, adding new credit, and having a shorter history.

- **New credit can lower your score.** In the short run, the combination of more available credit and more inquiries on your account can increase your risk profile and lower your score. This is most sensitive for those without a long credit history. The bottom line is that you should only add new credit when it makes sense, not just to have another card or to get an incentive gift.

- **Use more than one type of credit.** To show you can manage credit cards, retail accounts, installment loans, and other types of credit, make sure you open a variety of accounts.

- **Accurate negative information stays on your credit report for seven to ten years.** However, it counts for less every time you add positive information to your report. Most credit scores look heavily at the last two years of history, not all seven.

- **Secured cards can help establish or reestablish credit.** These cards are backed by your savings and build a positive payment history with the bureaus. A positive payment history improves your score.

- **Cosigning for anyone is dangerous to your credit score.** If they default, you may not know about it for months. You will not only be responsible for the debt, but your credit score will suffer as well.

For Dummies: Bestselling Book Series for Beginners

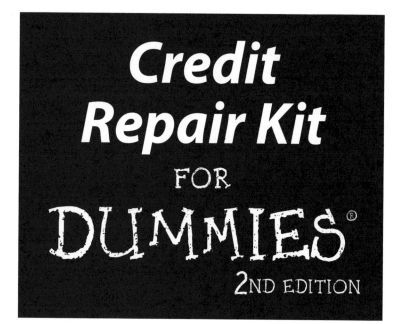

Credit Repair Kit

FOR

DUMMIES®

2ND EDITION

by Steve Bucci

President of the MMI Financial Education Foundation

WILEY

Wiley Publishing, Inc.

Credit Repair Kit For Dummies®, 2nd Edition

Published by
Wiley Publishing, Inc.
111 River St.
Hoboken, NJ 07030-5774
www.wiley.com

Copyright © 2008 by Wiley Publishing, Inc., Indianapolis, Indiana

Published by Wiley Publishing, Inc., Indianapolis, Indiana

Published simultaneously in Canada

For general information on our other products and services, please contact our Customer Care Department within the U.S. at 800-762-2974, outside the U.S. at 317-572-3993, or fax 317-572-4002.

For technical support, please visit www.wiley.com/techsupport.

Wiley also publishes its books in a variety of electronic formats. Some content that appears in print may not be available in electronic books.

Library of Congress Control Number: 2008930528

ISBN: 978-0-470-27673-0

Manufactured in the United States of America

10 9 8 7 6 5 4 3 2

WILEY

About the Author

Steve Bucci is president of the Houston, Texas–based Money Management International Financial Education Foundation, a nonprofit organization that operates to educate the general public on sound personal financial skills and money-management principles by partnering with national organizations that develop, deliver, and support programs that teach those skills and principles. The organization also sponsors research projects on personal financial issues of national importance.

Steve writes a popular weekly column as the Debt Advisor for the financial megasite Bankrate.com. His column is featured frequently on America Online, Yahoo! Personal Finance, and other Web sites. The Scripps-Howard newspaper syndicate distributes his column nationally. He is a regular contributor to the Comcast Cable program *Your Morning Show.*

Steve was formerly president of Consumer Credit Counseling Service of Southern New England, and he founded the Consumer Credit Counseling Service of Rhode Island and the University of Rhode Island Center for Personal Financial Education.

He began his career in counseling at the Yale Psychiatric Institute before switching to management consulting and then developing both publicly- and privately-offered investment products in the insurance and financial-services industries. Steve returned to helping individuals in 1991, this time using his financial and management experience when he launched Rhode Island's first private, nonprofit, financial counseling agency.

Steve has served as director of the CDNE Education Foundation, the National Foundation for Credit Counseling, and the Better Business Bureau of Rhode Island, National Network Non-Profit Services. He was named Visiting Executive in Residence at the University of Rhode Island and is a member of the Jump$tart Coalition for Financial Literacy and the American Savings and Education Council. Steve graduated from East Providence Senior High School and the University of Rhode Island at Kingston, where he received his BA and MA degrees. He and his wife, Barbara, live with their two cats, Pea-head and Stinky, at Sand Hill Cove in the seaside community of Narragansett, Rhode Island.

Dedication

This book is dedicated to my widely dispersed family: my wife and friend, Barbara; my brother Jim and his wife Betty who live in Florida (this year); my sons, Geoff, who lives in San Diego, and Steve and his wife Grace, who live in Washington, D.C.; and my mom who stays home. I also want to dedicate at least a part of this book to the memory of Big Al (also known as Alexander the Great) who passed away to kitty heaven suddenly — with his boots on, as they say — while chasing a mouse across a frozen pond.

Author's Acknowledgments

I want to thank John Wiley and Sons for asking me to update this book — not only because so much has changed in the last two years, but also because it represents a vindication of sorts of a holistic approach to repairing credit. This method relies on addressing the root causes of your credit problems as a way of building a sound financial base, improved credit, and a better life for you and your family. No successful person I know of works alone. Certainly, in my case, I received the support, help, and encouragement of a large number of colleagues.

My thanks to them all, and my particular thanks to Ivan Hand of Money Management International, who continues to support my balancing my work at the MMI Foundation with projects like this book; Susan and Ken at Ken Scott Communications, who helped me with updates and offered valuable insights and advice; Patricia LaSalle, a remarkable intern from the University of Rhode Island who balances work, family, and school and still found the time to work with me on the CD content; Helen Iasimone who helped me understand foreclosure options while saving uncounted families from losing their homes; Jim Triggs for his bankruptcy expertise; Ron Ramos who provides invaluable perspective when I lose mine; my credit reporting and scoring gurus Craig Watts at Fair Isaac and Rod Griffin at Experian; Jessica Faust, my agent; and my editors at John Wiley & Sons, especially Chad Sievers, Tracy Boggier, and Christy Pingleton.

Publisher's Acknowledgments

We're proud of this book; please send us your comments through our Dummies online registration form located at www.dummies.com/register/.

Some of the people who helped bring this book to market include the following:

Acquisitions, Editorial, and Media Development

Project Editor: Chad R. Sievers
  (Previous Edition: Elizabeth Kuball)

Acquisitions Editor: Tracy Boggier

Copy Editor: Christy Pingleton

Editorial Program Coordinator: Erin Calligan Mooney

Technical Editor: Shashin M. Shah, CFA, CFP

Media Development Producer: Jenny Swisher

Editorial Manager: Michelle Hacker

Editorial Assistants: Joe Niesen, Jennette ElNaggar

Cover Photos: © Steven Puetzer/Getty Images

Cartoons: Rich Tennant
  (www.the5thwave.com)

Composition Services

Project Coordinator: Erin Smith

Layout and Graphics: Carrie A. Cesavice, Reuben W. Davis, Nikki Gately, Melissa K. Jester, Christine Williams

Proofreader: Nancy L. Reinhardt

Indexer: Potomac Indexing, LLC

Publishing and Editorial for Consumer Dummies

  Diane Graves Steele, Vice President and Publisher, Consumer Dummies

  Joyce Pepple, Acquisitions Director, Consumer Dummies

  Kristin A. Cocks, Product Development Director, Consumer Dummies

  Michael Spring, Vice President and Publisher, Travel

  Kelly Regan, Editorial Director, Travel

Publishing for Technology Dummies

  Andy Cummings, Vice President and Publisher, Dummies Technology/General User

Composition Services

  Gerry Fahey, Vice President of Production Services

  Debbie Stailey, Director of Composition Services

Contents at a Glance

Table of Contents

Part II: Navigating with Your Own Credit GPS............ 83

Chapter 5: Getting a Copy of Your Credit Road Map 85

Chapter 6: Understanding the Parts of Your Credit Report. 95

Part III: Houston, We Have A Problem: Doing Damage Control 113

Chapter 7: Sprucing Up Your Credit Report. 115

Foreword

All the warnings in the previous edition of this helpful book have become today's reality. The credit crisis is upon us — making this updated version of *Credit Repair Kit For Dummies* more useful and necessary than ever before.

Consumer bankruptcy filings are soaring. Home foreclosures are creating statistics not seen since the Depression. The housing "piggy bank" has cracked, limiting consumers' ability to refinance and use the cash to pay off debt. Credit card balances are overwhelming many households, as finance charges and late fees pile up.

The mountain of debt that so many Americans have built for themselves is now crashing down upon them. People of all ages and income levels are impacted — from seniors trying to pay medical bills and manage rising food costs to college graduates dealing with unprecedented credit card debt and student loans. Millions of families are unexpectedly faced with higher monthly mortgage payments or the prospect of losing their homes, mostly because they didn't understand the consequences of credit decisions they made in haste or out of ignorance — oftentimes decisions that were made years ago.

But the situation is far from hopeless. The fact that you have picked up this book is a very good start.

America is a country that believes in second chances. We don't have debtors' prisons. On the other hand, we can't expect the government to use our tax dollars to bail us out of our personal financial problems. So it's up to *you* to get organized to deal with your debt — and start a new, better organized, and more positive financial life.

Credit Repair Kit For Dummies, 2nd Edition, recognizes that now you need more than a basic understanding of how credit works. Those chapters dealing with the basics make this book a great gift for someone starting out in real life. But today you also need to know how to deal with creditors, how to stave off a foreclosure, how to make decisions about bankruptcy under the new laws, and how to avoid the tempting but fraudulent offers to fix your credit problems.

All that and more is covered in this newly updated version. As we've all learned, personal finances are now very public. Your money decisions can make you a statistic — either one of those who see their financial lives crumble, or, hopefully, one of the many success stories upon which our country is built. It's up to you to make smart, well-informed choices to set you on the path — or bring you back to the road — toward financial success.

It's so easy to get off to a bad start. Few schools teach kids about money. Their first lessons come from sitting in a car seat and watching Mom put a card into a machine in the bank's drive-thru. Money doesn't grow on trees anymore; it comes out of ATMs! By the time teens are ready for college, they're handed credit card applications along with their books and the school sweatshirt.

In my years as a nationally syndicated personal finance columnist for the _Chicago Sun-Times,_ I've heard so many sad stories about lives ruined by debt. It's like quicksand — easy to walk into and very tough to pull yourself out of. And if you aren't careful, you could fall into an even worse trap: unscrupulous "fix-it" companies that actually make your situation even worse.

That's why I'm delighted you've picked up this book. Written by a pro in language you can understand, it will give you honest answers to all your credit questions. Whether you're just starting out in life or feeling overwhelmed by financial problems, this is the resource that will guide you to the correct answers.

Steve Bucci is currently the president of the Money Management International Financial Education Foundation, www.mmifoundation.org, which provides funds and materials for essential money management education. In addition, he is helping to build one of the nation's largest credit counseling services, Money Management International (MMI). MMI is not only accredited by the Council on Accreditation, but is also a member of both the Association of Independent Consumer Credit Counseling Agencies and the National Foundation for Consumer Credit — the umbrella associations for credit counseling nationwide. In addition, all of their counselors are certified — and trained to help you find the best way out of debt.

But isn't it better to avoid credit problems in the first place? That's why this book should be must reading for everyone — from high school students and their parents, to senior citizens. After all, as Benjamin Franklin said in _Poor Richard's Almanac:_ "Creditors have better memories than debtors."

If you don't use credit wisely, your creditors and the collectors they assign to your case will make your life miserable. But if you understand and manage your credit well, you have started down the road to financial success.

Terry Savage

Nationally Syndicated _Chicago Sun-Times_ Columnist

Author of: _The Savage Truth on Money_ and _The Savage Number: How Much Money Do You Need to Retire?_ (both published by Wiley)

Introduction

Since the first edition of this book came out around two years ago, the credit world has been turned upside down. The subprime mortgage crisis and credit meltdown almost overnight moved credit from extremely loose to as tight as my belt after a two-week cruise. The value of the dollar has dropped to new lows, making everything from gas to imports to foods more expensive. You may have faced this increase in prices along with a credit crunch and discovered the real value of an emergency savings account in making ends meet. At the same time, you've probably discovered that you can't count on the equity in your home as savings.

You may have found that filing for Chapter 7 bankruptcy has become much harder. For those of you forced into Chapter 13, the result has been a very unpleasant three- to five-year budget crunch as the reality of living under tight spending constraints has become apparent.

Millions of you have had personal data stolen. I believe you haven't seen the full size of this problem yet. Theft of personal information remains high, but actual use of the stolen data remains low. How long this inconsistency will remain is anyone's guess. However, you need to be prepared to protect your identity and to quickly stop any damage that identity thieves may impose.

A major event for those of you new to credit is that you're now a major expansion market for credit-related products. Whether just new to credit or new to the United States, you're one of nearly 40 million customers being under-served. In others words, you aren't buying or using enough credit products as far as the financial services industry is concerned. Today, the focus on marketing to you is growing, and you need more information to make sense of it all.

Credit Repair Kit For Dummies, 2nd Edition, comes at a critical time. Credit continues to play an ever-changing role in your life, whether you use a credit card or not. Insurance, employment, entertainment, home buying or renting, getting an education with college loans, and more are more dependent than ever on you having good credit. The reward for good credit has never been higher. The penalties for bad credit, often unseen or even unrecognized, have never been greater. No wonder you and so many others are looking for up-to-date, useful, and proven answers from a trusted and known resource. And you need not look any further than this book.

About This Book

I am pleased to be able to continue to serve as your guide. In the last two decades, I've helped and advised thousands of shell-shocked credit refugees, and I've received feedback from readers of my popular Internet column that appears in newspapers all over the country. I've helped individuals and families work through all aspects of financial challenges, from creating a household budget for the first time to negotiating the complexities of bankruptcy.

In *Credit Repair Kit For Dummies,* 2nd Edition, I share what I've learned so you can get things right the first time or, if it's too late for that, get back on track as soon as possible. The advice in this book is for *anyone* seeking easy-to-understand, no-nonsense, straightforward advice about repairing credit. But I don't limit my focus to turning around a less-than-stellar credit report. I pack the pages with plenty of powerful action plans for what is even better than repairing credit . . . *avoiding* bad credit.

So, why this book?

- ✔ Because while so much has changed, the basis for successful credit has remained the same — and I give you all the tools and insight you need to build, rebuild, and maintain great credit.

- ✔ Because you may be drowning in collection calls and notices — and this book reveals your rights to fend off the callers.

- ✔ Because you may need the advice of an experienced advisor to guide you through your debt situation — and this book tells you how to find a good credit, HUD, or bankruptcy counseling agency.

- ✔ Because one in four of you may have inaccurate data in your credit record — and this book offers tips on cleaning up your credit report.

- ✔ Because you may be one of the millions of people who just last year were victims of personal data theft — and this book provides valuable information to protect your identity.

- ✔ Because you may be on the brink of credit trouble — and this book gives you budgeting and spending advice that can pull you back from the edge.

- ✔ Because you may be in serious credit despair — and this book offers you solid and level-headed advice about your options, including bankruptcy.

- ✔ Because the time is right for you to make a difference in your credit and your financial peace of mind — and this book helps you do just that.

Conventions Used in This Book

To make this book as simple to follow and as convenient as possible, I use the following conventions throughout:

- ✔ All Web addresses and e-mail addresses appear in `monofont`.
- ✔ I use **bold** for all keywords in bulleted lists and for steps in numbered lists.
- ✔ New terms appear in *italics* and are closely followed by easy-to-understand definitions.

What You're Not to Read

Although I hope you read every word I've written, I understand your life is busy and you want to read only the need-to-know info. You can safely skip the sidebars, which are shaded gray boxes containing text. These provide supporting or entertaining information that isn't critical to your understanding of the topic. You can also skip anything marked by a Technical Stuff icon.

Foolish Assumptions

I assume that you're reading this book because you or someone you care about is at a point in life where credit is important. This doesn't mean that anyone's credit must be out of control to benefit from this book. You may just be wise enough to know that up-to-date knowledge can ensure healthy credit. An understanding of your credit and how the credit system works may be especially important during certain life situations. I assume that this book is of value to you if you're

- ✔ Concerned about your ability to buy, sell, or remain in your home
- ✔ Establishing credit for the first time
- ✔ Considering a bankruptcy
- ✔ Already in or will soon be in a marriage or partnership
- ✔ Recently divorced or soon will be
- ✔ Saddled with a student loan
- ✔ Hunting for a job
- ✔ Concerned that your personal info has been compromised or stolen
- ✔ Dealing with medical issues and bills
- ✔ Coping with the loss of a spouse or life partner
- ✔ Wanting to know more about maintaining good credit
- ✔ Concerned about the credit status of a loved one

I assume that you don't have a formal education in credit or personal finance. If you do, however, I believe you can still find practical insights in this book based on my experience and that of others whom I've helped.

How This Book Is Organized

This book is divided into five major parts with numerous chapters. At your fingertips is everything you need to get your credit back on the right track with simple, easy-to-understand tips and action steps.

Part 1: You Can't Fix Something You Don't Understand: A Credit Owner's Manual

In this part, I give you the lowdown on what's really important about your personal credit, and I explain how your credit behavior is reported to the credit bureaus. I give you valuable info about your credit reports and credit scores so that you'll have a first-rate understanding of how the great American credit machine works. Lastly, I help you decide whether getting outside help is smart and, if so, how to find the very best at the lowest cost.

Part II: Navigating with Your Own Credit GPS

I have a GPS in my car and I wouldn't take a trip anywhere unfamiliar without it. Part II is your GPS for navigating credit. You know where you want to go, but you also need to know where you're starting from. Your credit report and your credit score can give you critical information to establish where you are and what road you need to take to get where you want to go.

Part III: Houston, We Have a Problem: Doing Damage Control

Millions of Americans are facing mortgage problems that were unthinkable two years ago when the first edition of this book came out. In this part, I detail options and solutions to foreclosure problems as well as the less dramatic, but still traumatic, debts that lead to bad credit and more debt problems. If you have damaged credit, you have damaged debts. You've come to the right part to get on top of both. And solving both is the only way to solve either one. The chapters in this part are dedicated to helping you permanently improve your credit as quickly as possible.

Part IV: Transforming Your Credit from Bad to Beautiful

This part is for all of you who ever wished you had a personal trainer to help you build fabulous credit and get your finances under control once and for all. Here I provide you with the underlying principles to build a plan that can get you to your financial goals. I also give you proven techniques to build strong credit, control your flabby finances, and avoid the agony of identity theft. I show you how to spend with confidence, stay within your means, and save for emergencies. I prepare you to deal with the many financial hurdles you may find along the marathon course of life, including marriage, divorce, unemployment, and more.

Part V: The Part of Tens

If you like pithy information and you want to improve your credit, this part is for you. I offer succinct information to help you avoid identity theft and keep your home out of foreclosure or minimize the damage if it comes to that. I also include ten ways to make your credit strong. **Bonus:** Check out the accompanying CD for ten tips on how to handle financial emergencies.

Appendixes

In Appendix A, I compile a list of commonly used terms that are helpful in your daily use of credit. Even though I define these terms in the text where they first appear, this is a place where you can look up a term that has you stumped. In Appendix B, I fill you in on the CD-ROM that comes with this book, letting you know what you can find there and how to access the info.

Icons Used in This Book

Icons are those little pictures you see sprinkled in the margins throughout this book. Here's what they mean:

The CD that comes with this book is jam-packed with all kinds of useful information that I reference throughout the chapters ahead. Whenever I mention a useful tool available on the CD, I use this icon.

Whether you're new to this country or just new to credit, this symbol alerts you to important concepts and actions that are vital to properly establishing credit.

This icon denotes critical information that you really need to take away with you. Considering the state of my own overcrowded memory, I wouldn't ask you to remember anything unless it was really important.

This image of a credit professional — okay, fine, of a Dummies Man — shows up whenever I go into more detail on a concept or rule. If you don't care about the details of how something works or where it came from, feel free to skip these gems.

This bull's-eye lets you know that you're reading on-target advice, often little-known insights or recommendations that I've picked up over the years.

This icon serves as a warning — telling you to avoid something that's potentially harmful. Take heed!

Where to Go from Here

You get to choose what happens next. This book is packed with information to help you at whatever state or stage your credit is in. You can go directly to the topics of most interest to you, or you can start at the beginning and take it from there. With the information in *Credit Repair Kit For Dummies,* 2nd Edition, I'm confident you can get on top of your credit, clean up your credit report, and stay on a positive path. I wish you all the best in achieving your life dreams, which increasingly require a good credit history to realize. You deserve it.

Finally, I want to again extend my invitation for you to contact me with any questions or concerns you may have. Please keep your questions as short and concise as possible. I'll be glad to make specific recommendations or forward your issues or concerns to appropriate resources if I can't help. You can e-mail me at CreditRepairForDummies@moneymanagement.org or you may write me at:

Steve Bucci, President
Money Management International Financial Education Foundation
9009 West Loop South, Suite 700
Houston, TX 77096-1719
Attention: *Credit Repair Kit For Dummies*

Part I

You Can't Fix Something You Don't Understand: A Credit Owner's Manual

The 5th Wave   By Rich Tennant

"I'd lend you advice on how to manage your money if you had a better credit score."

In this part . . .

I begin at the beginning — I tell you in straightforward terms what credit is and how it's becoming more important in many areas of everyday life. I help you to see yourself as lenders, insurers, and employers see you, through the looking glass of credit reports and credit scores.

I explain how to establish credit the right way for those new to credit or new to America. For those with existing credit files, I give details on reporting and scoring so you know the true score and what you can and can't do to improve your credit. Solutions to problems with mortgages, credit counselors, credit bureaus, and more are demystified so you can clearly see what options are in your best interest. In this part, you discover how you can improve your credit report for maximum benefit to you, and I include details on what you can do to get the very best credit score.

Chapter 1

The Lowdown on Credit Essentials: Just What You Need to Know

In This Chapter

▶ Seeing yourself as lenders see you

▶ Understanding credit reports and credit scores

▶ Establishing credit for the first time

▶ Handling mortgage problems

▶ Living happily ever after

*W*hatever did people do before there was credit? In the olden days, it was much more difficult for the average person to buy the goods and services that are taken for granted today — things like a car, a home, and a college education, to name a few. Imagine if first-time home-buyers had to save $267,000 (the national average for the cost of a new home in 2008, according to the Federal Housing Finance Board) before taking ownership and stepping over the threshold. If that were the case, they'd likely be using walkers to enter their new abodes.

Credit is a powerful tool. It can be used to move mountains. Unfortunately, it can also bury you beneath one if you use it improperly. Credit doesn't come with an instruction manual or a warning label. The subject generally isn't well-taught in schools or, for that matter, in the family, either. So where do you get an understanding of this genie in a bottle before you make your three wishes? You're holding the answer in your hands.

For nearly two decades I've been helping people just like you recover from the aftereffects of credit gone bad. The best of my experience is contained within the pages of this book. I firmly believe that if you know the rules of the credit game, you stand a much better chance of getting a good score. We all make mistakes, and this applies to credit use as much as anything else. The important thing is to know how to recover from your mistakes without compounding the damage.

I start with the basics so you can better understand the principles and concepts behind credit. Consider this chapter your jumping-off point to this book and to the world of credit. My goal is to make your credit the best it can be and keep it that way. Not just for the sake of having good credit, but so you can live the American dream of having a decent job, a place to call home, and whatever else you desire for yourself and those you love.

Defining Credit: Spending Tomorrow's Money Today

Credit has its origins in the Latin word *credo,* which means, "I believe." The real underlying issues of credit are: Do you do what you promise? Are you believable and trustworthy? Have you worked hard to have a good reputation? Little is more precious to a person than being believed — and that's what credit is all about.

You (and Webster's) can also define credit as:

✔ Recognition given for some action or quality; a source of pride or honor; trustworthiness; credibility

✔ Permission for a customer to have goods or services that will be paid for at a later date

✔ The reputation of a person or firm for paying bills or other financial obligations

The concept of credit is simple: You receive something *now* in return for your promise to pay for it *later.* Credit doesn't increase your income. It allows you to conveniently spend money that you've already saved — or to spend the money today that you know you'll earn tomorrow.

Because businesses make money when you use credit, they encourage you to use it as often as possible. In order for creditors to make as much money as possible, they want you to spend as much as you can, as fast as you can. Helping you to spend your future earnings today is their basic plan. This plan may make them very happy — but it may not do the same for you.

Many types of credit are available to consumers today, which is no surprise to you. I suspect you receive as many offers for various types of credit cards and lines of credit as I do. But despite the endless variations and terms that seem to exist, most credit can be classified as one of two major types:

- ✔ **Secured credit:** As the name implies, *security* is involved — that is, the lender has some protection if you default on the loan. Your secured loan is backed by property, not just your word. House mortgages and car loans fall in this category. Generally, the interest rates for secured credit are lower and the *term* (the length of time before you have to pay it all off) may be longer because the risk of loss is lessened by the lender's ability to take whatever you put up for security.

- ✔ **Unsecured credit:** This type of credit is usually more expensive, shorter-term, and considered a higher risk by the lender. Because it is backed by your promise to repay it — but not by an asset — lenders are more vulnerable if you default. Credit cards fall into this category.

Chances are, you've always looked at credit from your own perspective — the viewpoint of the *borrower.* From where you're standing, you may be the customer who should be catered to. Consumer spending is two-thirds of the U.S economy, and much of that is generated by using lines of credit or credit cards. Whether you use credit as a convenience or because you need to spread out your payments, you keep the economy humming and people employed. Right? From the lender's perspective, however, you represent a risk. Yes, your business is sought after, but the lender takes a chance by giving you something now for a promise to pay later. If you fail to keep your promise, the lender loses.

The degree of doubt between the lender making money and losing money dictates the terms of the credit. But how does a lender gauge the likelihood of your paying on time and as promised? The lender needs to know three things about you to gauge the risk you represent:

- ✔ **Your character:** Do you do what you promise? Are you reliable and honest?

- ✔ **Your capacity:** How much debt can you handle given your income and other obligations?

- ✔ **Your collateral:** What cash or property could be used to repay the debt if your income dries up?

But where can this information be had — especially if the lender doesn't know your sterling attributes firsthand? The answer: your credit report and, increasingly, your credit score. That's why, before you open up that line of credit that allows you to buy the new dining room suite on a 90-day-same-as-cash special, you have to fill out and sign some paperwork and wait a few minutes for your credit to check out.

Sometimes, however, an unscrupulous creditor may try to take advantage of you and charge you more than the market price for the credit you want. Why? Because they like to make money. So, how do *you* know if you're being overcharged? The same way the lenders decide whether to offer you credit and what to charge you for it: by knowing what's in your credit report and your credit score.

Meeting the Cast of Characters in the Credit Story

Before I delve into the saga of credit and all its complicated plot twists, allow me to introduce the characters. In most lending transactions, three players have lead roles: the buyer (that's you), the lender, and the credit reporter.

The buyer: I want that now!

The cycle of credit begins with the buyer — a person who wants something (that's you!). A house, a car, a plasma TV . . . it doesn't matter what it is that you want. The definitive factor is that paying for it upfront is either inconvenient or impossible. Maybe you just don't have the cash with you and you want the item now, perhaps because it's on sale. Or maybe you haven't even earned the money to pay for the purchase, but you know you will and you don't want to pass up the chance.

"Hmm," you calculate as you gaze longingly at the coveted find. "I really want to get this now. If I wait until I have the money, it might be sold or the price might have gone up, so it only makes sense to buy it now." Or, if you're generous (or making excuses), you might say, "My sweetie would love this — and *me* — if I bought this. Who cares that I don't have the money right now? I will someday. I just know it."

Enter creditors, stage right.

The creditors: Heroes to the rescue

The creditor spots your desire a mile away, and it stirs the compassionate capitalist within him. "Hey," says the person with the power to extend you credit, "no need for you to do without. We have financing. We just need to take down a little information, do a quick credit check, and you can walk out the door with this thing you're lusting for."

If businesses can't sell you something or lend you money, they can't make a profit. So believe it or not, they really do want to loan you money. But there's that risk factor: They need to find out how risky a proposition you may be. In order to get the rundown on your credit risk, they call the credit bureau.

Enter credit bureau, stage left.

The credit bureaus: In a supporting role

The merchant most likely contacts one of three major credit-reporting bureaus — Equifax, Experian, or TransUnion — to get the credit lowdown on you. The credit bureaus make the current lending system work by providing fast, reliable, and inexpensive information about you to lenders and others.

The information in your credit report is reported by lenders doing business with one or more bureaus and put into what is the equivalent of your electronic credit history file folder. This file of data is called your *credit report,* and I devote a good portion of this book to credit reports. (See Chapter 2 for the full-blown story.)

Over the years, as more information has built up in credit reports and faster decision-making has been found to result in more sales, lenders have increasingly looked for shortcuts in the underwriting process that still offer protection from bad lending decisions. This need was met by the *credit score,* a shorthand version of all the information in your credit report. The credit score predicts the likelihood of your defaulting on a loan. The lower the score, the more likely you are to default. The higher the score, the better the odds for an on-time payback. By far, the most-used score today is the FICO score, which I cover in detail in Chapter 2. FICO scores range from 300 to 850.

Knowledge is power: Knowing your rights

When it comes to credit, you have rights — a lot of them. Two big laws address your rights pertaining to your credit standing:

✔ **Fair Credit Reporting Act (FCRA):** The Fair Credit Reporting Act ensures fairness in lending.

✔ **Fair and Accurate Credit Transactions Act (FACTA, or the FACT Act):** The FACT Act updated some sections of the FCRA (though not all, so both acts still stand on the books). It addresses credit-report accuracy and entitles you to access your data and dispute it. It also addresses the problem of identity theft and gives you leverage to deal with this crime if it happens to you.

I discuss these laws throughout this book, but if you want the nitty-gritty details, you can find copies of these acts on the accompanying CD.

In Chapter 5, I tell you about an additional 20 bureaus that have information about you. They're known as the *national specialty consumer reporting bureaus,* and they contain information on everything from how much you gamble to what medical condition you may have.

Understanding the Consequences of Bad Credit

Over the last 17 years, I've seen the underside of credit up close. During that time, I started a local credit-counseling agency that grew into a regional consumer resource and helped thousands of individuals and couples from all walks of life with credit issues. During the last few years, I've gotten questions from consumers just like you from all over the country — questions about their credit-related problems and opportunities — through my weekly "Debt Advisor" column that appears in newspapers and on the financial mega-asite Bankrate.com. I've witnessed time and again the devastating effects of credit gone bad.

Aside from the obvious increase in borrowing costs and maybe a hassle getting a credit card, what are the very real costs of bad credit? The extra interest you have to pay is only the tip of the iceberg. The real cost of bad credit is in reduced opportunities, family stress, and having to associate with lenders who, more often than not, see you as a mark to be taken for a ride and dumped before you do it to them. And, believe me, they're better at it than you are. In this section, I fill you in on some of the unpleasant consequences of bad credit.

Paying fees

From your perspective as the borrower in trouble, paying fees makes no sense at all. You're having a short-term problem making ends meet, so what do your creditors do to help you? They add some fat fees onto your balance. Thank you very much.

How do these fees help you? They don't. The fees helps the *creditor* in two ways:

- They focus your attention on *their* bill, instead of someone else's.
- The creditor gets compensated for the extra risk you've just become.

As bad as the fees can be on your credit cards, they can be even worse on your secured loans. If you fall three months behind in your house payment, you can be hit with huge fees to the tune of thousands of dollars.

Secured lenders tend to be low-key. Don't let that calm voice or polite, non-threatening letter lull you into complacency. They're low-key because they don't *have* to shout — they'll very quietly take your home or other collateral, unlike the credit-card guys, who can be heard from across the street. Pay attention to the quiet guy, and take action.

Late fees, over-limit fees, legal fees, repo fees, penalty fees, deficiency payments, and default rates: When the fees show up, it's time to get serious. Call the creditor and ask to have the fees waived. Explain your plan to get current (make any past-due payments) and let them know that you need their help, not their fees. Chapter 13 of this book helps you put together a budget so you know exactly how much you can afford. If you have difficulty developing a budget, your creditors may accept a debt-management plan, which you work out with the help of a credit-counseling agency (see Chapter 3). Take action early enough in the game while you and your account are still considered valuable assets, and you're more likely to have success getting the fees removed.

Being charged higher interest rates

Consider two home-buyers: one with a credit score of 760, the other with a credit score of 659. The happy new homeowner with the lower score won't be so happy to learn that, because of that lower score, he'll pay more than $90,000 more in interest over the life of the loan. Why? Because the mortgage company offers an interest rate of 5.3 percent to the individual with the 760 score, and an interest rate of 6.6 percent to the borrower with the 659 score.

The concept works basically the same in any lending situation. What impact would these scores have on a new car loan? A 36-month interest rate is more than *50 percent higher* for the person with the 659 score versus the 760 score!

Your credit score is based on your credit actions yesterday, last year, and maybe even ten years ago. If you miss a payment or two, that low-interest-rate credit card on which you're carrying a high balance can take your breath away. Watch the rate climb to the mid- to upper-20s or even 30-something — percent, that is! After all, you made a mistake and might stop paying altogether. So the lender is going to make money on interest while it can.

You think that getting your interest rate hiked for a minor infraction is unfair? That's not the end of it. Under the policy of *universal default,* if you have an issue with one lender, all your other lenders can hike their rates as well. Yes, even though you're still paying the others on time and as agreed! In fact, some companies even use a deteriorated credit score as reason to escalate your rates to the penalty level. Even though you're paying that loan on time, a change in your credit score (perhaps from too many account inquiries or carrying higher balances) gives the creditor that has a universal default policy full rein to hike up your interest rates. All the more reason to pay all bills on time and keep track of your credit report and credit score on a regular basis.

Losing employment opportunities

Prospective lenders aren't the only ones who judge you based on your credit report and credit score. Potential employers check out your credit report, too. Why is that, you ask? Businesses reason that the way you handle your finances is a reflection of your behavior in other areas of your life. If you're late paying your bills, you may be late for work. If you default on your car loan, you may not follow through with an important assignment.

Even if your credit woes can be explained, bad credit is a distraction from the employer's perspective, and it detracts from worker productivity. Recent research shows that employees with credit problems are significantly less productive on the job than those without.

Increasingly, credit checks are a standard part of the hiring — and even promotion — process at companies large and small throughout the United States. And from the employer's perspective, it's easier to hire someone with good credit than to bother to find out what's going on with someone whose credit is bad.

Increased insurance premiums

The brain trusts at the insurance companies (known as *actuaries*) love their numbers. They sniff out a trend, sometimes even before it happens, and slap a charge on it faster than my cat can catch a mouse — and, let me tell you, she's *fast!* The fact that a strong correlation exists between bad credit and reported claims hasn't escaped the attention of these people. The upshot: Bad credit will cost you a bundle in insurance-premium increases and may result in you being denied insurance.

Some states have gotten very excited about safe drivers and homeowners getting premium increases with no claims being reported. About 50 percent of states have restricted the use of credit-based insurance scores (and to a lesser extent, credit reports) in setting insurance prices. To find out whether scores and to what extent credit reports are used in your state, contact your local state insurance department. The states are still battling with this issue and it's difficult to say whether current laws will be overturned or upheld, or whether more will be added.

I'm not talking about your garden-variety credit score here. Fair Isaac has developed an Insurance Score. This score is calculated by taking information from your credit report, but the formula is different from the one used to figure your typical credit score. Insurance scores range from 500 to 997 with 626 to 775 being average. The Federal Trade Commission recently weighed in on the topic when a study they conducted found that these scores are effective predictors of the claims that consumers will file.

Getting a divorce

Would your better half dump you because of bad credit? Maybe not, but one thing is sure: Half of all marriages end in divorce, and the biggest cause of fighting in marriages is due to financial issues — as in bad credit.

Spouses want to be proud of their mates. And with credit playing a bigger role in so many aspects of modern American life, living with bad credit has to be a real blow to your image and self-esteem. I advise couples who are serious about pursuing a life together to talk about their attitudes on money and credit use. Sweeping this topic under the rug is too easy. Having a credit card refused for payment (often in front of others), worrying about which card still has available credit, or getting collection calls in the sanctuary of your home can be part of the credit nightmare you face as a couple. If you can't seem to find the words to talk about this sensitive topic or agree on a solution, get some professional advice before it becomes too late (see Chapter 3 for more information).

As a former counselor, I've seen too many people ruin otherwise promising marriages over money and credit. I can't help but offer some advice on bad credit and marriage:

- Get a credit report before you marry.
- Discuss money and credit and agree on goals.
- Find out if your honey is a spender or a saver.
- Fix your credit before it fixes you (as in "My cat is going to get fixed").

I cover couples and credit in more detail in Chapter 14.

The Ultimate in Secured Credit: Mortgages

Over the last few years, the mortgage market has been turned on its head. Credit has gone from amazingly loose to amazingly tight. People who took out mortgages with rates and payments that reset with market conditions have been stunned by the rapid increase in interest rates as a result. Many mortgages were oversold to people who relied on increasing property values to allow them to continue to refinance periodically and avoid high-interest-rate resets. Others have been unable to keep up with payments because of an unrelated financial problem. Either way, millions of homeowners have found themselves unable to refinance due to falling real estate prices and are trying to keep their heads above the financial waters that are rising higher and higher.

This section looks at what help is available and some pointers you need to remember. Check out Chapter 9 for more detail on mortgage issues and how a foreclosure can affect your credit score.

Knowing the type of mortgage you have

Today's market has a wide number of types of mortgages. So what kind of mortgage do you have? Will your payments increase or stay the same? How long? Knowing this information is important so you can make plans or take action ahead of time. If you have any doubt, start by contacting your loan servicer and asking. Following are some common types:

- **ARMs (Adjustable Rate Mortgages):** Mortgages that have adjustable rates from the start, which means your payments change over time based on preset interest rates usually up to certain preset caps.

- **Hybrid ARMs:** These mortgage payments stay the same for a few years, and then turn into adjustable loans. Common varieties are called 2/28 or 3/27 hybrid ARMs: The first number is the number of years the loan has a fixed rate and the second number is the number of years for which the loan has an adjustable rate. Some others are 5/1 or 3/1 hybrid ARMs: The first number again refers to the number of years the loan has a fixed rate, but the second number indicates how often the rate changes. In a 3/1 hybrid ARM, for example, the interest rate and payment are fixed for three years, then adjust every year thereafter.

- **Fixed rate mortgages:** Also called *traditional mortgages,* the rate is fixed for the life of the loan, often 15, 20, or 30 years. Usually payments don't vary unless you include taxes and/or insurance in your payment to your servicer.

Coping if you can't make your payments

If you're having trouble keeping up with your mortgage payments, you're probably worried sick about potentially losing your home. Rather than sitting helplessly, you can take some action. Consider doing the following if you're having a difficult time making your payments:

- **Find out whether you can refinance to a fixed-rate loan with a lower payment.** Check your mortgage documents first for prepayment penalties. Prepayment penalties may require large payments to the original loan holder if you pay off the loan early. After you know this info, contact your loan servicer and find out your options. The earlier you call the better. More programs are available to you if you begin before you default (miss a payment or pay less than is due) rather than waiting.

✔ **Contact a HUD-certified counseling agency.** Make sure you have all your options clearly explained to you. Furthermore, an agency can give you referrals to any programs for which you may be eligible.

Don't go through the foreclosure prevention process alone. A counselor with a housing counseling agency can help you to assess your situation, provide answers to your questions, give you options from which to choose, and help you know what to ask for from your lender. Very often, credit counseling agencies also provide housing counseling under a grant from HUD at no cost to you. Be sure you are dealing with a HUD-certified office. See Chapter 3 for more details on what to look for. Or consider contacting the NeighborWorks Center for Foreclosure Solutions at 888-995-HOPE or www.nw.org.

Avoiding default and foreclosure

Foreclosure can be a shattering experience. Beyond the financial loss, your pride and self-esteem can take a major hit. Moreover, foreclosures can really put a major dent in your credit history.

Being 90 days past due is a critical number in the transition from mortgage delinquency to the beginning of the foreclosure process. Most mortgages have a 14-day grace period, so your mortgage payment is due on the 15th of each month rather than the first. However, after you're delinquent (make a payment after the grace period has ended or only make a partial payment), the grace period goes away, so your next payment is now due the first of the next month with no grace period, period! Many homeowners are surprised when they think their payment won't be seriously past due for another two weeks, and they receive a foreclosure notice instead.

If you're running late on making payments, don't assume a foreclosure is inevitable. The sooner you look for help, the more options there will be that fit your situation. Even late in a delinquency, help can still be had, but you have to ask for it. Here are some alternatives you can pursue:

✔ **Forbearance:** This may be an option if your income is reduced temporarily, for example, your overtime is cut but you expect it to resume in the near future. Your mortgage payments may be reduced or even suspended for a period of time. Both you and the servicer need to agree on the time. Forbearance won't help if your financial situation has changed permanently and you can't afford your regular payments.

✔ **Repayment plan:** This may be an option if you've only missed a payment or two due to a temporary problem that is now resolved, and you can afford your payment but not the arrearage in one lump sum. Ask the loan servicer for a set amount of time to repay the amount you are behind by adding part of what you owe to your regular payment.

✔ **Loan modification:** If you can't afford your current payment, either because it has gone up or your income has gone down, this option may be for you. It entails a permanent change to one or more of the terms of the mortgage to make your payments affordable. Modifications may include reducing your interest rate, extending the term of your loan, or adding missed payments to the end of the loan or the loan balance. Before you ask for forbearance or a loan modification, be prepared to show that you are making a good-faith effort to pay your mortgage. For example, if you can show that you've reduced other expenses, your loan servicer may be more likely to negotiate with you. A HUD counselor can help you prepare for this.

✔ **Selling your home:** Depending on the real estate market in your area, selling your home may be an option. If your home's value is less than the amount owed, you can ask for a short sale or deed-in-lieu of foreclosure in which your lender takes back the property title and cancels the remainder of your debt. These may result in credit damage and perhaps a tax liability, but they are better for both you and the lender than long-term delinquency followed by a foreclosure.

✔ **Bankruptcy:** If other debts are making it impossible to make your mortgage payments and you have little or no equity, a personal bankruptcy may be worth looking into. A Chapter 7 bankruptcy is usually a last resort because it stays on your credit report for 10 years and can make it more expensive or difficult to get credit, qualify to buy another home, get life insurance, or even get a job. A Chapter 13 bankruptcy may be a less damaging alternative. In Chapter 13, the court approves a repayment plan that allows you to use your future income toward payment of your debts during a three-to-five-year period rather than surrender the property. To find out more about filing bankruptcy, flip to Chapter 11.

Dealing with a Thin Credit File

Are you new to credit? Is your credit history file a tad thin? (No, your credit history hasn't been on a diet.) A *thin file* means that you don't have enough information in your credit file on which to base a credit score or make an underwriting decision. Typically people who have just graduated from school, who are recently divorced or widowed, or who are new to this country have a thin file. The good news is this group of newbies is so large and potentially profitable in today's comparatively saturated credit market that they've been given their own name — the *underbanked.* Basically the underbanked are individuals who don't have access to the basics of the banking system such as checking and savings accounts and credit services.

Don't confuse underbanked with subprime. The folks in the underbanked group don't have blemished credit histories. They simply don't have much, if any, credit history. A better term may be *pre-prime!*

This section takes a closer look at some of the subgroups among the under-banked who have thin credit files and discusses some important points. Check out Chapter 4 for more in-depth coverage.

When you're new to the country

Those individuals new to the United States may bring old attitudes about banks with them. But the reality is that not only does the Statue of Liberty welcome you, so do many banks and lenders. Furthermore, many immigrants have to overcome misconceptions and understand that in this country banks are safe, insured for deposits, currency doesn't become worthless overnight, and the government is unlikely to nationalize the banks!

Social classes don't carry much weight in American banking. Anyone who walks into a bank or credit union gets treated with respect, regardless of what they do for a living. In fact, in many states with large enough concentrations of immigrants, banking services are being offered in different languages and in informal community settings, not just traditional banking offices.

Credit is essential to making a full and comfortable life in the United States. Lending, employment, insurance, and more are tied into establishing a positive credit history. The American dream, if you will, is intimately related to the credit system. So where to start? Here are some things to consider:

- ✔ You don't need a social security number to open a bank account if you are a foreign national. A consular ID or taxpayer identification number is sufficient with many banks.
- ✔ Credit bureaus don't require a social security number to establish a credit history for you. Name, address, and date of birth all come before social security number when it comes to linking credit histories with individuals.
- ✔ Credit doesn't consider race, national origin, gender, or any of those discriminatory categories.
- ✔ Building a relationship with a mainstream lender can help you avoid overpaying for credit products.

After one of life's many transitions

People who have just graduated or who just went through a divorce also often have thin credit files. If you fall into this category, you're probably looking for ways to build your credit history. In order to begin your journey, I suggest you set some long-term and interim goals as your destinations. Financial goals, like traveling goals, make sense, if only to keep you from wandering aimlessly. A car, a better apartment, a home, a vacation are all good goals and reasons to save your money and use credit wisely. (Check out the section, "Setting your financial goals" later in this chapter for more info.)

You can also do the following to help you begin to build credit:

- ✔ **Establish credit easily by using a secured credit card.** You make a deposit into an insured bank account and are given a credit card with a limit up to the amount of your deposit. This guarantees payment and allows you to have positive credit reported in your name. Soon, you'll qualify for an unsecured card and larger credit lines.

- ✔ **Open a passbook loan.** With a passbook loan, you make a deposit into a savings account and take out a small loan, using the account as security. There is no credit card, just a lump sum payment to you. But you can build a credit history when you make your payments on time, over time. Plus, the secured nature of the loan keeps costs very low. Credit unions, in particular, like these little starter loans.

Identity Theft: The Crime That Turns Good Credit Bad

Companies and schools seem to be losing the war on hackers and laptop thieves who are reported to be compromising databases with alarming frequency. Identity theft can devastate your credit and your ability to get loans, employment, insurance, and some security clearances and licenses without your ever having done anything to deserve it. An identity theft can also put you on the defensive, burdening you with the responsibility of proving that you are not the person collectors are after. Chapter 15 specifically addresses these issues, but for an overview, read on.

Protecting your identity from theft

To avoid the havoc wreaked by identity theft, your best bet is to avoid being a victim of identity theft altogether. Consider these tips:

- ✔ **Protect your financial information at home.** Don't leave credit-card numbers and statements, Social Security information, bank-account information, and other financial data unprotected. Most identity theft is low-tech (that is, paper-based). And most is carried out by people you know: friends, relatives (I've always worried about some of my aunts), acquaintances, co-workers, and people you invite into your home for a variety of reasons.

Shred statements before putting them in the trash and lock your sensitive information away. Using your computer more (as long as you use it properly and password-protect information) is an even better way to avoid theft.

✔ **Watch the mail.** Most people think that no one is watching their unprotected mailboxes. And most are right, but that leaves the rest of you with sensitive account numbers and documents containing your Social Security number sitting all day in an unlocked mailbox outside your home or apartment. By comparison, electronic bill paying is much safer.

Taking action if you're victimized

If you're a victim of identity theft, you may first discover that fact through a collection call on an account you never opened, or unusual activity on a credit card or credit report. When you suspect your identity has been compromised, respond immediately. Here are some tips:

✔ **Write down everything.** This process may not be quick or simple, but it is critical.

✔ **Call any creditors affected and close your accounts.** Don't forget ATM and debit cards — you have higher limits of liability for these than you do credit cards, so they're particularly important.

✔ **Freeze your credit report.** (You can unfreeze it later.)

✔ **Call the police and make out a report.** Some creditors and collectors require this to take action. Be sure to get a copy of the report.

Taking Charge of Your Credit

Now that you have a better understanding of the uses, perils, and pitfalls of credit, you *can* take charge of your credit! By following some very basic actions — some of which have an element of fun and inspiration — you can harness the power of credit to your advantage:

✔ Borrowing when it suits your needs without paying outrageous interest rates

✔ Taking advantage of lucrative lending offers such as "same-as-cash" and "no-money-down" offers typically available only to those with stellar credit histories

✔ Achieving your life dreams, whether owning that vine-covered cottage or sending your offspring to an Ivy League university

It all begins with the simple steps I cover in the following sections.

Setting your financial goals

Your financial goals serve as a powerful incentive to you and keep you on course. You've heard the saying, "If you don't know where you're going, any road will take you there." Well, if you don't have clear objectives when it comes to how you want to spend and save your money, you risk veering off on that rocky and perilous path to bad credit. Your goals — whether as grand as starting your own business or as modest as buying a new refrigerator — help you keep your eye on what's important to you and guide you to your destination. Chapter 13 helps you put together a list of your goals for both the near and far-off future.

Creating a budget

Call it a spending plan, if you like, but however you refer to it, be sure to see it as a positive *enabler,* rather than a restriction or a barrier. The purpose of the budget is to get you to arrive at your goal. If, for example, your goal is to take a beach vacation next year, putting money aside each paycheck and limiting spending on restaurants and clothing are as important in getting you there as filling the gas tank before you leave for the shore.

Start with an understanding of how much income you have to work with, and then allocate it as necessary for living expenses. If you have debt, set aside part of your income to retire that debt just as quickly as you can.

Then, just as important as your expenses and debt commitment, be sure you contribute to your own savings plans: one toward an emergency fund (in case of job loss or illness, for example); the others, for your goals (your kids, your honey, your retirement). Make saving as automatic as possible (an IRA or 401[k] for retirement, for example); the money can come right out of your paycheck. Use payroll deduction as an easy way to do this — and try to put at least half of your future raises in savings. You can spend the other half. In Chapter 13, I walk you through creating your own personal budget.

Obtaining and maintaining your credit reports and credit score

Like your annual medical exam, checking your credit reports serves as your routine credit checkup — only you're wise to schedule this exam every four months. Get it more often if you have a need — a big purchase on the horizon or a job change, for example. Pay for it, if you have to. It won't kill you. For information about ordering your credit reports and score, read Chapter 5.

Read your credit reports — every word. Errors do happen and when you're dealing with billions of pieces of data a month, they can happen a lot. Do you count your change when you check out at the supermarket or a restaurant? Your credit report is no small change. Dispute the errors, outdated information, and negative stuff that belongs to someone else's report.

Check for signs of identity theft and take immediate action if you discover evidence that someone else is using your good name. Chapter 15 of this book addresses identity theft in detail.

Being a good credit citizen

You're already so many other good things: a good person, a mother or father, a boyfriend or girlfriend, a spouse, a sibling, a worker. Do you really need someone telling you to be a good borrower, too? The answer: Yes.

I bet you knew I was going to say that, didn't you? The reason is not about you, but about the environment you're in. Taking the credit that is offered, using the credit that is offered, even not using credit at all can put you at a disadvantage. So how do you know what's "good"? You weren't born with the credit gene that enabled you to understand the correct path to follow like so many migrating birds.

Being a good credit citizen means being responsible as a borrower, responsible to yourself and those who share your life. This starts with goals, a future vision of your life, and knowing which financial tools to use, in what measure, and when.

Here are my top ten good-citizen credit practices:

- ✔ Set goals.
- ✔ Know what's in your credit report and dispute out-of-date, inaccurate, or just plain wrong information.
- ✔ Know what your credit score is, what it means, and what you can do to make it better or keep it great.
- ✔ Have a spending plan or budget.
- ✔ Use long-term credit for long-term uses. Don't use a home-equity line to buy sneakers or eat out (see Chapter 12 for more on home-equity lines).
- ✔ Use short-term credit for short-term uses. Pay off your credit-card balances as quickly as you can.
- ✔ Save money for future goals and needs.
- ✔ Pay your bills on time.

✔ Pay at least the amount due. Always set a time by which you will pay off a debt; don't let the creditor set the time for you, because it may be forever.

✔ Watch out for the seven warning signs of bad credit and get help as soon as you think you may need it — not as a last resort:

- Using credit cards for daily expenses and not paying the balance every month

- Not knowing how much you owe

- Using cash advances to pay credit-card bills or for daily expenses

- Only paying the minimum due on credit cards, or paying less than the minimum

- Getting calls from your creditors

- Spending more than 20 percent of your take-home pay on credit payments, excluding your mortgage

- Arguing about money at home

Chapter 2

The 4-1-1 on Credit Reports and Scores

Many people used to put their credit reports in the same category as IQ results, SAT scores, school report cards, job reviews, and cholesterol readings — in other words, information that's important only when a particular situation arises. As soon as the situation goes away, then so does the need to monitor it. Sort of like my diet. Once my belt stops cutting off my circulation, I can stop counting my calories. Right? Wrong! The same applies to watching your credit report and keeping track of your score periodically.

Today, with tightening credit, a larger-than-usual need to refinance a home by a larger-than-usual percentage of the population, and credit-card debt at very high levels, your credit report and score have moved to center stage. And that doesn't begin to touch on the other problems that can be exacerbated by a low score or negative credit file. Insurance rates are rising and homeowners' insurance is getting not only expensive but, in some places near the water, also hard to find. What's in your credit report and score can make an important difference here as well. So in this chapter, I explain why you need to be on frequent and intimate terms with your credit report.

Understanding Why a Credit Report Is Important

Your credit report doesn't come into play just when you want to borrow money. A bad credit report may affect what you pay for insurance, whether you can rent the apartment of your choice, or whether you'll be hired for certain jobs. Heck, a particularly finance-conscious romantic prospect might even nix you for a bad credit history!

It's a fact, Jack: Your credit score can cost you thousands of dollars and deny you opportunities you never even knew you missed. Clearly, what you don't know *can* hurt you. Consider two hypothetical life situations to illustrate my point:

✔ Say you signed up for a dating service. Now, what if all the information available to your prospective dates is given to them by people you've dated in the past? What if the quality of the dates you get in the future is directly tied to what all the people you've dumped (or been dumped by) say about you? Starting to sweat a little?

✔ Say you're applying for a job. Your salary, job title, and the size of your office will be tied directly to what's on your résumé. But what if you didn't write your résumé — your past employers did, and what if they mixed up your personnel file with the file of that person who was fired for sexual harassment? Can you imagine walking into that job interview without any idea what your former boss may have reported or whether it was correct?

Meeting your life partner, landing a great job — these situations are ones in which you have a great deal of personal interest in a successful outcome. Kind of like getting a good mortgage rate so you can afford or keep that dream home.

I'm not saying you're guaranteed to *like* the outcome of your date with Sylvia or the job interview — but at least you know it's based on information you're privy to. Likewise with your credit report. You can't rewrite your own credit history, but you *can* be knowledgeable about what a credit report is and how much weight it carries as you try to negotiate your way through the financial universe. You *can* be savvy to situations that could cost you thousands of dollars more or deny you opportunities. And you *can* catch inaccuracies on your report (a common situation) and correct them.

There is no excuse for not knowing what's in your credit report. Getting the information is fast and easy. You should have a current copy of your credit report from each of the three credit bureaus (Equifax, Experian, and TransUnion). And don't even think about saying you can't afford it, because you can now request your credit report from each credit bureau once a year for *free. Free! I think I just heard my father smile!*

So, what's in your report? Is the information correct — or even yours? And if not, what can you do to fix it? Settle in for some facts that will open your eyes and save you money, time, and frustration.

What Is a Credit Report, Anyway?

In its most basic sense, your credit report is your financial life history of borrowing money. This information is gathered, managed, maintained, and shared by credit-reporting bureaus or agencies. Trust me: You don't have to lift a finger to create it or disseminate it. There are actually as many as 20 credit-reporting bureaus; most are specialty reporting agencies (I introduce you to some of these at the end of this chapter and others in Chapter 5). The following three are considered the biggies:

- ✔ **Equifax** (www.equifax.com; 800-685-1111)
- ✔ **Experian** (www.experian.com; 888-397-3742)
- ✔ **TransUnion** (www.transunion.com; 800-888-4213)

This section details the items in your credit report and who uses this information.

What your credit report says about you

As a snapshot of your financial life, your credit report may also indirectly predict your potential behaviors in other areas of your life. The fact that you have a history of making credit-card payments late may tell a prospective landlord that you're likely to be late with your rent, too. A history of defaulted loans may suggest to a potential boss that you aren't someone who follows through with commitments. If you have a foreclosure in your file, it may tell someone that you may take on more than you can handle or are just one unlucky duck. If you've declared bankruptcy because your finances are out of control, perhaps you're out of control in other ways, too.

This snapshot, which brings into focus the details of your spending and borrowing and even suggests your personal life patterns, also paints a *bigger* picture of two important factors — characteristics that are critical to employers, landlords, lenders, and others. I cover these two critical characteristics in the following sections.

Do you do what you promise?

Your credit history is an indicator of whether you're someone who follows through with commitments — a characteristic important to most people, whether they're looking for a reliable worker, a responsible nanny, a dependable renter, or a faithful mate. Needless to say, a person or company considering lending you a sizeable sum of money will want to know the same.

Based in large part on your history of following through with your financial promises, you're assigned a credit score. People with higher scores generally get the best terms, including lower interest rates and reduced minimum down payments. People with lower credit scores may not get credit in today's economy, unless they pay higher interest rates and possibly additional fees or insurance. And even then, they may not qualify at all, for anything, under tight approval guidelines.

Do you do it on time?

When it comes to your credit score, following through with your promises is only half of the game. The other half is doing it on time. It's a fact in the lending business that the more overdue the payment, the more likely it will not be paid at all — or paid in full. This is why, as you get further behind in your payments, lenders become more anxious about collecting the amount you owe. In fact, if you're sufficiently delinquent, the lender may want you to pay back the entire amount at once rather than as originally scheduled. (When it comes to money, your creditors' faith in you is only 30 to 90 days long. Car dealers, notoriously short on faith, see the end of the world happening in credit terms in a payment that's late by as little as two weeks.) So, the longer you take to do what you promised, the more it costs you and the more damage you do to your credit score.

Uncovering your credit report's details

Many people believe that your credit report contains the intimate personal details of your life, ferreted out from interviews with your neighbors, your ex, and your business associates. Not true! You can rest assured that your credit report doesn't reveal whether you tend to drink too much at office parties, whether you sport a tattoo, or whether you had an eye lift or indulged in a wild fling on your last vacation to Mexico.

The information in your credit report is specific, purely factual, and limited in scope. What it lacks in scope, however, it makes up for in sheer volume of material and the length of time it covers. When I talk to high school, college, or technical-school students, I tell them that if they cut a class, chances are no one will notice, but if they fail to pay a bill on time, a multibillion-dollar industry will notice, record it, and tell everyone who asks about them for the next seven years!

Here's the short take on what's in your credit report:

- ✔ **Personal identification information** such as your name, Social Security number, date of birth, addresses (present and past), and your most recent employment history.

    Be consistent with your information, especially how you spell your name and address. Name, address, and date of birth are the most common sources used to identify which file is yours. Social security number is fourth.

- ✔ **Public-record information** on tax liens, judgments, bankruptcies, child-support orders, and other official information.

- ✔ **Collection activity** for accounts that have been sent to collection agencies for handling.

- ✔ **Information about each credit account,** open or closed (also known as *trade lines*), such as whom you owe, the type of account (such as a mortgage or installment account), whether the account is *joint* (shared with another person) or just in your name, how much you owe, your monthly payment, how you've paid (on time or late), and your credit limits.

- ✔ **A list of the companies that have requested your credit file for the purpose of granting you credit.** Requests are known as *inquiries* and are one of two types:

    - *Soft inquiries* are those made for promotional purposes (for instance, when a credit-card issuer wants to send you a hot offer). These don't appear on the version of your credit report that lenders see. They will be on the consumer's copy that you get.

    - *Hard inquiries* are those made in response to a request from you for more or new credit. These inquiries *do* appear on the lender's copy of your credit report.

- ✔ **An optional message from you** that can be up to 100 words in length and that explains any extenuating circumstances for any negative listings on your report.

- ✔ **An optional credit score.** Your credit score is, strictly speaking, not part of your credit report but an add-on that you have to ask for. Your score will be different for each credit report due to data differences. (I cover the importance of your credit score later in this chapter.)

Credit reports are easy to read, although there's still room for improvement. Each of the three major credit-reporting agencies reports credit information in its own unique format. The credit-reporting agencies are competing with each other for business, so they have to differentiate their products.

Among the list of items *not* included in your credit report are your lifestyle choices, religion, national origin, political affiliation, sexual preferences, friends, and relatives. Additionally, the three major credit-reporting agencies do not collect or transmit data on your medical history, checking or savings accounts, brokerage accounts, or similar financial records.

On the CD, you can view a sample credit report from TransUnion. You can see sample credit reports from Equifax and Experian online:

- ✔ **Equifax:** Go to www.equifax.com and, from the View All Products drop-down menu, click on Products and then Equifax Credit Report; and then click on See Equifax Credit Report Sample.
- ✔ **Experian:** Go to www.experian.com/consumer_online_products/ credit_report.html and click on View Sample Report.

Who uses the info in your credit report

Every day, businesses rely on the information in your credit report to help them decide whether to lend you money and at what price (otherwise known as the *interest rate* and *loan terms*). But because the information in your credit report can be sliced and diced many ways, your report becomes an important tool that serves different purposes for different people:

- ✔ For a lender, your credit report is a tool to determine how likely and able you are to repay a loan, and it's an indicator of how much interest and what fees to charge you based on the risk profile you represent — if you qualify for a loan or refinance at all!
- ✔ For an insurance company, your credit report is a tool to predict how likely you are to have an accident or have your house burn down.
- ✔ For an employer, your credit report is a tool to predict whether you'll be a reliable and trustworthy employee.
- ✔ For a landlord, your credit report is a tool to determine whether you're likely to pay the rent on time or at all.
- ✔ For you, your credit report is a tool to help you understand how you've handled your finances in the past and how you're likely to handle them in the future.

Many different types of people can look at this information and make an increasing number of significant decisions that can affect your life. That's why double-checking this info is essential. Establishing a positive credit history as soon as possible can help with jobs, insurance, and more.

Understanding How Bad Stuff Gets in Your Credit Report

Whether you're new to the world of credit or you're an experienced borrower, you need to keep a few key concepts in mind as you look over your credit report. Like the person who can't see the forest because there are too many trees, when you get your hands on your credit report you may be blinded by the amount of information. In the following sections, I help you focus on what matters and let go of what doesn't.

Nobody's perfect: Don't expect a straight-A report card

You aren't perfect. (I hate to have to be the one to tell you this, but if you aren't married, someone had to!) The same goes for your credit report — and lack of perfection isn't a big deal as long as your credit report shows more smooth patches than bumps. No matter how early you mail off that bill payment, it can still arrive late or get lost, which means you can expect to find some negative information on your credit report from time to time. The good news is that you can still be eligible for plenty of loans at competitive rates and terms without having a flawless credit report or qualifying for credit sainthood.

But how many bad marks are okay? How long do they stay? And how will they be interpreted by lenders who view your report? For example, say you're a well-heeled, easygoing gal and you loan your boyfriend $5,000 for a very worthy cause. He promises to pay you back monthly over two years. But after four months without a payment, it's likely that two things will happen: He'll no longer be your sweetie, and you'll have mentally written off any chance of collecting the debt. Plus, if you're smart, you'll think twice before loaning money to a friend again. You may even mention the negative experience to your friends, especially if they're thinking of floating him a loan.

If you were to run into your ex-boyfriend sometime down the road, you'd probably mention the $5,000 — after all, you want your money back, and he still owes you! Whether you'd ask him to join you for dinner is another matter and may depend on his showing you some good-faith gesture!

In business, as in love, trust and faithful performance are keys to success. A creditor can tell your future and current creditors any repayment information that is correct and accurate through your credit report, in the same way that you could warn your friends about your ex-boyfriend. That information or warning may be modified at any time, as long as the new information is correct and accurate.

Just how much does a mistake cost you when it comes to your credit report? Well, it depends on your history. Along with the credit report, and all the information that it contains, lenders can also buy a *credit score* based on the information in the report. That score comes from a mathematical equation that evaluates much of the information on your credit report at that particular credit bureau. By comparing this information to the patterns in zillions of past credit reports, the score tells the lender your level of future credit risk. (Check out the section "Fleshing out credit score components" later in this chapter for more info on credit scores.)

People with a lot of information in their credit files find that a lot of good credit experiences lessen the effect of a single negative item. Score one for the old folks with long credit histories! If you're a young person or a new immigrant with only a few trade lines and a few months of credit history (sometimes called a *thin file*), a negative event will have a much larger effect in relation to the information available. Many young people think the world is stacked against them. In this case, it's true — but to be fair, it's also stacked against anyone with a limited credit history, regardless of your age or what country you come from.

Checking for errors: Creditors aren't perfect, either

Other people make mistakes, too. Even banks and credit-card payment processors! Considering that about 4.5 billion pieces of data are added to credit reports every month, it shouldn't be a big surprise that incorrect info may show up on your credit report. And I won't even get into the unrelated problem of errors caused as a result of identify theft. (I address this at length in Chapter 15.) A number of conflicting studies have been done on what percentage of reports contain errors and, of those, how many were serious enough to affect either the terms under which credit was granted or whether it was granted at all. So, you may or may not have errors on your report. And they may or may not be serious. But unless you're feeling really lucky, I strongly suggest you find out what's in your report.

Still, credit-reporting agencies have a vested interest in the accuracy of the information they report. They sell it, and their profits are on the line if their information is consistently inaccurate. If credit-reporting agencies consistently provide error-riddled data, those who grant credit won't be as eager to pay money to get or use a bureau's credit reports.

Getting a copy of your credit report gives you a chance to check for these errors and — better yet — get them corrected! You can have inaccurate information removed by one of two methods: contacting the credit bureau or contacting the creditor.

Contacting the credit bureau

If you notice incorrect information on your credit report, contact the credit bureau that reported the inaccurate information. Each of the three major bureaus allows you to dispute information in your credit report on its Web site, or you can call the bureau's toll-free number (see "What Is a Credit Report, Anyway?" earlier in this chapter). If you make your dispute online, you'll need to have a copy of your credit report available; there is information on the report that will allow the bureau to confirm your identity without a signature. If you opt to call the toll-free number, you're unlikely to get a live person on the other end — this stuff is heavily automated — but you'll be told what information and documentation you need in order to submit a written request. After you properly notify the credit bureau, you can count on action.

Credit-reporting agencies are required by the Fair Credit Reporting Act (FCRA) to investigate any disputed listings. The credit bureau must verify the item in question with the creditor *at no cost* to you, the consumer. The law requires that the creditor respond and verify the entry within 30 days, or the information must be removed from your credit report, and the credit-reporting agency has to notify you of the outcome. If information in the report has been changed or deleted, you also get a *free* copy of the revised report.

Contacting the creditor

Another way to remove inaccurate information from your credit report is outlined under the Fair and Accurate Credit Transactions Act (commonly referred to as the FACT Act or FACTA), passed in 2003 and rolled out in pieces through 2005. Under these new FACT Act provisions, you can deal directly with the creditor who reported the negative information in the first place. Contact information is contained on your latest billing statement from that creditor.

I strongly suggest you do everything in writing, return-receipt requested. After you dispute the information, the reporting creditor must look into the matter and cannot continue to report the negative information while it's investigating your dispute.

For new delinquencies, the FACT Act requires that you be notified if negative information is reported to a credit bureau. That said, you may have to look closely to even see this new notice. Anyone who extends credit to you must send you a one-time notice either before or not later than 30 days after negative information — including late payments, missed payments, partial payments, or any other form of default — is furnished to a credit bureau. This includes collection agencies, as long as they report to a credit bureau. The notice may look something like this:

> ✔ **Before negative information is reported:** "We may report information about your account to credit bureaus. Late payments, missed payments, or other defaults on your account may be reflected in your credit report."

> ✔ **After negative information is reported:** "We have told a credit bureau about a late payment, missed payment, or other default on your account. This information may be reflected in your credit report."

The notice is not a substitute for your own close monitoring of your credit reports, bank accounts, and credit-card statements.

Looking at the accurate information

Most of the information in your credit report will be accurate. A popular misconception is that data stays on your credit report for seven years and then drops off. What really happens is that negative data stays on your credit report for seven years, although a few items are different, such as a Chapter 7 bankruptcy, which stays on your report for ten years. Even though the negative info is out there for a long time, as the months and years roll by, the info becomes less important to your credit profile. The fact that you were late in paying your credit-card bill one time three years ago will not concern most creditors. Positive information, however — the good stuff everyone likes to see — stays on your report for a much longer time. Some positive data may be on your report for 10, 20, or even 30 years, depending on whether you keep your account open and depending on each bureau's policy.

Negative information may be used by unscrupulous lenders as a reason to put you into a higher-cost (and more profitable for them) loan, even though you qualify for a less-expensive one. This is just one example of a situation in which understanding your credit score can save you money. The scenario can go something like this: You're looking for a loan for a big-ticket item. Instead of going from bank to bank and wasting days of precious free time or risking being turned down after filling out long applications and explaining about the $5,000 your ex-boyfriend owes you, you go to a trusted financial advisor who knows how these things work. She pulls your credit report and shops for a loan for you. The answer that you're given is that this is "a great deal considering your credit score." Translated, this means you're being charged a higher-than-market rate because of your imperfect credit score. If you don't know what your score is and what rate that score entitles you to in the marketplace, you may be taken advantage of. So read on and get the skinny on credit scores, which have a big effect on your interest rates and terms.

Deciphering Your Credit Score

With billions of pieces of data floating around, it's little wonder that the people who use this data to make decisions turned to computers to help make sense of it all. Starting back in the 1950s, some companies, including one called Fair Isaac Corporation, began to model credit data in hopes of predicting payment behavior. (A *model* uses a series of formulas based on some basic assumptions to simulate and understand future behavior or to make predictions. Weathermen use models to predict your weather for tomorrow. Usually, the credit guys are more accurate because they're predicting the likelihood of something bad happening in the next year or so.) Until recently, the three major credit bureaus offered different scoring models created for them by Fair Isaac — the developers of the *FICO score*. Each one called the score by a proprietary name. Now they also use an identical credit scoring model called the VantageScore. (For more info on the development of credit scores, see Chapter 5.) Your credit score is a three-digit number that rules a good portion of your financial life, for better or worse.

You may have no credit score at all if you don't have enough of a credit history. Understanding what your credit score is made up of is an important step in ensuring that yours is the best it can be. This section takes a closer look at the two main types of credit scores — FICO and VantageScore — and helps you understand what makes them up.

Fleshing out credit score components

In order for a score to be calculated, you need to have at least one account open and reporting for a period of time. In this category the Vantage people have the current edge. They require only one account to be open for at least three months and to have been updated in the last 12 months before generating a score. FICO requires the account to have been open for at least six months and to have been updated in the last six months. Although having no credit history makes it difficult for you to get credit initially, you'll find it a lot easier to build credit for the first time than to repair a bad credit history (which is like being two runs down in a ballgame and trying to catch up). In this section, I give you the skinny on both main types of scores.

What constitutes a FICO score?

The most widely used of these credit scores is the FICO score. Until recently, the proprietary formula for FICO scores was a well-guarded secret. Creditors were concerned that if you knew the formula, you might be tempted to manipulate the info to distort the outcome in your favor. Well, that may or may not be the case, but if creditors are looking for good behavior on your part, it only makes sense to tell you what constitutes good behavior. In 2001, Fair Isaac agreed with me, with a little help from some regulators, and disclosed the factors and weightings used to determine your credit score.

FICO scores range from 300 to 850. The higher the number, the better the credit rating. All the ranges change with time and experience. Based on the general population's FICO scores, the ranges and percentages of scores are as follows. FICO takes into account more than 20 factors when building your score and the importance of each one is dependent on the other factors and the volume of data and length of your history. Your FICO score is made up of five components (see Figure 2-1):

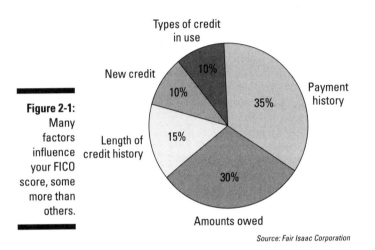

Figure 2-1:
Many factors influence your FICO score, some more than others.

Source: Fair Isaac Corporation

✔ **Paying on time (35 percent):** Payment history is considered the most significant factor when determining whether an individual is a good credit risk. This category includes the number and severity of any late payments, the amount past due, and whether the accounts were repaid as agreed. The more problems, the lower the score.

✔ **Amount and type of debt (30 percent):** The amount owed is the next most important factor in your credit score. This includes the total amount you owe; the amount you owe by account type (such as revolving, installment, or mortgage); the number of accounts on which you're carrying a balance; and the proportion of the credit lines used. For example, in the case of installment credit, *proportion of balance* means the amount remaining on the loan in relation to the original amount of the loan. For revolving debt, such as a credit card, it's the amount you currently owe in relation to your credit limit. You want a low balance amount owed in relation to your amount of credit available. Having credit cards with no balances ups your limits and your score.

✔ **The length of time you've been using credit (15 percent):** The number of years you've been using credit and the type of accounts you have also influence your score. Accounts that have been open for at least two years help to increase your score.

✔ **The variety of accounts (10 percent):** The mix of credit accounts is a part of each of the other factors. Riskier types of credit mean lower scores. For example, if most of your debt is in the form of revolving credit or finance-company loans, your score will be lower than if your debt is from student loans and mortgage loans. Also, the lender gives more weight to your performance on its type of loan. So, a credit-card issuer looks at your experience with other cards more closely and a mortgagee pays closer attention to how you pay mortgages or secured loans. An ideal mix of accounts has many types of different credit used.

✔ **The number and types of accounts you've opened recently, generally in the last 6 months or so (10 percent):** The number of new credit applications you've filled out, any increases in credit lines requested by you (unsolicited ones don't count), and the types and number of new credit accounts you have affect your credit score. The reasoning is that if you're applying for several accounts at the same time, and you're approved for them, you may not be able to afford your new debt load.

What constitutes a VantageScore?

A relatively new and up-and-coming entrant to the scoring field is the VantageScore. Vantage needs three months of history and an update in the last 12 months for a score. VantageScore's range is from 501 to 990. Your VantageScore is made up of six components (see Figure 2-2):

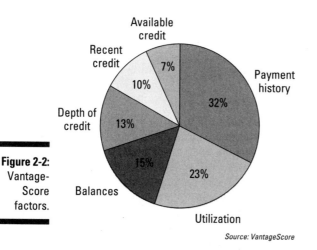

Figure 2-2:
Vantage-
Score
factors.

Source: VantageScore

✔ **Payment history (32 percent):** Once again, the most significant factor when determining whether an individual is a good credit risk. This includes satisfactory, delinquent, and derogatory items.

✔ **Utilization (23 percent):** The percentage of credit available to you that you have used or that you owe on accounts. Using a large proportion of your overall available credit is a negative.

- ✔ **Balances (15 percent):** This includes the amount of recently reported current and delinquent balances. Balances that have been increased recently can be an indication of risk and lower your score.

- ✔ **Depth of credit (13 percent):** The length of history and types of credit used are included. A long history with mixed types of credit is best.

- ✔ **Recent credit (10 percent):** The number of recently opened credit accounts and all new inquiries. New accounts initially lower your score. It's not clear at first why you want more credit. However, after you use the accounts and pay on time, they can help raise your score by adding positive information.

- ✔ **Available credit (7 percent):** The amount of credit available on all your accounts. Using a low percentage of the total amount of credit available to you is a good thing.

If you're trying to build a credit history for the first time, you're an immigrant, or you're in the FBI's Witness Protection Program and you're looking for your first unsecured credit card in your new name, look for a lender that uses a VantageScore to grant credit once you have established a credit record. Examples of ways to start a credit history include using a secured card or a passbook loan. (Check out Chapter 4 for more info.)

If you're too thin: The Expansion score

It used to be that if you didn't have much information in your credit file, known as a *thin file* in the business, you were in a pickle. Lenders had a more difficult time assessing your risk because they couldn't get a score for you. Well, thank heavens for Yankee ingenuity, because just as soon as a problem shows up, so does a solution.

FICO calls it their *Expansion score*. Essentially, it's a credit-risk score based upon nontraditional consumer credit data (in other words, it's not based on data from the three major national credit bureaus). The purpose of this new score is to predict the credit risk of consumers who don't have a traditional FICO score. The use of FICO Expansion scores gives millions of new consumers without extensive credit histories an opportunity to access credit including:

- ✔ Young people just entering the credit market

- ✔ New arrivals and immigrants to the United States

- ✔ People who previously had mostly joint credit and are now widowed or divorced

- ✔ People who've used cash rather than credit most or all of the time

Examining Specialized Credit Bureaus

In the world of credit reports, there are the "big three" credit-reporting bureaus: Equifax, Experian, and TransUnion. But specialty credit-reporting bureaus, which are covered by the FCRA and the FACT Act, also exist. In fact, to allow for the large number and to allow for even more to come under the law, they aren't specifically named by the Federal Trade Commission as the big three are — the list would be too long and it would change frequently. Specialized credit bureaus report data about you in areas such as gambling, checking, medical, and insurance experience.

Exploring all these specialized bureaus would require a book of its own, but I do want to give you a sampling of what's out there. In the following sections, I fill you in on two types that are worth knowing about.

Getting to know national check registries

One of my favorite stories as a kid was the original 1932 *Tarzan, The Ape Man,* in which the big guy goes to the elephant graveyard. The legend was that when elephants knew they were going to die, they all went to this big, secret graveyard to do it — and it was full of ivory! Well, where do checks go when they bounce? To the bounced-check graveyard, of course, and it must be full of rubber!

There are three main repositories of information on your checking-account activity. They contain only *negative* information about your history — banks only report the bad news to them. Each of these repositories has a database of information that its members, retailers, and other subscribers use to help make decisions regarding the acceptance of checks or the opening of accounts. This information helps members reduce their financial losses from returned checks, improve customer service, and safeguard against identity theft and fraud. Three of the repositories are

- ✔ **Chex Systems** (www.consumerdebit.com/consumerinfo/us/en/chexsystems/report/index.htm; 800-428-9623)
- ✔ **Shared Check Authorization Network (SCAN)** (www.consumerdebit.com/consumerinfo/us/en/index.htm; 800-262-7771)
- ✔ **TeleCheck** (www.telecheck.com; 800-835-3243)

Maybe working with all that negative information has rubbed off on these companies, but they aren't as easy to deal with as the other relatively consumer-friendly credit bureaus. They're regulated under the FACT Act, so you can get a free copy of your report and dispute errors as you can with the other credit bureaus.

But you can't get a report online. You must call a toll-free phone number and go through a menu before you finally get to a live person, who will then request lots of information, including the usual identification information such as your driver's license number, Social Security number, and some check-specific data such as checking-account routing and checking-account numbers. After you submit your request, the report follows by mail in 10 to 15 days.

You can look at sample reports from two of the major check-reporting bureaus online:

- ✔ **ChexSystems:** Go to www.consumerdebit.com and, under Consumer Assistance, click on Sample Consumer Report. Then, next to ChexSystems report, click on View Sample.

- ✔ **SCAN:** Go to www.consumerdebit.com and, under Consumer Assistance, click on Sample Consumer Report. Then, next to SCAN report, click on View Sample.

Gambling with Central Credit Services

When you want credit, usually you want it now. Well, at least one credit grantor couldn't agree with you more! Every minute you go without credit can cost them money. Who are these guys? Why, they're none other than your friendly neighborhood casino or bingo parlor. And — what are the odds? — there's a credit-reporting agency just to serve their needs!

Getting credit casino-style

The gaming industry is thrilled with Central Credit Services (CCS). And why not? In its own words, "Services from CCS help put more cash on the floor." Personally, I like cash in my pocket, rather than on the floor, but I'm not fussy.

Need a credit line of $10,000, $50,000, maybe $1 million or more? Have a credit score of 300? Want the money fast, in cash, with no hassles, fees, or interest? How about 45 days, interest-free, to repay whatever you draw from the line of credit with no strings attached? Oh, I almost forgot. How about dinner and a suite at the best hotel in town because you were such a good customer and borrowed lots of money?

Sound like a lender's nightmare? Welcome to the world of Global Cash Access, the parent company of Central Credit Services, and owner of the largest gaming-patron, credit-bureau database in the world. Every day thousands of gaming patrons make just such requests from casinos all over the

United States and around the world. Instant financial reports on new and sea-
soned gamblers have to be available quickly, or the patron (the best patrons
are sometimes affectionately called *whales* by the casinos) will migrate to
another casino.

Gamblers live in a culture of their own. It's no wonder they have a unique
credit-granting system. Central Credit is the big Kahuna of what is called the
gaming-patron credit-database industry.

Making bets with markers

When a gambler needs cash at a casino, he can either go to an ATM and pay
through the nose for a cash advance, or he can stroll into the casino credit
department and ask for a *marker*. The super-sophisticated modern gaming systems not only give you a card with a unique number — similar to what you get
with your garden-variety ATM card — but the card ties into your file that contains your name, picture, birth date, Social Security number, and *casino rating*
(how much you bet, how long you play, and if you win or lose) for that day and
for your previous trips to the casino. Use this card at an automated cashier's
window and be sure to smile for the camera, because it may use face-matching
technology to be sure you are who you're supposed to be.

A marker entitles you to interest-free chips or cash with very generous repayment provisions. Gamblers think only a chump would use an ATM or her
own money when the free stuff is available and comes along with oodles of
customer service, freebies, and, yes, even that most elusive of commodities . . . RESPECT. *Capisce?* What a deal! (I tried this out myself when I was
researching this section at the Atlantis Casino in the Bahamas and at Planet
Hollywood in Las Vegas and I almost felt like I was Bond, yes, James Bond,
when I tossed my card on the green velvet and asked the croupier for a
marker in front of some impressed and impressive ladies!)

How does Central Credit Services do it? A worldwide network of casinos
accumulates each patron's marker experience and makes it available in
much the same way that creditors report your experience to the three credit-
reporting bureaus. If you're late paying a marker, have too many markers
outstanding at the same time, or have a derogatory notation (for example,
you punched a dealer in the nose), it all gets tracked in the Central Credit
database. This data, accumulated worldwide from casinos and gaming establishments, along with information from consumer credit bureaus and bank-
reporting agencies, is entered into your patron record.

The stakes are high for both you and the casino. We're not talking about the
lender losing out on a monthly 1 percent interest income ($500 on a $50,000
cash advance). We're talking about the whole $50,000 as potential income

to the casino if you lose it all. These are big numbers with big risks and big rewards. About 80 percent of a casino's profit comes from 20 percent of its customers. And they don't use credit cards — they use markers. So speed and accuracy in making underwriting decisions are critical to successfully doing business with some very particular people, whether you're in Vegas, the Bahamas, or Monte Carlo. In fact, the competition for business is so stiff and so profitable that to minimize the risk of a patron going next door to gamble, the goal is to offer the patron preapproved credit during the check-in process at the front desk. Now, that's what I call a welcome gift amenity!

You can contact Central Credit Services at its headquarters in — where else? — Las Vegas. Here's CCS's info: 3525 E. Post Rd., Suite 120, Las Vegas, NV 89120; phone 702-855-3000 or 702-262-5000.

Chapter 3

Getting Help for Free

....

In This Chapter

▶ Deciding when you're in too deep to go it alone

▶ Seeing what a credit-counseling agency can do for you

▶ Evaluating the merits of credit-counseling agencies

▶ Finding out what credit counseling should (and shouldn't) cost

....

*I*n the United States, money is the last taboo. Bad breath, substance abuse, even erectile dysfunction — no problem. Credit or money issues? Unacceptable! So much of your self-image is expressed in terms of financial worth that admitting to having bad credit is worse than saying that you still sleep with your teddy bear. It just isn't what 21st-century U.S. society expects of attractive, robust, successful adults like you.

Getting advice from someone with lots of experience is a smart thing to do. Getting it for free is pure genius. Yet when it comes to seeking help for money or credit problems, many people avoid it. Why? Because seeking help means stepping into the unknown, not to mention that having to ask for help can be downright embarrassing. Society doesn't expect you to ask for directions or read assembly instructions. When you ask for help with your credit, you reveal your vulnerabilities and shortcomings by admitting that you don't know or don't understand what's going on and you may actually have made a mistake or two. Well, welcome to the real world where not everything is simple and can be learned or solved in 30 minutes.

This is where a professional credit-counseling agency can help. In a nutshell, a credit-counseling agency can analyze and suggest changes to your financial situation by looking at your goals, income, expenses, and debts. The best credit counselors can help you understand the roots of your debt problem, what to do to solve it, and how to ensure that it never happens again. And — surprise — the very best do it for free!

Sounds great, right? There's just one catch: You have to be able to figure out not only which agencies are the best, but also which of those agencies is best for you. In this chapter, I show you how.

Figuring Out Whether (or Not) to Ask for Help

If you're asking yourself whether you need to turn to a credit counselor for help, you're no doubt feeling some financial pressure — even if it's only a vague pinch. To help decide, ask yourself — or yourself and your partner if you're not in this alone — some key questions:

✔ **Are you overwhelmed?** You know you're overwhelmed when:

- You check your caller ID because the calls may be from creditors. (See Chapter 8 for more info.)

- You fight with your partner about money or credit.

- Your financial concerns keep you from sleeping soundly or make getting up in the morning a chore.

✔ **Are you dealing with multiple problems at the same time?** You know your financial problems are snowballing if:

- Multiple creditors are hounding you. (Check out Chapter 8.)

- Three or more situations (for example, financial, medical, and marital) are creating stress in your life.

✔ **Are you (or you and your partner) in conflict regarding the solution?** You may be arguing over:

- Increasing income to meet your lifestyle. (Refer to Chapter 13.)

- Decreasing expenses to adjust your lifestyle to meet your income.

- Getting a loan to pay off debt. (Flip to Chapter 8 for more.)

- Filing for bankruptcy. (Refer to Chapter 11.)

✔ **Are you 60 or more days late on your mortgage?** No matter what, you need to see a counselor now! A miscalculation can cost you

- Thousands of dollars.

- Even your home. (See Chapter 9 to avoid a foreclosure.)

✔ **Are you considering bankruptcy?** Getting counseling before you file is smart; otherwise, you may not know

- Whether bankruptcy is really right for you

- Whether another way out exists that is less damaging to your credit

> ✔ **Are you new to the United States and have you been rejected for credit?** You may need help if:
>
> - You don't understand how credit works in the United States.
>
> - You need to establish credit.
>
> - You want to get on with the American Dream as soon as possible. (Refer to Chapter 4 for more info.)

If you answered yes to any of these questions, you stand to benefit from talking to a professional who can help you see what your options are. In the following sections, I walk you through some of these issues.

Situations you can handle on your own

In the following sections, I outline three credit situations that you can probably resolve without much help. However, if you answered yes to any of the questions in the preceding section, do not pass go and do not collect $200 — go straight to getting help from someone you can trust.

Be sure that, if you go it alone, you

> ✔ Identify the cause of the problem and resolve it.
>
> ✔ Know how much money you have available to work with.
>
> ✔ Act quickly.

Credit cards

If you can't make this month's payment or if you've missed a month's payment already on your credit card, be proactive. As long as you know what you can afford, and you don't mind explaining your situation over the phone, you can get quick results. Here's what to do: Call the toll-free customer-service number and tell them who you are, what happened, and how you'd like to handle it. If you need a break from having to make payments, say so. If you can make up the missed payments over the next month or two, make an offer (just make sure your offer is something you can make good on).

Usually, if you're proactive and contact the credit-card company before they contact you, this approach will establish you as a good customer who needs and deserves some special consideration — much better than a customer who's behind in payments, doesn't call, and may be a collection risk.

Be careful about asking for a payment to be stretched out for more than a month or two. If you need three months to catch up, you may get it — or even qualify for a longer hardship program — but the creditor may close your account, which hurts your credit.

You may be asked to do more than you think you can. Do *not* agree to anything you don't think you can deliver. Saying that something isn't possible, and explaining why, is much better than caving in but not being able to follow through. Ask to talk to a supervisor — he or she may have more authority to bend the rules.

Mortgages

If you're within the grace period allowed in your loan documents and you have the money to make up the shortfall, just send it in. If you're past the grace period, you have varying amounts of time to make up the deficit, depending on the state you live in. Say you're behind on your monthly payment of $1,000. If you can only send in $500 extra with the next month's $1,000 payment, you'll still be short $500, right? Wrong. You may be behind the full $2,000 if the bank doesn't accept either payment because you didn't catch up in full. So, the gist is, if you aren't far behind and you can catch up in one shot, do it. Otherwise, don't delay — see "Choosing the Right Credit-Counseling Agency for You" later in this chapter and get help.

Mortgage lenders count delinquency times differently than credit card issuers do. As soon as you're late, the 15-day grace period is counted as 15 days late. After you're 90 days late from the due date (not the grace period), all the rules change and you're in big danger of a foreclosure! (Check out Chapter 9 to find out what a foreclosure can do to your credit and how to avoid it.)

Student loans

Getting a short-term waiver isn't difficult if you have a good reason for not being able to pay. Unemployment, a low-paying job, illness, a return to school — each of these reasons may qualify you for a short-term waiver, but only if you give the lender a call before you get into a default situation. The student-loan people are usually very forgiving as long as they think you're playing it straight with them.

If you don't have enough money to apply to your financial problem, you won't be able to satisfy your creditors. But don't despair: There's a way to find it. The first step in addressing a financial problem is to maximize your sources of income and minimize your expenses. A spending plan or a budget helps you with that. Turn to Chapter 13 for more on budgeting.

Problems you'll need some help with

Certain situations create more financial stress than others. Credit counseling can help with these four types of problems that can wreak the most havoc:

✔ **Multiple bill collectors:** Most people can handle one or two collectors. But when you get to five, ten, or even more, you're pulled in many directions at once by their conflicting demands. It only takes one unreasonable creditor to make your situation impossible.

✔ **Joint credit problems:** Credit problems are exacerbated when you share them with someone who doesn't see things the way you do. Compromising is hard enough in good times; in stressful situations, finding solutions agreeable to everyone can be much more difficult.

✔ **Debts that are backed by assets:** If you take out a loan to buy a car, your loan is secured by that car. If you take out a loan to buy a house, your loan is secured by the house. In other words, *security* is what you stand to lose if you don't or can't pay back the money you borrowed. For example, if you don't make your car payment, the lender can take your car. If you don't pay your mortgage, the lender can take your house. If you don't pay your credit-card bill, the lender doesn't have any collateral it can take, because it has no security beyond your word and your willingness to pay as agreed.

As a general rule, the more security lenders have, the less willing they are to work with you to solve what is clearly "your problem." It's easier than most people think to lose assets if you're not making payments. Often, the rules are complex and not well explained by the lender. Because the loans are secured (by the assets, like the car or the house), the lenders tend not to get very excited about deficits. They can't lose — but you can! If you can't come up with the entire deficit quickly, get help before things snowball. This is especially true for cars. They can be repossessed if you're even a week or two late on a payment.

✔ **Bankruptcy:** The law requires that you get credit counseling before you file for bankruptcy and credit education before you're discharged. Be sure to pick a good agency that does a lot of this stuff. It should be fast, efficient, and cost effective. Otherwise you could run into problems and delays later on. See Chapter 11 on bankruptcy for more info.

Working with an Agency

A legitimate, certified credit counselor may be just the help you need to begin resolving your financial woes. A credit-counseling agency serves as an objective party to help you sort through your problems, see your situation through the eyes of professional, give you some credit education, offer personalized budgeting advice, and design a customized plan to get you out of debt — all for nothing or next to nothing.

A brief update on credit counseling in the U.S.

In the beginning, credit-counseling agencies were generally community-based groups that specialized in helping local residents through financial-education classes, personal budgeting, and customized plans (often called *debt-management plans*) to get the individual out of debt. Credit counselors were serious and sometimes difficult people to deal with. Filled with the burning spirit often found in small, messianic, nonprofit agencies, they required the debt-shocked people who showed up on their doorsteps to fill out endless forms. Then, even after extensive counseling, the counselors sent the consumers home to think over their recommendations and be sure they weren't rushing to an inappropriate solution. A less-than-positive customer-service experience, to say the least.

In the mid-1990s, some enterprising people figured out how to make money in this industry. Similarly to what has happened recently in the subprime mortgage market, some charged huge fees, advised inappropriate solutions (to get more huge fees), and left a trail of personal and financial devastation in their wake. This new industry was made up of ultraprofitable debt mills, which had the resources to dominate the advertising media while operating on the edge of the nonprofit laws. Don't get discouraged, however; legitimate credit-counseling agencies are still out there and customer service has improved greatly. Most agencies are now open evenings and weekends. They do business over the phone and over the Internet, as well as in person, and they have quality standards for their services. In many ways, they've become more technologically based but have retained their mission and customer-focused values. They're much better organizations than they were even as recently as four years ago. From a consumer credit-counseling service, you can not only get help for your immediate credit problem, but also get information and guidance that will set you in the right direction for a debt-free future.

The IRS and state regulators have stepped up enforcement of laws and are weeding out the bad apples. The government tends to move slowly, so be sure to exercise caution when choosing an agency (see "Choosing the Right Agency for You" later in this chapter).

Beware of services that overcharge and under-serve the credit-impaired, offering a product based on technology rather than public-service, mission-oriented values. If you're already up to your eyeballs in debt, avoid these debt mills like the plague! You need the maximum help for the minimum cost and you won't find it with them. (I help you differentiate the good guys from the bad guys later in this chapter.)

What credit-counseling agencies do and how they work

A credit-counseling agency analyzes your sources of income and your expenses. The agency

    ✔ Details what you owe

    ✔ Gives you an organized picture of your financial situation

    ✔ Provides options that match your resources, lifestyle, and goals

    ✔ Tells you the steps you need to take to reach those goals

Whether you first contact a credit-counseling agency by phone, e-mail, or in person, the counselor asks you why you're there, what you'd like to accomplish at the meeting, and what your short- and long-term goals are.

Then some fairly detailed data-gathering takes place. You're asked about your income sources and tax deductions, as well as your monthly expenses. Having a good idea about what your monthly expenses are is very helpful, but it isn't a requirement — if you don't know, the credit counselor can help you estimate them. A quick subtraction of expenses from income tells you how much you have available for monthly debt service, if any. The counselor suggests ways to adjust your expenses or income to get you to a *positive cash-flow* position (one in which more money is coming into your household than is going out).

Next, you and the counselor go over all the debts you have to pay. The positive cash flow from the earlier calculation is applied to the amount you have to pay out. If anything is left over, you're basically done — you leave with an action plan and a budget you can follow to keep your expenses in line with your income. If the result is negative (you have more expenses than you have income), you and your counselor rework the expenses to free up cash flow and your counselor tells you what your debt service fee would be under a *debt-management plan* (see the "Debt-management plans" section, later in this chapter, for more detail).

This process of reducing your expenses and increasing your income continues until you and the counselor get to a positive cash flow or it becomes apparent that, no matter what you do, the numbers just don't work in your favor. If you can't get to a positive cash flow, the counselor refers you to an attorney or other community resources for additional help.

Everything I describe in this section can be done through snail mail or e-mail, over the phone, or via a Web site. Often, the process involves more than one of these methods over a series of contacts and days. For example, you might start out on the Internet filling out a contact form and answering questions, you might follow up with a phone call to clarify and discuss matters further, and then you might go into an office or use the mail to finalize your solutions. The method of contact you use is just a matter of what you're most comfortable with — one method isn't better than another.

You get to make all the choices about what happens next, whether it's tightening your belt, cutting out piano lessons to stretch household income, or seeing an attorney to pursue legal remedies. It's your life and it's your money, so you get to pick the approach that works for you.

What a credit-counseling agency can offer you

Alas, no magic wand exists to make all your financial problems disappear, but a good certified credit counselor can always offer solutions. Expect more than one solution, and expect some solutions you don't like. Your counselor can give you a balanced perspective of what you need to do, how long it will take, and what resources are available to help you along the way. Your counselor will probably discuss bankruptcy, as well as other solutions. The key: The counselor proposes solutions not only in light of your current situation, but also in light of your future needs.

Goal setting for the future

A good credit counselor offers solutions with your future goals in focus. A solution that works best for you is one that not only deals with current issues but also takes into account how you see your future. For example, if you're planning to buy a house, get a security clearance at work, or send your triplets to college in five years, that future goal affects the course of action that best fits your needs.

Improved communication with your family

For about 75 percent of the approximately 2 million people who bare their souls to credit counselors each year, advice and direction are all they need. One unexpected byproduct is improved financial communication. For many couples and families, credit counseling is the first time that goals, spending priorities, and even some secrets such as hidden debts are openly discussed.

An action plan that works for you

Expect to have a customized *action plan* when you're finished with your credit counselor. To be useful, an action plan has to fit you and the way you live. If it doesn't, you won't follow it. You don't wear clothes that are too tight — and you won't follow a poorly fitted financial plan. A comfortable budget designed with your spending and saving style in mind is more likely to be something you'll follow.

If you're struggling toward the abyss of debt, a good credit-counseling agency can help you understand how you landed in your predicament, what you need to do to correct the problem, and how to maintain your good financial reputation. For example, one man I worked with was having trouble making ends meet and didn't know why. When a budget was created, it turned out that although he thought he was spending less than $100 a month on food, he was really spending over $700 eating out with his girlfriend! A few words with his honey, and he was back on track again.

An often overlooked aspect of using a nonprofit credit-counseling agency is that they know a lot about other community resources that may be able to help. Doing due diligence before making referrals to other resources, whether community, legal, or otherwise, is part of a good agency's service.

The credit-counseling process isn't something you can breeze through in 15 minutes, because the plan you walk away with is tailor-made for you and your financial situation.

Periodic checkups

Expect some fine-tuning as you go. Although your counselor anticipates as much as possible when developing your plan, he can't foresee the future. Murphy's Law applies to credit counseling in spades. Not only can things go wrong, but with limited financial resources, every bump in the road feels much worse. Ongoing involvement with your credit-counseling agency as you navigate this credit-repair journey helps you stay the course. Expect the agency to make this easier for you by giving you names, e-mail addresses, and phone numbers of people to contact beyond the agency for more help. You should be able to go back to your counselor for additional suggestions and referrals as you go along, although most people, when they have a workable plan in hand, are off on their own.

Debt-management plans

For about 25 percent of those who turn to credit counselors, more than advice is prescribed. In these cases, in addition to the action plan (see "An action plan that works for you," earlier in this chapter), a debt-management plan is recommended. A debt-management plan (sometimes called a *debt-repayment plan*) involves the agency as an intermediary (for a small monthly fee it handles both communications and payments on your behalf) and it includes revised payments that:

- ✔ Are acceptable to all your creditors
- ✔ Leave you enough money to handle your living expenses
- ✔ Generally get you out of debt in two to five years

An alternative to bankruptcy. A workout plan. Debt consolidation. An interest-rate-reduction plan. All these descriptions have been attributed to debt-management plans. In fact, debt-management plans offer all these benefits — and perhaps a lot more. Here's how: When creditors realize that you can't meet the original terms of your credit cards or other loan agreements, they also realize that they're better off working with you through your credit counselor. Under a debt-management plan, your creditors are likely to be open to a number of solutions that are to your advantage. These include:

- ✔ Stretching out your payments so that the combination of *principal* (the amount you originally borrowed) and interest will pay off your balance in 60 months or less

---

The value of an intermediary

Some people wonder why a credit-counseling agency has to serve as an intermediary as part of the debt-management plan. Why can't the agency just set up a plan and leave you to follow it on your own, without paying them a monthly fee?

The answer is twofold:

✔ **Most people hit a bump or two in the repayment road.** Through its ongoing involvement, your credit-counseling agency can explain your situation to the creditor, dispassionately and professionally. Many plans would blow up at the first misstep without the trusted intermediary to smooth strained communications.

✔ **The creditors want the credit-counseling agencies involved.** Agencies can be easily reached for questions, the agencies' checks don't bounce, and the agencies don't get excited and yell over the phone the way consumers have been known to do.

✔ Changing your monthly payments to an amount you can afford to pay

✔ Reducing your interest rate and/or any fees associated with your loan

✔ Stopping creditors from hounding you day and night

Why would creditors be willing to do all these things for you? Because if they don't do some or all of them, and if you really can't make the payments, they'll spend a lot more money on collections than they'd give you in concessions. Plus, maybe you'll file bankruptcy — and then your creditors may *never* get their money.

The critical point here is that the creditor has to believe that you can't make the payments as agreed. But how does the creditor believe that without staking out your house or apartment to verify that you aren't drinking champagne and driving a new Corvette? The creditor generally takes the word of the nonprofit credit-counseling agency you've gone to for help. Still, being lenders, they may not be able to resist checking your credit report from time to time while you're on a debt management plan to make sure you haven't opened new lines of credit.

Sounds like a good deal: lower interest rates, smaller payments, and all. Well, the debt-management plan isn't a free lunch. The minuses may include

✔ A possible negative impact on your credit report (although just being in a debt-management plan doesn't affect your FICO score)

✔ An increase in interest rates (unless you pay in full and through the credit-counseling agency you originally signed up with)

✔ Restricted access to credit during the term of the plan

✔ Difficulty in changing credit-counseling agencies after you begin a debt-management plan

The bottom line is this: If you're in debt crisis or you're concerned you may be getting close to it, a debt-management plan from a good credit-counseling agency may be just the solution. If you're just shopping for an interest-rate reduction or a consolidation-loan alternative, a debt-management plan may *not* be in your best interest.

Protection for your financial reputation

Think of your credit report as your electronic financial reputation. If you do what you promise, the report is good. If you don't do what you promise, your report gets ugly. A credit-counseling agency can help you, through a debt-management plan, to renegotiate the terms of debt *before* your bad credit behavior hits your credit report and ruins your reputation.

A faster repair process

If you already have a bad credit report, credit counseling can help you restore your financial reputation faster. For example, say you were five months late on a $200 monthly payment. Your next bill will show $1,200 due, and your credit report will show that you're five months late. Typically, after three on-time payments of the new agreed-upon amount (the amount in your debt-management plan, which may be less than $200 and may be at a reduced interest rate), your account may be reported to the credit bureau as "current." That's a good thing!

Steering clear of debt-settlement plans

Debt settlement is not the same as credit counseling or a debt-management plan. Debt settlement is, in the opinion of many experts, an unethical approach to solving your financial issue. It is sometimes advertised as a way to save money, but it can be one of the most expensive methods of all! In a *debt-settlement plan,* you pay money to a company that holds your money without making any payments until your credit is trashed, the creditor gives up hounding you, and the creditor is supposedly ready to take less than the face value of the debt.

This course of action will *severely* damage your credit for years to come. If that's not enough to scare you off, consider this: Often, if you actually get to a settlement, the amount forgiven by the creditor becomes income to you! You guessed it: The IRS wants taxes on the forgiven amount — which can, in some cases, add up to thousands of dollars due on April 15 to Uncle Sam. And those agents at the IRS don't go away! Even if you later decide to go the bankruptcy route, the IRS still gets its money.

Debt settlement is an unsavory business in which the worst players keep all your money if you miss a payment to them. My advice: Don't do it!

To reach the current-account or on-time stage on your credit report without credit-counseling assistance, you would have to make your current payment of $200 each month, plus a monthly late charge in addition to many more payments above $200 — until the $1,200 deficit was made up. In addition, under the terms of a debt-management plan, creditors often eliminate over-limit and late fees, as well as reducing your interest rate — which you'd be hard-pressed to get them to give you on your own. The net effect is that more of your money goes to reducing your debt load faster.

Choosing the Right Agency for You

You've done the hardest part already; deciding to look for assistance isn't easy. Now all you need to do is follow a few simple guidelines that can help you choose the best agency, and you'll be on the road to credit wellness.

But how do you separate the debt mills (which may exacerbate your credit woes) from the genuine nonprofit services that help people and families regain financial control and credit health? Don't fret — in this section, I help you identify the real community servants and arm you with the right questions to ask to make sure you get the help you need.

What to look for in a credit-counseling agency

The best way to be sure you're working with a legitimate nonprofit organization is to ask if the agency is currently accredited by the Council on Accreditation (COA). COA is the largest third-party accreditor of nonprofits and does a very comprehensive, agency-wide audit of practices, safeguards, and policies before certifying an agency. Perfectly good nonprofits are out there that *aren't* accredited, but no dishonest agencies *are*.

Good questions to ask a credit-counseling agency before you start working with them include the following:

> ✔ **Is your organization not-for-profit?** Some nonprofits are shams, so the fact that an agency is nonprofit doesn't mean it's good. So, be sure to ask about affiliations with organizations you know (like local housing authorities, the United Way, the military, or governmental agencies such as the U.S. Department of Housing and Urban Development [HUD] or the Federal Reserve). You can verify nonprofit status by calling your state agency that regulates charities or by checking on www.guidestar. org, which has a database of 1.7 million nonprofits you can check for free.

✔ **Are your counselors certified? Who provides the certification?** Certification of credit counselors by an independent third-party organization is a sign that the organization is committed to adhering to quality standards set for the credit-counseling profession. (See "Looking for accreditation," later in this chapter, for more information.)

✔ **What fees will I be charged?** Do not, under any circumstance, work with an agency that charges a large upfront fee. Some agencies promise to allow you to earn the fee back over a period of time — walk away. The conditions and timing may make it unlikely that you'll earn it back. Besides, you need the cash more than the agency does! And don't forget, the best agencies counsel you for free. If they recommend a debt-management plan, the agency may charge a setup fee and a low monthly fee you can afford. (See "Paying the Piper: The Cost of Counseling," later in this chapter, for more info on counseling fees.)

✔ **How long will the counseling take?** Anything less than 30 to 45 minutes will just deal with surface issues and won't help you to set new goals, understand how you got into debt in the first place, and figure out how to stay out of debt in the future.

✔ **What lifestyle changes will I need to make to be successful?** To be successful in getting out of debt, you probably have to make changes in your spending habits. The agency should help you learn to budget, set financial goals, and begin a savings program.

Any agency that you're considering should be willing to discuss all these issues with you. If the organization is not willing to answer or does not spend the time to give satisfactory responses, find a different agency.

With all the different choices out there, take your time and do your research before choosing a credit-counseling agency. You want to choose an agency that is reputable, works with your interests and needs in mind, and expresses interest in helping you improve your financial situation in both the short- and long-term.

What should you expect when you turn to a credit-counseling agency for help? Check out the following list:

✔ **Agency accreditation and certified counselors:** Insist on independently certified counselors and an independently accredited agency. Mr. Goodwrench who works on your car is certified, Mr. Goodbucks who works on your spending plan and credit should be, too! (See the "Looking for accreditation" section of this chapter for details about two accreditation services.)

If you're looking for an agency to help with prefiling bankruptcy counseling, be sure to ask whether they've been approved by the Executive Office of the U.S. Trustee (EOUST). Only an agency so certified can give a certificate that will allow you and your attorney to make your bankruptcy filing.

After you've requested the certificate, be sure to ask how long it will take to get your certificate before you begin. Delays can be expensive and frustrating. Also, be sure you're using an agency that does a lot of bankruptcy counseling and can deliver your certificate at once — preferably via e-mail to you or directly to your attorney.

✔ **Professional service and basic courtesy:** You should be treated professionally, the same as if you were meeting with a certified public accountant (CPA) or an attorney. The office décor may not meet the standards of a high-powered law firm, but the service level should. Look for friendliness and patience. Following a courteous greeting, you should be given the opportunity to explain in detail what issues brought you to the agency and what help you would like.

✔ **Thoroughness:** Expect to answer questions about what deductions come out of your paycheck, what you spend in detail, and what you owe to whom. Expect some questions that you hadn't thought of.

✔ **Multiple written solutions:** Expect to get more than one choice to address your concerns. Expect these solutions in writing. You should also get a written budget or spending plan that is based on your situation, not general guidelines.

✔ **Appropriate fees:** Upfront fees, if any, should be no more than $75. Better yet, the agency will offer low, pay-as-you-go, monthly fees no greater than $50 a month. The agency gets paid as you get help, and it has an incentive to keep you happy. (See "Paying the Piper: The Cost of Counseling," later in this chapter.)

✔ **Willingness to spend time:** A good credit counselor works efficiently but takes the time necessary to understand your problem and to educate you. A ten-minute phone conversation or e-mail exchange isn't counseling. The real value of counseling (as opposed to being jammed into a debt-management plan) is understanding how you got where you are. You're provided a range of options and come away with a workable plan that includes a detailed analysis of income and expenses.

Making sense of agency claims

What can a credit-counseling agency really do for you? In the blitz of hype, promises, and vaguely misleading ads, the answer is confusing at times. As long as you commit the time, pay the fees, and don't run up your credit cards, here are the kinds of valid claims you can expect from an agency:

✔ **Some interest concessions (reduction in your interest rates):** One or two of your interest rates may go down a lot; others may go down just a little — your interest rates depend on your creditors, not on the agency.

The agency has more clout in persuading the creditor to offer some leeway than you would have on your own. For example, one major creditor I know reviews each debt-management plan, line by line, and offers interest concessions based on your need, as well as its corporate policy. An agency that takes the time to explain your situation to that creditor may be able to save you a few percentage points.

✔ **Cessation or reduction of collection calls:** The agency will likely be able to persuade your creditors to stop the haranguing calls from the collection companies. The calls usually stop after you've made payments for about three months, though some creditors will stop calling you as soon as your debt-management plan is in place. Very few, if any, creditors will continue calling you if they're getting paid regularly.

✔ **Waiver of late charges and over-limit fees:** The agency can usually arrange to have these charges waived after a plan is launched.

✔ **Current-account status on your credit report:** With the help of a credit counselor and a good debt-management plan, your accounts may be brought to a current status on your credit report within three months. The federal regulators allow creditors to re-age your account for good reason once every five years. Every month that your payment is short or missing, your account ages from 30 days late to 60 days late and so on. When an account is _re-aged,_ it's brought up to current or pays-as-agreed status in one shot — but only once in a 60-month period. Usually, three successive payments do the trick, even if you're more than three payments behind.

✔ **Halting of court actions for wage garnishment:** If court actions to garnish your wages are pending, those may still go ahead, but the actions will often stop just before the court order is executed. Your creditors will want to be ready to collect if you fail to pay, but most creditors recognize that, by taking your wages, they're inviting you to file bankruptcy — and if you file bankruptcy, they don't get any of the money you owe.

✔ **Improvement of bad-credit status:** If you have damaged credit when you start the process with your credit counselor, it will improve.

✔ **Referrals to helpful resources:** Your credit counselor is armed to supply you with referrals to community or professional resources to help you with everything from marriage counseling to job placement to substance abuse.

✔ **A personalized budget:** A written plan to help you budget your money and spend it based on your personal priorities is something that will provide benefit for years to come. This last item is, in my opinion, the most important and valuable. If you don't have a budget that allows you to spend your money on the things you decide you need, save some for a rainy day, and find ways to resist all the temptations that seduce you every day, nothing else you get from a credit counselor will help.

Some agency claims are just plain ridiculous. Here are samples of what a credit-counseling agency may promise but will *not* be able to do:

✔ Make you debt-free today.

✔ Reduce your debt up to 60 percent in seconds.

✔ Stop embarrassing collection calls as soon as you call an agency.

✔ Give you money in your pocket at the end of the month.

✔ Erase all your debts and save you thousands of dollars.

To add to the confusion, some of the terms used in ads have meanings that are very different from what you may think they mean at first glance. For example, consider the true meaning behind the following:

✔ "Not-for-Profit" doesn't mean inexpensive — or even honest.

✔ "IRS 501 (c) (3) approved" doesn't mean the agency has been investigated and approved by the IRS. It means the agency *told* the IRS it qualified for tax exemption under the tax code.

✔ "The agency has established relationships with creditors" doesn't mean it'll get a special deal for you. Creditors take money from anyone who will give it to them, and that's an "established relationship."

✔ "You'll get out of debt fast without repayment to your creditors" doesn't mean you can walk away from all your bills with the agency's settlement program. The agency is ignoring secured creditors (such as mortgage holders, child support, IRS debts, student loans, and others).

Seeking referrals

Finding an aboveboard agency can seem bewildering at times — even with the tips and warnings I provide in the previous sections. Sometimes, the decision can be made a bit easier when you know what reliable sources think of the place you're considering. In the following sections, I give you some places to turn for more information.

Looking for accreditation

Both the Council on Accreditation (COA; www.coanet.org) and the International Standards Organization (ISO; www.iso.org) accredit nonprofit credit-counseling agencies. COA specializes in nonprofit and government agencies in the United States. ISO is best known for standardizing for-profit and manufacturing companies worldwide. It also accredits nonprofits. ISO uses the same standards of quality for both.

Key aspects of accreditation include checking whether:

- ✔ Client funds are being handled appropriately.
- ✔ The agency is licensed to conduct business in the state you live in.
- ✔ The agency has a trained and certified staff.

Being accredited is a feather in an organization's cap and you can expect to see it prominently displayed on its Web site or informational materials. Just to be safe, ask if the accreditation is current — just because an agency was accredited years ago doesn't mean it is today.

Turning to Uncle Sam

Every state has a consumer-protection office, which can offer references to credit-counseling agencies. In some states, this office is part of the attorney general's office; in other states, it's the responsibility of the local district attorney. Either way, you can use today's equivalent of *The Untouchables* G-Man Elliott Ness to check out the agencies you're investigating. These public servants can tell you about complaints filed and legal action taken against credit-counseling agencies in your area.

While I'm on the topic of helpful civil servants, I always like to mention congressional delegations. Because the best credit-counseling agencies offer local education and information programs, often in conjunction with other community resources, those agencies are likely to have worked with the local congressperson's office in the past. Your elected officials like to refer constituents to organizations that are safe and won't cost them votes. They count votes, you count money — same thing! Explain to your congressperson that you'd like help finding a reputable credit-counseling agency in your area. (You won't be the first one to ask.) Your congressperson may want to contact the agency first, and then get back to you.

You can find the phone numbers for your state's consumer-protection office and congresspeople in the "Government" section of your Yellow Pages or in the blue pages of your phone book.

Seeking help from the Better Business Bureau

The Better Business Bureau (BBB) is a good source of information about complaints against companies and organizations in your area. However, the BBB isn't a judge of quality or an accrediting body and, as such, can't vouch for one agency over another. It's not unusual for businesses to have some complaints against them. But you should be on the lookout for the *number* of complaints relative to the size of the organization. A small agency with 5 complaints may be far worse to do business with than a very large one with 50. You don't want to do business with a dishonest company or even an honest company that's not very good at what it does!

Like many nonprofits, some local BBBs are hard-pressed to keep up their funding levels. As more companies go national or even global, fewer are available to fund local BBBs. They get their operating expenses covered from membership fees from the same companies they rate; as a result, I'm not as comfortable using the BBB as a main source of referral as I used to be in the past. However, most do a good job.

Tracking down information online

For the computer-comfortable, GuideStar provides a great Web site (www.guidestar.org) that puts together and distributes information on more than 1 million nonprofit organizations. The service has been around for over a decade and gets its funding from some of the biggest foundation names in the United States, including the Carnegie Corporation of New York, the Ford Foundation, the W. K. Kellogg Foundation, the Lilly Endowment, and so on — which just means it already has all the money it needs, so I feel comfortable recommending it to you!

At the site, plug in the name of the company in question, sign in, and you'll have access to IRS tax returns, a financial summary, and the names of those on the board of directors. Red flags include excessive salaries for the bosses (a salary for a large company boss can be larger than yours, but it shouldn't be excessive when compared to others in the same-size company in the same business), relatives of the bosses on the payroll, a lot more revenue than expenses, and any for-profit companies receiving big payments or that are owned by the bosses.

Paying the Piper: The Cost of Counseling

Credit counseling does entail a number of costs. Some are financial, others are personal, and some may affect you for years to come. Don't get nervous — *not* getting the help you need has costs, too, some of them devastating (paying more for credit and insurance, losing job opportunities, getting a divorce, dodging phone calls).

Who would ask someone who can't pay his bills or afford groceries to pay a fat counseling fee? No one you want to deal with, that's for sure. Legitimate credit counselors charge *very little* for their services — or nothing at all.

Credit counseling is one of those rare industries in which the more you pay, the worse service you're likely to receive. Why? Because the best agencies understand that you're having trouble paying bills and that every dollar you pay them is a dollar you can't send to your creditors. So the agency keeps its fees as low as possible. But how can they do this and still offer good service and attract qualified staff? Well, they get donations and grants from others, especially creditors, to keep their pricing as low as possible. A little like Robin Hood, the credit-counseling agency gets funding from the rich companies and gives affordable services to you!

For about 75 percent of people who seek credit counseling, the pain and suffering is brief. In the hour or so they spend with the counselor, they arrive at a solution and obtain the information they need to yield a huge change in behavior. And off they go, having paid little or nothing for their brief session with the credit counselor, but wiser for the experience. The other 25 percent of people who visit a credit counselor benefit from a debt-management plan. Because a debt-management plan is an ongoing program that takes months to work through, a small monthly fee — $10 to $50, depending on the complexity and your ability to pay — may be charged. This fee is affordable and makes more sense than a fat, upfront fee that may cause you to slip farther behind in your bill payments.

Table 3-1 outlines the fees you should expect to pay, as well as fees that you can safely consider unreasonable. If the agency you've approached charges you fees that fall in the "Unreasonable" column, find another agency.

Table 3-1	The Costs of Credit-Counseling Services	
	Reasonable	*Unreasonable*
Counseling*	Free to $50	Your first-month debt-management-plan payment ($100 to $1,000)
One-time setup fee*	Free to $75	More than $100
Monthly fee	$15 to $50	More than $75

*There may be other optional charges for things like getting a copy of your credit report or educational materials (such as books), but you should have the choice to say, "No thanks."

Some agencies try to justify large fees by saying you can earn it all back, plus more, through their incentive programs. If you hear this pitch, walk away — incentive programs don't work. In addition, some agencies ask for a percentage of the money you save on interest and fees. If this sounds familiar, walk away. You need the money more than the agency does — and if the agency doesn't understand that, it doesn't understand credit counseling.

I said there were personal costs, too: Admitting to a stranger that you need help is humbling. Realizing you haven't exactly been communicating with your spouse about money matters — and then having to do so — can be daunting. Lastly, changing behavior isn't easy. Yet more than 2 million individuals and families seek credit counseling each year — and grow a bit because of it.

How are credit counselors compensated?

Offering a quality hour of credit counseling costs a lot — but you won't be paying for it. You can't afford to cover what your credit-counseling agency's help, rent, and overhead costs, so the agency accepts donations from your creditors, who *can* afford it. This situation has never bothered me, because creditors understand the risks and costs of lending. They have to take some responsibility for the damage done by generous, risk-based lending rules — or in some cases, the lack thereof — and for not providing much in the way of instruction for the proper use of their products.

Be assured, however, that despite the fact that good credit-counseling agencies are being subsidized by your lender, the agencies will work for you to come up with the best solution acceptable to all parties and, if push comes to shove, will put your interests over those of the creditors every time. Finally, individual counselors should never be compensated based on the outcome of a counseling session. In reputable agencies, they are paid salaries or hourly rates based on helping you find an appropriate solution, not selling either a product or a debt-management plan.

Chapter 4

Identifying Credit Issues for the Underbanked and Newcomers

Credit is as American as apple pie. However, getting the credit you need is easier said than done — particularly if you're new to the credit system. Whether you're seeking credit for the first time, perhaps as an immigrant to the United States or a recent high school or college graduate, or starting over, such as after a divorce, obtaining the credit you need can be a stressful endeavor. You may feel like you're fighting a battle you just can't win.

Not to worry though. In this chapter I help you understand why establishing a credit history and financial services relationships are essential to getting the credit you need. Your confidence gets a boost when I show you the size and importance of the underbanked market (people like you whose financial needs aren't being met) to lenders, so you know just where you stand. I also debunk some credit myths that you may have brought with you from another country or been taught right here at home. And in case you make an early mistake or two, I give you some tips on how to make corrections and get back on the road to good credit quickly. Credit is as American as mom and apple pie, so take your seat at the table and help yourself to a big piece of the American dream . . . credit.

Defining the Underbanked Consumer

Just who and what is the underbanked market? In the broadest sense, the term *underbanked* refers to anyone whose financial needs aren't currently being fully met, including those individuals who are under-served by the credit industry. Among those individuals included in this catchall category are

- ✔ **Immigrants:** Legal or not, to be financially successful in the United States you need to establish a U.S. credit history.

- ✔ **Consumers new to credit:** The longer you wait to establish a credit history, the longer you pay more for basic services like check-cashing and short-term (payday) loans. Some examples include Gen Ys who are taking their place in society and Gen Xers and Boomers who are starting life over for reasons ranging from divorce to death of a spouse or life partner.

- ✔ **Cash-paying households:** You live in a cash economy, with many of your financial decisions driven by the realities of whatever the next day brings, be it good or bad. Incomes tend to be moderate, assets few, and the money comes and goes. "Cash in hand" is comforting for many.

- ✔ **Those individuals without strong banking relationships for whatever reason:** This group includes rugged individualists, people who really like their privacy, as well as students and individuals reentering the credit market after a long absence.

If you fall into one of these categories, you represent a fundamentally different market from your banked counterparts. Over the years, you have found ways to address your financial service needs outside of the mainstream system — through check-cashers, payday lenders, retailers, friends, and family.

Don't confuse the underbanked with the subprime market. Just because you're new to credit in no way means that you have a poor credit history. As a market segment, you collectively represent the full spectrum of credit risks that my friends at VantageScore refer to as high risk to superprime (see Chapter 2 for more info). You make up one of the largest untapped credit markets in the United States — estimated at between 40 and 50 million people. Financial service providers want to offer you their full range of products and services in order to expand their customer base and profits.

Overcoming Old Attitudes about Banking and Credit

Depending on your culture or what your friends and family may have told you, you may not be comfortable with using credit. However, rest assured, many people safely use credit on a daily basis. Doing so can often increase their enjoyment of life and all it has to offer. The following list spells out

Why banks want to do business with you

Why do banks do anything? To make money, of course. Oh yes, they talk about a lasting relationship and desire to help the community, but why else would they do so except to make money in those communities? Now this isn't necessarily a bad thing. You're already paying a price for using cash and nontraditional financial products. Why not pay less and get into the mainstream banking and credit world? It can be tricky if you don't know the rules and expensive if you make a mistake, but by following the suggestions in this chapter, you'll know everything necessary to join in.

With hundreds of millions of dollars in profits at stake, some of the biggest and best names in the financial services industry are vying to get you to try their products and services, hoping you'll like them and become long-term customers. Why do they like long-term customers? You guessed it; they're more profitable. Selling something new to someone who knows you is easier than selling to a stranger. So banks want your business. Most are not out there trying to rip you off with high fees and penalties; instead, they want you to use their products to your advantage.

So, now that you know you're a valued customer in a large market segment that banks want to do business with, you should expect to be well-treated, respected, and yes, maybe even spoiled just a little. Anything less and you can just move on to the next player who may know better how to treat a valuable customer like you.

some commonly held misconceptions about banking and credit, and debunks the myths:

- ✔ **Banks are not safe places to put money because they can close and go out of business, causing you to lose all your money.** Not so. All depository institutions (like banks) are insured by the full faith and credit of the U.S. government. No one has ever lost a penny of money that was in a federally insured depository account.

- ✔ **Currency is unsafe because it can decrease in value or become worthless overnight.** When you deposit money into a U.S. bank, it is deposited in dollars. The dollar, while subject to fluctuations in value, is the most stable and trusted currency in the world. For example, Arab sheiks price their oil in dollars. The dollar is used as the currency of a number of countries in the Caribbean and Central America. More countries hold more bonds denominated in dollars than any other currency. So, it's safe!

- ✔ **The government can nationalize your bank and your account.** The government only steps in and takes over a bank if it is about to fail. If the government takes over your bank, a very rare occurrence, your deposits are guaranteed by an agency of the U.S. government like the Federal Deposit Insurance Corporation (FDIC) or the National Credit Union Administration (NCUA).

> ✓ **You need to be rich to be a respected customer of a bank.** Not so. Adding new customers is a top priority for banks, and the size of your account, no matter how small your deposits may be, doesn't determine your value as a customer. It never hurts to be a big depositor, but in the United States no one knows who will be successful tomorrow, so everyone gets treated well. If a bank doesn't respect you on your terms, you should take your money to a competing bank.

> ✓ **Cash has many advantages over credit or debit cards.** A lost or stolen card is protected against misuse by another person (most have a liability of $50 or less); lost or stolen cash is gone. Unlike cash, using a card creates a record that can be followed. This isn't a cause for concern — the government isn't interested in tracking or spying on its citizens as a matter of course. Rather, this record constitutes the credit history you need to up your credit score. Payments for defective goods or services purchased with a credit card may be disputed and recovered, unlike cash payments.

> ✓ **I have only a consular ID, not a Social Security number. I can't build a credit history.** Not true. You can establish a credit history and use credit without a Social Security number. A Social Security number is not even in the top three match criteria used to place a credit history in the right credit bureau file. Your name, date of birth, and address are more important, so be sure to report them correctly and the same way each time you use credit.

The following sections explain why you need credit and why it's safe. Hopefully, this information can ease your potential anxiety about any misconceptions you may have.

Why you need credit

What do you hope to achieve in your life? Maybe you want a good job, a safe place to live, a car, some financial security, and a better life for your kids. Sounds pretty straightforward, doesn't it? Yet the reality of life in the United States is that to accomplish goals like these, you need good credit.

For starters, consider that good job. Say the company you want to work for has narrowed the field down to you and a couple of other candidates. How does the boss make a choice? This is where having a credit history may come into play. People can lie about their experience (ADP Screening and Selection Services says that about 30 to 41 percent of applicants lie on their resumes) and they can fake being nice, but a good credit history is tough to fake. As one employer put it, "When you think about it, people who have good credit keep their promises and are responsible, so it makes sense that if their credit is good, they may be more honest." So, all other things being equal, the job may go to the candidate with the best credit history.

To a greater or lesser degree, the same thing happens when you try to rent an apartment, get a security clearance, buy insurance, apply for a college loan, or earn a promotion at work. In all these circumstances, the person making the decision may check your credit history as part of the qualification process. Being underbanked and relying on cash may keep you out of the race for the things you want. It pays to understand how to build good credit and use the banking and financial system to your best advantage.

Why credit is safe

The credit industry didn't become the huge and powerful entity that it is without addressing the question of safety. Many laws have been implemented along the way to ensure the safety of credit users, and, as a result, you have access to one of the fairest and most market-driven credit systems in the world. The following laws play a major role in protecting borrowers in the United States:

- ✔ **The Fair and Accurate Credit Transaction Act (the FACT Act, also known as FACTA)** gives you lots of rights when it comes to how your credit is reported and what you can do to correct mistakes. It also gives you rights and remedies in the event that your identity is stolen, making you even more secure.

- ✔ **The Fair Debt Collection Practices Act** protects you — not the debt collector — and spells out what those guys can and can't do when they try to collect a debt. If they step over the line, you can sue them for big bucks.

- ✔ **The Truth in Lending laws** assure you that you won't find any hidden surprises when you borrow money. All the costs of doing so must be spelled out for you before you sign a contract.

Using credit is made even safer by additional laws governing purchases made with credit. Consider the following:

- ✔ If you use a credit card to purchase a service or a product and it fails to live up to your expectations, you can get a refund from the credit card issuer rather than the company you bought it from.

- ✔ If a card is stolen and used without your permission, you aren't liable for any charges under normal circumstances. Try that with cash!

- ✔ A single credit card can have a limit of several thousand dollars. Carrying that much cash in your pocket is an invitation for a bump on the head.

Recognizing What Your Credit History Doesn't Say about You

With all the information available to companies, the government, and others, you may easily think a huge dossier about your every movement is housed in your credit report. To clarify: A credit history is nothing more than a snapshot of your financial life to date.

The credit industry can be especially intimidating for newcomers. Keeping track of the information that can make or break your chances of getting credit may seem mind-boggling. However, identifying what is and isn't in your credit history may put you at ease. The good news is that only information sent into the credit bureaus by people with whom you choose to do business ends up in your file. And even then not all your information is reported. Some companies or service providers don't report credit activity at all. Doctors, hospitals, grocery stores, and others rarely, if ever, send any information to the credit bureaus. Other items that are not in your credit report include

- ✔ Your gender
- ✔ Your race or ethnicity
- ✔ Your country of national origin
- ✔ Your religion
- ✔ Your political affiliation
- ✔ Your checking- or savings-account information or major purchases that were paid in full with cash or check
- ✔ Business accounts (unless you're on record as being personally liable for the debt)
- ✔ Details about your personal lifestyle or friends
- ✔ Bankruptcies that are more than ten years old
- ✔ Charge-offs or debts placed for collection that are more than seven years old
- ✔ Your credit score (Although your credit score is generated based on information in your credit report, it is not part of the report itself.)

You have many legal rights to dispute out-of-date or inaccurate information in your credit report. These provisions are detailed in the FACT Act, which is spelled out on the accompanying CD. Check out Chapter 5 for more specific info about what *does* appear in your credit history.

Starting Your Credit Building on the Right Foot

You're ready to begin building your own credit, but you're not quite sure where to start. Take a deep breath and get ready for the ride. The Chinese say that a journey begins with a single step. Just goes to show how wrong people can be for thousands of years. The journey begins when you see a destination in your mind. Then, after packing your lunch and other essentials, you take a first step. You start slow and build up a credit history over a period of time. How much time depends on how active you are and which scoring model is used to rate your credit file.

Don't fret though. This section walks you through these steps to help you begin your credit journey down the right path.

Establishing credit without a Social Security number

You don't need a Social Security number to start building credit. In fact, a frequent objection to beginning to establish a credit history, and thereby a credit score, is the lack of a social security number, driver's license, or voter registration card. However, none of these items are required to establish a successful and envious credit record at any of the three major credit bureaus.

I recently spoke with a bureau representative and asked how incoming records are matched to files. He told me that when a credit bureau receives a new data line, the bureau matches the data with the following items, in the order shown:

1. Your name

2. Your birth date

3. Your address

4. Your Social Security number

So, no number? No problem. The bureaus can use plenty of other matching points to get your information in the right file. Do try to be consistent though! For example, make sure you use the same name every time you apply for or use credit.

Setting goals before you set out

Figuring out what your goals are prior to seeking out credit is an important step for anyone, but especially for the underbanked. Setting your goals and writing them down allows you to see what you need to do financially to achieve credit success.

To begin setting your goals, I suggest you and anyone you may be sharing your life with follow these steps. (That person may be a spouse, life partner, parent, family member, or trusted advisor. Who the person is isn't as important as the fact that he or she shares a desire to help you reach a goal and is committed to doing what it takes to do so.)

1. **Get together for some uninterrupted thinking time and dream about the future as you want to live it.**

   Set aside some time when you won't be interrupted to set goals. Get a sitter for the kids or do this when they're asleep. Allow at least an hour, and set an endpoint so you finish before one of you gets exhausted. You can always come back to this later after some reflection.

2. **Write down some short- (one year or less), medium- (one to five years), and long- (more than five years) term goals.**

   Some typical goals people have shared with me include: Beginning to save this year, beginning to save next year, getting out of debt in the next year, and repairing bad credit. Others would like to receive guidance with financial matters and find out about financial topics such as bank checking accounts, certificates of deposit (CDs), children's college accounts, retirement accounts, and bank savings accounts.

   Writing down your goals serves two purposes:

   - It clarifies what each person is talking about.
   - It makes your goals feel like real promises rather than just whims.

3. **Assign goals to each person and then make a list of those actions that need to be taken to reach each goal.**

   For example, if you want to reestablish your credit so you can get a good apartment and a better job, how do you do this? Some basic steps are to get a copy of your credit report at www.annualcreditreport. com and determine what needs to be paid or disputed and removed to improve your credit. Then make sure you make payments on time on all your accounts. It's simple, but it works. Chapter 13 has more suggestions and details about budgeting and goal setting.

4. **Track your progress.**

   Periodically talking about or reviewing progress to your goals is not only an incentive to keep up the good work, but it's an opportunity to celebrate your interim success.

A real-life couple: How goals can help

I love using examples to illustrate and clarify a concept. To help me with this, I invented Roland and Carlotta, two recently engaged young people who are new to credit and wanting to get a head start in their new lives. They begin by spending an hour one evening imagining what they want their futures to look like and then setting goals to make it happen.

Carlotta and Roland want to get married in a year, and they agree they want a better apartment, and eventually a small house for the new family they'd like to start as soon as they're able. Roland wants a better job than the hourly one he currently has and would really like to buy a better car. Carlotta wants to decorate their new place and buy some new furniture for it. Carlotta wants to establish credit for herself and Roland needs to repair his credit. Notice that you don't need to be in complete agreement on all the specifics as long as you can agree on the concept. You can make adjustments as you get closer to your goals.

Goal	Roland	Carlotta
Short term:	Get married	Plan a wedding and get married
		Establish credit
	Open savings and checking accounts	
Medium term:	Get a better apartment	Get a bigger apartment
	Repair credit	Furnish and decorate apartment
	Get a better job	
	Buy a car	
Long Term:	Buy a house	Buy a house
	Have six children	Start a family

Having a relationship with a bank

When a person says, "That's as good as money in the bank," he or she means that's as good as it gets. Having money in the bank is a good thing and the situation you want to be in. Being underbanked, you may not have a relationship with a bank or credit union. I can't stress enough how important this is to your ultimate success. You want to develop a relationship with a bank by setting up at least a checking account, not just so you have a place to take out a loan, avoid high interest charges, or get a platinum credit card to impress your friends, but more importantly, because you need a place to put the money you earn but don't spend right away. Saving is essential to your success.

Spending what you make or using credit to supplement your income is a recipe for disaster. There is no substitute for savings when life throws you a curveball. Chapter 14 has more detail on what you can do when times get tough. But without savings, even life's little bumps are hard to absorb.

Why you need to save

Everything is going along okay. What money comes in, goes out, and debt is under control. You may be a little short at the moment and your credit card balances may be building, but you figure that will all end as soon as you get that next promotion in six months. Then, your car breaks and costs $500 to repair, your tooth breaks at lunch and suddenly you need $900 for a crown and a day's work is lost, and your rent goes up by $100 a month. Where does the money come from if you have no savings?

You can use credit if you have any left. But if you do, you may be paying a high interest rate and getting close to your card limit. After that happens, your credit card issuer may be able to raise your rates even though you didn't miss a payment, so that $2,000 balance you've been carrying at 12 percent is now at 30 percent, and your minimum payment is huge.

If you don't have access to credit or savings, you have fewer choices. You may have to carpool, have the tooth removed rather than crowned, and be forced to move to less-expensive housing. That's why you need savings — because credit and good luck truly are never enough for you to be financially successful.

How to get started saving

Fortunately, getting started to save is easy, painless, and automatic as soon as you get going. The key is not to focus on how you're going to save six months' worth of living expenses, which could test even a saint. (For your information, St. Matthew the Apostle is the patron saint of money managers.) What I want you to do is start with a small savings program but make it automatic.

To get started saving, take the following steps:

1. **Go to a bank or credit union that is near where you live and ask about automatic deposit savings and checking accounts.**

   Most likely you don't have much to put in them, at least right now, but that doesn't matter. Limited funds are no excuse for not saving. Tell the bank you don't want any fees because you'll be using automatic deposit. If the bank charges a fee, go to another bank or credit union. Banks usually waive all fees for people who save regularly through payroll deductions.

2. **After you open two accounts, one checking and one savings, go to your human resources department or payroll person at work and say that you want your pay automatically deposited into these two accounts.**

   For example: You want all your take-home pay minus $5 (or more if you can) put into checking and the remaining $5 put into your savings account. At the end of the first pay period, you will have saved $5. Not a huge sum, but you're starting a habit that will grow and add up with time.

If direct deposit isn't available through your employer, you can have the bank automatically transfer money monthly from your checking account into your savings account.

3. **When you get that next raise or promotion, have half the increase automatically deposited into each account.**

Now you're making a smart financial move — increasing your savings by using the extra money from your raise before you have an opportunity to spend it! Do the same thing for IRS tax refunds and so on. In no time you'll have a cushion that will get you over life's bumps without stretching your credit or causing potential damage to your credit history!

Unless you're very vigilant about putting aside cash for savings, you're likely to end the month having spent what you brought in. To secure your financial future, stop cashing paychecks and get automatic deposit and automatic savings. You owe it to yourself, your sweetie, and your future.

Using prepaid and reloadable cards

When trying to build your credit, you may want to consider using prepaid and reloadable cards. These cards are fairly new to the underbanked market. They're neither a credit card nor a debit card; rather, they exist somewhere in between. You deposit money onto the cards at locations throughout the nation and then use them as you would a credit or debit card.

The following list outlines their major advantages:

- ✔ You can use money without getting hit over the head for the cash in your pocket.

- ✔ Many prepaid cards are accepted just the same as a MasterCard or Visa.

- ✔ You need no credit record or credit check, just your name, address, telephone number, and the ability to pay a one-time fulfillment fee. Non-U.S. citizens can provide an alternative form of ID, such as a driver's license, passport, or alien registration. Funds may post to your account within 30 minutes.

- ✔ Prepaid credit cards offer convenience, ease of availability, guaranteed approval, and other features that can make them ideal substitutes for credit cards.

- ✔ Prepaid cards are loaded with your own money — no credit here.

- ✔ You can use them on the Internet, on the phone, and in many other places just like a credit or debit card.

- ✔ They can help with financial discipline and the building of good financial habits.

Some prepaid cards claim to report to major credit bureaus but to my knowledge, at the time of this printing, they don't report to any of the big three national bureaus. Secondly, the fees for use can be high. Despite these facts, prepaid cards can still be useful.

Fattening up your credit file

You're not alone if your credit file is underweight. Today, up to 50 million U.S. adults — nearly 25 percent of the credit-eligible consumers in the United States — come back from credit inquiries to the major bureaus either as no-hits or as thin files. If you fit this category, don't worry. You can take action to move yourself along the credit history road. The following options work well for underbanked individuals:

- ✔ **Order some checks.** A check order means you must be using checks and a quick review of the check registries shows whether you have any bounced checks. Therefore, the system assumes you are using the checks successfully to pay bills and gives you some points for good check-writing.

- ✔ **Continue using your foreign credit card if you have one.** If you had an existing banking relationship before you came to the United States, you may be surprised to learn that it doesn't carry over into your U.S. credit file. A Visa card from a foreign bank does not generate a record on an American credit report. And the American credit bureaus can't import data from other countries either. However, you can still use your impeccable credit experience overseas to your advantage. You can either continue to use your foreign credit card here, or you can make an arrangement with a multinational bank to give you a letter extolling your virtues so the local underwriters will approve the issue of an American credit card that is listed with American credit bureaus.

  Global scoring is expected in the future, and, in fact, FICO has a proven Global Score that is accurate in every country in the world except France (surprise!). However, it isn't yet being used in any country of the world.

- ✔ **Ask that an Expansion score be used to score your application for credit.** This is a one-time snapshot of about 90 non-credit databases that tell whether you pay your obligations as agreed. Reporting real-time information rather than keeping a warehouse full of dated material may be the future of credit reporting. (Check out Chapter 2 for more info.)

- ✔ **Make use of your newly established savings account and take out a loan that is secured by your savings.** These loans, sometimes referred to as *passbook savings loans*, are a great way to build your credit. The loan is considered an installment loan because you're borrowing a specific amount with a defined monthly payment. Pay each month on time and you'll be well on your way to establishing your credit history.

✔ **Get a secured credit card.** These cards are a cross between a credit card and a prepaid card. After you've established a savings account and built up the balance, you can ask the bank to give you a credit card that is backed by your deposit in their bank. Sometimes you may qualify for a credit line in excess of the amount you have on deposit.

Each month you receive a billing statement and you can either pay the amount due or use some of the money on deposit to do so. Many credit issuers will eventually move you into a traditional credit card after a period of successful use of the secured card. The best part is that, unlike most prepaid cards, secure cards are reported to the three major credit reporting bureaus and can help you build a history and a score. They can be had for low or no fees if you shop around.

Chapter 18 offers more in-depth ways a person can build a good credit history. And Chapter 7 can help you keep it looking good.

Avoiding scams and unnecessary fees

Unfortunately, being new to something leaves you open to abuse by people who know the rules better than you do and decide to take advantage of your lack of knowledge. Scams perpetuated on immigrants and people who are new to credit have been around forever and are not about to go away. This section lists several scams that you're likely to run into, along with some guidelines on how to handle them.

Immigration consultants

The number of scam artists who prey on Spanish speakers and others who come to the United States in hopes of making a home here is increasing. Many have been swindled out of hundreds and even thousands of dollars by people claiming to be immigration "consultants." These so-called consultants may offer legal advice and fill out immigration paperwork.

Typical scams may include charging exorbitant fees for immigration services and then failing to file any documents; filing false asylum claims for people who don't understand English; and charging fees to prepare applications for nonexistent immigration programs or for real programs that you don't qualify for, such as asylum or labor certification.

If one of these consultants contacts you, be sure to get references and check them out carefully. Ask local social service agencies or low-cost attorneys if they can get you similar services for less.

Generally, they're neither qualified nor authorized to provide these services. The term *notary public* in Spanish, *notario publico,* refers to an attorney who has been trained to handle complex legal documents. Unscrupulous notaries deliberately play upon the language barrier to trick Spanish speakers into thinking they have legal expertise (which they don't) to match their high fees.

Payday loans

When the underbanked don't have savings or credit but do have an unexpected expense, what are they to do? An entire industry has arisen to answer this question. In a nutshell, if you have no options, are extremely vulnerable, and need to act quickly, someone will be glad to take advantage of you. Payday lenders charge a very high interest rate or fee for a short-term loan guaranteed by your next paycheck. Individuals without other credit resources are favorite targets of these extremely high-interest-rate loans. Payday loan establishments charge a fee for loaning you money based on the amount of your paycheck, and in return you must give them a post-dated check.

It's not unusual for the person seeking such a loan to need additional money after the original post-dated check is cashed by the payday loan shop. In worse shape yet are those who don't have the money in their account to cover the check written for the loan. This requires seeking an additional loan to cover the old one. Before you know it, a vicious cycle has begun with several high-fee, high-interest loans and no real way to pay them off. Payday lenders don't even report your loan experience to the credit bureaus, so even if you have a good experience you receive no credit-history-building benefit from using one of these outfits.

Refund Anticipation Loans (RALs)

Refund Anticipation Loans (RALs) are as bad as payday loans. RALs are high-fee loans that are secured by your tax refund that may, and the operative word here is *may*, get you your refund a week or so earlier than having it direct-deposited after filing your return electronically with the IRS. The real downside is that the person selling you the loan has an incentive to inflate your tax refund to get you to take out a higher loan.

If your actual refund is less than what you borrowed, you owe the difference plus a hefty interest rate. A much better idea is to open a bank account and have any refund direct-deposited. You get it fast, free, and with no surprises.

Check-cashing for a high fee

Going to a check-cashing place instead of a bank or credit union is like shopping at the most expensive store in town in the worst possible neighborhood. Check cashers are often located in places that are rife with crime. Why? Because everyone coming out has a pocket full of cash. A bank or credit union with which you have an account won't charge you to cash a check and you don't have to take all the cash with you when you leave — you can deposit it in your savings and checking accounts.

If you see a guard at the bank, remember that the guard is there to protect you! Not to give you a hard time. You are the valuable customer that the bank wants to take care of.

Instant credit rating

Credit repair companies may offer you either a new identity or a repaired credit rating for only a few hundred dollars — usually upfront. Don't spend the money. The new identity is often illegal and the instant credit repair doesn't exist.

Foreign bank accounts

Usually a letter or e-mail comes to say that you have been chosen, lucky you, to help a foreign rich person get some money into the United States and that you will receive a fat percentage of the amount for your small trouble because you are trustworthy. Most of these come from Nigeria but they can originate anywhere. If you don't know the person, don't do it.

Overcoming Credit Fears and Mistakes

Everyone makes mistakes, even the lenders and bureaus, so a mistake isn't a big deal if you deal with it quickly. The key is to get on top of the problem fast before they get bigger and smellier. Chapter 7 discusses what to do if you run afoul of the credit reporting system. Chapter 8 addresses what to do if you end up owing more than you can pay and have to deal with collectors.

As a person new to credit and maybe even new to the United States, you may be a tad scared of having to deal with credit and all that potentially can come along with it. Bill collectors aren't above using threats of deportation or imprisonment if they think it will help collect a bill. The truth is they can't do either. You won't be deported and you won't go to jail, no matter what they say. How do I know for sure? Well, these guys get paid for collecting the money due their employers. If they were to actually deport you or put you in jail, which they legally can't, they wouldn't get their money, would they?

You can find complete copies of the FACT Act and the Fair Debt Collection Practices Act, both of which spell out your rights, on the CD. Collectors may try to scare you — heck, they try to scare me — but if you understand your basic rights, you can overcome any mistakes quickly and easily.

If you're a credit newbie, keep these basic tips in mind for dealing with mistakes:

> ✔ **Do it fast.** Outstanding credit and debt issues don't improve with age. If you're proactive and make the call to solve a problem before you're called, then you'll get a much better reception and improve your chances of a favorable resolution.

✔ **Check your statements every month and challenge anything you don't understand or remember.** Errors may be disputed on your statements but often there are time limits. Also some errors may turn out to be the beginning of an identity theft. The sooner you notice a problem and challenge it, the better.

✔ **Do everything in writing.** You may resolve simple problems over the phone. But to protect your rights in a dispute, you need to make your case in writing. So if it's important, do it in writing and keep good records.

✔ **Keep good notes of names and times.** Keeping notes on who promised what to whom not only keeps you from making more mistakes, but it also tells the other person that you know what you're doing. So when the manager says this is the first time you've called, you can say, "You are mistaken, I called on these occasions and I spoke to these people who told me these things."

✔ **Never lose your temper.** Nothing can derail your effort to resolve a mistake or error faster than raising your voice. After you escalate the volume, you'll be directed to someone who does "loud" professionally or you will be politely ignored. Either way, you lose. Call back if you need to, but don't lose control.

✔ **Safeguard your identity.** Newbies to America or credit often come from a culture of sharing. Whether you shared with your family in Mexico or you shared with your roommate at Harvard, the time for sharing information and credit is over. Identity theft is a serious and growing crime in the United States. It can take years to unravel and cost thousands of dollars to fix. In Chapter 15, I tell you how to safeguard your identity.

The short version is to be careful with your personal identification information, mail, computer passwords, and bank account information. Shred your financial mail. Also, if you invite people into your home, be sure to clean up any account statements and check deposit slips. Even someone you know well could be tempted with your personal financial information. This sort of temptation is like leaving twenty dollar bills all over the floor and furniture. Certainly not something you'd do. So don't.

Check out Chapter 7 for more information on what to do if you run afoul of the credit reporting system. If you do end up owing more than you can pay and have to deal with collectors, Chapter 8 has you covered.

Building from checking to credit to a business

A solid credit report and a good credit score can not only help you in employment, borrowing, and getting a credit card, a decent apartment, and insurance, but they can also form the first building block to starting a new business. With good credit, savings, and the stability that savings brings, you're a prime candidate to step up to that business you may always have wanted to pass on to your offspring.

Good personal credit is essential. If you want to start a new business, you can't be financially successful doing so unless you move from the underbanked to traditional banking. That big piece of the American Dream called credit is now yours to enjoy. Welcome to the table. And be sure to bring the family! For more information about starting your own business, check out *Small Business For Dummies,* 3rd Edition, by Eric Tyson (Wiley).

Part II
Navigating with Your Own Credit GPS

The 5th Wave   By Rich Tennant

"No, Mrs. Moskowitz. There's just no way we can list the unpaid debt of gratitude your son owes you on his credit history."

In this part . . .

1 focus on helping you determine exactly where you are in terms of your credit history — your credit report and credit scores. I show you how to get your credit report for free, tell you when it's best for you to do so, and explain what your credit report and credit scores really mean to you and your future.

I discuss the various components that go into building a good FICO and VantageScore. I help you determine whether your credit scores measure up and how you can improve them. I tell you about the other credit reporters in the sectors of insurance, medicine, gambling, employment, checking, and even renting. Finally, I help you understand what your credit report contains, how information gets there, how you can dispute information, and who can access the information besides you.

Chapter 5

Getting a Copy of Your Credit Road Map

In This Chapter

▶ Finding out how to get your credit reports (and why you need them)

▶ Navigating the murky waters of credit scoring

▶ Seeking more specialized credit data

*R*ecognizing the value of good credit is an important first step in gaining control of your financial life, getting the best interest rates, and even landing that next job or promotion. And every year the value of good credit seems to increase, just like a good investment, as more people, including potential employers and businesses you hope to borrow money from and get credit from, use the information in your reports to help predict future behavior. Getting your hands on the same information makes sense to make sure it is accurate and complete and — heavens protect us — not someone else's.

But how do you get a copy of your credit report so you can be sure it's accurate, up-to-date, and complete? And how do you do it without being charged for extras you don't want or need? In this chapter, I tell you the who, what, where, when, and — most importantly — the *how* of getting your hands on your credit report. You not only find out about the three largest and most well-known of the credit bureaus, but you also get familiar with the data repositories that report traditional credit and more. Finally, especially if you are new to credit or a recent immigrant trying to establish yourself financially in the United States, you discover the lesser-known places where data pertaining to you and your life resides.

So come along with me on a trip that will take you from the portals of the big credit bureaus to the bounced-check graveyard and even to the cashiers' cages in Las Vegas! This chapter is all about your information — where it's kept and how you can get it.

Requesting Copies of Your Credit Reports

Button up your overcoat. Wait an hour after eating before swimming. Stop crossing your eyes or they'll stay that way. These are some of the bits of advice you got while you were growing up. I don't know about you, but my mother never told me to get a copy of all three of my credit reports. Well, call me "Mom," but you really should check each of them, at least annually.

Three main sources of credit information dominate the credit industry today. They are Equifax, Experian, and TransUnion. These credit bureaus are basically huge databases of information. Within the databases are hundreds of millions of individual files on folks just like you and me. Where does all that information come from? Lenders, bill collectors, courts, public utilities, and others who provide goods and services to you today and get paid down the road supply this information.

Credit-reporting bureaus don't put data in your file. They simply maintain the files with the data that others report. In the following sections, I tell you why you need to request your copies, where to go to get your reports, what kind of information you'll need to provide, what to watch out for, and when you should check your reports.

Why requesting copies is important

Getting copies of your credit reports from the three credit bureaus is essential to verify your information and to protect your identity. Each month, all the companies that report payment history information to the credit bureaus have numerous chances to mix up, misreport, or misfile that information. They don't mess up all the time, but they do occasionally, and these errors are why reviewing your credit report at least once a year is so important — even if you've never had credit problems. You need to make sure that this info is correct. If it isn't, it can be very costly to you (you may not get the loans you want, the terms you want, or you may have to pay much higher interest than you should have to pay) and to the lender (if the lender doesn't get its money back and subsequently has to raise your rates on your next loan).

Many people assume that if they get a copy of their credit report from one of the bureaus, they've done everything they need to do. But the reality is that the information Equifax has is slightly different from the information Experian has, and the information Experian has is slightly different from the information TransUnion has. You generally won't see major differences from one report to the next. However, because not all creditors report to all bureaus, if you're new to credit, the differences may be important enough that a few missing account histories or *trade lines,* as they're called in the business, can have a noticeable impact. Also, you could have a perfectly clean Experian report while your TransUnion report could have some negative items on it in error, or vice versa.

Even though it means a bit more effort and hassle, getting and reviewing copies of all three of your credit reports is absolutely essential to keeping your credit in good shape. But don't despair! This isn't a big deal because under the Fair and Accurate Credit Transactions Act (commonly referred to as the FACT Act or FACTA), every American is entitled to one free credit report from each of the three bureaus per year. Not since the days of the elusive nickel beer and the free lunch has there been this much excitement in credit reporting. You're also entitled to an additional free report from each of the bureaus if:

- ✔ You were denied credit within the last 60 days.
- ✔ You are unemployed and planning to seek employment within the next 60 days.
- ✔ You're on welfare.
- ✔ You're a victim of fraud or identity theft and have reported it to the police.

Where to get your reports

The FACT Act now requires each of the credit bureaus to provide you with a free copy of your credit report each year, but don't expect them to come knocking on your door, offering you your free copy. You have to ask for it.

That said, getting a copy of your credit report from any of the big-three credit bureaus is simple. You can get things started with a phone call, a visit to the bureau's Web site, or through the mail. Here's the contact information for the three major credit-reporting bureaus:

- ✔ **Equifax,** P.O. Box 740241, Atlanta, GA 30374; phone 800-685-1111; Web site www.equifax.com
- ✔ **Experian,** P.O. Box 2104, Allen, TX 75013-2104; phone 888-397-3742; Web site www.experian.com
- ✔ **TransUnion,** 2 Baldwin Place, P.O. Box 1000, Chester, PA 19022; phone 800-888-4213; Web site www.transunion.com

The big-three bureaus have set up a central source where you can get your free credit report. If you go to any of the bureau Web sites, they'll redirect you to this central source. So why even go the individual sites? Because each site has some informational and educational features, and they're the places for you to order (at a cost) a credit score in addition to a free credit report. If you want to skip the individual sites and go to the central source that allows you to pick up all three reports, here's the information you need:

Who else can get their hands on your report?

Anyone can get a copy of your credit report if they have a *permissible purpose* — in other words, if the person has a valid reason to review your report — *and* if you've given that person your permission to do so. The permission part can often be lost in the fine print of a credit-card application or at the bottom of an employment application.

What counts as a permissible purpose under the law? Here are some examples:

- **Credit approval:** When you apply for credit (whether that's filling out a credit-card application or applying for a car loan, student loan, or mortgage), the creditor or lender has the right to get a copy of your credit report. This only makes sense — they need to know whether you're likely to pay them back or whether you have a history of defaulting on loans.

- **Renting an apartment:** Likewise, it only makes sense that a landlord would like to know if you pay your bills on time before giving you the keys to an expensive piece of real estate. For that reason, most rental applications ask for permission to access your credit file and also any tenant history information that may be available.

- **Employment:** When you apply for a job, that prospective employer can get a copy of your credit report. Although this may be less obvious than the applying-for-credit reason, your financial history says a lot about what kind of employee you might turn out to be. If you're irresponsible with money, the logic goes, you may be irresponsible at work as well.

- **Insurance underwriting:** When you apply for car, homeowner's, renter's, medical, or any other kind of insurance, the insurance company has the right to get a copy of your credit report. Depending on the type of insurance you apply for and the state in which you live, the insurer may get a copy of your credit report and use the information in it to help predict

the likelihood not of a default in premium payments but of your likelihood of filing a claim. Insurers and their actuaries believe there is a strong relationship between past financial performance and future claim experience.

- **Issuing a professional license:** Licensing authorities take their responsibilities very seriously. Before allowing you to become licensed — or, in other words, approved to perform a specific job — they want to know all they can about your background and how you've conducted yourself in the past. If, for instance, you want a license to sell stocks and bonds and deal with someone else's life savings, it makes sense to see how you handle your own money. Want a gambling license? Same thing applies.

- **A court order or subpoena:** If a court orders you to appear before the court or subpoenas information about you, the court can also get access to your credit file.

- **Reviewing or collecting an existing account:** When an account is overdue and sent to a collector for action, the collector wants to know who else you owe money to and what kind of payer they're dealing with. In some cases, if a person moves a lot, they use the information in the credit report to find a current address or phone number. (The industry term for this is called *skip tracing*.) However, even if you're current in your payments to your credit-card issuers, mortgage company, or other creditors, your creditors may look at your account from time to time to determine if your credit quality is deteriorating or, on the brighter side, to increase your limits.

- **If you owe the Internal Revenue Service money:** If you owe the tax guys and don't come across with the payment in the time specified, they'll look in your credit report to find out if you have assets to attach or sell. Some examples of things they look for are real estate, cars, bank accounts, and so on.

Annual Credit Report Request Service
P.O. Box 105281
Atlanta, GA 30348-5281
Phone 877-322-8228
Web site www.annualcreditreport.com

I strongly suggest that you get a copy of your report from each of the three bureaus.

What you'll need to give in order to get your reports

Whether you contact a credit bureau directly to get a copy of your report, or you go through the central source to get all three at once (see the preceding section), you'll need to provide information that lets them know that you are who you say you are. The information requested will vary from one bureau to the next, but the following is a list of some information you're likely to be asked for:

- ✔ Your Social Security number
- ✔ You credit-card account numbers
- ✔ Your former addresses and the dates you lived there
- ✔ Your employment history
- ✔ Your favorite drink (just kidding)

When you order your credit report, the bureaus may try to sell you a credit score as well. See "Getting a Copy of Your Credit Score," later in this chapter, for more information on this.

When to get copies of your credit reports

The information in your credit report is used for many purposes — from granting a mortgage to getting homeowner's insurance to renting an apartment — so you should get copies of all three of the big-three (Equifax, Experian, TransUnion) at least once a year. If you're planning to make a big purchase, look for a job, or buy insurance, get your report up to six months in advance; this will give you time to dispute any errors that may have ended up on your report (like from your sister's last bankruptcy) before people start checking out your credit. As you get within a month or two of the loan application date, get your report again in case new errors have slipped into your file.

Real-estate closings can be delayed, mortgage rates can go up, and job opportunities can be lost if there is incorrect negative information on your credit report. So give yourself time to get the report and correct it before going forward with your plans.

You should get a copy of your report when you're planning to:

✔ Buy or lease a car

✔ Buy a house

✔ Refinance a mortgage

✔ Rent an apartment

✔ Apply for a job

✔ Apply for a professional license (such as a license to sell securities or insurance)

✔ Apply for a security clearance

✔ Join the military

✔ Be up for a promotion

✔ Get married

✔ Get divorced

✔ Switch insurance companies or buy new insurance

Even if none of the preceding situations applies to you, I still recommend that you get copies of all three of your reports annually. Why? Because people may be making decisions about your future and using your credit information without your knowing it (for example, you may be considered for a promotion at work). Because you can get one copy of each report free once a year, I recommend that, every four months, you order a report from one of the three bureaus, rotating through them so that you'll have three separate chances, at spaced intervals, to see if something unexpected has shown up.

Getting a Copy of Your Credit Score

Getting your hands on your credit report is one thing — but getting a copy of your credit score is not as straightforward as you may think. And a misstep here can cost you more money and give you less-than-accurate information.

A credit score is an additional component used in most credit reviews. When lenders order your credit report, they also order your credit score. A credit score summarizes your risk of default in a three-digit score that ranges from 300 to 850.

You can only get a copy of your FICO score if you're ordering a credit report at the same time. But unlike your credit report, which you get for free once a year, you have to pay for a copy of your credit score. Not just any credit score will do. You want your FICO score, which is the credit score most lenders use.

You can only get your FICO credit score from two places:

- ✔ **myFICO.com** (phone 800-319-4433; Web site `www.myfico.com`)
- ✔ **Equifax** (P.O. Box 740241, Atlanta, GA 30374; phone 800-685-1111; Web site `www.equifax.com`)

The other credit-reporting bureaus — Experian and TransUnion — offer credit scores, but not the *FICO* credit score. (See the sidebar "The Credit Score Conundrum" for more info on the various credit scores available and who sells what.)

The only credit bureau that can provide you the FICO credit score used by most lenders along with its credit report is Equifax.

If your lender uses TransUnion or Experian to make a lending decision (you can find out which bureau they use by asking the lender), you want to get a copy of your TransUnion or Experian credit report, and then get your FICO score (from myFICO.com).

The credit score conundrum

The notion of summing up a person's creditworthiness with a single, three-digit number is the brainchild of Fair Isaac, the company that developed the FICO scoring measures. Equifax bought the rights to market the FICO formula along with its credit data to its customers; however, Experian and TransUnion did not buy these rights. Fair Isaac, wanting to make three sales rather than just one, developed similar, but differently named, formulas to sell to Experian and TransUnion. So while Experian and TransUnion offer credit scores that were developed by the same company that developed the FICO score, the scores they offer are slightly different from the original FICO score.

And just in case that's not confusing enough, yet another score exists — the VantageScore — that isn't a product of Fair Isaac at all, but rather is a FICO competitor.

So, which credit score is the right one for you? My advice is to try to get the same score that your lender will be using. How do you know which one that is? Ask them! They'll tell you. If you aren't working with a specific lender and just want the most widely used score, then FICO is the one for you. (This may change in the future, however, as this is a very competitive business.)

Tracking Down Specialty Reports: From Rental History to Gambling

In addition to the big-three credit-reporting bureaus, there are other, lesser-known, specialty reporting agencies. As the name implies, they specialize in a subset of credit-related data, covering areas such as gambling, checking accounts, medical claims, and insurance. If you're being underwritten for credit or other permissible purposes like auto insurance, renting an apartment, or a promotion at work in one of these areas, the person reviewing your application will most likely request a report from a specialty agency in addition to a traditional credit report from one of the big-three credit bureaus.

The information these specialty credit bureaus collect can have an impact on you. Among the better-known specialty report providers are the insurance bureaus, such as Choice Trust, which sells its CLUE products based on your auto and homeowner insurance claims history, as well as information for background employment and rental checks; the Medical Information Bureau (MIB), which accumulates and sells your medical-insurance claims history report; and ChexSystems, SCAN, and TeleCheck, all of which sell various check-verification products. Included in the growing list of companies that report on you are those that specialize in rental history, workers' compensation claims, and gambling history.

You have the right to request and obtain your credit reports from these agencies for free annually, just as you do with the traditional credit bureaus. Some contain only negative information — or they may have absolutely no information about you at all (you've *really* never been to a casino?). Table 5-1 provides the contact information for the major specialty bureaus to get you started — call the number for any bureau you want a report from, and ask how to order a free copy.

Table 5-1	Specialty Credit-Reporting Bureaus	
Category	*Bureau Name*	*Contact Info*
Casinos	Central Credit Services	702-855-3000 or 800-833-7110
Checking accounts	Certegy/Equifax	800-437-5120
	CheckCenter/CrossCheck	800-843-0760
	CheckRite	800-466-2748
	ChexSystems	800-428-9623
	International Check Services	800-526-5380
	SCAN	
	TeleCheck	

Category	Bureau Name	Contact Info
Employment	ChoiceTrust Employment Reports	866-527-2600
Insurance	CLUE Auto History	866-312-8076
	CLUE Homeowners' History	866-312-8076
	ISO's A-Plus Auto and Property Databases	800-709-8842
Medical information	Medical Information Bureau (MIB)	617-426-3660
Rental information	Accufax	800-256-8898
	American Tenant Screen	800-888-1287
	ChoicePoint Tenant History Reports	877-448-5732
	National Tenant Network	800-228-0989
	Tenant Data Services	800-228-1837
	Tenant Screening Services	800-296-5050
	UD Registry	818-785-3905
Mortgage financing	Innovis	800-540-2505

Getting a global credit report

As people move from country to country, they increasingly need to establish and access local credit sources. Thus, credit reporting and credit scoring are going global. Although the Fair Isaac Global Credit Score isn't in wide use at present, this score is sure to gain followers in the near future. Using credit information from databases overseas, Fair Isaac can give an accurate credit score that will help establish credit in 20 countries at the time of this writing. Of course, France is not one of them. *Quel dommage.*

If you're new to the United States and trying to develop credit, ask a major international bank in your home country to provide you with a copy of your credit report. This may be useful in helping to establish a credit relationship in the United States.

For all their wanting to look technically advanced, most bankers are anything but. Credit is being used in every country in the world. Those non-U.S. records are capable of being used to allow a credit history established in Canada or Turkey to be used by an American lender to make a credit decision. The technology and network are there; the bankers aren't — yet. My prediction is that in the near future, hopefully before this edition is revised again, a new resident of the United States will be able to choose a bank that has international operations (any one of the big bank names should do) and ask them to grant him access to products and credit based on his past credit record in his previous country. In the meantime, a non-U.S. credit report — say, from Citibank in Berlin — will be one more item in your favor to help the New York Citibank office favorably underwrite your request for credit in the United States.

Chapter 6

Understanding the Parts
of Your Credit Report

In This Chapter

▶ Interpreting the data on your credit report

▶ Understanding the terminology

▶ Comprehending credit scores

▶ Comparing your credit score to the population-at-large

"**I**s this thing a phone book?" "Okay, what do these terms mean? And where does it say whether I'm doing a good job, anyway?" "How do I tell whether I'm passing or flunking?" "Can't I just Google it?" I confess: At first glance — and for the first-time reader — a credit report, with its huge volume of information and its industry jargon, can be a little overwhelming. All those columns, numbers, terms, and historical information. . . . But trust me — daunting though it may appear, your credit report is no Code of Hammurabi. Although the format and terms may vary by credit bureau or credit-report reseller, the detail in your credit report is in a pretty basic language that I can have you speaking in no time. And you don't need to get an advanced degree, learn a complex code, or pass a secret initiation ritual to do it.

In this chapter, I walk you through the basic outline of a credit report, breaking it down into its various parts and explaining its terms and components. I also shine a light on the credit score and help you understand the different kinds of scores that are available.

Give me the time it takes to read this chapter, and I'll have you whipping through your credit report, feeling confident that you know where you stand in the eyes of your creditors, insurance company, employer, and anyone else who looks at your report. If you have a copy of your credit report from one or more of the three major credit-reporting agencies — Equifax, Experian, or TransUnion — you can follow along with this chapter. (If you don't yet have a copy of your report, turn to Chapter 5 for information on how to get one.)

What's not in your credit report?

With all the information available on the Internet and in data files, you can easily become concerned about what exactly is in your credit report and what isn't. In order to set the record straight and put you at ease from the beginning, your credit report from Equifax, Experian, or TransUnion does *not* contain:

- ✔ Your gender
- ✔ Your race or ethnicity
- ✔ Your national origin
- ✔ Your religious preference
- ✔ Your political affiliation
- ✔ Your checking- or savings-account information or major purchases that were paid in full with cash or check
- ✔ Business accounts (unless you're on record as being personally liable for the debt)
- ✔ Details about your personal lifestyle or friends
- ✔ Bankruptcies that are more than ten years old
- ✔ Charge-offs or debts placed for collection that are more than seven years old
- ✔ Your credit score (Although your credit score is generated based on information in your credit report, it is not part of the report itself.)

Before you get too comfortable with what's not disclosed in your credit report, be aware of this. *Indirect disclosure* may allow some of your personal information to get passed on. Medical information is one example. Even though credit bureaus do not report medical history, detail on your credit report may give away information indicating that you have a medical condition. Here's how: Say you're paying a collection agency for an overdue debt for a hospital stay. The account noted on your credit report will read: Medical Collection. You apply for a job. As part of its background check, your prospective employer requests a copy of your credit report. They easily deduce that you have (or had) a medical condition. A week later, you get a letter saying the position has been filled.

Okay, so this is a pretty extreme example. But it illustrates that, without disclosing medical reports or particulars about a health condition, the detail on your credit report *can* reveal personal information that is legally restricted from your file. Some other disclosures that can happen include employment history you forgot to mention to a prospective employer, frequent changes of addresses (which may make you look unstable), and multiple inquiries from Central Credit for gambling lines of credit (which could raise a question for a lender or an employer).

Perusing Your Credit Report

Perhaps the best way to get a handle on how your credit report comes together is to take it apart — starting from the outside and working in. First, I help you to understand the big picture. Then I talk about each part in more detail.

Each credit report contains the following elements:

- Personal profile
- Accounts summary
- Public records (which include public records, negative remarks, collections, and late payments)
- Credit inquiries
- Account history
- Credit score (optional)
- Your 100-word statement (optional; see Chapter 7 for more information on writing a 100-word statement)

Note: The three credit-reporting agencies use slightly different names for each of these sections.

I cover each of these items in the following sections. For a sample credit report from TransUnion, check out the CD. For information on where to find samples of the Equifax and Experian reports online, turn to Chapter 2.

Personal profile: It's all about you

This section of your credit report may be labeled "Personal Profile" or "Personal Information," depending on which credit bureau issued the report.

Appearing first in the order of credit-report elements, your profile section contains the key components that help you make sure that the report is actually about *you:* your name (and any of your previous names), Social Security number, address(es), and current and previous employers.

Be sure to check this section and make sure all the information is correct. An error could cause someone else's credit history to end up on your report.

Account summary: An overview of your financial history

This section of your credit report may be labeled "Account Summary" or "Credit Summary," and it may follow the "Personal Profile" section or appear later in the report. It may also be the first part of the "Account History" section (covered later in this chapter), depending on which bureau's report you're looking at.

This information illustrates your history in broad terms. It includes summaries of open and closed accounts, credit limits, total balance of all accounts, payment history, and number of credit inquiries. Why a summary? Well, lenders are people, too (sort of), and they'd rather read one page and go to lunch than read 60-plus pages of eye-glazing detail (my longest personal credit report was 66 pages). But don't worry: If you're hungry for painstaking detail of your payment past, you're certain to find it in the "Account History" section of the credit report.

If something in the summary section looks like it's not yours, if it's too old (see the "Knowing how long items stay on your credit report" sidebar, later in this chapter), or if a paid loan still shows a balance, make a note to check it out in the "Account History" section.

Public records: Tallying up your days in court

This section is one you'd probably rather skip if you had the choice. No wonder some reports title this section "Negative Remarks"! Public records are only negative items that come from — you guessed it — a public record (for example, from a court proceeding). If you're lucky, this section will be empty. Some examples include bankruptcy, tax liens, judgments, and, in some states, child-support information.

Credit inquiries: Tracking who wants your credit report

Knock, knock. Who's there? This section shows who's been knocking on the credit bureau's door, asking if you were home. According to the Fair Credit Reporting Act (FCRA), those with a permissible purpose specifically listed in the law may receive credit information. This includes businesses and individuals you've given permission to, such as your employer, insurance company, or lender, as well as yourself.

This section includes the date of the inquiry and how long the inquiry will remain on your report. An inquiry that you initiated, say, to shop for or obtain credit, stays on your report for two years.

On the credit report that you request, information about those who inquired for the purposes of extending a preapproved credit offer are included for your information only. These inquiries are not revealed to creditors and do not affect your ability to obtain credit.

Who's the fairest of them all?

I pulled all my own credit reports and scores from the bureaus' Web sites and from Fair Isaac's www.myfico.com. Each had a little different presentation and some were easier to read than others. The myFICO site gives you what I think is the best summary of your score, how you did on the major components, things hurting and helping your score, and some averages so you know where you fall nationally. They also provide significantly less detail than the bureau sites. This reflects their orientation as a scoring-focused group as opposed to the bureaus with their data warehouse perspective. So if you want to know more about your score or your data, just look in the right mirror.

Account history: Think of it as a payment credit-oscopy

Your "Account History" section, sometimes titled "Account Information," is the heart of your credit report. It shows all open and closed accounts with excruciating detail about payment history, balances, and account status over the last seven years.

How is this section different from the "Account Summary" section (earlier in this chapter)? Well, if the summary is like getting your blood, temperature, and weight taken when you go to the doctor, this is the in-depth diagnostic testing that follows. Take a deep breath; you won't feel a thing!

Each credit-reporting bureau displays this detail in its own unique way, using some different terms. I take them one-by-one, and then I make a fourth stop and show you the version of the reports you get from myFICO.com when you request your credit score.

Equifax's version

Equifax reports its "Account History" by type of account. These include mortgages, installment accounts, revolving accounts, and so on. Account numbers are shortened for protection of account information. A short summary at the beginning of each account includes your "Account Status," which indicates whether you've paid as agreed or are late (and if so, how late).

Here's a list of the information that Equifax reports in its "Account History" section:

- ✓ **Account Number:** That long alphanumeric string that is unique to this card or loan.
- ✓ **Account Owner:** Indicates whether the account is an individual or joint account.

- ✔ **Type:** The account type. Here are the account types you may find:

  - **Installment account:** Installment accounts are loans that are for a set amount of money and often a set period of time. Your mortgage and car payment, for example, are on installment — you may have a set amount to pay at the same time each month until the debt is paid off.

  - **Revolving account:** Unlike installment accounts, balances of revolving accounts don't have to be paid off in a set amount of time, and as you pay off a part of the balance, the amount available for new purchases increases. Your credit cards fall into this category.

  - **Other account:** This category may include personal loans — for example, if you've gone to your local bank and taken out a loan to cover something like a computer or a vacation.

  - **Collections account:** These are accounts that have been sold or turned over to a collection agency, usually when the account is more than 180 days past due.

- ✔ **Term Duration:** The total number of payments you're expected to make on your loan (for example, 60 payments for a five-year car loan).

- ✔ **Date Open:** The date on which you opened the account.

- ✔ **Date Reported:** The latest report from the lender, whether provided monthly, quarterly, or less frequently.

- ✔ **Date of Last Payment:** The date listed here may be different from the date reported. If you're in arrears, your last payment may be September 2005 and the last date reported may be December 2005. If you had no activity on a credit-card account for six months, the last payment date could be June 2005 and the last reported date could be December 2005.

- ✔ **Scheduled Payment Amount:** This information only applies to installment accounts, in which a set amount of money is due at a set time every month.

- ✔ **Creditor Classification:** The type of creditor.

- ✔ **Charge-off Amount:** Debt or portions of debt that were written off by the creditor because of nonpayment and inability to get the money from you. You want this amount to be *zero*. Any amount — no matter how small — is not a good thing to have on your record.

- ✔ **Balloon-Payment Amount:** The big lump-sum payment at the end of some loans. Your loan may or may not have one.

- ✔ **Date Closed:** The date you or the lender terminated an active account.

- ✔ **Date of First Delinquency:** Blank is best.

- ✔ **Comments:** Additional information about the closed account. Some examples can be "Account Transferred or Sold," "Paid," "Zero Balance," "Account Closed at Consumer's Request," and so on.

✔ **Current Status:** Provides the payment status and refers to whether you've paid or are paying as you said you would. You may see terms such as "Pays," "Paid as Agreed," or "*X* Days Past Due."

✔ **High Credit:** The highest amount of credit used by you.

✔ **Credit Limit:** Your maximum limit for this account.

✔ **Term's Frequency:** How often your payment is due (weekly, monthly, and so on).

✔ **Balance:** The amount owed to a creditor on an account.

✔ **Amount Past Due:** The amount of money owed that should have been paid by now but hasn't been.

✔ **Actual Payment Amount:** The amount of money that you paid.

✔ **Date of Last Activity:** The last time you used the account.

✔ **Months Reviewed:** How many months are in the history section below (up to 81).

✔ **Activity Description:** For example, Paid and Closed.

✔ **Deferred Payment Start Date:** Some accounts have no payment for a year or other promotional terms.

✔ **Balloon-Payment Date:** When that big lump-sum payment at the end of some loans is due. Your loan may or may not have one.

✔ **Type of Loan:** For example, Auto.

✔ **81-Month Payment History:** Equifax will show each month's status for the last seven years of payment history. Terms used in reporting the status include the following:

- Pays as Agreed
- 30 (30 to 59 days past due)
- 60 (60 to 89 days past due)
- 90 (90 to 119 days past due)
- 120 (120 to 149 days past due)
- 150 (150 to 179 days past due)
- 180+ (180 or more days past due)
- CA (collection account)
- F (foreclosure)
- VS (voluntary surrender)
- R (repossession)
- CO (charge-off)

Experian's version

On Experian's credit report, all accounts — satisfactory or adverse — are grouped respectively in the "Account History" section. For security, the complete number does not appear.

Here's a list of the information that Experian reports in its "Account History" section. Accounts are listed within each category type, for example, "Potentially Negative Items" (public records, collection agencies, and so forth) and "Accounts in Good Standing." Then, within each major category, the accounts are alphabetically listed by creditor:

- **Status:** Open or closed and oldest late item, if any.

- **Date Open:** The date on which you opened the account.

- **Reported Since:** First reported date.

- **Date of Status:** Last time the status was updated.

- **Last Reported:** Last time the update (which might be new or old) was reported.

- **Account Type:** Specifies whether it's an installment account, a revolving account, and so on (see "Equifax's version" for definitions of these terms).

- **Terms:** The total number of payments you're expected to make on your loan (a 30-year mortgage would be 360, for example).

- **Monthly Payment:** The last reported minimum payment that you owe(d). This is typically applicable for installment loans such as auto loans or mortgages, if reported at all.

- **Responsibility:** Individual, joint, authorized user, and so forth.

- **Credit Limit:** The highest dollar credit limit you've ever been approved for.

- **High Balance:** The most you've ever owed on the account.

- **Recent Balance Information:** The amount you owe. Sometimes balance information is on the report, and sometimes it's not — this is not because the credit bureau wants to save trees, but because some creditors don't want their competition to know what a big spender and great customer you really are.

- **Recent Payment:** Your most recent payment in dollars. This contrasts the Monthly Payment category.

- **Account History:** Whether you've been late, and, if so, how often.

- **Your Statement:** This is where you tell your side of the story. For example, you may contest an account that shows you haven't paid as agreed when you contend that you didn't receive the services for which you were charged.

- **Account History:** Comments that the creditor may have sent to the bureau about this account.

On a closed account, a Status Detail Note indicates when the account will stop being reported.

TransUnion's version

TransUnion reports its account histories in two groupings, "Adverse Accounts" and "Satisfactory Accounts." Account numbers may be displayed in full. Contact information for the creditor, including mailing address and maybe a phone number, are also included (handy, if you don't have quick access to this information).

Here's a list of the information that TransUnion reports in its "Account History" section:

- ✔ **Loan Type:** This refers to whether the account is a credit card, line of credit, conventional real-estate mortgage, home-equity loan, charge account (retail account), or other designation. In the case of mortgages, the information includes the name and address of the loan servicer.

- ✔ **Late Payments:** These are grouped under three headings of 30, 60, or 90 days old.

- ✔ **Remark:** Indicates whether the account is open or closed.

- ✔ **Balance:** Your current balance at the time the account was last reported.

- ✔ **Date Updated:** The date of the latest report from the lender. Some lenders report every month, some report quarterly, others report less frequently.

- ✔ **High Balance:** The most you've ever owed on the account.

- ✔ **Collateral:** The security (such as a house) pledged for the payment of a loan. Collateral is typically listed for mortgages; the listing shows the property address of the collateral securing the loan.

- ✔ **Credit Limit:** The maximum amount you've been approved to borrow.

- ✔ **Past Due:** The amount of money overdue on the account.

- ✔ **Terms:** The total number of payments you're expected to make on your loan (180 for a 15-year mortgage, for example).

- ✔ **Payment Status:** Indicates whether you've paid what you owe as you promised. Typical positive descriptions include "Paid," "Paying as Agreed," and "Unrated."

- ✔ **Account Type:** May be different from the loan type; further defines the loan type (for example, a conventional real-estate mortgage [loan type] may be a mortgage account [account type]).

- ✔ **Responsibility:** Lists individuals who are named on the debt — and indicates whether the account is individual or joint. It is *not* a reflection of how responsible you are.

✔ **Date Opened:** The date on which you opened the account.

✔ **Date Closed:** The date on which the account was closed.

✔ **Date Paid:** The date the loan was paid off; may be different from the date closed depending on the circumstances (for example, if you opted out of a rate increase and closed your account, you would still have time to pay it off over the original terms).

myFICO.com's version

When you order your credit reports from myFICO.com, the first big difference you see is in the material before you get to the credit details. It makes some sense that more emphasis is placed on other matters because this site isn't a data warehouse like the big three. You receive about seven pages of summary information providing an overview of how lenders see you, how you did on four of the main rating factors, your score, and tips on what may be hurting and helping your score plus sample rates you should expect if you run out and apply for a loan that day. Clearly, this report focuses more on how data is used than data itself. The "Account Details" are less detailed than the ones you get from the bureaus, and they focus more on the last two years of activity. Here's a list of the information that myFICO.com reports:

✔ **Date Opened:** The date on which you first opened the account.

✔ **Date of Last Activity:** The most recent lender report.

✔ **Date Paid Out:** The date you made your final payment.

✔ **Account Number:** A shortened or crossed-out version of the real thing.

✔ **Account Type:** The type of account, such as overdraft checking account (the line of credit you have associated with your checking account to keep from bouncing checks), revolving account, open account, and so on.

✔ **Credit Limit:** The maximum amount you can borrow in this account.

✔ **Largest Past Balance:** Your highest (non–past-due) balance in the past.

✔ **Credit Type:** Type of account, such as revolving or installment.

✔ **Account Holder:** Individual, Joint, and so forth.

At the end of this information for each account, a box contains more detail important to the creditor — and to you. Within the box, you find:

✔ The balance

✔ The current status of the loan (such as "Paid as Agreed")

✔ The amount past due, if any

This information is followed by the monthly payment history and a two-year payment-history summary box showing any late payments by age of delinquency (30, 60, or 90 or more days late).

Credit score

Depending on which report you order, your credit score may be indicated as "FICO Score," "VantageScore," "Plus Score," or "Score Power."

Your *credit score* is a three-digit number that considers more than 20 variables in a complex calculation and provides an indication of your overall creditworthiness. Many scores are marketed today, and they can be very confusing — each giving different numbers based on different scales. See Chapter 2 for more details on the VantageScore and FICO score.

The most important score for you to get your hands on is the FICO score — the one that your prospective lenders, employers, and other business and personal partners are looking at. You get a FICO score if you order any of the credit bureau reports from myFICO.com or if you order the Equifax report from the credit bureau directly.

The credit score appears in different places, depending on the source you order it from. Although it may be in the front or back of the report, it's prominently featured with an explanation based on the reason codes I cover later in this chapter.

Your optional 100-word statement: Getting the last word

You have the right to add a statement of up to 100 words to your credit report, and the credit bureaus are required to include this statement whenever your credit report is accessed by anyone. This statement is helpful in explaining any extenuating circumstances, and it allows you an opportunity to document any disagreement with data provided by creditors.

Use this privilege with some care. Your statement may draw attention to an event that is far enough in the past that a lender would not have cared about it or noticed it otherwise. Your comments may stay on the report as long as the account does — and that may be too long. You can get the statement taken off, however, by notifying the bureau.

Examining Your Credit Score

Just as you would fuss a bit to get ready for a date or special occasion, when you're being courted by a lender, you want to be sure all your data is buttoned, neat and pretty. Take a minute to look at yourself from a lender's point of view. How do you look in their eyes? Along with your credit report, lenders can buy a credit score based on the information in the report. How many times have you heard someone say, "She's a perfect ten"! High praise indeed. Well, lenders think of you based on your credit-score number — specifically, how you measure up to the perfect FICO score of 850 or VantageScore of 901.

Your credit score is a three-digit number that speaks volumes about your financial life. The pages of information contained in your credit report are boiled down to a number that gives those who want it fast a quick snapshot of your creditworthiness. The credit score used by the vast majority of lenders is called the FICO score. Your credit history can earn you a FICO score ranging from 300 (the lowest; in other words, the *worst* score you can get) to 850 (meaning if credit scores were IQ assessments, you'd be Einstein!).

Credit scores can have a huge impact on your financial status. A high score can help qualify you for great rewards — including easy access to credit, good terms on loans, and the best insurance rates — and it can even help you get a job. Prospective employers often request your credit report and score.

If you want to make sense of your credit report, understanding the role of the credit score in lending makes sense. Score usage has grown from occasional to essential in modern lending and risk management. Because of the volume of transactions and the rapid response consumers are accustomed to — especially those who use online tools — credit scores have become a virtual necessity for busy lenders who can size up a prospective borrower in the time it takes to glance at the one three-digit number.

Is credit scoring fair to minorities?

Scoring doesn't consider your gender, race, nationality, or marital status. The Equal Credit Opportunity Act doesn't allow lenders to consider gender, race, nationality, or marital status when underwriting credit. Independent studies have shown that credit scoring is not unfair to minorities or people with little credit history. In fact, recent developments in scoring have allowed scores to be generated with less credit history than ever before, and in some cases by using payment and other information that resides in databases other than those of the credit bureaus. In other words, as much as possible is being done to make scores a more accurate and consistent measure of repayment potential for everyone.

Understanding the main credit-score models

More than one credit score exists, and understanding the differences between them is important. Why? Because you want to be sure that the score you see is the same score your lender sees.

The big daddy of credit scores is the trademarked FICO score developed by Fair Isaac. Although each of the three credit bureaus has a proprietary score also developed by Fair Isaac, it's not the same trademarked FICO score that most lenders use. Because the bureaus make money selling *their* proprietary scores, they push these scores on their Web sites. As a result, you'll see multiple names, including "Score Power," "Score Plus," and others.

Recently the three bureaus got together and agreed on a common scoring product (in addition to their own, of course) called the VantageScore. The vendor of this score touts that it is more predictive because it was designed to make maximum use of the data contained in all three bureau files. And who knows a bureau file better than the bureaus! The Vantage people tell me they can offer an accurate score for those new to credit, such as immigrants, recent graduates, and so on, with only one account and three months of history. The VantageScore is still only lightly used compared to Fair Isaac as of the writing of this book. Who has the best crystal ball? Stay tuned.

 Don't get hung up on a number. Be as good as you can be, but don't get excited and kick the dog over a 790 instead of an 800. The most important thing is to know what your *lenders* know about your credit score and what's in the credit report they're looking at. On this topic, you want to be on the same page as they are.

In Chapter 2, I go into more detail about the credit scores. The main points to keep in mind are:

- ✔ Your score is different for each credit bureau report, if only because each bureau has different data about you in its files.

- ✔ Be sure you know which score you're getting: a FICO score or a proprietary bureau score.

- ✔ You improve your credit score by improving your credit history, not the other way around.

- ✔ Because credit reports commonly have errors, you're likely to have a faulty credit score. Dispute errors and outdated items to get the most accurate score possible.

If you're in a rush and can't wait the 30 or so days a credit bureau takes to resolve a dispute, thereby giving you a more accurate score, consider a *rapid rescorer*. These are credit-score and credit-report resellers who will add verifiable corrections to your report quickly and give you a new report and score, as the name suggests, rapidly. They can often get your lender a new, updated score . . . well, rapidly!

Telling a good score from a bad one

Good score ranges change over time as the history of the population changes. Not like Napoleon history, but credit and payment history. The subprime problems of 2008 caused a lot of the population that had high scores to move much lower on the scoring ladder.

So, what's a good score? Essentially, it's one that's good enough to get you what you want at a price you can afford. My best advice is to try and stay within the upper categories and not slip into the lower ones.

FICO likes to give you a picture of where you stand in comparison to others using an eight-bar chart (see Figure 6-1). You can tell these guys were never teachers — more like statisticians!

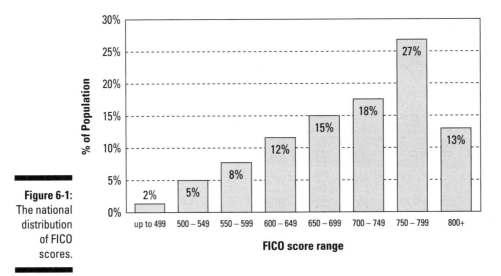

Figure 6-1:
The national distribution of FICO scores.

Source: Fair Isaac Corporation

In the current environment, the difference in loan terms between 750 and 800+ (the top two groups) may be small, but the difference between 599 and 600, which represent two lower groups, is very large. Moving *between* groups (say, from 700 to 750) is more important than moving *within* them (say, from 700 to 749). And most of the lending risk, as well as the high pricing to offset it, is seen in the lower groups.

Meanwhile, Vantage uses an A to F grading system. Under their scale, you can estimate your place in the credit pecking order like this:

- ✔ **A: Super Prime** — The top 12.8 percent of the population is in this category with scores ranging from 901 to 990.

- ✔ **B: Prime Plus** — Forty-five percent of the population is Prime Plus or better. Prime Plus scores range from 801 to 900.

- ✔ **C: Prime** — The top 70 percent of the population is Prime or better. Prime scores range from 701 to 800.

- ✔ **D: Non-Prime** — The lowest 30 percent of the population is Non-Prime or lower. Non-Prime scores range from 601 to 700.

- ✔ **E:** No, there is no "E." I think one of the developers was a former school teacher.

- ✔ **F: High Risk** — The lowest 8.8 percent of the population is High Risk. High Risk scores range from 501 to 600.

So how high is high enough? In a time of relatively easy credit, such as in 2006, the saying was that all you needed was a pulse to get a loan. Although this may not be totally true, getting a loan in 2006 was certainly easier than it is today.

What we don't know is whether the future will hold the same, easier, or tighter credit requirements. Over time, the standard for lending has swung in a pendulum from easy to tight and back again. So, keeping your credit as clean as you can is all the more important because today's record will be there for seven years, while tomorrow's credit market will surely change one way or the other.

Connecting risk-based pricing to your credit score

Most lending today is done on a modified version of *risk-based pricing*. Risk-based pricing used to mean that rather than saying "no" to a bad-risk customer, lenders would say "yes" and still make money on the risky loan because they'd charge you a high interest rate and fees. This allowed more people to get more loans — if at a higher cost — at lower scores. That was until the subprime mess turned risky loans into losses at any interest rate. So while your score and credit report may get you a higher or lower interest rate, if they're too weak under tight credit conditions, they may get you a "no thank you" instead.

What do credit-score groupings look like in the market as of early 2008? As an example, take a $300,000, 30-year, fixed-rate mortgage. Remember the actual rates for your loan today will be different. This example is meant to illustrate the magnitude of difference between scores and rates. The rates would look like this:

Score	Rate	Monthly Payment
500–579	10.22 percent	$2,682
580–619	9.259 percent	$2,470
620–659	6.624 percent	$1,921
660–699	5.814 percent	$1,763
700–759	5.530 percent	$1,709
760–850	5.308 percent	$1,667

Maintaining the highest credit score possible can save you hundreds of dollars a month in mortgage loan payments. And while the number of dollars you save with smaller loans may not be as high as that associated with a mortgage loan, a high credit score will save you money in interest charges for any amount of money you plan to borrow.

Knowing the reason for reason statements

Along with your credit score, you get up to four reason statements on your credit-score report. What's the reason for reason statements? Well, a lender can't make money turning down business, so if your score is getting in the way of commerce, knowing the reason why can help identify how to correct the situation and get those fees and loans flowing again!

The creditors get what is called a *reason code,* and you get the interpreted version of that, which is called the *reason statement.* For example, if a reason code reveals that your lower-than-desired score is because of an inordinate number of open accounts used to the max and not because you never pay on time, the lender may be more willing to take you on.

Some 60 different codes give you and your lender a hint about what's causing your credit troubles. Additionally, they may be helpful in allowing you to determine whether your credit report contains errors and where the errors exist because they highlight areas that lower your score.

The reason codes are interpreted by the bureaus. Typically, following whatever section your credit score is in, both positive and negative reasons for your score are listed, with tips to help increase your score muscle. According to Fair Isaac, the ten most frequently given score reasons (specific wording may vary) are

✔ Serious delinquency

✔ Serious delinquency, and public record or collection filed

✔ Derogatory public record or collection filed

✔ Time since delinquency is too recent or unknown

✔ Level of delinquency on accounts

✔ Number of accounts with delinquency

✔ Amount owed on accounts

✔ Proportion of balances to credit limits on revolving accounts is too high

✔ Length of time accounts have been established

✔ Too many accounts with balances

Part III

Houston, We Have A Problem: Doing Damage Control

The 5th Wave   By Rich Tennant

Tell Her Highness I think the people from the collection agency are here.

In this part . . .

Managing credit problems so that damage is minimized is what this part is all about. First, I cover your rights under the Fair and Accurate Credit Transaction Act (the FACT Act or FACTA). I explain how it entitles you to an accurate, up-to-date credit report, and how it provides clout in getting the bureaus and creditors to correct your credit information. Whatever your current situation, I show you how to stop your credit from deteriorating further and begin to build a positive report and credit score as quickly as possible.

You discover how the FACT Act controls what collectors can and can't do, and how to keep them from hounding you while getting the best outcomes from lawyers and the courts. I include up-to-date suggestions and options for anyone dealing with or considering a mortgage foreclosure. Finally, I help you sort out whether you're eligible for or should consider bankruptcy and how to best recover from it.

Chapter 7

Sprucing Up Your Credit Report

. . . .

In This Chapter

▶ Keeping your credit report clean — why it's so important

▶ Understanding your rights under the FACT Act

▶ Identifying what shouldn't be in your credit report

▶ Getting errors out of your credit report

▶ Placing positive information in your file

. . . .

*I*f you're like most Americans, you value your privacy in an increasingly public world. This is particularly true where financial matters are concerned. For better or worse, many people's self-image is based on their financial situation and its perception by others. Looking a little wealthier than you are doesn't hurt, after all (unless, of course, you look too good and your relatives begin to think you should be bailing them out of financial scrapes). And if you have some credit blemishes, you certainly don't want everyone to see them —not even your own family members.

Despite your desire to restrict access to the more-intimate details of your personal financial history, your credit report and score are accessible to much of the world. More and more decisions are being made impersonally from long distances, by people or programs that only know you from your credit file and, in some cases, from globally-based companies. In this environment of full financial nudity and disclosure, the best you can hope for is that your credit profile be as accurate as possible. At the very least, you should demand that your financial record is your own and not someone else's.

Congress has done its part by tightening up the laws around personal data and giving you sweeping rights through an update to portions of the Fair Credit Reporting Act (FCRA). The new legislation is called the Fair and Accurate Credit Transactions Act (the FACT Act or FACTA for short). All you need to do is understand and exercise the rights granted by this law — and that is exactly what this chapter will help you do — discover the ins and outs of sprucing up your credit report.

Knowing Why a Clean Report Is Vital

The detail in your credit report is used to determine much more than a loan approval or an interest rate. The people who make decisions that affect you try to find acceptable social, political, and business reasons for making those decisions. They look for independent and valid data — void of discrimination, favoritism, or prejudice — to help them come to a conclusion. So if you have a dirty report with incorrect info, you may end up paying higher interest rates or not even be approved for a loan. That's why having a clean report is important.

And among the best and biggest sources of data available today are the credit-reporting databases. The information in your credit report has been found to be a good predictor of future financial and non-financial behavior in your life. Among the kinds of decisions being made about you based at least in part on what's in your credit report are whether to

- ✔ Give you credit and on what terms
- ✔ Hire you for a new job
- ✔ Give you a promotion at work
- ✔ Give you insurance coverage
- ✔ Grant you a professional license in your line of work
- ✔ Qualify you for security clearance for your job or in the military

So, if you're borrowing, looking for work, seeking career advancement, renewing insurance, getting licensed, or, to put it otherwise, if you're a living, breathing member of our society, to get the most you can from the 21st-century American financial system, you want to make sure that your credit information is accurate, current, and, yes, about *you.*

Examining Your Credit Report for Problems

The task of repairing your credit is a lot easier than some people may lead you to believe. All it takes is some time, patience, and persistence. The problem usually comes in when people don't just want to repair or rebuild their credit, but when they want their credit to be better than it really is — and, usually, instantly so. Faking it is a losing game, and I don't recommend it.

You want to keep a close eye on your credit report for any potential problems because not only are errors fairly common but they are important. Your credit history is being used to make an increasingly large number of decisions about your future, financial and otherwise, from lending to insurance to employment. And the GAO has found that about 25 percent of reports have serious errors. To examine your report, arm yourself with the information in your credit reports (one from each of the three major bureaus), as well as your FICO score from myFICO.com. (Chapter 4 shows you how to get these reports and your score.) There are other scores out there that you can get; however, FICO is still used the most often. If you apply for a loan and the lender uses a different score, such as Vantage, you may want to get that one as well. But for our purposes here, I suggest you use the FICO as your benchmark to gauge your repair progress.

When you have your credit report, you're poised to take the necessary steps to clean up the information that's there — removing outdated or inaccurate details, adding positive information, and even increasing your credit score. By doing all this, you can put yourself in a better position to receive credit and earn the most attractive interest rates when you borrow.

As you study your credit report, you may be surprised by how many accounts you find. Because your credit report includes negative information for the past seven years (longer exceptions, such as government debts and bankruptcy, also exist) and positive information for much longer, you're likely to see accounts, referred to as *trade lines,* that you've forgotten about and perhaps even some you didn't realize you still had. Many creditors don't close accounts — even if you haven't used them in years. Retailers in particular are famous for this. Ever the optimists, they continue to hope you'll show up in the store or online and buy something using the ease and convenience of their card. Plus, they get lower transaction costs and better data when you use their in-house card. Still, your task is to weed through the trade lines — current and ancient alike — and identify errors and inaccuracies. (For a rundown on all the different sections of your credit report, turn to Chapter 5.)

Here's what you should look for in particular:

- ✔ **Make sure your name is spelled correctly and your Social Security number is correct.** With all the data moving through the financial reporting system, a "Jr." or "Sr." can easily be missed, or confusion over a "II" or "III" designation may occur. Although variations on your name are okay (for example, my report shows both Stephen and Steve), make sure that your address and date of birth are also correct. Your social security number is actually the fourth matching criteria after name, address, and date of birth.

- ✔ **Check to see which of your accounts are shown on your credit report.** Remember that your credit report may not show all your accounts. Why? Because creditors may only supply information to one (or none) of the three major credit bureaus, particularly if they only use one bureau's report to make credit decisions.

- ✔ **Look to see if accounts are showing the activity they ought to.** If you see accounts that are familiar but activity that isn't — such as a late-payment notation when you're certain you've never been late — you'll want to report that error to the credit bureau. Also, if you see accounts you don't recognize, it may be a simple mix-up or something more serious, like identity theft. Again, contact the bureau and find out.

✔ **Scan for accounts from a bank or store with which you have never done business.** Someone else's account information may have been added to your credit report because of a misspelled name or incorrect Social Security number.

✔ **Identify and verify any accounts that show negative activity.** *Negative activity* can include anything from a missed or late payment to a charge-off or bankruptcy notation. Be sure this negative information is really yours and really accurate. For example, an unpaid charge-off and a paid charge-off differ greatly from one another, even though both are negative.

✔ **Bank and store mergers can result in multiple entries for the same account, so be sure that an account that moved from one source to another is listed only once.** Multiple entries can make it look like you have excessive amounts of credit available.

✔ **Look for any overdraft protection lines of credit.** These lines of credit often outlive the account they're protecting. Closing these lines of credit can be helpful if you have a lot of credit available.

✔ **Check out all the addresses shown on your reports.** Incorrect addresses can lead to incorrect information ending up in your file.

If an account isn't listed and you believe it would be a positive addition to your credit report, write the credit bureau and ask them to add this information to your report. Although the bureau isn't required to do so, it may add verifiable accounts for a fee. After you add the account to your report, keep in mind that the account may not be updated if the creditor does not generally report to that credit bureau. I include a form letter on the CD to help you get started.

Some lenders offer a rapid rescore product for sale. This service was developed by the three national bureaus. For a fee, the lender will model changes to the information in your credit report. If the change gives a positive result, then as soon as it is made, the lender can order a rapid rescoring within 72 hours. Actions may include paying down a balance to less than 50 percent of your maximum limit or making changes such as closing a card.

Using the FACT Act to Get Your Credit Record Clean and Keep It That Way

The FACT Act of 2003 is about getting the facts about you straight. It includes new sections intended to help consumers fight the growing crime of identity theft. How so? By redefining and setting new credit-reporting standards for accuracy, privacy, limits on information sharing, and consumer rights to disclosure. For example, one small aspect of the act prohibits the showing of your entire account number on credit- and debit-card receipts. Now only the last five digits can be shown.

The FACT Act offers you, the consumer and credit-user, expanded rights regarding your credit report, granting you more empowerment than perhaps at any time in our modern history of credit. In addition to requiring lenders and credit bureaus to play a greater role in protecting you, the FACT Act offers consumer rights. You now can

- ✔ **Receive a free credit report.** You're entitled to a free copy of your credit information once a year (see Chapter 5 for information on how to get a copy of each of your reports). You can get additional free reports if you believe your identity has been stolen or you have been on the receiving end of bad news caused by information in your credit file. They call this *adverse action* in the credit business.

- ✔ **Limit access to your credit report.** Only people and institutions with a need recognized by the FCRA and further limited by the FACT Act — usually generated by an application with a creditor, insurer, employer, landlord, or other business — are permitted access to your credit report.

- ✔ **Require your consent before anyone is provided with your credit reports or specialty reports that contain medical information.** Your employer, prospective employers, creditors, insurers — anyone — needs your permission before he can access your private information.

- ✔ **Have access to all information in your file.** Ask and you shall receive. You must be given the information in your file, as well as a list of everyone who has recently requested access to it. Creditors are also required to give you an early-warning notice if any negative information is placed on your credit report.

- ✔ **Be informed if your report has been used against you.** Anyone who uses information in your credit file and takes action against you — such as denying an application for credit, insurance, or employment — must reveal that the information in your credit report was used to make the decision. Recently, this rule was expanded to require that you be notified if you're approved for credit at a higher interest rate than first offered.

- ✔ **Dispute inaccurate information.** After you say that your report contains inaccurate information, the credit bureau must investigate the items — usually within 30 days — and give you a written report of the investigation and a copy of the revisions made to your report if the investigation results in any change.

- ✔ **Place a statement on your report.** You may include 100-word statements in your report, explaining extenuating circumstances or noting your disagreement with items on your report.

✔ **Have inaccurate information corrected or deleted.** Inaccurate or unverified information has to be removed from your file, usually within 30 days after you dispute it. If the reported information is later found to be valid, it can be reinserted into your report, in which case you must be given a written notice telling you of the reinsertion. The notice must include the name, address, and phone number of the information source.

✔ **Have outdated information removed.** In most cases, information more than seven years old — ten years for bankruptcies — should be deleted from your credit report. If it is not, you may demand that it be dropped.

✔ **Exclude your name from lists for unsolicited credit and insurance offers.** Although creditors and insurers may use file information as the basis for sending you unsolicited offers of credit or insurance, they must also include a toll-free phone number for you to call if you want your name and address removed from future lists. The opt-out toll-free number for all national credit-reporting agencies is 888-567-8688.

✔ **Initiate a fraud alert by calling one of the three credit bureaus.** If your identity is stolen, you just have to make one phone call to a credit bureau (as opposed to having to contact each one of the three credit bureaus individually). A *fraud alert* requires the credit grantor to exercise enhanced levels of protection, such as taking additional steps to verify you are who you claim to be, for your information.

A growing number of states have enacted Credit Freeze legislation responding to growing consumer sentiment. The bureaus now allow you to *freeze* your credit report for any reason. This allows you to lock the door to any unauthorized review or use of your credit information without you specifically allowing it. The only exception is, of course, if Uncle Sam wants to see your credit record. Those G-men have master keys to every lock in town! Generally, you can freeze, and then unfreeze or thaw, your information as your needs warrant. You may be charged a small fee, but the process is effective.

✔ **Receive damages from violators.** If those who report information to the credit bureaus don't follow the law, you can sue them in state or federal court. Some people have, and they've collected millions of dollars!

✔ **When deployed overseas, active-duty military personnel can place a special alert on their files to protect their credit.** Known as the Active Duty Alert, it requires a business seeing the alert on your credit report to verify your identity before issuing credit in your name. The business may try to contact you directly, but if you're on deployment, that may be impossible. As a result, the law allows you to use a personal representative to place or remove an alert. Active Duty Alerts are effective for one year and may be renewed. The alert also cuts down on your junk mail. Your name will be removed from the nationwide consumer reporting companies' marketing lists for prescreened offers of credit and insurance for two years. Sweet!

I cover the FACT Act in more detail in Chapter 15, where I also discuss the details of combating identity theft.

Disputing Inaccurate Information

You can't legally remove accurate and timely info from your credit report — whether it's good or bad. But the law does allow you to request an investigation of any information in your file that you believe is outdated, inaccurate, or incomplete. You won't be charged for this, and you can do it yourself at little or no cost. *Note:* Inaccurate data serves no purpose for anyone in the credit-report chain. The credit bureaus, the lenders, and you all want the information in your report to be accurate.

In the following sections, I let you know how to file a dispute with the credit bureaus, as well as with the creditor in question.

Understanding the dispute process

The process for disputing and correcting inaccurate information has been made as easy as possible by the credit bureaus. Your role is to check your reports at least once a year and, if you see information that looks unfamiliar or wrong, file a dispute.

If you don't have any major purchases or life changes (like a move, new job, and so on) pending in the next 6 to 12 months, I suggest that you stagger ordering your credit reports so you get an updated one every 4 months. This helps you become aware of any possible fraud or identity theft faster. If you have things coming up in your life sooner, I'd get them all at once.

Here's what happens when you dispute information: After a dispute is received, the bureau contacts the source that provided the data. That source has 30 days in which to respond. If the source cannot verify the data within the time allowed, whether it's because the information never existed, they can't find it, or Helen (the data retriever) is on vacation, the information must be removed from your report. If, on the other hand, the information is verified, it stays on your report. In either case, you're notified in writing of any actions that occur as a result of your dispute.

Under the FCRA, both the credit bureau and the organization that provided the information to the credit bureau — such as a bank or credit-card company — have responsibilities for correcting inaccurate or incomplete information in your credit report.

For the complete story on the FCRA or the FACT Act . . .

If you just can't get enough of this stuff, the complete text of the FCRA and the FACT Act is at the Federal Trade Commission's Web site (www.ftc.gov) and on the CD. You can also contact the FTC at: Federal Trade Commission, Consumer Response Center, FCRA, Washington, DC 20580; phone 877-382-4367.

If that doesn't satisfy you, contact your state or local consumer-protection agency or your state attorney general to find out more about your rights.

If you disagree with the findings, you can contact the company that placed the erroneous report yourself and try to get them to change it. Be sure to ask how the investigation was conducted and who was contacted. You also have the right to add a statement to your report or a specific trade line saying why you disagree.

If you place a statement on your report, be sure to keep track of the time it's out there so it doesn't outlast the negative data it explains and cause you further problems.

Countering the credit bureaus

Not all the bureaus have the same information in their files. So if, for example, you look at your Experian credit report, see an inaccuracy, follow the dispute process, and have it corrected, you may not be out of the woods. TransUnion or Equifax may have *different* inaccurate information. So, you need to get all three reports to see which reports contain *which* false data.

If the same error appears on two or all three reports, you only need to dispute it once; if the information is inaccurate, the credit bureau will report this finding to the other two bureaus on your behalf. But, being a cautious person by nature, I suggest that you double-check.

Correcting all three reports is important, because some lenders or business-people purchase the three-in-one report that includes a credit score and credit-history information from each of the three bureaus. Each of the three credit bureaus has slightly different procedures for consumers to file disputes, but all three allow you to dispute inaccurate or out-of-date information by phone, online, or by mail:

✔ **Equifax:** Call 800-685-1111, and be sure to have your ten-digit credit-report confirmation number (on your report) available. You can also dispute by mail at Equifax Information Services LLC, P.O. Box 740256, Atlanta, GA 30374 (no confirmation number is required on written correspondence) or online at www.equifax.com.

✔ **Experian:** You can dispute by phone at 888-397-3742; online at www.experian.com; or by mail at P.O. Box 2104, Allen, TX 75013-2104.

✔ **TransUnion:** You can dispute any information by phone at 800-916-8800; online at www.transunion.com; or by mail at TransUnion Consumer Solutions, P.O. Box 2000, Chester, PA 19022-2000 (be sure to include your TransUnion file number, available on your TransUnion credit report).

While initiating a dispute by phone may be the easiest route, most experts suggest that you do everything in writing or online to create a trail of documentation you can point to if things go wrong or get lost.

If you choose to dispute items on your credit report via mail, write a letter stating which item(s) you're disputing. Include any facts that support and explain your case, and include copies (not originals) of documents that support your position. Enclose a copy of your credit report with the items in question circled. Be sure to provide your complete name and address, and tell them what your desired action is (correction or deletion).

Figure 7-1 is a sample letter disputing information on your report. (It's also available on the CD, along with other letters you may find useful.)

If you're contacting the credit bureau by mail, send your letter by certified mail, return-receipt requested, so you can document the fact that your dispute letter was mailed and received. Keep copies of your dispute letter and enclosures.

Fixing your credit can be a lot like taking a bath

The ancient Greek Archimedes was famous for leaping from his bath crying, "Eureka!" when he found a solution to a problem. Picture your credit history like a bath tub. The more history, the more water in the tub. Adding negative information adds a drop of food coloring to the water. The more water in the tub or credit data in your report, the less color change. As you add positive credit history, the negative will be further diluted and, "Eureka!" you will have cleaned up your credit standing.

Your Full Name   Date
Current Address
Current Phone Number
Attention: **[Insert the name of the credit reporting agency]**
            [Add agency address here]

Dear Sir or Madam:

This letter is a formal request to correct inaccurate or out-of-date information contained in my credit file. The item(s) listed below *(is/are)* **[Select and insert appropriate word(s): *inaccurate, incorrect, incomplete, erroneous, misleading,* or *outdated*]**. I have enclosed a copy of the credit report your organization provided to me on **[insert date of report here]** and circled in red the item(s) in question.

Credit Report Number: **[Insert number from credit report containing error]**
Line Item: **[Insert name of creditor, account number, or line item number]**
Item Description: **[This information is found on your credit report]**
Requested Correction: **[Describe exactly what you want. If you want an item deleted, say so and explain why. If you want an item corrected or updated, provide the correct information such as names, dates, amounts, and so forth and any evidence to support your claim]**.

In accordance with the federal Fair Credit Reporting Act (FCRA), I respectfully request you investigate my claim and, if after your investigation, you find my claim to be valid and accurate, I request that you immediately **[*delete, update, correct*]** the item. Furthermore, I request that you supply a corrected copy of my credit profile to me and all creditors who have received a copy within the last six months, or the last two years for employment purposes. Additionally, please provide me with the name, address, and telephone number of each credit grantor or other subscriber that you provided a copy of my credit report to within the past six months.

If your investigation shows the information to be accurate, I respectfully request that you forward to me a description of the procedure used to determine the accuracy and completeness of the item in question within 15 days of the completion of your reinvestigation as required by the Fair Credit Reporting Act.

I thank you for your consideration and cooperation. If you have any questions concerning this matter I can be reached at **[insert daytime phone number including area code]**.

Sincerely,

Signature, Printed Name

Figure 7-1:
A sample letter to a credit bureau disputing information on your report.

The credit-reporting agency must forward all relevant data you provide to the company that originally provided the information. When the company receives the request for verification from the credit bureau, it must investigate, review all relevant information provided, and report the results to the credit bureau.

- ✔ **If the information is found to be inaccurate,** all nationwide bureaus are notified so they can correct this information in your file.

- ✔ **If the company cannot verify the accuracy of the information you're disputing,** the information must be deleted from your file.

- ✔ **If the disputed information is incomplete,** the credit bureau must update it. For example, if you were once late in making payments, but your file doesn't show that you've caught up, the bureau must show that you're now current in your payments.

- ✔ **If the disputed information in your file shows an account that belongs to another person,** the bureau must delete it.

When the investigation is complete, the credit bureau must give you the written results and a free copy of your updated credit report if the dispute results in a change of information. If an item is changed or removed, the bureau cannot put the disputed information back in your report unless the company providing that information subsequently verifies its accuracy and completeness. Then the credit bureau must give you written notice that includes the name, address, and phone number of the company that provided the verification.

Avoiding a frivolous dispute

The credit bureau must investigate the disputed items in question — usually within 30 days — unless it considers your dispute frivolous. If the bureau considers your request frivolous, they're required to notify you within five business days; the bureau must tell you why it considers your dispute frivolous and explain what you must do to convert the dispute into one that will start a reinvestigation.

So how can you make sure your dispute isn't seen as frivolous? If you send a long list of disputes — for example, all the negative information on your credit report — you may give the appearance of trying to overwhelm the credit-reporting agency with requests and they may refuse to honor your request. For this reason, you're better off sending only a few disputes in a single letter.

You may think this sounds silly. You, overwhelming a huge credit bureau. Well, some shady companies try to do just that, hoping to tie up the investigation process long enough for a new score to be calculated without the disputed (but accurate) negative information included. The bureaus consequently need procedures to handle this situation. And that's the story of frivolity at the bureaus!

You can request that the bureau send notices of corrections to anyone who received your report in the past six months. If you've applied for a job, you can have a corrected copy of your report sent to anyone who received a copy during the past *two years* for employment purposes.

If you aren't satisfied with the results of your dispute, you can dispute the item directly with the creditor (see "Contacting the creditor," later in this chapter). Be sure to include copies of all the information you have. You also have the right to include a 100-word statement of the dispute in your report and in future reports. Submit the written statement to the credit-reporting agencies, which are required to include it in your report (see "Adding a 100-word statement," later in this chapter). Depending on each bureau's rules, this statement can stay on your report indefinitely, so don't forget about it!

When the negative information in your report is accurate, only the passage of time can assure its removal. Most accurate negative information stays on your report for seven years, but certain exceptions to the seven-year rule exist:

- ✔ Criminal convictions may be reported without any time limitation.

- ✔ Chapter 7 bankruptcy information may be kept on your report for ten years.

- ✔ IRS liens remain on your credit report indefinitely, until removed by the IRS.

- ✔ An inquiry in response to an application for a job with a salary of more than $75,000 has no time limit.

- ✔ An inquiry because of an application for more than $150,000 worth of credit or life insurance has no time limit.

- ✔ A lawsuit or an unpaid judgment against you can be reported for seven years or until the statute of limitations runs out, whichever is longer.

If you're unhappy with the results of your dispute and think you have been treated unfairly or have not been taken seriously, contact the Federal Trade Commission (FTC). The FTC works to prevent fraudulent, deceptive, and unfair business practices in the marketplace and to provide information to help consumers spot, stop, and avoid them. To file a complaint or to get free information on consumer issues, visit www.ftc.gov or call 877-382-4357 (TTY 866-653-4261).

Contacting the creditor

Any financial institution that submits negative information about you to a national credit-reporting agency has to tell you so. This gives you a heads-up to jump on errors earlier than under the old laws.

Challenging data you aren't sure about

The dispute process is protected from abuse by the law. You don't want to dispute information that you know is accurate or claim that an account listing is the result of identity theft when you know that is not the case. However, you can dispute any listing in good faith if you're uncertain of its validity — in other words, if you can't find records that confirm the item, you don't recall the status, or you're simply uncertain that the information has been reported correctly.

Follow the dispute processes outlined in this chapter, and explain why you believe the item is questionable. Just as you might challenge a word that you aren't familiar with in a game of Scrabble with friends, disputing information about which you aren't completely sure is okay. Disputing information that you know is correct is *not* okay.

You have a right to direct access to the furnisher of the disputed information. The actual contact process varies and can be as simple as walking into the credit department and explaining the problem or calling the company's toll-free number or visiting its Web site (many companies' Web sites also have information on reporting fraud).

After you've contacted the creditor, it must investigate the dispute and report the results back to you following the same guidelines that the credit bureaus have to follow (see the preceding section), including responding in the same time frame as the credit-reporting agencies.

Best of all, the creditor cannot continue to report the negative information without noting that it is in dispute. And if the information that's been disputed was reported as the result of a possible identity theft, then it can't be reported at all while the investigation is pending.

Again, as with the credit bureaus, the creditor must respond to your request within 30 days. If there is no response, the item in dispute is removed or corrected. If the creditor finds the information to be inaccurate, it must be corrected. If the information is outdated or someone else's, it must be removed. The result must be submitted to each credit-reporting agency with which the creditor has shared the incorrect information. If your dispute is not found to be valid, you can add the 100-word statement mentioned earlier in this chapter to your report, explaining why you dispute the claim.

Be sure to keep good records such as names, dates of contact, and copies of letters and e-mails. Any company can experience what I call "bureaucratic memory loss." So if you get a response like, "we never heard of this before, who were you speaking to?" you'll have the answer handy. Good record keeping will keep these delays and irritations to a minimum.

Adding Info to Your Credit Report

Not enough information in your credit report can also be a problem. The best way to get positive information inserted into your credit report is to make payments to your creditors on time and in the full amount each month. Do so for a year or more, and you'll have made great strides in improving your credit history and your credit score.

If you're new to this country or have little or no credit data in bureau files, you have a couple options to get information added. Those two options include

✔ **A Global FICO score:** If you have verifiable credit information from outside the United States, you may be able to have that information used for credit-granting purposes. Ask your lender if it can use the Global FICO score. The Global Score is valid across multiple geographic regions, excluding (why am I not surprised?) France. Credit reporting and scoring are becoming global; however, international credit reporting still has a long way to go to meet American standards and ease of use. If you don't have a Social Security number, you can use a Consular ID to set up a Taxpayer Identification number to establish a credit record.

✔ **Expansion Score:** The elves at Fair Isaac developed a variation on the traditional FICO score called the Expansion Score. I cover this in more detail in Chapter 2. To paraphrase the old Star Trek mission, the FICO people search for new sources of credit life (that don't report to the bureaus, such as cell phone records) and boldly use them to generate a score where no bureau has gone before.

You can also add some information to your credit report yourself. I cover a few of your options in the following sections.

Getting good accounts added to your report

If you have good accounts that aren't showing up on your credit reports, you can request that they be added. For example, if you have a loan through your credit union and the credit union does not report to the major credit bureaus, you can request that the bureaus verify the account and add it to your report. Those deferred payment plans at your local furniture store are another source that can be included. You may be charged a fee to do this, but it may be worth the cost if the account will improve your credit standing and get you a better interest rate.

Opening new credit accounts

Another way to insert information is to open new credit accounts. Opening types of accounts that are not already on your credit report is particularly helpful. For example, you may have several credit cards, so you could add an installment account — which can increase your "Type of Credit Used" profile (see Chapter 2 for more information).

Be careful when using this tactic to improve your credit score. You may do more harm than good if you open an account with a large amount of available credit — this is likely to push your available credit over the limit of what is acceptable by lenders. Also, do this well in advance of applying for a loan as opening a new account may have a short-term negative impact on your score.

Adding a 100-word statement

Don't like what others are saying about you? You can add a 100-word statement to explain certain items on your credit report. Although a statement won't change your credit score, it may help answer questions that a lender or employer may have when reviewing your report. Yes, the score is important, but so is the analysis by the person looking at your record. This statement can be used to accomplish several things:

- ✔ **Explain a series of past late payments, collections, or charge-offs.** These may be due to a life event such as a job loss, divorce, or illness.

- ✔ **Dispute information that you believe is incorrect, but that the credit-reporting agency will not remove from your report.**

- ✔ **Tell your side of a negative report.** For example, you may have ordered a product that was not delivered on time or was unsatisfactory to you and you refused to pay for it. Although the situation was not resolved in your favor, you may be able to explain it more clearly in your 100-word note.

Do these 100-word statements really help? It depends on who is reviewing your credit report and what you say. The statement will stay on your report at least as long as the disputed item does and at least one credit-reporting agency — TransUnion — thinks it's important enough to offer you help in writing it (call 800-916-8800 for help from TransUnion).

If you decide to put a statement on your report, be sure that your statement doesn't outlive its usefulness. As old information becomes less of a factor in your score, or even drops off your report, statements can highlight past payment problems better forgotten, especially if the credit report shows no recent delinquencies. Your outdated statement could call attention to past situations that no longer apply, and it may hurt more than it helps.

Steering Clear of Credit-Repair Companies

If you're desperate for ways to speed up the recovery process, you may suddenly be looking at credit-repair companies as your last hope (even though you can repair your credit on your own). You may be asking yourself, "Why not?" Well, the answer is this:

✔ **Credit-repair companies can get you into a lot of trouble.** Most credit-repair companies use one of two strategies. Their first strategy is to challenge everything on your credit report, or at least such a large portion of it that the credit bureau and the creditors will not be able to respond to their disputes within the legal time frame allowed. As a result, the items not verified will come off your credit report in 30 days. Sounds good, right? Not really. Although credit bureaus may be slow, they're tireless machines. So at some point in the near future, the information that was removed will be verified and it will reappear on your credit report. If you're thinking, "Yeah, but I can get a loan while the information is deleted," consider this: When the information comes back on your report, you can be considered to have committed fraud. Ouch!

Their other strategy is to establish a new identity for you, using an employer identification number (EIN). The idea is that, with your new identification, you'll begin to develop a good credit report and leave behind all the bad stuff. But savvy creditors usually see through this ploy when a credit report shows very limited or no activity. Some credit-repair agencies suggest that you use the EIN as a Social Security number. If you're able to pull this off, you'll get into trouble and find yourself facing all sorts of legal unpleasantness. Why? Because you've essentially established a false identity and gotten credit under false pretenses. Nice.

If you do what the credit-repair company tells you to do, and if any of it turns out to be against the law, you — yes you, your mother's favorite child — can be prosecuted!

✔ **Credit-repair companies have a terrible track record of delivering what they promise.** Unlike credit counseling, which has also come under fire for having disreputable elements, credit repair is a much more recent phenomenon and the industry has not adopted independent standards of conduct. In fact, the industry has such a poor reputation that it has a very restrictive federal law named after it. The Credit Repair Organizations Act has as one of its two objectives "to protect the public from unfair or deceptive advertising and business practices by credit repair organizations." Need I say more?

✔ **Credit-repair companies are expensive.** And if you are someone like me, famous for frugality, this is not a small objection. Typically, the cost is at least $400. Chances are, if you're in a situation where you need help repairing your credit report, that money can serve you better by paying off some debt. If you're short on time and long on money with bad credit, why not hire someone to improve your credit for you? Certainly you could ask an attorney or accountant to help you through the process of improving your credit, but it will not be cheap and unless you have other business with these professionals, I would question why anyone with their credentials would apply their considerable talents and egos to such a mundane task. If you were to ask your lawyer to wash your car, chances are you'd get a big "no thanks," even of you were willing to pay the attorney her hourly rate. The same should be true of your request to repair your credit. But the hidden answer to this question is that it's very difficult to know with whom you're sharing all the information on your credit and financial histories. When you consider the damage they might cause you, I'm sure you can see that it's not worth the price — in any sense of the word.

Cleaning up your credit report is not as difficult as you may have heard. Erase the past? No. But you can make sure all the good stuff that may have been missed is added to your reports, that the old bad stuff is removed, and that no one else's information is on your report.

Chapter 8

Making Bad Credit and Debts Behave

*W*hen I was still counseling clients with credit problems, I was once called into a difficult counseling session. The client was upset and refused to leave, and I was asked to move him along so the next client could come into the office. A mountain of a man, with hands like sledgehammers, the client sat across from the seemingly very small desk. I thought I was going to the hospital that day. He insisted that we find a solution for him, no matter how long it took. He just couldn't stand the pressure anymore. I tell you this story to illustrate the fact that credit trouble can scare people silly — even big, strong people. And no wonder: Bad credit can threaten you and your family's economic safety in ways that rival the damage done by a thief who breaks into your home. A poor credit record can rob you of a good home, an affordable car, and an income. So it's understandable that this big guy felt overwhelmed and needed little me to help put a stop to his credit and collection woes.

If credit worries aren't bad enough, collection worries are even worse. Just the name *collectors* sounds intimidating. Who are these guys, and why don't they leave you alone? Why can't they just be a little more understanding? Collection activity can drive even the most assured person into an anxiety attack. But it doesn't have to be that way if you know how things work and how to make the best of a bad situation. You can keep your head while others around you are losing theirs.

The Fair Debt Collection Practices Act (FDCPA) can be your friend. This law was enacted to amend the Consumer Credit Protection Act to prohibit abusive practices by debt collectors. That's right, our stalwart elected protectors in

Washington, D.C., responded to what they termed the "abundant evidence of the use of abusive, deceptive, and unfair debt collection practices by many debt collectors" in the United States. Hey, they're talking about the *collector*, not you! A lot of Web sites and publications offer information about the act. If you're interested in the details, go to the source: the Federal Trade Commission Web site (www.ftc.gov).

If you believe you're in credit trouble and you feel your anxiety level spiraling, this chapter's for you. Relax, take a calming breath, and read on. In this chapter, I reveal how to put the brakes on runaway spending and park your pocketbook until you regain control of your financial situation. I show you how to communicate to your creditors to gain their support instead of putting them on the defensive. I explain how the collection process works, get you through it with as little pain and damage as possible, and minimize the impact on your credit report. Finally, I offer some simple but very effective steps to make sure you don't ever find yourself in credit or debt trouble again.

Taking Actions That Help Instead of Hurt

Let me just remind you of that infamous credit score I explain at length in Chapter 2 — you know, the one that prospective lenders, employers, insurers, and life partners may use to evaluate your worthiness — credit and otherwise. The Big Daddy of credit scores, FICO, is calculated based on massive amounts of data grouped into five categories. Three of the five have nothing to do with late payments. Like an iceberg floating in the sea, 50 percent of your score comes from items below the surface. These three are

- How much money you owe
- How many new credit lines you have
- What types of credit you use

In other words, you may never have made a late payment in your life but you can still have a credit score that causes other people to think twice about your reliability and stability. What can you do to get yourself in better financial shape without triggering any of these scoring factors? Read on.

Putting the brakes on your charging

First and foremost, if you see yourself getting in credit trouble, stop charging until you get back on solid ground. How much you owe is 30 percent of your credit score. Some tips to remember:

- **Keep balances on your credit cards below 50 percent of their limits if possible.** High outstanding debt near a card's max can adversely affect your score.

> ✔ **Pay off debt rather than move it around if you can.** The most effective way to improve your score in this category is to reduce your outstanding credit balances.
>
> ✔ **Don't close unused credit cards.** Closing unused credit cards messes with your ratio of credit card debt to available credit.

Leveraging new credit lines to your advantage

Spreading debt over more credit lines can help keep monthly payments manageable and avoid missed payments. One strategy is to transfer balances to new lines with attractive rates. This can be a temporary help, but it will result in some inquiries on your report that could possibly affect your credit score. One additional credit inquiry may take less than five points off your score. But if you have a thin credit file or are an immigrant, opening several new credit accounts in a short period of time may not be helpful. Industry statistics show that six inquiries or more on your credit report mean that you may be eight times more likely to declare bankruptcy than if you had no inquiries on your report.

This may sound like a Catch-22. How can you look for a better deal and improve your credit situation if *looking* counts against you? Don't despair — the solution is *rate shopping*. The folks behind the credit-score model realize this and show mercy to loan shoppers. If you want to shop around for the best credit line or loan opportunity, confine your shopping excursion to 14-day chunks — or find a loan within 30 days — and the inquiries won't affect your score.

Your credit score doesn't take into account any inquiries from businesses with whom you did not apply for credit (like all those unsolicited preapproved offers that come in the mail), inquiries from prospective or current employers, or your own requests to see your credit report.

Working for the right credit mix

Having a mix of credit from different sources is a good thing. Each type of credit (credit cards, retail accounts, installment loans, mortgage, consumer finance accounts, and so on) shows that you can handle different repayment obligations, such as a minimum payment on a credit card or a set payment on an installment loan. You do *not* need to have one of each type. Overall, however, installment accounts (mortgage, auto) help your score the most.

The credit mix usually isn't a huge factor in determining your score — but it is more important for those with shorter credit histories or a less-than-average amount of information on which to base a score.

Closing an account you wish you never met doesn't make it go away. A closed account will still show up on your credit report and may be considered in computing the score.

Communicating with Your Creditors

For many people, communication isn't easy. When dealing with creditors, communication can be even more difficult because of the associated emotion, guilt, and anger; basically, you have a recipe for conflict and communication breakdown.

From your end of the phone line, the situation looks like this: You're a responsible adult who has been a good customer for a long time. A series of unfortunate, unexpected, and undeserved events has descended upon you like a flock of unwanted relatives. You've tried for months to overcome your payment problems before asking for help. You can't seem to catch up. You're at the end of your rope — dangling at the edge of a cliff. But with some help, you know you can pull yourself out.

From the creditor's end of the phone line, the scenario looks like this: You made an agreement and broke it. Everyone else pays their bills on time — why shouldn't you? You may be overspending and living it up beyond your means. You need to catch up on payments as fast as possible. If you don't come through with your payments, their business will be hurt and they'll be calling their own creditors.

See how the same scenario can be seen so completely differently? And before you accuse me of being soft on the creditor, let me just reassure you — I *am* on your side! I just know that you'll be more successful in getting the outcome you want if you're able to see the situation from your creditor's perspective. For whatever reason, you haven't been able to keep all the promises you made to your creditors. Although this doesn't mean you're a bad person, it does indicate that doing business with you may have a higher risk associated with it than doing business with someone else.

So now it's *your* job to assure your creditor otherwise. Is resolution possible here? Yes — if you do your homework, offer a solution, and follow through with what you promise. Where do you start? What do you say? To minimize negative perceptions, be proactive from the start and follow the steps in this section.

Contacting your creditor promptly

Early inquiries for solutions are much more productive and much less upsetting for everyone. From the creditor's point of view, there are three types of customers:

✔ Good customers who pay as agreed

✔ Good customers with a temporary problem who are willing to work things out

✔ Bad customers who have to be chased

If you can't be the first type, you want to be the second.

The best time to let your creditors know you're in trouble is as soon as you *know* a negative situation is on the horizon. Don't wait until you've missed a payment — or more — on that credit card or auto loan. Don't wait for the phone to ring or the letter to come and *then* give your story. Get in touch *before* the payment is late. By preempting the bad-news announcement, you increase the odds that your negative event won't show up on your credit report!

Don't call if you only *think* you may miss the payment. This used to be a good thing to do before the policy of universal default came on the scene. *Universal default* is a risk-management practice that got started after a rash of bankruptcy filings in the mid to late 1990s surprised some of the financial guys in the credit business. Not wanting to be surprised a second time, they developed a type of early-warning system that not only tries to predict when something bad is going to happen, but tries to offset the risk with higher rates (also before the bad event happens). If you're perceived as a higher risk — whether you miss a payment or not — you can get whacked with a very high interest rate on this and any other loan or card that has that feature buried in the fine print.

Explaining your situation

Depending on your preference, you may choose to contact the creditor by phone, in writing, via e-mail, or through the creditor's Web site. In some cases, communication can even be handled through intermediaries. Whatever method you use, you need to explain your situation as clearly and effectively as possible, assuring the creditor that, despite your temporary difficulties, you intend to get back on financial track as quickly as possible.

But what do you want to say? How can you get the help you need and deserve? Here are some elements you want to communicate (using a phone conversation as an example):

✔ **Begin the conversation on a positive note.** Say something nice about the company and your relationship to it — for example, "I've been a customer for years and always had great products/service from you."

✔ **Get the person's name.** Use it. Why? Because this puts a human dimension on the dialogue and may help personalize your call. Don't say "you" or "you people."

✔ **Briefly (in a minute or so) explain your circumstances.** For example, you lost your job, you have no savings, and you have only unemployment for income.

✔ **Stick to the facts.** Skip all the gory details that may bias the listener in ways you can't anticipate. For example, you can simply say, "My company was recently downsized and they laid off a lot of us in the accounting division." In this day and age, such circumstances are all too common — and understandable. Don't digress with detail or emotional commentary such as, "Of course, they only laid off those of us who refused to kiss up to the supervisor — funny how they kept that hot little intern who spent a lot of time behind closed doors with him."

Offering a solution

After you've effectively given your side of the story, are you ready to throw yourself on the mercy of your creditor? Not a chance! Now you're ready to provide a resolution to this unpleasant situation. Yes, this is a critical and very positive step in the communication process. Your lender will be relieved that you've taken the responsibility to come up with a workable plan that makes you look like a person in control. Plus, you'll have *more* control over the outcome if you present a repayment plan that actually works for you. (You may even be able to negotiate a concession or two in your favor — see the section "Negotiating a payback arrangement" later in this chapter.)

Whatever your proposed plan, be sure to cover these bases:

✔ **Assure the creditor that you're already taking steps to resolve the problem** *now*.

✔ **Offer an estimate of how long you realistically need to rectify the situation.** Not "soon" or "I don't know."

✔ **Propose a specific payment figure and plan that you can manage.** Don't ask the creditor to suggest a payment. You won't like the answer.

✔ **Offer specifics.** Avoid saying, "I can't afford the $300-a-month payment right now. You're going to have to accept less." That's not a plan. "Could we reduce the monthly payment to $150 for the next four months? I would even be able to pay $75 twice a month. Then in four months, I believe I can return to $300, which will only extend the length of the loan by two months." Now, *that's* a plan. It shows that you're sensitive to the creditor's situation and you're making a fair effort to make good.

✔ **Don't overpromise.** You may feel intimidated or embarrassed. But in the end, the creditor will not be happy if you promise a certain payment and fail to deliver.

If you prefer to handle things in writing, check out Figure 8-1 for an example of a letter you may send. The same letter is on the CD, along with other letters you may find useful as starting points.

Date

Creditor Name
Creditor Address
City, State ZIP

RE: Account #:
        Name on Account:
        Balance:
        Regular Monthly Payment:

To Whom It May Concern:

To date I have remained current with the monthly
payment on the account listed above. My financial
situation has recently changed and I am unable to
continue to pay this amount. *Briefly describe financial
hardship (for example, I have been laid off and my current income covers
only my basic living expenses).*

My intent is to honor my obligation with you and
propose paying $XXX per month for the time being.
I will contact you when my financial situation
improves and I am able to increase this amount.

Thank you for your patience and assistance with
this matter. Please contact me in writing at the
address below by *Insert Date 2 Weeks from Date of Letter* with
your response.

Sincerely,

Your Name
Your Address
City, State ZIP
Your Phone

Figure 8-1:
Proposing
something
is always
better than
hiding out
and hoping
the creditor
will forget
what
you owe.

Covering all the bases

After you propose your plan and the terms have been agreed upon, ask for a letter with the new agreement to be mailed or e-mailed to you so there is no misunderstanding. If that doesn't seem to be forthcoming from your contact, or if you don't receive written documentation of the new terms in a few days, follow up yourself, stating the agreement in writing.

Reducing Expenses to Clear Credit Woes

I'm not going to lie to you: Cutting expenses is no fun! But after you've done it successfully, you'll feel much better. So, if you can reduce or even eliminate your credit challenge by doing without for a while, not having fun will turn out to be worth the effort. This section helps you take some steps to lower your expenses.

Coming up with a spending plan

The best way I know to cut expenses and set yourself on the road to credit recovery is to develop a detailed spending plan. I'm not proposing anything that will leave scars or hurt you permanently. A *spending plan* can tell you just how much available cash you have to meet your obligations — and have some fun, too. It allows you to say with certainty that you can afford $50 and not $60 on your monthly entertainment expenses, unless you're willing to reduce your spending on something else. For more on developing such a plan, turn to Chapter 13.

Creating a spending plan is easy — but putting it in writing is critical in determining what you need to change! The CD includes forms to help you. And if you still feel overwhelmed, Chapter 3 offers advice on choosing a good credit counselor who can help you with this process. (Believe it or not, there *are* people who love putting together budgets.)

Cutting the fat from your budget

The simplest way to cut expenses is much like cutting calories when you're on a diet. When slimming down, you eat the stuff that's low in calories and skip the cake. When cutting expenses, do things that have a low cost (shop at the bargain grocery store with coupons in hand) and lay off the expensive stuff (cancel that reservation to your town's hot new restaurant).

Speaking of calories and entertainment, one of the biggest entertainment expenses in American families is eating out. If you add up your monthly expense for restaurant food, you may be shocked. Cut that expense by eating in or packing a lunch. Make eating at home fun by involving the entire family in preparing some of the dishes you'd order at that fancy restaurant. You'll be surprised to see your monthly food budget shrink by as much as 25 to 50 percent.

Some entertainment cutbacks to consider are

- **Shopping as entertainment:** Cruising the mall often leads to purchases of nonessential items. You and I know that most entertainment shopping is for *wants,* not needs.

- **Movies, theater, sports events, and concerts:** You know how much even a night at the movies can cost — especially after you add up the cost of the ticket, popcorn, and drink. Don't even talk about season tickets to a major sporting event. If you're afraid you'll become uncultured or uncool, look for free concerts and plays in your community. Use the television or video rentals at home for your sports and movie fixes. Many local libraries allow you to check out movies for free.

- **Hobbies:** If your favorite pastimes come with a high price tag — golf or gambling, for example — consider switching to something that demands a little less of an investment — such as bike-riding (if you already own the bike) or bird-watching (as long as it doesn't mean a trip to Costa Rica).

  You're not giving up doing something you love forever — just until you resolve your current financial situation.

Finally, take a look at your monthly expenses and determine whether you can trim back anywhere. Some places to look are

- **Cellphone expenses:** Perhaps you can combine several phones onto one plan, switch providers, or switch to a less-expensive plan.

- **Cable TV:** Cut back the cable and spend more time reading, talking, or otherwise enjoying different pursuits.

- **Eating out:** Most people eat out so much they forget how much it costs. Even that $4-a-day latte becomes a $1,000 a year expense. After taxes!

- **Utilities:** Get energy-efficient lights, turn up or down your thermostat (depending on the time of year), and adjust the temperature on your water heater downward.

The savings from cutting back on expenses may not seem like much at first, but they'll add up quicker than you may realize. And before you believe you can't go another day without a grande triple latte, you'll have reached your goal of regaining control of your finances and stabilizing your credit situation.

Look at work for help to increase your cash flow

If you want to increase your cash flow and aren't thrilled about getting a second (or third) job, you may not have to look far. Consider the following suggestions with your job to increase your cash flow:

✔ **Take a look at your payroll deductions.** If you get a tax refund each April, see your employer and add deductions to increase your take-home pay; if you'll end up writing a check to the IRS, don't do it.

✔ **Free up some money in your retirement plan.** I'm not suggesting you take money out of the plan — that would result in some ugly penalties! But you may temporarily reduce or stop your contributions if that closes the gap.

Paying Your Bills on Time and in Full

I recognize that if you're reading this chapter, there is at least a chance that not paying your bills on time may be what got you into a bad-credit situation in the first place. But this simple act is the most important thing you can do to keep bad credit from getting worse. This section lays out what you need to do to help you pay your bills on time and keep creditors off your back.

Getting organized

Nothing is quite so frustrating as getting hit with a $35 late-payment fee on your credit-card statement when you're trying to cut expenses. And the absolute *worst* is when all seven of your credit-card issuers notice you're late and bring all your accounts to the default rate of 30 percent! Getting organized is a surefire way to avoid unnecessary late payments. Here are some options for getting organized:

✔ **Pay bills as soon as you receive them.** Make a pact with yourself to get the mail, sit down immediately (or at least when you get back inside your house), and write checks or go online to pay any bills *that day.*

✔ **Mark a calendar with due dates for all bills.** Allow at least a week for bills that are mailed and a few days for bills that are paid online. Place the calendar where you'll see it every day, so you won't miss any due dates.

✔ **Set up a filing system.** Place bills in folders marked with the day of the month that they need to be paid. The trick is remembering to place the bills in the folders and to check the folders on a daily or weekly basis.

Experiment, find a solution that works for you, and get those bills paid.

Ending paycheck-to-paycheck living

If you live paycheck to paycheck, you may find it difficult to pay all bills on time and in full every month because money is so tight. Consider these tips:

✔ **Ask your creditor to change the due date.** You can request that it fall when you have the money to pay the bill in full and on time.

✔ **Start a savings account.** Wait, what does this have to do with living paycheck to paycheck? Plenty. If you're living paycheck to paycheck, having some savings is even more critical. How else do you have money to replace the muffler or pay that doctor bill for your child? (Later in this chapter, I delve further into the importance of savings.)

✔ **Follow the advice in the "Reducing Expenses to Clear Credit Woes" section, earlier in this chapter.** Doing so can help you loosen up the money flow so you have more flexibility making payments.

Yours, Mine, and Ours: Dealing with Joint Debt

The joining of two people in marriage usually means the joining of finances as well, particularly if you live in a community-property state. *Community-property states* generally treat any property (other than a gift or inheritance) and debt that has been acquired *after* you were wed as owned (or owed) by both of you equally, no matter who earned the money or incurred the debt. Currently there are 9¾ community-property states: Arizona, California, Idaho, Louisiana, Nevada, New Mexico, Texas, Washington, and Wisconsin. Alaska has an opt-in provision (so I count it as half). Puerto Rico has community property but is not a state (so I count it as one-quarter).

Talking to your creditors is hard, but talking to your sweetie about money may be even more daunting. Dealing with joint debt isn't necessarily twice as difficult as dealing with debt alone — it can easily be 20 times harder! If you're trying to keep your bad credit from getting worse and you have some joint debt involved, you may well feel as though your situation is out of control. And it may be.

The most helpful tool at your disposal is communication. Here's what you and your partner need to discuss:

- ✔ **Agreeing on goals:** Starting here is important. This conversation is about the future (where all your problems are solved), and setting goals gives you a shared positive future that you both buy into, as the impetus to make some changes in your lives. Goals may include saving for college tuitions, retirement, or vacations. Keep in mind that your goals will change over time. Refer back to these shared goals as you continue talking ("If we want to go to the Caribbean for our big anniversary, then we need to . . ."). In the goal-setting process you don't have to be specific the first time around. After you get through all the steps that follow, I suggest you go back to the goals and put a price tag and date on each. Then rework the savings and spending plan to see how many you can fit in and what needs to be cut or delayed.

- ✔ **Eliminating debt:** Keep in mind you're trying to keep bad credit from getting worse here, so determining the best way to eliminate and avoid adding to debt is a priority. How much can be allotted each month for paying off debt? While paying down debt, agree that neither one of you will add to credit-card balances.

- ✔ **Paying bills:** If possible, pay bills together so you both know how much you owe each month and where your money is going. Decisions that need to be made, such as how much to pay on a particular credit-card balance, can be determined together.

- ✔ **Keeping track of check-writing:** Make sure that checks written by each of you are recorded in one place so that you can keep up with your balance. The same goes for using your ATM or debit card — you both need to be recording expenses. If you have two separate accounts, decide who pays what and let each other know how things are going with your respective bills.

- ✔ **Saving:** Come to an agreement as to how much you can afford to put aside in savings each month. At an early point in your financial life, it may only be $5 or $10 a paycheck. The key is to start a habit. It *will* add up with time.

Now that you have the good feelings flowing and a plan in place, make a commitment with your significant other to track your progress, communicate regularly about your finances, and avoid making large purchases without discussing them with each other first.

Knowing What Collectors Can and Can't Do

Let me begin by demystifying the power of collectors. I'm told that collectors are people just like you and me, but with a tough job to do. My personal experience over some 15 years of helping people who are dealing with debt is that this is sometimes, but not always, the case. Although some professionals in the debt-collection field see collections as no more than an extension of customer service to customers in trouble, others see collections as a power trip and use unfair and abusive collection practices.

The FDCPA law doesn't apply to what are called *in-house collectors,* the people working for the original creditor to whom the debt is owed. In-house collectors are governed by individual state laws. Most, however, use the federal rules as benchmarks to be on the safe side in case they're called to task for their actions.

The FDCPA sets the rules for outside collection agencies and prevents abuse and intimidation of individuals in debt. Very strict regulations exist governing what a collector *may* and may not do, as well as what a collector *must* do.

First for the *must:* If you're contacted about a debt by phone, the collector has five working days to send you a written notification of the amount of debt owed and the name of the creditor who referred the debt to the collector. The notice has to say that this is an attempt to collect a debt and that any information obtained will be used for that purpose. The written notice also must disclose that you have the right to dispute the debt within 30 days of receiving it.

Post-dated checks: Good for the collector, bad for you

At some point in the collection process, you may be asked to send post-dated checks to the creditor. The logic here is that, with the post-dated checks in hand, the collector will not have to call you to remind you to send in any payments you may have agreed to. It also covers the collector in case you "forget" to send a check at the appointed time.

This practice is akin to putting a piece of bacon on your dog's nose and telling him not to eat it. Giving a collector a post-dated check is almost always a bad idea, because there is a tremendous temptation on the part of the collector to cash the check too early, even though she isn't supposed to. If she cashes the check early and the money isn't in the account yet, the check will bounce, and the collector will be upset. If she cashes the check early and the money is there but the collector gets it sooner than you planned, all your other checks may start to bounce.

Fighting harassment

Getting harassed by a collections agency? You aren't the first. If you complain to the Federal Trade Commission (FTC), which watches over the collection industry, you'll be among 25,000 others who lodge collection complaints annually. Some consumers have even taken collectors who overstep the law to court, where some of the consumers have won very large settlements.

To file a complaint against a collector who is harassing you, contact the FTC at www.ftc.gov or 877-382-4357. The FTC won't follow up for you on your specific case, but your complaint will help others by allowing for patterns of possible law violations to surface.

Other things you can do about harassment or abuse include the following:

✔ **Take a deep breath.** Always be professional and as calm as you can manage, and never raise your voice. Take notes during each call. Be prepared with facts and dates, and know what you're going to say before you say it. After all, the collectors do!

✔ **Ask for a name.** Always get the name of the person calling you, and ask for full contact information including the name of the company and the manager of the office making the call. Do this before things get out of hand.

✔ **Just say no.** If the collector goes over the top or breaks a rule (threatens, yells, uses obscene language), you can tell him to stop it and call back when he can act in a businesslike manner. Keep a record of the call and behavior.

✔ **Contact the original creditor.** Even though you aren't in good graces at the moment, a complaint here can get action. No business wants past or future customers scared away by an abusive collector. The original debt holder may take the debt back and deal with you directly if you make a good case. Plus, they may save on collection expenses!

✔ **Contact the collection manager.** Remember, you were smart enough to ask for the manager's name when you were first contacted, so use it. Your complaint may be the one that gets the abuser canned. No collection agency wants to be sued because of a bully who can't be professional.

✔ **Tell them to tell it to your lawyer.** This is a double-edged sword. After you tell a collector to contact your attorney, all contact with you ends. Usually, the collection agency sends the debt to its own lawyer.

A debt collector is *not* allowed to

✔ **Use threats.** Whether in writing or over the phone, a collector must use businesslike language. Any threatening, abusive, or obscene language is not allowed.

✔ **Annoy you.** An annoying collector — isn't that a redundancy? The rule means that the collector is not allowed to make repetitive or excessively frequent phone calls to annoy or harass you.

- **Deceive you.** No trick or treat. The collector cannot pretend to be taking a survey or pose as a long-lost school friend or anyone else in order to get you on the phone.

- **Lie about the consequences.** They can't say you've committed a crime or that you'll be arrested if you don't send payment.

- **Make idle threats.** You can't be threatened with illegal actions or actions that they have no intention of taking. If they have no intention of taking you to court, they can't threaten to.

The debt collector *may*

- **Contact you directly unless you tell them to contact your attorney and give them the attorney's contact information.** You can also declare that you don't want to be contacted again about this matter. In this case, the file will usually go straight to a collection attorney.

- **Contact you by phone between 8 a.m. and 9 p.m.** The collector can only contact you outside those hours if you offer permission.

- **Call you at work.** If you tell the collector that your employer prohibits it, the collector must not call you at work.

- **Contact you by mail.** The collector cannot put information on the outside of the envelope that indicates a collection attempt.

- **Contact others to get information on where you live and work.** The collector can't say anything about the debt, though. The sticky part is that if the collector calls your mother and *she* asks who they are, they can state their name and the name of their employer.

- **Boost your bill.** The addition of any charges to your bill agreed to under the original terms of your loan is allowed. That's the fine print that few people read in all new accounts. This includes endless fees and the costs of collection.

- **Ask for a post-dated check.** Depending on the state in which you live, the collector may be entitled to ask for post-dated checks. Check your state guidelines — although it may be permitted, providing a post-dated check is not in your best interest (see the nearby sidebar for more information).

- **Report your delinquency to the credit bureaus.** A delinquency showing up on your credit report as a negative lowers your credit score.

- **Raise your interest rate.** You may be hit with a penalty rate. You can't pay the current bill, so why would they increase your interest rate to 20 to 30 percent? Because you're a higher risk than they thought — and because they can.

- **Repossess your purchase.** This is almost always a bad deal for you because the creditor determines the value of the repossessed item — and the creditor can charge you for costs incurred in reselling it, too.

✔ **Take you to court.** The collector may decide to obtain a judgment against you in a court of law. Depending on your state laws, this can be a prelude to garnishing your wages or placing a lien on your home. It further damages your credit report.

✔ **Revise the terms of the contract.** Some collectors can offer to allow you to make up your shortfall over time by adding an amount to future payments. Some, to their credit, offer hardship programs, but usually only if you ask. Be sure to get any revisions or agreements in writing, particularly if communications are, at best, strained — you'll need documentation to ensure the agreement is honored.

✔ **Accept or offer a settlement for less than the full amount.** If a lower amount is agreed upon, the collector usually wants the settlement at once and in a single payment. This will generally be reported negatively on your credit report as "settled." Depending on the amount of the write-off (usually a $600 threshold), you may get a 1099C in the mail at tax time. The forgiven portion of the debt is considered income to you, and taxes are due on it. (Check out Chapter 10 for more on settlements.)

Taking Charge of the Collection Process

The best way to deal with the collection process is to take positive action as early in the game as possible. Debts do not improve with age, and they certainly don't go away if you ignore them. In fact, as debts age, they get bigger and uglier and harder to satisfy.

Accounts that are 30 to 90 days *delinquent* (overdue) are usually handled by people working for the company from which you bought your product or service. If you're contacted by a third-party collector early in the process, chances are the company hired them because of their tact and effectiveness rather than their skill at offending people. Outside or third-party collectors are covered by the FDCPA and must abide by those rules (see the preceding section). The biggest difference with an in-house or inside collector is that these guys may want to keep you as a customer as well as collect the money due. However, if the business determines it's unlikely to get payment from you, your customer status becomes less and less of a factor in working things out (that is, they don't really care how nice they are).

 Calling the creditors before they call you is always better because it places you in a much different category than you'll find yourself in if they do the dialing. Good faith will be on your side, but even that will fade if you don't deliver on your commitments.

This section walks you through what to do to give you the greatest chance of success when dealing with collectors.

Asking for verification

When you get a call or a letter claiming you have a past-due financial obligation, make sure you verify its accuracy. Here's what you do. Even if you're sure you owe the money, ask for details — which account, what the bill was for, the age of the debt, when the statement was mailed to you. Doing so never hurts. Why? Check out these two good reasons:

- ✔ **The collector may be wrong.** Creditors make mistakes — asking for a little proof is reasonable. You're not denying you owe the debt; you're just making sure they have the right customer and the right account.

- ✔ **You may be the victim of a scam.** There are people out there who will call or write and say you owe money — and maybe you do — but not to them. They may even have proprietary information that persuades you that they must be legitimate. They may not be. Get the facts in writing through the U.S. mail before you act. Having the information mailed opens scammers up to mail fraud charges.

The FDCPA rules say that you have 30 days to respond to a collection attempt, and you're well within your rights to dispute the debt. To do so, use certified mail with a return receipt. All you need to do is ask that they provide proof of the debt. Keep copies of everything you send. When you dispute the debt, the collector must stop all activity and provide you with proof of your obligation before reinitiating contact. Meanwhile, the clock is running during the dispute period, and your credit is still aging — time spent here will count as additional time past due if the debt is verified. If the verification process takes two weeks when all is said and done, that time may push your account into the 60-day delinquency category on your credit report. So try to resolve matters as quickly as possible when you're sure the debt is yours.

Knowing when debts fade away: Statutes of limitations

The United States is the land of the present, the here and now. As a result, people tend to let the past, well, be history. And so too it is with old debts. Every state has a statute of limitations (SOL). After a debt is between 2 and 15 years old without a payment having been made, it becomes history as far as the law is concerned.

Each state has its own SOL rules so I include a chart on the CD to help demystify things. Overage debts can't be enforced in a court of law. This turns even the fiercest collector into all bark and no bite.

Here's what to do if you think you may have an old debt that qualifies for SOL treatment:

- ✔ **Verify when your last payment was made.** Use your credit report or, if you keep checking records for seven years like I do, look in the back of the drawer. You don't want to see any recent payments here. A payment will reset the clock on the SOL. Say it has been 6 years and 51 weeks since your last payment and the SOL is 7 years. If you make a payment, the 7 year period starts again. So expect some pressure from the collector to get you to send in anything as the date approaches.

- ✔ **Check the CD to see if you may qualify for SOL status.** The info on the CD isn't a legal guarantee, but it is grounds for you to see a lawyer if you believe your debt qualifies.

- ✔ **Make an appointment to see an attorney to verify your status.** Yes, I suggest that you see a lawyer even though it may cost you some cash. This is a legal matter and only a lawyer can slam the lid on a dead debt.

- ✔ **Have the attorney write a letter.** The letter will include your documentation of the age of the item, that it is over the limit, that you don't intend to pay a penny and, here's the crusher, that all future contact must go through the attorney. No collector I know of will bother to try to collect an uncollectable debt from a lawyer. And they can't go around the attorney once they are notified you have a lawyer, or they can be sued. Yes, by your attorney!

Negotiating a payback arrangement

When you and the collector are in agreement that all the particulars of the debt are legitimate, it's time for you to make an offer to resolve the obligation — whether the cause of the delinquency was an unintended error or unfortunate circumstance. For tips on devising a payback plan, see the earlier section, "Offering a solution."

You want to convey your concern and reassure the collector that you're sincere in your commitment. But that doesn't mean you shouldn't negotiate some concessions. For example, you may want the creditor to:

- ✔ **Keep it from the credit bureaus.** If, for example, you're able to pay off your obligation and you're just 30 to 60 days past due, ask that your oversight not be reported to the credit bureau.

- ✔ **Waive late fees.** It doesn't hurt to ask the creditor if they'll waive the late fees. Be sure to tell them that, if they do, you'll be happy to get off the phone so you can run to the post office to mail your check. Most — not all — will agree.

✔ **Give you a lower interest rate.** Not the ideal time to try to get a better interest rate? Actually, it is. The lender wants to get what is called a *promise to pay* from you to resolve your situation. So ask for a break on the interest rate in order to help you become current faster. On a delinquent credit-card account, for example, you may be looking at a 30 percent default interest rate. The lender knows that adding this much to a strained budget will increase the chances of a larger and more costly default, or even a bankruptcy if you feel hopeless. The bottom line is that lenders will often help if you're sincere.

If you're 90 days or more past due, you're on thinner ice because you're more seriously late and three months of fees will probably be in the $100 vicinity. You may just ask for bureau-reporting forgiveness (that costs them nothing). If, on the other hand, your situation is such that you can't pay back the money right now, you may not have a leg to stand on when it comes to asking for favors. You may just have to set your sights on a reasonable repayment plan that you can live with.

If you're under extreme financial duress, go a step further and ask if the creditor has a hardship program. You may have to meet some qualifications, but if you do, you could see your interest rate drop dramatically, perhaps even to zero, and have your payments lowered for six months to a year.

Keeping your promise

Following through with whatever promise you make is essential. From the collector's perspective, you've already broken your original agreement to make payments. Breaking a second agreement will place you squarely in the not-to-be-trusted category.

Collecting on a mortgage

An overdue mortgage payment is definitely a different animal from other types of overdue accounts. The rules for mortgages are very different because the debt is secured by a piece of collateral — namely, your home. Never allow your mortgage payment to be 90 days past due. The reason? After your payment is 90 days overdue, you have to pay all the money past due — three months, plus the regular payment — or the foreclosure process begins. Send in less and you'll get it back.

Remember, after you're late on the first payment, the 15-day grace period no longer applies. Be careful not to cross the 90-day mark by mistake, thinking you still have 15 days to go. For more information, see Chapter 9.

Contact a good HUD-certified counseling agency and get help before you miss your second payment. You can find listings of approved housing counseling agencies by state at www.hud. gov or by calling 800-569-4287.

If you're in the military: Drop and give me your debt

In Chapter 7, I discuss the rules of engagement between the financial system and military personnel. Generally speaking, there are some significant safeguards built into the Fair and Accurate Credit Transactions Act (also known as the FACT Act or FACTA) and a rewrite of the Soldiers and Sailors Civil Relief Act (SSCRA). Here's what you need to know about your rights when it comes to debt collection:

✔ **Delayed court hearings:** If a creditor summons you to court for a hearing, the date can be held off by at least a 90-day stay (but you need to request it). The judge can grant additional delays as the case warrants.

✔ **Interest rate reductions:** The interest rates on pre-service loans and obligations cannot exceed 6 percent; interest due in excess of 6 percent per year must be forgiven, not just deferred. But you have to ask the lender for the reduction in writing and include a copy of your military orders.

✔ **Eviction protection:** You cannot be evicted from rental property for not paying the rent (if the monthly rent is $1,200 or less) without proper court action. The law gives you other special protections if the rent is between $1,200 and $2,400.

✔ **Lease termination:** Housing leases entered into before you started active duty may be terminated without penalty if you're under orders for a permanent change of station or deployed for at least 90 days. You don't need a military termination clause in your lease.

✔ **Auto lease cancellations:** You can cancel automobile leases if your orders are for 180 days or more, even if the auto is for a family member.

Write to anyone attempting to contact you for the purposes of collecting a debt, let them know your situation, and specifically ask for their cooperation according to the SSCRA. If you have a spouse at home, you may have him or her follow up on your behalf — be sure to mention that in your initial letter.

Most military units have a financial specialist who may be able to help further. If that fails, contact a lawyer or an accredited credit-counseling agency and ask them to act on your behalf. The lawyer may be expensive, but should be worth it. The credit counselors will be free or low-cost and most will try to help you by e-mail or through their Web sites.

To make sure you and the collector are clear on what you promised, get or put the particulars in writing. Get the names, addresses, and phone numbers of everyone you talk to, and include a written copy of your agreement with the payment. Asking for an e-mail confirming the arrangement is a reasonable request. A letter is a little more challenging because the delivery time may cause you to delay acting on your promise for another five days or so. The collector wants you to act today. So if this is the case, confirm all the agreements in a quick note with names and times (don't forget to keep your copy), and send it off with your payment.

If you feel any payment plan may push you over the financial edge, work on a *spending plan* (see Chapter 13 for more information). After you've established your goals, identified your sources of income, and tackled your living expenses, you can discover what you can actually afford for debt service.

 If this topic is too intimidating, if two or more of you are involved and you just can't seem to communicate on money matters, or you just want help getting started, a reputable credit-counseling agency can help you with a spending plan. (See Chapter 3 for help finding an agency.)

Saving your credit score by using a credit-counseling agency

If you're having trouble catching up to a "current" or "paid as agreed" status, consider the credit-counseling route. Using a credit-counseling agency may get you current faster. Often, many national creditors will bring an account to a current status after three on-time payments of the agreed-upon payment when you work through a credit counselor. This concession on the part of many lenders normally does not require making up the past-due amount, and it may also be at a lower interest rate. *Note:* Fair Isaac's FICO score doesn't take points away for using a credit-counseling agency. For an entire chapter on finding and using a credit counselor, head to Chapter 3.

Handling Those Collection Phone Calls

You have some late bills, but you waited too long to call the collectors. Now you're starting to receive calls about making payments. You may find yourself in the middle of a recurring nightmare of insatiable callers who will not go away, but who seem to take strength from your inability to give them what they want.

This does not have to be the case. The FDCPA protects debtors from harassment from collectors — particularly where it involves the use and abuse of the telephone. Armed with your knowledge of the rules and a plan of action, as I describe in this section, you can handle those calls before they handle you.

Deciding whether to answer the phone

If a collector has been pursuing you, you may find yourself reluctant to answer the phone for any number of reasons. You may have had a hard day at work, you may be overtired, or you may not be feeling in control of your emotions at the moment. Or if you've been contacted by the collector and you've already explained that you're doing your best and that's all you can do, having the same conversation again and again may feel frustrating and unproductive, especially if the collector is on the overbearing side.

You don't have to pick up the phone. But keep in mind that, although answering machines or caller ID can help you screen calls (and may help you with your sanity), they won't help you avoid or solve your debt. If the collector can't reach you by phone, he'll find another way to contact you.

Don't answer the phone if you know you won't be able to have an effective conversation. (For tips on what to say, see the following section.)

Preparing to answer collection calls

If you decide to answer the phone and talk to the collector, you need to make sure you're prepared. The best way to be prepared is to write down the key points you want to cover with the collectors. Having a plan in mind helps you keep on track and in control of the call. It also helps you not to overpromise and under-deliver, never to lose your temper, and not to stand for any abuse. Lastly, if you start to feel overwhelmed or backed into a corner, get outside professional help.

Even though it may not feel this way, you aren't the first or only person to have gone through debt collections. It happens all the time, and you *will* get through it.

If you're late on some bills, expect that sooner or later you'll get a call from a collector. If you've decided to pick up the phone, here's what you need to do:

- ✓ **Get the caller's name and contact information.**

- ✓ **Use the collector's name.**

- ✓ **Ask for proof of the debt.** Mistakes happen, and crooks call to get money from people all the time. (see "Asking for verification," earlier in this chapter, for more information).

- ✓ **Explain your situation.** Provide a very short story of why you're behind and what you're able do, if anything, about the debt.

- ✓ **Make an offer.** You can make an offer for a period of time. Say you owe $1,000. If you offer to pay $50 per pay period for the next 20 weeks, that may do it. Or you may offer to pay $25 per pay period until your next raise in three months, at which time you'll pay them $75 per pay period. Offering the amount you're able to pay is always better than waiting for the collector to demand a certain amount. (See "Negotiating a payback arrangement," earlier in this chapter.)

✔ **Don't agree to a commitment you can't keep.** Be realistic or you may find yourself agreeing to something you know you can't follow through on. (See "Keeping your promise," earlier in this chapter.)

✔ **Get it in writing.** If you come to an agreement, ask for it to be put in writing so it's clear to both parties. If the collector won't do that, write the letter yourself (keeping a copy for your records) and send it to the collector by certified mail (return receipt) so you have proof that the collector received it.

Knowing what not to say

Saying the *wrong* thing in a conversation with a collector not only may be unproductive, it can also elevate the conversation into a hostile confrontation that could end up causing you more harm. No matter how adversarial your caller seems, here are some definite don'ts:

✔ Don't let yourself get drawn into a shouting match.

✔ Don't make threats.

✔ Don't say you're getting a lawyer if you don't intend to.

✔ Don't say you're going to file bankruptcy if you don't plan to.

✔ Don't lie for sympathy (for example, "My mother's in the hospital," when your mother's kicking up her heels by the pool in Boca). When you're caught in a falsehood once, you'll have a hard time being believed again.

Identifying Escalation Options That Help

When you're dealing with a debt collector, you may arrive at a sticking point and recognize that she doesn't have the authority to do what you're asking. Instead of stopping at that frustrating dead end, you're better off tactfully suggesting that you'd like to take your situation to a higher authority — one who is empowered to make decisions. This is known as *escalating* the issue. In this section, I show you how to do this, as well as how to contact other people who may be able to help you when the manager doesn't do the trick.

Asking to speak to the manager

Collection representatives who just won't warm to your proposed payment plan may have one of several reasons. They may

- ✔ Not believe you're offering your best effort to repay
- ✔ Have a quota to fill and your offer won't do it
- ✔ Have strict rules regarding permissible payment options
- ✔ Be having a bad day and just not feel helpful
- ✔ Have just been yelled at for coming in late

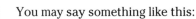

A manager has more flexibility and may even see the bigger picture of a best offer. By asking to speak to the manager, you take the pressure off the little guy and free him to attack another customer while you and the boss work things out. If you look at it as though you're helping everyone, you may have an easier time escalating the problem to management.

You may say something like this:

> I understand that you've done your best to try to resolve this issue satisfactorily. But I'd like to speak to someone who has the authority to make exceptions/waive policy/take my offer to a higher level. It's not fair of me to ask you to go against company policy and take the payment I'm offering. So, please let me speak to a manager.

If the collector doesn't want to let you go, tell her you'll call back on your own and ask someone else. Thank her for trying and say good-bye, nicely. Going over the same ground with the same person will quickly wear thin on one of you.

Approaching the creditor

Surprise! Your original creditor may still talk to you even after sending your bill to a collector. A lot depends on how you left them. If there were bad feelings or you lost it with a customer-service rep, chances are you won't be welcomed back. But if the transition from inside collections to an outside agency was more matter-of-fact, they may be willing to talk with you.

So why would you want to approach the creditor directly? If you're not getting anywhere with the debt collector, the creditor may be willing to work something out with you. After all, they just want their money.

Creditors either place a debt for collection (and pay a commission based on results) or they sell the debt outright. The former is more common. If your debt has been sold, calling the lender won't do any good. But you may well have more room to negotiate because debts are not sold at full value. So a smaller-than-owed payment may still be profitable for the collector.

Calling in a credit counselor

On your own, you can get to a manager. But the manager can't change policy that was set in the corporate headquarters. Very often, the "big guys" have already set a special collection policy that applies only to the legitimate credit-counseling agencies with whom they've established a working relationship. Thus, when a credit counselor gets involved, she may be able to deal with a special department that handles only credit-counseling accounts — and is much more sympathetic than the line collector or manager. So in one leap, you escalate to high-level corporate policymakers.

Talk to a credit counselor from an accredited agency. Chapter 3 explains how to pick one from a crowded field. The cost is lower than an attorney and the advice is practical rather than legal. The professional analysis of your financial dilemma and your options is valuable. As an intermediary, the credit counselor can deal with your creditors on your behalf and may be able to administer a favorable workout plan (often referred to as a *debt-management plan*) while you follow a fairly strict budget.

Referring the matter to your lawyer

A good lawyer can work wonders with the more complex legal situations people face from time to time. Like showing up to a gunfight with the second-fastest gun, hiring a so-so lawyer isn't worth the effort. The best attorney for you is one who specializes in debt law. The drawbacks: Lawyers are expensive, and after *you* start down a legal path, so do the collectors.

Get an attorney who specializes in representing debtors. She knows the routine, has the letters on file, and may even know the collection agency or company. Besides sheltering you from having to deal directly with the collectors, the attorney helps slow down the freight train of events heading your way. She knows what will be acceptable to the collector, collection lawyer, or judge (if things get that far).

Chapter 9

Avoiding a Foreclosure

. . . .

In This Chapter

▶ Figuring out what foreclosure involves and finding help

▶ Exploring short- and long-term solutions

▶ Facing foreclosure if it happens

▶ Settling the score if your house is worth less than what you owe

. . . .

Homeownership is very much a part of the American dream. Granted, some people do prefer to rent or live with others, but if you're one of those people who have made the commitment to purchase a home, you probably consider anything else less than ideal. You worked hard to save for a down payment, and you take pride in knowing you're a homeowner.

Unfortunately, life throws some curveballs. If the purchase of a home is one of life's successes, then the loss of a home can be one of life's failures. When you default on most types of credit, all you end up with is a late fee or a small credit report ding. However, in the case of a mortgage, a seemingly small mistake or miscalculation compounded by inaction caused by embarrassment, indecision, or misinformation can cost you a huge negative on your credit report and score, as well as your home and tens of thousands of dollars.

A mortgage default is reported like most other negative items on your credit report for the usual seven-year period. Future loan underwriters and credit grantors view it as a more serious event because of the size of the obligation and the possible serious consequences to the lender if a mortgage fails. When lenders look at your credit report, they give special emphasis to how you have performed on similar types of loans. So a car lender pays special attention to car payments, and a mortgage lender looks hard at your mortgage history. If you're one of those people who think owning a home is the only way to live, be sure to pay special attention to your home loan payment record and this chapter.

Given the meltdown of the subprime mortgage industry and the general tightening of credit it has produced, this chapter is a critical one for any homeowner who is under financial stress. Money, self-esteem, and the very roof over your family's head are at stake in addition to your good credit when a possible foreclosure is looming. This chapter provides you with the advice you need to prevent foreclosure from becoming a reality, if possible, or to make the best of a bad situation if it's unavoidable. Options to save a delinquent mortgage have changed greatly in the last year or so and continue to offer more help to borrowers in trouble. However, the need to get help and get it early is still critical. Fortunately, help *is* available, and this chapter will guide you through the process of getting it.

Understanding that Mortgages Are a Different Credit Animal

Mortgages are quite different from other consumer loans. This is partly due to their huge size — a lot of money is on the line — and partly because they're backed by what historically has been the gold standard in collateral, your home. Furthermore, mortgages are not only underwritten differently from other types of credit, but they also have a different collection process, generally called the *foreclosure process.* When you default on a mortgage, the lender forecloses, or terminates the mortgage, and your house is consequently taken away from you.

From a credit score and credit reporting standpoint, mortgage defaults are among the most serious negatives out there. Because of that, they can trigger universal default clauses in your credit cards, which means your low rate can go up to a rate of 30 percent and make your already difficult life even more expensive. I tell you more about this later.

Obviously, foreclosures put a serious hit on your credit score and history. To ensure you minimize this hit, this section gives you an overview on how mortgages differ from typical credit, and how mortgages and your credit go hand in hand. Here you can find valuable information to help you understand when a late mortgage payment can quickly cause you problems and what you can do to get help.

Seeing a foreclosure coming

In order for you to get a firm grasp on everything related to mortgages and your credit, you first need to understand what leads up to mortgage foreclosures. What exactly makes them tick? To start, some basic terminology can help you keep everything in focus. The following people and processes related to mortgages can have an impact on your credit:

✔ **Mortgage broker/banker/lender:** The person you worked with to fill out the mortgage paperwork and get your loan closed. This person typically, but not always, sells your loan to an investor.

- ✔ **Investor:** The owner of the loan and the one who makes the rules.

- ✔ **Insurer:** The one who insures the lender/investor in case the loan becomes delinquent.

- ✔ **Mortgage servicer:** The one who is responsible for customer service, processing payments, and working with delinquent customers. This is the one you talk to and who knows what can be done and what exceptions can be made.

- ✔ **Loss mitigation:** The process of working with a customer to find a permanent solution to resolve delinquency. Also known as Homeownership Preservation.

- ✔ **Foreclosure:** Legal action to force the sale of a home.

So how exactly does a servicer foreclose? The key words that you need to be aware of in the process are *quickly* and *quietly. Unless you speak up, it can all be over in as little as 120 days, depending on your state's laws.*

A lender has a lot of money on the line with your mortgage, and the longer you're delinquent, the greater the risk that the lender will lose money on a defaulted loan. The result is that the mortgage lender has a much lower tolerance for your delinquency than, say, a credit card issuer. Here's an example: As long as you're less than 180 days past due on a credit card, it's not the end of the world. Generally, you can just pay the minimum due along with a late fee and go on your way. If it's really your lucky day, you might get the lender to waive the late fee and not report the delinquency. For a mortgage, however, once you're just 60 days late you're well on your way to the edge of a cliff, and you may not even be aware of it.

The key number to avoid in a mortgage delinquency is 90 days late, not 180. After 90 days, unless you get some help or work out an arrangement, the servicer will generally require the entire arrearage to be paid at once and may not accept partial payments. A 90-day mortgage delinquency on a credit report is very serious. To make matters worse, many people don't understand when the 90 days is up. It's not as simple as you may think, so I cover it in detail in the next section of this chapter.

Many mortgages are packaged into large securities and sold to investors. Because the actual lender is often far removed from your community and your home, they use a servicer to collect your payments and work out any problems. The servicers don't have their own money at risk, so they don't get too excited about the prospect of a delinquency. Unlike the credit card guys who have little recourse in a default except to intimidate you into paying, mortgagees speak softly and may not even be heard over all the noise that your other creditors are likely to be creating in a financially stressful situation. Mortgagees won't call you at work or at night, and they won't yell or threaten you over the phone. On the contrary, the tone of their messages, often letters, is concerned, low-key, and polite — and then you lose your home. But if you know where to get help, what to ask for and what to avoid, this can all change for the better. Needless to say, it pays to know the rules and what to ask and listen for.

Counting to 90

A major difference between mortgages and credit cards (or other types of consumer loans) is the amount of time you're allowed to be late. What's the "magic number"? After you're 90 days late on a mortgage, unless you take action, the servicer requires you to pay the entire overdue balance at once. If you fail to do so, they proceed to foreclosure.

Up until then, you may be able to make partial payments on your own. If you're 30 or 60 days late and you make a partial payment, the servicer usually credits your account with the payment. If, however, you cross the 90-day mark and then send in a month or two's worth of overdue payments rather than the entire amount due, the servicer may send the money back and the clock keeps ticking.

 Furthermore, a fact you may not be aware of is that once you're late on your first payment, your grace period disappears. (A grace period is a period of time that is specified in your mortgage loan agreement during which a default will not occur even though the payment is past due.) The grace period only applies to loans that are up-to-date, or current. The following example illustrates how this works.

Say your loan papers state that your due date is March 1. Assuming you have a typical two-week grace period, this means your payment actually has to be in by March 15. If you don't submit your payment by March 15, you miss that window of opportunity and lose your grace period. Your April payment is now due April 1. April 15 is no longer an option. In other words, no more grace period in April. If you pay April's payment on or before April 1, you will get your grace period back for May and thereafter, as long as your payments stay on time.

If you lose your grace period, the counting of the number of days you are late begins on the first of the month, rather than the 15th. So if you don't send in a payment on March 15, April 1, or May 1, then on May 2, you need to catch up all the payments for March 1, April 1, and May 1, plus any fees and penalties (which can be hundreds of dollars or more), all at once. This is a huge amount for someone in financial difficulties. If you don't, then on May 2 the formal foreclosure process can start and you may incur fees for collection costs, attorneys, title searches, filings, and more. Once the foreclosure process begins, and it's up to the investor when this actually kicks in, the loan servicer can do what is called an acceleration of the loan. This means that the servicer can ask for the entire balance of the loan, not just the late part, to stop the foreclosure.

A foreclosure in a *non-judicial state* (one where the foreclosure process doesn't go through the courts until the very end) can happen very quickly. Here's an example: After 30 days, you get a late notice; at 60 days late, you receive a demand letter; at 90 days, you receive an acceleration notice; and by 120 days, the foreclosure and sale/auction can be scheduled. Table 9-1 illustrates HUD's time guidelines for their lenders by state. These are estimates, and a foreclosure may take less time than allotted by HUD under these guidelines.

Table 9-1		HUD's Time Guidelines			
State	*Days[1] from Foreclosure Initiation to Sale*	*Foreclosure Method*	*State*	*Days[1] from Foreclosure Initiation to Sale*	*Foreclosure Method*
Alabama	85	Non-judicial	Nebraska	155	Non-judicial
Alaska	140	Non-judicial	Nevada	155	Non-judicial
Arizona	125	Non-judicial	New Hampshire	110	Non-judicial
Arkansas	130	Non-judicial	New Jersey	300	Judicial
California	135	Non-judicial	New Mexico	250	Judicial
Colorado	130	Non-judicial	New York	280	Judicial
Connecticut	220	Judicial	North Carolina	120	Non-judicial
Delaware	250	Judicial	North Dakota	190	Judicial
Florida	170	Judicial	Ohio	265	Judicial
Georgia	80	Non-judicial	Oklahoma	250	Judicial
Guam	250	Non-judicial	Oregon	180	Non-judicial
Hawaii	140	Non-judicial	Pennsylvania	300	Judicial

(continued)

Table 9-1 *(continued)*

State	Days[1] from Foreclosure Initiation to Sale	Foreclosure Method	State	Days[1] from Foreclosure Initiation to Sale	Foreclosure Method
Illinois	275	Judicial	Rhode Island	85	Non-judicial
Indiana	265	Judicial	South Carolina	215	Judicial
Iowa2	315	Judicial	South Dakota	205	Judicial
Kansas	180	Judicial	Tennessee	90	Non-judicial
Kentucky	265	Judicial	Texas	90	Non-judicial
Louisiana	220	Judicial	Utah	165	Non-judicial
Maine	355	Judicial	Vermont	360	Judicial
Maryland	85	Judicial	Virgin Isles	325	Judicial
Massachusetts	135	Judicial	Virginia	60	Non-judicial
Michigan	75	Non-judicial	Washington	160	Non-judicial
Minnesota	110	Non-judicial	West Virginia	145	Non-judicial
Mississippi	130	Non-judicial	Wisconsin	310	Judicial
Missouri	85	Non-judicial	Wyoming	100	Non-judicial
Montana	205	Non-judicial			

1 State foreclosure time frames are in calendar days.

2 State time frame represents the standard elapsed time for a judicial foreclosure without redemption. A longer time frame may be allowed if a borrower files a written demand to delay the sale.

Knowing where to turn for help

If you're having trouble making your mortgage payment on time, time is of the essence. Getting your mortgage issue resolved fast is critical. Remember, the mortgage company doesn't want your house; they just want to keep your loan *performing*, up-to-date or current. Following are a few ideas on who to turn to for help (along with some tips on who *not* to turn to!). The essential point however, is to not wait but take action. You can work directly with your servicer, but they may only offer you what they think is the easiest solution, not the one you need, because they don't know your situation in detail. I strongly recommend that you use a third-party intermediary that is approved by HUD. They are cheap, know what to ask for, and can help guide you through what can seem like an insurmountable problem.

Your mortgage servicing company

When you can't pay your mortgage on time, you can directly contact your mortgage company. When you contact them for help, look at it as though you're trying to solve two problems — yours and theirs! Ask to speak with the loss mitigation department, also referred to as the workout department or the homeownership retention department. This area is able to do more and deals with complex issues better than the standard collection department, who usually only offers to make catch-up payment arrangements. You can find the contact information for your servicer in your loan documents, on your monthly statement, or in correspondence you receive from them. When you call, get names and extension numbers so you can try to keep a single point of contact and continuity. This may not be possible, but knowing who you talked to, when, and what was agreed is important. Keep good notes!

To keep the call simple, I suggest you do some homework before you call and know what it will take and for how long to remedy your situation. Write out what happened, what changed, what you need, and how to contact you or your counselor if you're working with one. This helps you keep from rambling and get to solutions faster. Then ask for what you need and also ask what other options may be available beyond the one they offer you.

Other available help

A number of housing counseling agencies are also available to help you work out a solution. I strongly recommend that you use one of these agencies to help you work out a deal with the servicers. They do this every day, and you don't. They know what to ask for and will take the time to understand what you really need. Although the contact information may change over time and new players are continually offering this service, you can look for resources through HUD's Web site at www.hud.gov, or contact Neighborworks' Project HOPE at 1-888-995-HOPE or www.nw.org. I suggest you call before you e-mail or visit an office for quickest service, or contact the National Foundation for Credit Counseling at www.housinghelpnow.org or 866-557-2227. Many credit counselors are also HUD-certified housing counselors.

Not-so-helpful "help"

Keep in mind as you look for answers and help that not everyone out there has the same objectives that you do. Some are only trying to help themselves. So proceed with caution and consider the following tips as you evaluate any prospective source of help:

- Don't panic.
- Find out whether you're dealing with a nonprofit organization.
- Don't make payments to anyone other than your servicer or their designee.
- Be wary of any organization other than your servicer that contacts you to help.
- Never sign a contract under pressure.
- Never sign away ownership of your property.
- Don't sign anything with blank lines or spaces.
- If English isn't your first language and a translator isn't provided, use your own.
- Get a second opinion from someone or an organization you know and trust.

If you're having trouble paying your mortgage, a predatory lender or foreclosure scam artist may try to get you to take out a high-risk, second mortgage on your property. If these marauders come a-calling, run the other way — fast! These lenders are dangerous because they charge high fees you can ill afford to pay, and they distract you from real solutions by wasting critical time that could be spent solving your problem.

If you receive an offer saying you've been preapproved for a loan, it means you've been preapproved only for the offer, not the actual loan. Don't waste too much time chasing preapproved offers.

Other things to watch for include

- **Phantom help:** A company that just wants to "help" charges you high fees for work you can do yourself, charges you for legal representation that never materializes, or offers you a loan even though you don't have the income to repay it.

- **Bailout:** This includes various schemes to get you to surrender your title to the house thinking you'll be able to remain as a renter and buy the house back.

✔ **Equity stripping:** A buyer purchases your home for the amount of the arrearage and flips the home for a quick profit, pocketing the equity in your home that otherwise would have been yours.

Alternatives to Going Down with the Ship

If you're having trouble making your mortgage payments, you should know that you're not alone, and you may have some options that can avoid the expense and upset of going though a foreclosure. Even if you can't or don't want to keep your house, you can lessen the damage to yourself, your family and your credit by taking positive action. You can take control of your situation and turn this ship around before it sinks.

Before you take any action, assess your situation as dispassionately as you can. If stress and anxiety make that impossible, I suggest you get a third-party professional such as a nonprofit HUD agency (see "Other available help," earlier in this chapter) or an attorney to help you do this. Your situation may not be as bad as you think, or it may be worse. What's important is to know for sure where you stand. For instance:

✔ Will the problem that has caused your mortgage delinquency be corrected soon? Is it just a short-term event?

✔ If it's a longer-term event, how much extra time will you need to get back on track financially?

✔ Is the event long-term enough to reconsider whether you can stand the stress until it's resolved and stay in your home?

✔ Is your situation serious enough that you want to get out of your home-ownership obligation?

To help you find the answers to these questions, you need what's called loss mitigation counseling help. *Loss mitigation counseling* is help to develop a solution that will allow you to catch up on your payments, modify your loan terms, or otherwise rectify your situation so you can afford to keep your home or lessen the damage caused by a foreclosure.

This section gives you some loss mitigation alternatives to foreclosing to protect your credit history.

Starting with short-term solutions

Perhaps you believe that you have a plan to resolve your problem and, as a result, catch up or at least resume payments in three to six months. If that's the case, consider the following suggestions:

✔ **Find a good credit counseling agency.** This has nothing to do with credit counseling, but with getting an objective assessment of your overall financial picture and whether you can realistically afford your mortgage payments or not. The counselor can help you build a revised budget that may free up cash for your mortgage, and an expert opinion can help to prioritize your debts and expenses. Many agencies are also HUD-certified and can work with your servicer to get a solution that works for your situation. See Chapter 3.

✔ **Ask about Mortgage Repayment Plans.** These entail the servicer setting up a structured payment plan (sometimes called a special forbearance plan) that will get the mortgage back on track in three to six months. Sometimes this can be a verbal agreement with your existing lender. If it is, I suggest that you document the terms in a letter and send it to the lender so you're both clear on the terms of what you're doing. Typically during a repayment plan period, full monthly mortgage payments are made along with a portion of the past-due payments until the mortgage loan is back to "current payment" status. The sooner you do this the less the damage to your credit report.

✔ **Check the HUD Web site at www.hud.gov for resources and help.** Don't forget to talk to your lender about your need for assistance, and do it soon. Some servicers have programs that are only for those who are not yet delinquent and other programs for borrowers who already are. To get the greatest number of options, get started as soon as you know you have a problem making mortgage payments as agreed, and be sure to ask for all the options they may have for you.

Considering solutions for long-term problems

For problems that will take longer than three to six months to remedy, you can ask for mortgage loan forbearance or loan modifications.

A *forbearance* temporarily modifies or eliminates payments that are made up at the end of the forbearance period. This is useful if you have a sale pending or a windfall is expected, but you can't afford the payments at present. This also prevents your credit from being damaged by a string of late payments.

A *loan modification* modifies the terms of the original mortgage permanently in a way that addresses your specific needs. This may involve changing one or more terms of the original mortgage agreement, such as adding delinquent payments and other costs to the loan balance, changing interest rates, and recalculating the loan. If this seems intimidating, use a HUD agency to deal with the servicer and offer solutions on your behalf. Clear communication is key here.

These modifications need to be in writing and approved by both the servicer and borrower because they're long-term and large in scope. You can expect goodwill to only go so far, so don't be surprised if the servicer asks for a fee of around 1 percent to cover the costs of processing a loan modification. After all, servicers always have an appetite for some immediate income for their banks or companies.

If you were delinquent on your loan before the modification, expect your credit history to show the prior delinquency. Mortgagees are very reluctant to change your credit history, but a modification and efforts to bring the mortgage current should show up on your credit report.

If you are also carrying credit card debt, being late on your mortgage or having a loan modification on your credit report may set you up for a hike in your interest rates under universal default rules. Review the default provisions of the credit cards that you use to carry a balance and consider closing those accounts that have universal default provisions before they raise your rates. Once the accounts are closed, your rates should stay the same during your repayment period. The small damage to your credit score from closing accounts will be a bargain compared to what could happen if you can't handle interest rates that may go to 30 percent or more. If you've had the cards for more than ten years, consider keeping them open if you can transfer the balances to cards without the universal default provision, as these long-history cards count for more on your score than ones you've had for a shorter period of time.

Looking at longer-than-long-term solutions

Some things take longer to resolve than anyone wants them to, and some can only be resolved by taking a step or two backwards before making any progress. Even when you can't solve your problem or just can't stand it any more, you still want to stay in control of the process. This can lessen damage and expenses and keep your dignity — and maybe your sanity — intact.

Following are some of the many options available. And don't forget that there may be newer options as well. Be sure to check out the resources mentioned in the section "Other available help," earlier in this chapter.

✓ **Sell your home:** You may be able to sell your home in a short sale if you have no equity left or a pre-foreclosure sale if the value of the house still exceeds the remainder of the mortgage.

- **Short sale:** In a short sale, you ask your lender for permission to sell your home for less than the mortgage value and the lender uses a real estate agent to sell the home. The lender may allow a sale for an amount lower than the total debt. This is generally cheaper for the bank and less stressing for the homeowner than a foreclosure. Because this is good for the investor, you can negotiate a bit. Ask that the loan deficiency be reported to the credit bureau as a zero balance rather than a charge-off.

Congress has passed a law called the Mortgage Forgiveness Debt Relief Act that affects how a principal residence foreclosure is handled for tax purposes. It exempts up to $2 million of forgiven mortgage debt, subject to certain conditions, from federal taxes. Normally you would have to pay income tax on that amount. I suggest that you check to see if you may have state taxes due as they weren't covered in this federal law. Check out the full text of the law in the CD. If you don't qualify under the law, seek legal advice to see how you can protect yourself.

- **Pre-foreclosure sale:** A pre-foreclosure sale arrangement allows you to defer mortgage payments that you can't afford while you sell your house. This also keeps late payments off your credit report.

✔ **Deed-in-lieu of property sale or foreclosure:** This is becoming more popular. It requires listing your home with a realtor. If the home is unable to be sold, you sign the home's title over to the lender and move out. Usually, to qualify for this option, you can't have a second mortgage, an equity loan, or another lien on the property.

Handling a foreclosure if one has started

Even if you've gone down the delinquency path and are in the legal process of being foreclosed upon, there may still be some things you can talk to the servicer about to try to work things out or buy you more time to come up with a solution or make a more dignified exit from the home. But once again, time is not your friend here, so don't wait!

✔ **Get a HUD-approved counselor involved and review loss mitigation options with your servicer.** Most want to help. (Check out "Alternatives to Going Down with the Ship" earlier in this chapter.)

✔ **Contact and keep contacting the servicer's loss mitigation staff until you get a solution you can live with.** If they don't offer workable suggestions, ask to speak to managers and vice presidents or higher. This is not a time to stand on protocol or accept "I'm sorry" for an answer.

✔ **See an attorney.** Ask for options. Review all the mortgage documents to be sure they were properly drawn and executed. The technical phase used here is "Truth in Lending Compliance." Ask about bankruptcy options and timing so you know all options available to you.

If none of these options work, you will go through the full foreclosure process. In short, the house will go to auction and be sold. The new owner will give you appropriate notice to leave the house per your state statute. A notice may be placed on your front door detailing the terms.

Dealing with Deficiencies

When all is said and done, you may still owe some money. If your home sells for less than the amount still owed on the mortgage and fees, then you may have what is called a *deficiency balance.* For example, say a borrower borrows $500,000 from a lender to purchase a home, but the borrower falls behind in payments, and the bank forecloses. The home is ultimately sold for $400,000. The $100,000 that the lender lost on the deal is called a *deficiency.* Current practice is to forgive this amount. There was a time when this wasn't always the case and it may change again in the future. The most important thing is to realize that your problems may not be over when you leave the home. The IRS may need to be dealt with if you don't qualify for mortgage debt forgiveness under their rules.

The following are some potential, and I stress *potential,* deficiencies you may face and what you can do to deal with them:

- ✔ **The lender could ask for a note.** This is not a current practice, but you should be aware of it for the future. This note isn't the kind your mother wrote to school. This note is a promise to pay an unsecured amount to cover the mortgage deficiency after the sale. Just like any loan, it has terms, interest rates, and payments due on certain dates. Many of these terms can be discussed before the sale takes place and may be modified to fit your situation. Use a lawyer if anyone suggests this to you.

- ✔ **The lender could send a demand letter.** Like asking for a note, this is not a current practice. A lender may send a demand for payment of any deficiency following the sale of a home. The lender uses a *demand letter* if they don't want to give you an unsecured loan for the balance due. In essence, the problem is all yours and you need to work out a way to pay the balance. Here again, if this ever happens, get an attorney to advise you.

- ✔ **The lender forgives the debt.** This is a current practice, but it could always change. The lender chooses to forgive the debt rather than pursue it. This is nice as far as it goes, but be prepared for the forgiven portion of the debt to be counted by the IRS as income through the issue of a 1099 form. Forms 1099 A and C, which are normally used to document unreported income, are used to report forgiven debt. The amount of the forgiven debt becomes taxable income in most cases unless you're covered by the Mortgage Forgiveness Debt Relief Act. If you're among the unforgiven and you get one of these and it is for a lot of money, I suggest you see an attorney ASAP for legal options. Remember, the law is federal and may not forgive state tax obligations.

- ✔ **The state you live in makes mortgages nonrecourse.** If you live in certain states, you may get a break relating to personal mortgage deficiencies. Some states have passed laws saying that you are not responsible for any mortgage deficiencies. Some effectively make the mortgage a nonrecourse loan. (*No-recourse* means the lender has no recourse to collecting money due other than the security on the loan.) You may not be personally liable. This protection may not apply to refinancing. See an attorney to find out whether this applies to you.

Subject to additions or deletions, the list of states that have passed some anti-deficiency protection legislation that offers at least some protection for borrowers includes Alaska, Arizona, California, Minnesota, Montana, North Dakota, Oregon, Texas, and Washington.

✔ **The IRS wants more taxes.** Even though a loan may be uncollectable or forgiven, it is not beyond the reach of the IRS. You see, the lender gets to take a loss on its taxes for the bad loan. Not wanting to miss a tax opportunity, the IRS considers the lender's loss to be your gain. So, you may owe taxes on the deficiency amount if you don't qualify for relief under the Mortgage Forgiveness Debt Relief Act. This law is scheduled to run until 2010, and then go away. This can be a very big number indeed.

A foreclosed borrower faced with a sizeable 1099 still has hope. If you file IRS Form 982, "Reduction of Tax Attributes Due to Discharge of Indebtedness" and you are insolvent at the time of the forgiven debt, the IRS may forgive the liability. Again, see your attorney for the details.

Chapter 10

Getting the Best You Can from Collectors, Lawyers, and the Courts

I'm a science fiction reader, and I write about credit. If I were to combine my hobby with my writing, I might come up with a "B" movie entitled "I Was Attacked by Flesh-Eating Credit." This may not be as far-fetched as it seems. The news often carries stories about "super-bugs" — bacteria and viruses that are resistant to antibiotics. Often spawned by overuse or misuse of medicines, these bugs can lead to very serious complications. The world of credit has the equivalent of super-bugs in the form of super-debts. In this chapter, I deal with these most virulent and resistant of debt obligations that infect and wreak havoc with your credit.

These debts are the realm of credit quacks, who offer miracle cures for your credit and debt ailments for a fraction of the true cost of their value. Claims of settling an IRS debt for pennies and removing valid charge-offs from your credit report are as bogus as those made by the old traveling medicine shows.

In this chapter I explain about charge-offs, judgments, and super-debts that can't be killed even by a bankruptcy. I tell you how to minimize damage to your credit and give you strategies for controlling and even eliminating these credit infections before they send your score to FICO's intensive care unit. So, step right up ladies and gentlemen. The show is about to begin, and it stars those delinquent debts that just won't go away.

Getting a Firm Grip on Charge-Offs

Along the collections road, you come to some significant stopping points where unresolved matters take a turn for the worse. You need to know what they are, how important they may be, and what lies around the next corner. Unpaid charge-offs and paid charge-offs can hit your credit report like a bad case of the flu. Understanding the different symptoms and remedies may save you points and money in the long run.

Some generalizations hold true for many types of unsecured debts like credit cards or personal loans. After a bill goes past its due date, it's technically late. Less than 30 days late is usually no big deal; 30 to 60 days late can cost you some fees and maybe an interest-rate raise; 90 days late can cost you more and often brings on the serious players in the collection department. After your debt ages to between 120 and 180 days past due, it enters a new phase known as the *charge-off*.

So what does a charge-off mean? When the collector or creditor *charges off* your account, the debt isn't canceled, nor does the interest stop accruing. It only means that the lender's accountants, regulators, or audit firm think your debt is so unlikely to be collected, they won't allow it to remain on the books as an asset of the company. So, for tax purposes, the creditor considers your account a loss. If you imagine that no one is happy about this turn of events, you are correct. And among those who should be the least happy is you. Why? Because you still owe the bill, while fees, credit damage, and interest continue to accrue.

This section covers the difference between unpaid and paid charge-offs and why it's worth paying a charge-off even if it stays on your credit report. It also explains the role a spending plan plays in getting these nasties under control.

Understanding unpaid charge-offs

A debt *charges off* when it gets so old its value is called into question (and so is your sincerity in paying it). If your creditor reports account histories to the credit bureaus, and most major ones do, the charge-off is considered a very serious negative. The credit-scoring crowd picks it up and your score begins to dive like a blood pressure monitor that has been unplugged. This usually occurs at 180 days past due, but sometimes a conservative auditor will charge a debt off earlier.

A charge-off doesn't mean that you no longer owe the debt — only that the creditor can't count it as an asset. The longer it remains unpaid, the more damage it does to your credit report.

An unpaid charge-off shows up on your credit report. Check out the next section for an example; the only difference is it's labeled "unpaid charge-off." When an account first charges off, there may be a lull in the phone calls you've been receiving or other collection attempts. The reason for this is that the debt is changing hands from the collectors who were unsuccessful trying to save the account to those who want to save some part of it.

Some time ago, I visited a major collection department and looked out over a room that contained a sea of cubicles. Each one was populated by a collector, many of whom wished they were somewhere else. As you may imagine, the younger or less-experienced staff are assigned the less-serious delinquencies. The longer-tenured, more-serious group of collectors gets the progressively older debts. Guess who gets the charge-offs? Yes indeed, it's the most-experienced, longest-serving collectors. These men and women have heard it all a thousand times before and have lasted in this business because they are efficient and effective. Collectors will continue to try to collect the money due; however, after they determine that you either can't or won't be sending a payment in, the account may be sold many times for decreasing dollars to increasingly hungry bottom-feeders you really don't want to deal with.

Paying for charge-offs

With a charge-off, the collector tries to get you to make a promise to pay the bill either in full or in a series of agreed-upon payments. The stakes for failure to live up to any agreement are higher here than they were when the debt was younger. So, I suggest you be sure that whatever you commit to, you can deliver. The best way I know of to do that is to prepare a budget (see Chapter 13) that takes into account all your income and all your expenses. Using a spending plan, you can identify areas that you can trim to allow more money to go toward debt payments. Without one, you'll be guessing. The key elements of a plan (see the CD for a sample of a spending plan outline) are as follows:

- ✔ List all your income.
- ✔ List all your expenses.
- ✔ Cut out all the expenses you can.
- ✔ Increase your income if possible.
- ✔ Keep doing this until you have enough to pay the bill in a reasonable amount of time.

After you know how much you can actually afford to pay, be sure you don't promise more than your plan says you can afford just to get off the phone. Be sincere, explain how you got to that number, and then send the payment in. Do it on time, every time. It's fine to ask for a reduction in fees and interest before you get started. Reductions in the amount owed are harder to get and covered in the next section.

Unlike a delinquent debt that, once paid, becomes current on your credit report, a charge-off never does. An unpaid charge-off becomes a paid charge-off. A paid charge-off isn't nearly as bad as its predecessor, the unpaid charge-off. It says that you had a problem — perhaps a serious one — but you paid the bill. Hallelujah! Now you can get a little boost on your credit report (check out Figure 10-1), and you're on the way to obtaining credit at a more reasonable rate. Why? Simple: You've established that, although you may be a high-risk borrower, you do pay your bills in the end. You're now out of intensive care, but still susceptible to a relapse until you establish an emergency savings account with some money to help you get through the next unexpected setback.

Equifax Credit Report ™ for **Melissa Carson**
As of: 08/07/2007
Available until:
Confirmation #: 123456789

Report Does Not Update
Print Report

Negative Accounts Show All Account Details

Accounts that contain a negative account status. Accounts not paid as agreed generally remain on your credit file for 7 years from the date the account first became past due leading to the current not paid status. Late Payment History generally remains on your credit file for 7 years from the date of the late payment.

Open Accounts

Account Name	Account Number	Date Opened	Balance	Date Reported	Past Due	Account Status	Credit Limit
XYZ BANKCARD Show Details	4873664803 16XXXX	08/2001	$0	07/2007	$287	PAYS 91-120 DAYS	$8,000

Closed Accounts

Account Name	Account Number	Date Opened	Balance	Date Reported	Past Due	Account Status	Credit Limit
ABC LOANS Show Details	31667XXXX	09/1997	$0	09/2003	$0	CHARGE-OFF	$0

Figure 10-1:
An image of a paid charge-off trade line on a credit report.

Settling Your Debt

No one likes to lose, especially when what's lost is money. For this reason, settling a debt is rarely easy. When your creditor allows you to pay off your debt for less than you originally borrowed, you are *settling a debt.* Your debt may or may not have been charged off. And although you didn't stiff the lender completely, your actions did result in a loss of profit for the company — not a positive incentive to do business with you in the future. This has a negative impact on your credit report, so you may want to consider what's more important to you — the money or the credit report. This section focuses on what happens if you agree to a debt settlement, and how to get a paid-as-agreed notification in your credit report.

Considering a debt settlement offer

Many businesses offer borrowers debt settlements when they think that they won't ever get their money, it becomes uneconomical to continue collections, or they think they can recover more by settling than by selling the debt to a third-party collection agency. The businesses at least get *something* rather than nothing, the borrowers get the collectors off their backs, and the debt does go away. And in seven years, it will go away from your credit report, too. A settled debt appears in the same place as the "paid charge-off" (refer to Figure 10-1).

If you accept debt settlement as a resolution, I strongly advise you to get the terms in writing and read them carefully before you send a penny. You need to be on your guard if you're trying to get a settlement or if you've been offered one. You're dealing with someone who knows settlements better than you do and won't mind that you're making a mistake that is to their advantage and may result in more of what you owe being collected. After you send the money, you have no leverage with the collector and any promises made orally that aren't in the written agreement are unlikely to be kept.

If an outside debt-settlement firm — one that you haven't previously dealt with regarding the debt — suddenly shows up as a knight in shining armor to save you by helping you get a settlement offer, run away. Because the industry has few standards and little regulation, make sure you're aware of the following risks:

- ✔ You pay the debt settlement company and they keep the money.
- ✔ They do what they say and you end up in court for breaking a law.
- ✔ They get sued and file for bankruptcy, with your money.

These guys may cause a lot more problems than they solve. Not what you need or have in mind at a time when your world is already shaky.

One last consideration regarding accepting a settlement: The IRS considers the difference between the amount owed and the amount paid as income. I know; it defies logic. But, depending on the size of your debt, the creditor or collector may report to the IRS how much money was forgiven in the settlement, in which case you become responsible for paying income taxes on that amount. For example, if you owe $5,000 and you work out a settlement where you pay only $3,000, then the $2,000 that was forgiven becomes taxable income on your next tax return. As the saying goes, only two things in life are certain — and one of them is taxes!

Obtaining a paid-as-agreed notation

When you find yourself in the world of paid charge-offs and settlements, you discover a lot of moving parts, many not exactly fair to you. So, if you still have the energy — and maybe a good lawyer — ask for the holy grail of concessions in return for paying the bill: a *paid-as-agreed notation* on your credit report. Your logic is that despite the fact that you didn't pay your debt *when* you agreed, you did pay the *amount* agreed — even if that amount was reduced in a settlement. If you don't get a paid-as-agreed notation, your credit report will show extra negatives and your score will be lowered.

Getting a paid-as-agreed notation when you haven't paid the full amount you originally owed isn't exactly kosher. But if you have the money and can pay off the debt, you can use the small amount of leverage you have (the payment) to ask the creditor to report the debt to the credit-reporting bureaus as "paid as agreed." This is easy enough for the creditor to do and costs them nothing.

This falls under the it-never-hurts-to-try category, so go for it — but get any agreement in writing from the creditor before making the payment. After the creditor has your money, you have no leverage.

Expired debts

Sometimes procrastination has a silver lining. When a debt reaches a certain age (as defined by the statutes of your state of residence), it's no longer collectible in a court of law. Each state has its own statute of limitations rules. Check out Chapter 8 for more on expired debts and statute of limitations.

Understanding Judgments and What They Mean to You

An unpaid charge-off often makes its way to a legal department sooner or later. That may result in a collection attorney taking your case to court, having a judgment entered against you, a day lost to court, additional legal expenses, and maybe — if it's just not your day — a wage garnishment of up to 25 percent of your take-home pay. This is about as much fun as a legal colonoscopy. If you get a court summons for a hearing on a debt issue (see Figure 10-2), don't file it, answer it!

SUM-120

ATTORNEY OR PARTY WITHOUT ATTORNEY (*Name, State Bar number, and address*):	FOR COURT USE ONLY
	SOLO PARA USO DE LA CORTE

TELEPHONE NO.:　　　　　　　FAX NO. (*Optional*):
E-MAIL ADDRESS (*Optional*):
ATTORNEY FOR (*Name*):

SUPERIOR COURT OF CALIFORNIA, COUNTY OF

STREET ADDRESS:
MAILING ADDRESS:
CITY AND ZIP CODE:
BRANCH NAME:

PLAINTIFF:
DEFENDANT:

SUMMONS (JOINT DEBTOR) *(CITACIÓN (DEUDOR CONJUNTO))*

CASE NUMBER:
(*Número del Caso*):

NOTICE! You have been sued. The court may decide against you without your being heard unless you respond within 30 days. Read the information below.

You have **30 CALENDAR DAYS** after this summons and legal papers are served on you to file a written response at this court and have a copy served on the plaintiff. A letter or phone call will not protect you. Your written response must be in proper legal form if you want the court to hear your case. There may be a court form that you can use for your response. You can find these court forms and more information at the California Courts Online Self-Help Center (www.courtinfo.ca.gov/selfhelp), your county law library, or the courthouse nearest you. If you cannot pay the filing fee, ask the court clerk for a fee waiver form. If you do not file your response on time, you may lose the case by default, and your wages, money, and property may be taken without further warning from the court.

There are other legal requirements. You may want to call an attorney right away. If you do not know an attorney, you may want to call an attorney referral service. If you cannot afford an attorney, you may be eligible for free legal services from a nonprofit legal services program. You can locate these nonprofit groups at the California Legal Services Web site (www.lawhelpcalifornia.org), the California Courts Online Self-Help Center (www.courtinfo.ca.gov/selfhelp), or by contacting your local court or county bar association.

¡AVISO! Lo han demandado. Si no responde dentro de 30 días, la corte puede decidir en su contra sin escuchar su versión. Lea la información a continuación.

Tiene 30 DÍAS DE CALENDARIO después de que le entreguen esta citación y papeles legales para presentar una respuesta por escrito en esta corte y hacer que se entregue una copia al demandante. Una carta o una llamada telefónica no lo protegen. Su respuesta por escrito tiene que estar en formato legal correcto si desea que procesen su caso en la corte. Es posible que haya un formulario que usted pueda usar para su respuesta. Puede encontrar estos formularios de la corte y más información en el Centro de Ayuda de las Cortes de California (www.courtinfo.ca.gov/selfhelp/espanol/), en la biblioteca de leyes de su condado o en la corte que le quede más cerca. Si no puede pagar la cuota de presentación, pida al secretario de la corte que le dé un formulario de exención de pago de cuotas. Si no presenta su respuesta a tiempo, puede perder el caso por incumplimiento y la corte le podrá quitar su sueldo, dinero y bienes sin más advertencia.

Hay otros requisitos legales. Es recomendable que llame a un abogado inmediatamente. Si no conoce a un abogado, puede llamar a un servicio de remisión a abogados. Si no puede pagar a un abogado, es posible que cumpla con los requisitos para obtener servicios legales gratuitos de un programa de servicios legales sin fines de lucro. Puede encontrar estos grupos sin fines de lucro en el sitio web de California Legal Services, (www.lawhelpcalifornia.org), en el Centro de Ayuda de las Cortes de California, (www.courtinfo.ca.gov/selfhelp/espanol/) o poniéndose en contacto con la corte o el colegio de abogados locales.

1. TO THE DEFENDANT (*name*):
(*AL DEMANDADO*):

You are hereby directed to file in this court, within **30** days after this summons is served on you, a written response to the Declaration or Affidavit accompanying this summons, giving any legal reason why you should not be required to pay the unpaid amount of: $　　　　　　on the judgment rendered by this court on (*date*):
against (*name each*):

Date:　　　　　　　　　　　　　　　　　　　　　Clerk, by _____, Deputy
(*Fecha*)　　　　　　　　　　　　　　　　　　　(*Secretario*)　　　　　　　(*Adjunto*)

(*For proof of service of this summons, use Proof of Service of Summons (form POS-010).*)
(*Para prueba de entrega de esta citación use el formulario Proof of Service of Summons, (POS-010).*)

2. **NOTICE TO THE PERSON SERVED:** You are served

(SEAL)

a. ☐ as an individual defendant.

b. ☐ as the person sued under the fictitious name of (*specify*):

c. ☐ on behalf of (*specify*):

under: ☐ CCP 416.10 (corporation)　　　☐ CCP 416.60 (minor)
☐ CCP 416.20 (defunct corporation)　☐ CCP 416.70 (conservatee)
☐ CCP 416.40 (association or partnership)　☐ CCP 416.90 (authorized person)
☐ other (*specify*):

d. ☐ by personal delivery on (*date*):

Page 1 of 1

Form Adopted for Mandatory Use
Judicial Council of California
SUM-120 [Rev. January 1, 2004]

SUMMONS (JOINT DEBTOR)

Code of Civil Procedure § 989
American LegalNet, Inc.
www.USCourtForms.com

Figure 10-2:
A sample
court
summons
letter.

This process begins with a letter, not a phone call. After so many months of phone assaults, a simple mute letter is easy to ignore. Don't! Your letter is a summons telling you that a court hearing will be held on a certain day in a certain place. I strongly suggest you show up with a plan and, if possible, have an attorney. A good plan includes

- ✔ A short explanation of why you haven't paid
- ✔ Any disputes about the bill or collection process so far
- ✔ A plan to repay the debt on terms you can afford
- ✔ Documentation that shows why you can't afford more

If the debt is valid and hasn't been collected, the court generally will issue an order confirming that you owe money and commanding you to pay it. You have just received a *judgment*. Sure, others along the way have pressured you to pay — everyone from the creditor to the collection agency — but now a court is involved. This means legal fees, public-record information on your credit report, and dealing with a system that has absolutely no sense of humor. (Your debt collector will look like Jerry Seinfeld in comparison to the court system.)

Figure 10-3 shows a copy of a typical judgment from a hearing on a debt issue. If you get one of these, you need to wake up and get a repayment plan going. If you *dishonor,* or ignore, a judgment, the next step is wage garnishment. (Check out the section "Understanding Wage Garnishments" later in this chapter for more info.)

The judgment itself doesn't put any money in the pocket of the lender or collector. It does, however, set you up for execution — not execution as in the electric chair (although you may feel as though you've received a death sentence), but a *judgment execution.* In essence, if you've received a judgment and you still don't pay, the lender can go back to the judge and get an execution order. Depending on the laws in your state, the order allows the creditor to:

- ✔ Garnish your wages, up to 25 percent.
- ✔ Place a lien on your home or other property for the amount owed. The lien is like having another mortgage on the property. Before the property can be sold free and clear, the lien has to be paid off.
- ✔ Repossess any property involved with the debt you owe (for example, your car if it's a car loan, or your house if it's a home loan).

A judgment is about the worst thing that can happen in the whole collection process. At this point, many people pull the bankruptcy card out of the deck and ask for a fresh deal. Unfortunately for many people who earn above the median income in their states, bankruptcy is no longer an attractive option (see Chapter 11). This is one of the reasons why I think consulting a professional early on in the game makes a lot of sense. If the option to file bankruptcy is not there, you want to know it upfront.

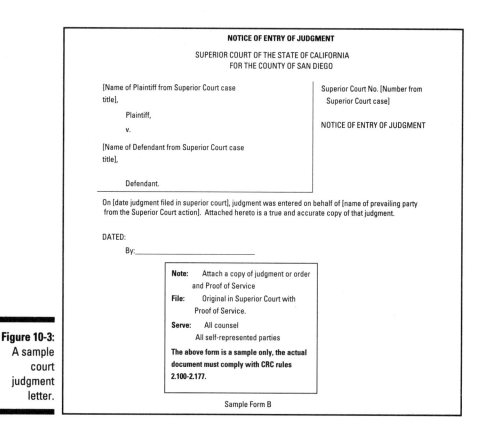

Figure 10-3:
A sample court judgment letter.

Dealing with IRS Debts, Student Loans, and Unpaid Child Support

IRS debts, student loans, and unpaid child support are among the more popular of a class of super-debts that aren't dischargeable in a bankruptcy and must be addressed to the creditor's satisfaction. That puts them in a special category, and I cover them in the following sections.

Slow and steady: Paying off an IRS debt

An IRS debt can be one of the easiest debt situations to deal with. First, the IRS knows *you* know who's in control, so they won't use the same high-pressure, strong-arm tactics that other collectors may. Besides, it's not their money they're chasing down — it's taxpayer money. So you'll probably be able to negotiate a reasonable repayment plan that you can manage over time. Figure 10-4 shows a sample of an IRS repayment form that covers repayment plans. As you can see, it's not scary, so don't wait too long before you act. IRS debts just keep growing with age. In fact, if you delay too long, the IRS will help you out by pulling any tax refunds you have coming straight into the treasury until the debt is paid — just what you wanted to hear, huh?

The slow-moving nature of the IRS can work against you, however. After you pay off the bill, the T-men at the IRS are off to the next taxpayer and have little time or energy to let the credit bureaus or (if they put a lien on your property to make the property security for the repayment) your town-hall clerk who takes liens off your property know that you've cleared the debt.

Keep good records of payments and discharges and follow up by checking your credit report and, if appropriate, the property records at your local town hall. Make sure that the records are updated, or you may miss an opportunity to sell your home or property because it has a big fat lien on it that shouldn't be there.

Installment Agreement Request

Form **9465**
(Rev. December 2007)
Department of the Treasury
Internal Revenue Service

► If you are filing this form with your tax return, attach it to the front of the return. Otherwise, see instructions.

OMB No. 1545-0074

Caution: *Do not file this form if you are currently making payments on an installment agreement. Instead, call 1-800-829-1040. If you are in bankruptcy or we have accepted your offer-in-compromise, see* **Bankruptcy or offer-in-compromise** *on page 2.*

1 Your first name and initial | Last name | Your social security number

 If a joint return, spouse's first name and initial | Last name | Spouse's social security number

 Your current address (number and street). If you have a P.O. box and no home delivery, enter your box number. | Apt. number

 City, town or post office, state, and ZIP code. If a foreign address, enter city, province or state, and country. Follow the country's practice for entering the postal code.

2 If this address is new since you filed your last tax return, check here . . . . ► ☐

3 ( ) _____
Your home phone number   Best time for us to call

4 ( ) _____
Your work phone number   Ext.   Best time for us to call

5 Name of your bank or other financial institution:

Address

City, state, and ZIP code

6 Your employer's name:

Address

City, state, and ZIP code

7 Enter the tax return for which you are making this request (for example, Form 1040) . . . ► _____

8 Enter the tax year for which you are making this request (for example, 2007) . . . . ► _____

9 Enter the total amount you owe as shown on your tax return (or notice) . . . . . | 9 |

10 Enter the amount of any payment you are making with your tax return (or notice). See instructions | 10 |

11 Enter the amount you can pay each month. **Make your payments as large as possible to limit interest and penalty charges.** The charges will continue until you pay in full . . . . | 11 |

12 Enter the day you want to make your payment each month. **Do not enter a day later than the 28th** ►

13 If you want to make your payments by electronic funds withdrawal from your checking account, see the instructions and fill in lines 13a and 13b. This is the most convenient way to make your payments and it will ensure that they are made on time.

► a Routing number

► b Account number

I authorize the U.S. Treasury and its designated Financial Agent to initiate a monthly ACH electronic funds withdrawal entry to the financial institution account indicated for payments of my federal taxes owed, and the financial institution to debit the entry to this account. This authorization is to remain in full force and effect until I notify the U.S. Treasury Financial Agent to terminate the authorization. To revoke payment, I must contact the U.S. Treasury Financial Agent at **1-800-829-1040** no later than 7 business days prior to the payment (settlement) date. I also authorize the financial institutions involved in the processing of the electronic payments of taxes to receive confidential information necessary to answer inquiries and resolve issues related to the payments.

Your signature | Date | Spouse's signature. If a joint return, **both** must sign. | Date

Figure 10-4:
A sample
IRS
repayment
form.

Why some lenders don't mind your judgments — and why you should

Some lenders won't consider you for a loan unless you have great credit. Others don't care if you have judgments or a bankruptcy against you. You may consider them saints to overlook a proven risk. Fact is, they probably don't mind the risk because they charge enough interest to still make money. Or they expect you to default and are ready to eat your lunch when you do.

Groucho Marx said it best when he quipped, "I don't care to belong to a club that accepts people like me as members." You really don't want a loan from a company that would lend money to a person with active unpaid judgments against him.

Educating yourself: Student loans

It used to be that student-loan collections were a joke. But no one is laughing anymore. They've been granted nondischargeable status in the bankruptcy law and lenders want their money for real. Depending on how many loans are involved — and you may have as many as one for each semester you were in school — the effect on your credit of being in default will vary. A lot of people ask me if they owe the money even if they didn't graduate or finish a semester. The answer is yes. They paid out money. What you did with it is of no interest (no pun intended) to them.

If you're in default on your student loans, what you assume to be one loan may be as many as eight or ten. Each loan, be it on a semester or yearly basis, is reported as a separate loan for each enrollment period. So four or five years of student loans may show up as eight or even ten separate trade lines in your credit report. If you end up in default, you may get a lot of negative information on your credit report, and your credit score may crash from all those negative individual loan entries.

A student loan isn't secured with collateral in the normal sense of the word. When you leave school, whether you graduate or not, certain situations, such as economic hardship or unemployment, may allow you to defer the payment of your loans until another time. However, when you're in default with a student loan, you can't defer payment of the loan and you may have to pay it all at once unless you come up with an acceptable repayment scheme. You also won't be eligible for further student aid, your school may withhold your transcripts, state and federal income tax refunds may be used to offset the loan amounts, and your wages (if and when you get a job) may be *attached* or *garnished.* (The loan people can go to court and have a judge order your employer to send them some of your wages each pay period until the loan is paid off. See "Understanding Wage Garnishments," later in this chapter.)

Delinquent student loans can be a big hiring issue. Getting a job with bad credit is a lot harder if your employer pulls a credit report to see whether you're reliable and stable. Not paying student loans is not only an objective negative, but it can also be a personal one as well. The person looking at your employment application had to pay his or her loans. Why shouldn't you? If you have any unpaid loans, explain early in the hiring process why you haven't paid and that you will as soon as you're employed.

Working with a student-loan creditor is essential to moving on with a normal life. Dealing with these folks is very much like dealing with the IRS: You need to get in contact, have a plan, make an offer to repay the loan, and follow through.

Kids first: Making child support a priority

Unpaid child support is another category of debt that lives as long as you do. Under the new bankruptcy law, child-support obligations cannot be discharged. And now the courts provide custodial parents the names of collection agencies that specialize in child-support debt — so your ex may work with a collection agency to come after you for what you owe.

Child support is a debt that will get you sent up the river if you continue not to pay it. Remember those courts and their limited sense of humor? Well, they have absolutely none in this sort of case. Not only will you have the collectors to deal with, but you may also end up with contempt-of-court charges filed against you, and then it's off to the hoosegow for you. This debt is not one you want hanging over you. Plus, it's sure to make a bad impression on any new employers. Make it your number-one priority to pay.

Understanding Wage Garnishments

All the types of debt in this chapter can lead to court and a judgment. If you receive a judgment and still don't pay the debt, your employer may be court-ordered to send part of your paycheck to pay off your creditors. Little is more essential to the working person than a source of income. Your paycheck provides for your family, makes the American dream possible, and strongly influences your feelings of self-worth. Take it away, or take away *enough* of it, and life may begin to seem impossible.

After the court orders a garnishment, it is still subject to some rules, as defined in the Consumer Credit Protection Act (CCPA). This section focuses on the main points, including how you can avoid wage garnishments. Remember, however, that state law can take precedence over federal law if the amounts allowed for garnishment are lower.

Avoiding wage garnishments

Before anyone can garnish your wages, a judgment from a court of law is necessary. You'll get a summons to appear in court for this. If the judgment isn't satisfied (that is, you don't pay what you owe), the lender can go back to court and execute the judgment they already have and get your wages garnished. You'll receive another summons if this happens.

Each state has its own debt-collection laws. Some states permit a lender to garnish your wages; others don't. Some states exempt large amounts or categories of assets from attachment or seizure by a creditor to pay your debt. Others may force you to sell things to satisfy a judgment. The best source for up-to-date information is your state's consumer-protection office. You can find a list of these offices at http://consumeraction.gov/state.shtml.

In many cases, you can avoid wage garnishments by keeping the following in mind:

- ✔ **Keep complete records of the collection process.** Be sure to keep a record of names, dates, copies of correspondence, summaries of conversations, and agreements and any disputes you may have had.

- ✔ **Show up in court when they tell you to.** Go to the hearings and speak up! If you have a reasonable story to tell the judge and a reasonable offer to make, you may be surprised at the result. The judge won't be happy that a collector is wasting his valuable time with a case that should have already been settled out of court.

Your state law may be lower than the federal maximum. The CCPA says your boss can't fire you for having a garnishment. However, the CCPA doesn't provide this protection for multiple wage garnishments. You can find much more information on minimum wages and wage garnishments at the Department of Labor Web site (www.dol.gov/dol/topic/wages/index.htm).

The CCPA doesn't apply to the following types of nondischargeable debts:

- ✔ **Child support and alimony:** The court offers no leniency in matters of support payments. The garnishment law allows up to 50 percent of your disposable earnings to be garnished for child support if you're supporting another spouse or child, or up to 60 percent if you're not. An additional 5 percent may be garnished for support payments more than 12 weeks in arrears.

> ✔ **Government-owed debts:** The garnishment restrictions don't apply to certain bankruptcy court orders or to debts due for federal or state taxes. A non-tax debt, like a credit card or personal loan, can be garnished at up to 15 percent and a student loan at up to 10 percent, cumulative multiple garnishments are subject to the 25 percent max. If a state wage garnishment law differs from the CCPA, the law resulting in the smaller garnishment must be observed. If you'd like to ask someone about the details and formulas, you can call the Department of Labor at their special toll-free garnishment number: 866-487-9243.

Knowing how much can be garnished

If you do receive a judgment, you may wonder how much the court can order your employer to garnish from your wages. The court uses *disposable earnings* (the amount left after legally required deductions like taxes, FICA, mandatory retirement withholding, and unemployment insurance) to figure your garnishment amount.

Whether you have one or more garnishments, the law sets the maximum amount that may be garnished in any workweek or pay period. Exceptions are made for support, bankruptcy, or any state or federal tax. The amount may not exceed the lesser of two figures: 25 percent of the employee's disposable earnings, or the amount by which an employee's disposable earnings are greater than 30 times the federal minimum wage (currently $5.85 an hour). See Table 10-1 for calculations of the latter.

Table 10-1: Maximum Garnishment of Disposable Earnings under Normal Circumstances* for the $5.85 Minimum Wage

Weekly	Biweekly	Semimonthly	Monthly
$175.50 or less: None	$351.00 or less: None	$380.25 or less: None	$760.50 or less: None
More than $175.50 but less than $234.00: Amount above $175.50	More than $351.00 but less than $468.00: Amount above $351.00	More than $380.25 but less than $507.00: Amount above $380.25	More than $760.50 but less than $1,014.00: Amount above $760.50
$234.00 or more: Maximum 25%	$468.00 or more: Maximum 25%	$507.00 or more: Maximum 25%	$1,014.00 or more: maximum 25%

*These restrictions don't apply to garnishments for child and/or spousal support, bankruptcy, or actions to recover state or federal taxes.
Source: U.S. Department of Labor

Taking Your Case to Court

I know how intimidating, embarrassing, and expensive it may be to take time off from work and go down to a courthouse that probably has no parking anyway. So does your creditor. Most of them count on this. They know that if you don't show up, they'll get just about anything they want from the judge. Considering what I just told you about garnishments, I strongly suggest you show up and tell your story to the judge. Be sure to bring:

✔ Statements from the account in question

✔ Records of phone calls and written correspondence with the creditor

✔ A payment plan you can afford

You can represent yourself, but you'll be at a significant disadvantage if you do. Trust me; your creditor is intimate with the ins and outs of the court process. If you can afford it, get an attorney. If you can't, go anyway — your presence and your genuine commitment to coming up with a workable way to repay your debt may just be all that you need.

You can show the court that you've made a good-faith effort to propose the best settlement you can afford. Be sure to back up what you're saying with your records and a reasonable payment plan that you offered but that was refused. If you went to a credit counselor along the way, mention it; if you can say that they thought your proposed settlement was reasonable, all the better. Of course, none of this reasonable stuff applies to overdue child support; unless your income has changed for the worse, you have to pay as agreed.

The following list shows the high points (or low points depending on your point of view) of the process for collections that have gone to an attorney for legal action.

1. **You receive a demand letter from an attorney demanding payment.**

   This letter will come in addition to all the letters you may have received from the creditor or collector. This demand letter gives you one last chance to try to resolve the problem before court action begins.

2. **A suit is brought in a court often within 10 to 30 days of the date of the demand letter.**

   This suit alerts the court of the situation and formally demands payment.

3. **You get served with a complaint.**

   You get a summons from a court to respond by a certain date and time. If you don't file an answer, then the Court is likely to enter a default judgment in the matter.

4. **The attorney will file for a default judgment if you don't answer the complaint.**

5. **If an answer is filed, the discovery process begins and a trial date is later set.**

If you respond to the suit, be sure to explain any discrepancies in the creditor's claims. If you can't, then be sure to show up at the court on the hearing date with all your documentation and a lawyer of your own if possible.

6. **If a judgment is awarded, the attorney attempts to locate and verify any of your assets.**

The attorney initiates bank levies, garnishment orders, liens, and so on to satisfy the judgment.

Understanding what happens may demystify the process and remove one more obstacle that keeps people from reacting until it's too late.

Chapter 11

The New Bankruptcy, It's Not Your Father's Oldsmobile

*T*he first time I heard the word bankruptcy, I was a kid playing Monopoly. After scooping up Connecticut, Vermont, and Oriental avenues, I found myself without an orange, beige, blue, pink, yellow, white, or green bill left when I landed on my uncle's Boardwalk — with a hotel. My only recourse was bankruptcy. Even then, it was bad news. But not as bad as "Go directly to jail. Do not pass Go. Do not collect $200." In the United States, people don't go to prison if they can't pay their bills (child support and IRS debts excepted). Instead, they file for bankruptcy.

Why does the United States, one of the most avowed capitalist countries in the world, even have a bankruptcy law? Because even the best capitalist tradition recognizes that sometimes people have to take big financial risks to get ahead or start a new business. If their ventures fail, they need not only protection from imprisonment, but also an escape clause to keep creditors from hounding them for the rest of their lives. Without this protection from harassment, the risk of using borrowed capital would be so high that few people would use it, and the economy would be the loser. So bankruptcy is good for the economy. Makes me feel patriotic just thinking of it.

Even though the everyday reality may be very different, this is still a land of hope and fresh starts. So when hope runs out and the creditors close in, bankruptcy offers that fresh start for those who need it and for anyone who can qualify. However, the start may not be quite as fresh as it was before

Congress passed a major rewrite of the bankruptcy statute. The current law has raised the bar for those who seek protection and, in many cases, lessened the protection available.

In this chapter, my goal is to give you an overview of how the law works. I help you figure out whether bankruptcy makes sense for you and to determine the cost in terms of your credit report. For how the details apply to your unique situation, be sure to seek competent legal help. I've seen too many people use bankruptcy for the wrong reasons — instead of providing them with a fresh start, it only locked them into a financial nightmare. So, if you're thinking about bankruptcy, or know someone who is, this is an opportunity to look past the legal fine print and consider what may be the most important financial decision you'll make in the next ten years.

Go directly to the next section. Do not pass Go. Do not collect $200.

Understanding Bankruptcy, Chapter and Verse

The bankruptcy law in this country may seem like a secret code. It *is,* after all, referred to as the Bankruptcy Code, and it contains all those mysterious chapters with numbers — 7, 11, 13 — rather than names. What do they really mean and how do you choose the right one? You came to the right place. But before you pick which chapter may be right for you, you first have to determine whether bankruptcy itself is right for you.

A financial or quality-of-life component factor usually figures in to the decision to file bankruptcy as well. If your wages are about to be garnished because of your inability to pay a bill — perhaps a totally unexpected and unasked-for medical bill — do you allow your family to suffer the financial consequences? For years? More than half of all those filing bankruptcy have sudden, uninsured medical expenses.

In a real sense, the reason for filing bankruptcy is to seek the protection of the court from your creditors. It's that simple. If you can't deal with the collectors on your own, call in the judge — and the judge will. This section gives you the lowdown on bankruptcy.

Defining bankruptcy types, chapter by chapter

The bankruptcy court allows for many kinds of bankruptcy, identified as chapters with numbers. A Chapter 9 bankruptcy, for example, is reserved for municipalities (cities and such). Chapter 12 allows farmers to reorganize their debt and keep their farms. Most people are familiar with Chapter 11 bankruptcy because of all the airlines and other companies taking advantage of it to reorganize and keep creditors off their backs until they can turn their companies around. Actually, individuals sometimes file for Chapter 11 bankruptcy, too.

But among all the various chapters, two are most commonly used by consumers who find themselves unable to fend off or satisfy the creditors:

- ✔ **Chapter 7:** Also known as *liquidation,* this is the most popular form of bankruptcy. It may require you to give up some assets (the liquidation part) and gets you out of almost all your liabilities.

- ✔ **Chapter 13:** Often referred to as *wage-earner bankruptcy,* this form of bankruptcy allows you to keep most of your assets and pay back what you can over a period of time, usually three to five years, under court supervision and protection.

The 2005 bankruptcy law: Tightening up on consumers

Bankruptcy law comes under the jurisdiction of the federal courts. States, however, can pass laws that deal with what is called the *debtor-creditor relationship* and, as a result, some property and other exemptions vary by state.

The Bankruptcy Abuse Prevention and Consumer Protection Act of 2005 has had a wide-ranging impact on bankruptcy in the United States. It was enacted because lenders convinced Congress (yes, the people you voted for) that some people had abused bankruptcy protection over the years. The act established restrictions to try to cut down on any such abuse in the future.

Here is a brief summary of the main provisions that may help you decide whether a bankruptcy may be worth pursuing in your situation:

- ✔ **You have to pass a means test to be eligible for Chapter 7.** Except in limited circumstances (check out the "Qualifying and Filing for Bankruptcy" section to see if you qualify), your net income has to be below the median income in your state of residence. The short version is that you have to prove to the court that even though you have above median income, you can't adhere to a Chapter 13 repayment plan.

- ✔ **You're required to get credit counseling from an "approved nonprofit budget and credit-counseling agency" before you can file.** The U.S. Trustee provides a master list of approved agencies you have to choose from. You can find out who is on the list by contacting the clerk of the court where your bankruptcy is to be filed. Also you can contact one of the three largest providers of bankruptcy counseling. (In the "Qualifying and Filing for Bankruptcy" section later in this chapter, I discuss why I think you should go with a large and experienced provider.) The three providers I list account for more than half of all bankruptcy counseling, with Money Management International being by far the largest.

- Money Management International, www.moneymanagement. org, www.bankruptcycertificate.com/home/home.php, 877-918-2227

- Greenpath, www.greenpathbk.com, 800-504-3397

- CCCS of Atlanta, www.cccsatl.org, 866-672-2227

✔ **After you file but before you're discharged from the bankruptcy, you must complete a course in financial management.** Again, I recommend one of the big three providers.

✔ **You're limited in what you can buy immediately before filing.** Having made the decision to file, you can't go out and spend up a storm or take cash advances and then not have to pay. Generally, the limits apply to the 90 days preceding your filing.

✔ **You have to wait a set amount of time after filing for bankruptcy before you can file again.** The law requires

- Eight years between Chapter 7 bankruptcies

- Two years between Chapter 13 bankruptcies

- Four years between Chapter 7 and Chapter 13 bankruptcies

✔ **Your *homestead exemption* (how much equity in your home you can keep out of your filing and keep for yourself) is limited by state law.** In addition, if you acquired your home less than 40 months before filing, you're allowed a maximum exemption of $125,000 — regardless of your state's exemption allowance.

✔ **Under Chapter 13 bankruptcy, you're allowed to spend only what the IRS guidelines allow.** The rest of your disposable income must be included in the plan and every year you have to document your income and expenses to see if you can pay more (or less).

✔ **Your attorney must certify that what you say in the documents you use in court is true.**

✔ **You will still owe all your past and future debts for taxes (incurred in the last three years or those unfiled or filed late), domestic support, drunk-driving injuries, or student loans.** Courts are extremely reluctant to discharge student loans, and the general policy is not to discharge them. In some very rare circumstances, older student loans can be discharged, if an "undue" hardship condition exists and you file a separate motion with the bankruptcy court and then appear before the judge to explain your hardship.

- ✔ **Domestic-support obligations are a priority debt that must be paid.** (A *priority debt* takes precedence over other debts you owe and is paid completely.) However, the *bankruptcy trustee* (the person appointed by the court to administer your Chapter 13 plan) receives administrative fees before your spouse, ex-spouse, or kids get their money. What a country.

- ✔ **You may be evicted if you don't pay your rent after you've filed for bankruptcy.**

- ✔ **You must provide your latest tax return to your creditors if they ask for it.** Before you can finalize your bankruptcy, you'll need to give information about your financial status to your creditors so they can see that you can't afford to pay what you owe. If you're filing for Chapter 13, you must provide your tax returns for the last four years.

Determining Whether Bankruptcy Is Right for You

Gone are the days of easily skipping out on debts or hiding a fortune in a palace in West Palm Beach with an unlimited homestead exemption. Declaring bankruptcy is no small decision. It's a change that can stay with you in some form for up to ten years. It's a decision that may affect your self-image for even longer. It's a condition that will redefine your credit report and certainly lower your credit score.

In other words, bankruptcy is a major life event, so it's something you want to consider very seriously. Don't get me wrong — it may just be the best alternative you have if you've suffered some serious financial setbacks. But before you take the plunge, invest time in carefully weighing all your options in this section.

Making the bankruptcy decision

As you consider bankruptcy, ask yourself this: Can you do anything more to help meet your obligations? Do you have hope of finding a solution to this mess that is acceptable to both you and your creditors? If you answered no to both questions, I think you're on the right track in considering bankruptcy.

I've known people who've answered no to both questions but still vowed they'd eat canned spaghetti for the rest of their lives before they would declare bankruptcy. (Most of them were from Sicily; I have some uncles from Sicily, and let me tell you, they hate canned spaghetti.) In the end, though, the decision is really only about money, not your honor, and money just isn't as important as your life (unless you're one of my Sicilian uncles).

Before you make the final decision to throw your credit and creditors off that financial cliff, I suggest you consider the following:

- **Make sure bankruptcy will solve your financial crisis.** Making all your debts and collectors go away may solve one problem. But will it solve *the* problem? If the problem is overspending, declaring bankruptcy won't help you in the long run. If you've been using credit to supplement your income for basic living expenses, bankruptcy won't help either.

  A good credit counselor should be able to help you consider this issue, as well as help you get your spending habits, expenses, and income level back in synch (see Chapter 3 for more on credit counselors).

- **Review and prioritize your goals.** Bankruptcy is a big step and its consequences will linger for years. To make the decision based only on immediate events without considering future impacts would be a mistake. How will this decision affect your chances of buying a home, getting married, getting divorced, getting a job? Describe your world as you would like to see it in the next five years, and ask yourself what impact a bankruptcy will have on that goal.

- **Consider your options.** Make a list of other ways to deal with your debts. Can you increase your income? Reduce your expenses? Stretch out your payments? Use your home equity to pay your bills for a while until things improve?

- **Get a professional, non-legal opinion.** Talk to a good credit counselor. You'll have to meet with a credit counselor anyway within six months before filing for bankruptcy. Expect this visit to give you options, an analysis of your spending and income, and an action plan. Make sure the credit counselor gives you a written budget or spending and action plan. This will go a long way toward answering the question of whether bankruptcy will help.

- **Get a professional legal opinion.** Find a lawyer who specializes in bankruptcies. Find out if you qualify for bankruptcy and, if so, which chapter. Make sure you understand what bankruptcy will and won't do for you. Ask about alternatives, including settlements or other options. While you're there, ask about the pluses and minuses of filing for bankruptcy on your own. Called *pro se,* the law allows you to represent yourself — and in some courts with sympathetic judges, this can be a moneysaver (in other courts, it can be a disaster). Your lawyer is the best one to guide you here.

- **Talk to your creditors.** Seriously. If you're considering a bankruptcy, let your lenders know and ask if they can offer any repayment plans you may not have heard about. This is a courtesy your creditor may appreciate. Don't expect too much, but talking to your creditors is always worth a shot. If you want, have your lawyer handle this task.

- **Talk to someone who cares about you.** Yes, even though this person is not a professional, he or she knows you and may have an important perspective. Avoid asking someone who would be personally affected by your choice (such as a person you owe money to, someone who owes you money, or a dependent).

- **Look in the mirror.** Given your current financial state, how do you see yourself? Consider your goals; weigh the options offered by your creditors, the credit counselor, and the lawyer, and be sure to consider the advice of others who care about you. Now you're ready to decide what is best for your future and your peace of mind. If you don't like what you see, go through the process until you do. Then do what you think is in your best interest.

Adding up the pluses and minuses

Like anything in life, bankruptcy is neither all good nor all bad. In the following sections, I let you know the good part about bankruptcy, as well as the harsh reality of the consequences.

The silver lining of filing bankruptcy

I'm always in favor of hearing the good news first. With bankruptcy, it's no different. Here are some of the positives of filing bankruptcy:

Finding a bankruptcy attorney

If you're considering filing bankruptcy, you want to make sure you have a qualified attorney. I always consider friends, family, or co-workers who have had a satisfied experience with an attorney as a good source of reference. I'm not suggesting that you put a note up on the company bulletin board, but someone who has already been through the bankruptcy process may be a good referral source.

The Internet also has some very good resources. Three that you may want to check out are

- American Bankruptcy Institute (www. abiworld.org)

- American Bar Association (www.abanet. org)

- Lawyers.com (www.lawyers.com)

If you have used a lawyer who handles other issues for you, ask for a referral to someone who either specializes in bankruptcy or does a lot of it. Don't use your cousin, the real-estate lawyer. Get a pro. Mistakes made here may keep a debt alive and that can be very costly and frustrating.

✔ **You get a fresh start.** The silver lining in a bankruptcy is that you get to begin again. The collection activity stops. The fees, penalty rates, and lawyers stop. In fact, in a Chapter 7 bankruptcy, virtually the entire debt may go away. Without the ability to call a stop to the madness of credit gone awry, some people would never — and I mean *never* — be able to live a normal life again. Bankruptcy can allow that to happen.

✔ **You get credit education.** Another plus of bankruptcy: The 2005 bankruptcy law says that anyone who files is required to get some credit education. This is an opportunity to look back at what happened and to rechart your financial and credit course going forward. If you take advantage of this opportunity, you'll walk away with a much better sense of how to manage your money — which means you'll be less likely to end up back where you started.

The not-so-pretty consequences of filing bankruptcy

As you can probably guess, filing bankruptcy comes with some pretty heavy consequences. I outline them for you here.

✔ **You may still owe money.** Bankruptcy may not wipe out *all* your debt. Some debts do not go away — even though you'd like them to — and they must be paid in full. The debts that don't disappear are

   • Federal, state, and local taxes

   • Child support

   • Alimony

   • Student loans from the government or a lender

   • Money owed as a result of drunk driving

✔ **Your credit score plummets.** Bankruptcy doesn't look good on your credit report. This event appears as a public record in your file and it stays there for up to ten years and sometimes more. Worse, it causes your credit score to plunge as many as 100 points. Declare bankruptcy and you're likely to see your score drop to 600 or worse. That is in the lowest 20 percent of all credit scores. Ouch!

✔ **Borrowing money becomes more difficult.** When a lender sees a score in the lowest percentile, your interest rates and terms escalate. In some cases, a lender will decline to give you credit because you no longer meet the underwriting guidelines.

Some lenders, however, specialize in giving loans to people with bad credit. They would be delighted to see you — the fact that you have just gone bankrupt is a big plus in their eyes. Why? Because under the law, you can't file a Chapter 7 bankruptcy again for eight long years. So while they get to charge you more interest as a risky borrower, you can't avoid repaying them by playing the bankruptcy card. If you fall behind, you can run, but you can't hide. Usually these lenders are very good at collecting overdue accounts. The bottom line: Avoid these guys at all costs. If you must borrow shortly after a bankruptcy, only use a reputable lender.

✔ **Renting an apartment may become more complicated.** Some landlords get credit reports on tenant applicants. They may refuse to rent to you, require a cosigner, or increase your required deposit if they see a bankruptcy.

✔ **Insurance becomes more costly.** A bankruptcy will cost you more in insurance premiums, particularly for homeowner's and auto insurance. The insurance mavens and their actuarial henchmen love credit scores and credit reports. All those dispassionate numbers lend themselves to justifying rate increases much better than real claims do. So even if you have no losses, your premiums may go up. Credit reports are used mostly by homeowner and auto insurers; some states don't allow credit to be a factor in setting rates, but most do.

✔ **Employment becomes dicier.** Even under ideal circumstances, job hunting can be stressful. When you consider the fact that many employers run a credit check before making a job offer, your stress level can increase as your opportunities decrease. As a practical matter, some licenses cannot be given to people who have filed for bankruptcy, and security clearances can be denied.

The killer here is the unasked and, therefore, unanswered question: What happened to cause you to seek bankruptcy protection and will you do it again? The behavior, events, or judgments you made that resulted in the filing are all concerns for prospective employers who may suspect your bankruptcy means you'd be an unreliable employee. These are the silent killers, because although you can't legally be denied employment because you filed a bankruptcy, the prospective employer rarely asks the questions to find out the reasons. Going on to the next candidate is just easier and legally safer.

✔ **Your self-image is likely to become tarnished.** Having a major life event go against you never helps. You may think you're made of steel or maybe something softer, but either way, bankruptcy can take its toll. Like it or not, a great deal of how most people view themselves is wrapped up in their financial persona. Most people think of themselves as responsible adults. Many people have been taught that responsible adults pay their bills and keep their promises. Even though you know it's okay to file for bankruptcy and that you have no choice in the matter from a practical standpoint, you may find that you have an internal conflict to deal with that you didn't expect.

Considering a debt-management plan first

One of the stops you're required to make on the road to getting help from the bankruptcy courts is a credit-counseling agency. The court has recognized the value of the work done by these agencies by requiring that you run your situation by them (*before* filing). The courts have also named them as one of the providers of financial-management education (*after* filing).

The idea is that you'll get an unbiased assessment of your financial condition, and that you may, upon reflection, change your mind or find a less-damaging way to handle your debt. Additionally, if a creditor refuses to negotiate with a credit counselor, the court can order that their debt get a 20-percent haircut.

Understanding what a debt-management plan is

One of the mainstays of the credit-counseling industry is the debt-management plan. You begin with an individually tailored spending plan that you create with the help of a credit counselor. A *debt-management plan* uses your available money to pay your creditors. It takes the equivalent of your disposable income after actual expenses and reallocates some or all of it to those creditors. The average debt-management plan may be set up for four to five years but in practice tends to be completed in about two years. (For more on debt-management plans, turn to Chapter 3.)

Seeing how a debt-management plan differs from bankruptcy

Under a debt-management plan, the money left (if any) after you've paid your living expenses and paid your creditors may go into your pocket or a savings plan for emergencies. Say your child gets sick and you have either a high deductible or no insurance. The money to pay for this emergency could come from your emergency savings account. If you file Chapter 13 bankruptcy, however, all your disposable income goes toward paying off your creditors. The amount you get to use for living expenses with minor adjustments comes from less-than-generous IRS guidelines.

Unlike the terms of a Chapter 7 or Chapter 13 bankruptcy, a debt-management plan is a voluntary arrangement between you and your creditors, using the credit-counseling agency as an intermediary. You can walk away from a debt-management plan at any time and still file for bankruptcy. Or, if you're on the receiving end of a windfall, you can pay off your creditors in one payment and be done with it.

Of course, your creditors don't have to accept the terms of the debt-management plan, whereas they *have* to accept it if you file bankruptcy. That said, most creditors do accept debt-management plans, because they know you'll be off to the courthouse to file bankruptcy if they say no.

Whereas a Chapter 7 bankruptcy liquidates many debts, a Chapter 13 bankruptcy forces creditors to accept a lower payment over a set period of time that may not cover what you originally owed. The difference between what was owed and what is paid under Chapter 13 is what the creditors lose. They also can't charge interest or fees under Chapter 13. A debt-management plan allows the creditors to collect finance charges, although many creditors reduce the rate to one that is more affordable and reflects your circumstances and your desire to repay the debt.

Perhaps one of the biggest differences between a Chapter 7 or 13 bankruptcy and a debt-management plan is the effect on your credit score. Bankruptcy has a large and not-too-positive impact on your score, which affects your ability to do lots of the things I mention earlier in this chapter for years after the *end* of your bankruptcy.

A debt-management plan, on the other hand, doesn't have the same negative impact on your credit score. In fact, many creditors don't report to the bureaus that your account is being handled by a credit-counseling agency. Those that do report it to the bureaus report it as a description of the account (for example, credit card, real estate mortgage, credit counseling), not as a payment history item (for example, "pays as agreed" or "*X* days late"). Payment history items count toward your credit score. Further, your credit report shows the credit-counseling account description only until you pay off the account or decide to discontinue the plan, at which point the notation is removed. The description is not reported for the next seven years.

More good news: Even while you're in a debt-management plan, the FICO scoring system does not subtract any points. That's right — your credit score is not affected. A credit-counseling notation on your file is perceived as a neutral item — not a negative or public-record item — and your creditor may report the account as "pays as agreed."

If you decide to try the debt-management-plan route rather than a Chapter 13 and the debt-management plan doesn't work out for you, you can always file for bankruptcy without any waiting period.

If it can work for you, a debt-management plan may be less restrictive and damaging to your credit report and score than bankruptcy. I suggest that when you get your mandatory counseling on the road to bankruptcy, you explore making a debt-management plan work for you. Your credit score will be glad you did.

Qualifying and Filing for Bankruptcy

At this point, you may have determined that bankruptcy remains your best or only viable way out of your financial corner. But although bankruptcy may be right for you, *you* may not qualify for bankruptcy. Both Chapter 7 and Chapter 13 bankruptcies are limited by new requirements, which I cover in the following sections. For a quick look at the new rules, see Figure 11-1.

Checking your eligibility for Chapter 7

The most popular form of bankruptcy in recent years, Chapter 7, is now restricted by new rules under the Bankruptcy Abuse Prevention and Consumer Protection Act of 2005. Chapter 7 has been so popular because of its effectiveness and efficacy in getting rid of debts and collectors. Under a Chapter 7, you receive relief from virtually all your debts, with a few exceptions, and you get it fast — like the same day (unlike a Chapter 13, which may take years before you get a discharge). I cover the major changes to Chapter 7 in the following sections.

NEW BANKRUPTCY CODE: FILING PROCEDURES			
Major Intent of Bankruptcy Reform	Cut down on abuse by requiring people who can pay all or some of their debt to do so.		
PROVISIONS			
In effect as of 4/2005			
Homestead Exemption (Sections: 308, 322, 330)	1) Exemption limited to $125,000 if property was acquired within the previous 1215 days (40 months). 2) Cap is not applied to a property transferred from debtor's previous principal residence if acquired prior to the 40 month period.		
In effect as of 10/17/2005			
Means Test	Used to determine if you qualify for Chapter 7 or Chapter 13 Bankruptcy		
	Test #1 Are family earnings over the median income for your state? See www.usdoj.gov/ust/eo/bapcpa for the approved income levels by family size. • If "No" Chapter 7 can be filed! • If "Yes", proceed to Test # 2.	*Test #2* Do you have monthly income in excess of expenses equal to at least $166.66/month to pay $10,000 of debt over 5 years? • If "Yes", Chapter 7 cannot be filed but Chapter 13 may be filed! • If "No", proceed to Test # 3.	*Test #3* Do you have monthly income in excess of expenses greater than $100/month to pay over the next 60 months to pay at least 25% of your unsecured debt? • If "No", you can file Chapter 7. • If "Yes", Chapter 7 cannot be filed but Chapter 13 may be filed!
Proof of Income	If filing Chapter 7 or Chapter 13 bankruptcy you must provide the court a copy of your most recent tax return or transcript of a tax return at least seven days prior to the 341 meeting.		
Counseling	You must have had approved financial counseling within the last 6 months.		
Child Support and Alimony	These debts increase to a number 1 priority and may not be discharged.		
Tithing	Up to 15% of your income can be given to charity. This may allow you to choose paying your creditor or your church in a Chapter 13 or getting your income low enough to qualify for Chapter 7.		

You have to pass the means test

The first hurdle in moving forward with Chapter 7 bankruptcy is meeting a means test. If you have too many means (that is, too much income), you can't declare Chapter 7. And, sorry, the courts won't take your word for it. You have to *prove* that your income really is as you said by handing in your most recent tax return. If your income is above the applicable median for your state of residence, you can't file for Chapter 7.

Do you have family income above the median for your family size in your state of residence? To find out, go to the census Web site (www.census. gov/hhes/www/income/medincsizeandstate.html).

If your income is above the average, don't give up just yet. Next, you want to determine whether you have *excess monthly income* of more than $166.66 to pay $10,000 of debt over five years. So what counts as excess income? You have to use the spending guidelines approved by the IRS. Allowable expenses are shown on the IRS Web site at www.irs.gov/businesses/small/ article/0,,id=104627,00.html. The IRS guidelines may be very tight for you. (I know from personal experience: My dad was an IRS agent and his idea of a reasonable allowance was $5 a week — even through college!)

If you're beginning to get a little worried, you may have good reason. The monthly allowances are tight. If you live in Alaska or Hawaii, I can offer a little ray of hope. These states have a separate schedule to account for increased living expenses. But don't get too excited: In Hawaii, for example, the extra food allowance per month is $2 to $5, depending on your income level.

If you *can* squeak the $166.66 a month out of your budget, the best you can do is to file under Chapter 13.

If you have less excess monthly income than the magic number of $166.66 a month left after IRS expense allowances, proceed to the next hurdle: Do you have an extra $100 a month over the next 60 months? And will that $6,000 account for at least 25 percent of your debt? If the answer to both questions is no, you can pass go and file for Chapter 7. If not, go directly to Chapter 13.

Tithing — giving money to your religious institution — is allowed in both Chapter 7 and Chapter 13 bankruptcies. You may donate up to 15 percent of your income and have it count as an expense that may lower your income. So much for rendering unto Caesar. Donating to your church, temple, or house of worship may just help you make the numbers work to become eligible for a Chapter 7 rather than a Chapter 13.

You have to go for counseling

At some point during the six months before you file for bankruptcy, you have to receive counseling from a court-approved credit counselor. The law leaves these requirements to the court (actually the Executive Office of the U.S. Trustee) to define. However, Congress did set certain minimum criteria. To be approved, a credit-counseling agency must

- ✔ Be nonprofit.
- ✔ Have an independent board of directors, the majority of whom are neither employed by the agency nor directly or indirectly benefiting financially from the outcome of a credit-counseling session.
- ✔ Charge "reasonable" fees and provide services, even if you can't afford to pay the reasonable fee.
- ✔ Disclose its funding sources, counselor qualifications, possible impact on your credit history, any cost imposed on you, and how those costs will be paid.
- ✔ Offer adequate counseling encompassing an analysis of your current situation, what brought you to your current situation, and options to solve your problem without incurring *negative amortization* of your debts. Negative amortization happens when you make payments on a debt, but the payments are too small to offset interest and fees on the account, so the debt grows instead of getting paid off.
- ✔ Train its counselors adequately but not pay them based on the outcome of the counseling.

The law also spells out minimum requirements for the personal financial-management course you must attend as part of the bankruptcy discharge process. The course may or may not be given by a credit-counseling agency; others are allowed to offer it if they qualify with the court, but all must:

- ✔ Provide experienced and trained personnel
- ✔ Incorporate relevant teaching methodologies and learning materials
- ✔ Be offered in an adequate facility or over the phone or Internet

Just because the court has approved the counseling agency does not make it the right one for you, so exercise caution when selecting. (See Chapter 3 for guidance in choosing a credit counselor.) You want someone who does a lot of this and has electronic-certificate-issuing capability. Why? Because if they get it wrong or if the certificate is delayed in getting to you, you could be facing costly delays in getting this matter successfully concluded.

Qualifying for Chapter 13

Because of the strict guidelines about who qualifies to file Chapter 7 bankruptcy, many more people will only qualify to file Chapter 13. The requirement for counseling and proof of income are the same for both types of bankruptcy, but although you must take the same means test, the outcome leads to different results.

Chapter 13 differs from Chapter 7 in that, after your income has been established and allowable expenses have been deducted, you must use all your disposable income toward the repayment of debt. *Disposable* is defined by taking your income and subtracting the IRS allowable expenses. The means test establishes whether your income is above the median for your state of residence. If your income is above the median average income level for your state, your disposable income gets disposed of (paid to your bankruptcy trustee who will forward it to your creditors) for the next five years, unless you can show that you can pay off 100 percent of the debt in less than 60 months.

Filing, then backing out

If you decide that bankruptcy is not for you *after* you've filed papers, you can ask the court to voluntarily dismiss your case before the discharge. For example, say you file a Chapter 7 and then find out that you have to give back that 3-carat diamond ring your sweetie gave you recently. Or in the case of a Chapter 13, you've been making payments and eating peanut butter for a month and can't go on. Or looking on the bright side, you get a windfall inheritance from a rich uncle and can pay off the Chapter 13 in one fell swoop.

No matter what the reason, you can call the whole thing off and get a dismissal. Keep in mind, however, that the credit-reporting bureaus will pick up the record of your filing and put the filing information out there even if you stop the process without getting out of any debts. The credit-reporting bureaus must also report that the filing was dismissed — but the record of your having filed a bankruptcy will stay on your credit report, and continue to lower your score, for the remainder of the reporting period (up to ten years). Both you and the creditor have the same rights and remedies as you had before your bankruptcy case was filed.

If you ask for a dismissal of your bankruptcy filing, you won't be the first to do so. In fact,

the law has a specific section that deals with people who not only change their minds, but also change them back again. Perhaps after backing out of the bankruptcy to save the diamond ring, your creditors turn up the collection heat to the point where you'd gladly give them the ring and your grandfather's watch if they'd just leave you alone.

Here's how the change works the second time around: In your first filing, after you file the paperwork with the courts, you get an automatic stay (or suspension) of collection activity on the part of your creditors. The length of time depends on the type of debt or action stayed and can vary in time allowed. But generally it's in place until you discharge your debts (that is, get rid of them). But if you refile after changing your mind, within one year of the original filing, the automatic stay (the stopping of all collection activity) is for only 30 days. So you have to get all your testing and counseling and paperwork done in the 30-day time period or the collectors and foreclosers return in force. If this is the third such filing in a year, you don't get *any* stay unless the court orders it.

So what this means is this: When you file for bankruptcy, do your best to make sure it's a decision you can live with for the long haul.

The current bankruptcy law is intended to require those who can afford to make payments toward their debt to do so.

Just as with Chapter 7, those filing for Chapter 13 bankruptcy must establish that their family income is either below or above the median for their state. The law allows that if your income is below the median for the state in which you reside, your disposable income may be paid to your creditors over the next three years. (To find out what the median income is for your state, check out www.census.gov/hhes/www/income/medincsizeandstate.html). Because your income is under the state median for where you live, you get a break and may only have to complete a three-year repayment plan. The creditors eat the rest of the debt. And there is no interest on any of the accounts involved.

If your income is above the median for your state, all the disposable income (income after allowable expenses) you have left over goes to the creditors over the term of your Chapter 13 program.

Managing Your Bankruptcy to Rebuild Your Credit

Declaring bankruptcy is more of a hassle than it used to be — and it's definitely harder to qualify for relief. But if you qualify and take the bankruptcy plunge, don't think you're out of the woods. You still have to live with the effects of bankruptcy on your credit report and your credit score, and the barriers that your new status creates. You're likely to discover that bankruptcy has an impact on your insurance rates as well as your ability to get hired or promoted.

Filing again for bankruptcy: A waiting game

Whether you file for bankruptcy via Chapter 7 or Chapter 13, be aware that you'll be restricted from doing so again within a significant period of time.

After you complete your Chapter 7 filing and the court discharges you and your debts, the clock starts to tick. You can't apply for protection of the court for another Chapter 7 — no matter what — for the next eight years. A Chapter 13 may not be filed within 4 years of a Chapter 7 discharge. In the case of Chapter 13, after you complete your filing, you can't file for a Chapter 13 again for the next two years or a Chapter 7 for the next four years.

Either way, it's important to be careful in your post-bankruptcy world because if a new astronomical debt with a super-aggressive collector comes along, you may not be able to refile for a Chapter 7 or 13 right away.

Your bankruptcy is not something you want to let take care of itself. Your bankruptcy status will remain on your credit report as the mother of all credit negatives for up to ten years — and that's a long time.

So, just how do you get a handle on your financial future now that you've nuked the past? You rebuild your credit as quickly as possible; and you use credit carefully as you go forward — bankruptcy may not be available to you again for years (see the nearby sidebar, "Filing again for bankruptcy: A waiting game"). This section shows you how to do so.

Preparing your statement

Now that your credit report shows a bankruptcy and will continue to for a long time, prepare for the consequences. To begin with, work on a short statement that describes your valid reasons for filing for bankruptcy. Businesspeople and potential lenders who have access to your credit report will want to know what happened so that they can judge whether to do business with you.

Note: This *statement* isn't the 100-word statement you can attach to your credit report — this is an actual verbal statement that you'll make when you're doing anything that requires someone to see your credit report (apply for a loan, apply for a job). Be sure to tell them about this before they see your credit report — but only if you're sure they'll be looking at it. (Why raise the issue if they'll never know about it otherwise?)

A tight and targeted statement explaining your bankruptcy is similar to the spiel you give a prospective employer when she asks why you left your previous position. Whatever your parting circumstances were, your explanation is always a positive spin on the truth. It's short, sweet, and rehearsed. Having it at the ready allows you to convey yourself as confident, professional, and reliable — just the sort of person she'd love to hire. Same deal here. Come up with a succinct statement that briefly explains your decision to declare bankruptcy.

 Although it's rare for one debt to push you over the edge, you're better off if you can attribute your situation to a single traumatic event. It may have been a divorce, a layoff, or an illness. Something beyond your control is a plus. Your efforts to pay the debts or deal with collectors are only of interest to you. All you need to say is that you tried everything you could think of to meet your obligations. End the short statement with some words of wisdom like: "I've learned a lot from this experience" or "I've become better at saving money as a result." Here's an example of a tight little speech that takes less than two minutes to share:

When you look at my credit report, I want you know that you'll see a bankruptcy there. It's not something I'm proud of, but because of an illness, I ended up with bills for $100,000. I felt terrible about having to declare bankruptcy, but I had no choice. I've increased my insurance coverage and savings so that this will never happen again. I certainly learned a painful lesson, but that's all behind me now.

Keeping some debt: How it helps and hurts

As part of your bankruptcy rights, you can request to keep some of your debt if you can show the court that you can afford to pay it. What? After all that trouble to relieve yourself of the terrible burden? Isn't that sort of like going through a knock-down divorce and remarrying your spouse? Why would you do that to yourself?

Beware of solicitations generated by your bankruptcy filing

After you declare bankruptcy, you'll likely face a flurry of solicitations and telemarketing calls from companies that receive notices of your filing. Many businesses use these bankruptcy notices as mailing lists for the high-cost credit products they're selling.

Be very careful of solicitations you receive following a bankruptcy filing. Read all the fine print and be suspicious of a company anxious to give you a new start. You're very vulnerable, both from a personal as well as a financial perspective. This may be a good time to opt out of the credit bureau and direct-marketing mailing programs that a lot of solicitors use to send you those preapproved offers. It wouldn't hurt to make sure you're in the Federal Trade Commission's National Do Not Call Registry as well (to register, go to www.donotcall.gov).

If you want your name and address removed from mailing lists obtained from the main consumer credit-reporting agencies, go to www.optoutprescreen.com or call 888-567-8688. The Direct Marketing Association can provide information about opting out of lists produced by companies that subscribe to their mail and telephone preference services. Contact them at the following addresses:

Direct Marketing Association Mail Preference Service P.O. Box 643 Carmel, NY 10512

Direct Marketing Association Telephone Preference Service P.O. Box 1559 Carmel, NY 10512

Include the following information with your request:

✔ Your first, middle, and last name (including Jr., Sr., III, and so forth)

✔ Your current address

✔ Your home phone number (only for the telephone preference service)

Believe it or not, there are some benefits to keeping some debt (and its associated credit lines). This is often referred to as *reaffirmation*. For starters, having some ready credit available when you walk out of the courthouse may be a good idea. Also a chunk of your credit score is based on longevity of accounts. Keeping an old account may help with the score-rebuilding process.

If you decide to keep some of your debt, make sure that you really *can* afford to pay and that the terms of the card, including your original unused credit limit, don't change going forward because of the bankruptcy.

Reaffirmations may not be the good deal they seem. A friend who declared bankruptcy was persuaded to reaffirm one debt so he could still have access to credit in his post-bankruptcy world. The card issuer reduced his credit line to the amount of the debt and raised his interest rate to the maximum. The result: He had no credit line left available to use and was stuck with a huge interest payment he couldn't afford. And after the first month, fees pushed him over his limit, so he began getting over-limit fees as well. And the creditor laughed all the way to the bank.

Working to repair your credit score

Your credit score is likely to suffer dramatically from a bankruptcy. The better your score originally, the more it will drop. If you had terrible credit before, a filing may not cause such a big drop. Either way, you'll likely have a very low score.

Now that your credit score has been decimated by bankruptcy, you want to take steps to repair it as best you can. In Chapter 5, I explain what factors influence your credit score. Here's how those factors are influenced by a bankruptcy:

- ✓ **Paying on time:** If you've gone bankrupt, this category may be heavily impacted. I say *may* be, because nearly half of all bankruptcies happen with no prior delinquencies. So you may have a long record of paying on time, with no delinquencies — just a bankruptcy. The more early problems you had, the lower your score will be.

- ✓ **Amount and proportion of credit used:** This category will also be affected. If you go bankrupt, you'll be closing most of your accounts — or your lenders will. Your available credit will drop to $0 in most cases.

- ✓ **The length of time you've been using credit:** Here again, your score will be damaged, because the history on your open accounts — if any remain open — will be shortened as a result of closing so many accounts.

✔ **The variety of accounts:** Chances are, you'll be left with only secured debt such as mortgages, student loans, or car loans. All your revolving and retail accounts may be gone, which means you won't have the variety of accounts that helps to boost your credit score.

✔ **The number and types of accounts you've opened recently:** After the bankruptcy, you may have more activity here than usual as you attempt to reestablish your credit. And your score will fall. (The more accounts you've opened recently, the lower your score.)

Keeping this in mind, a helpful tactic is to take steps to improve your credit in these five areas. And — don't forget — creditors don't necessarily report to all three of the credit bureaus. Now more than ever, you want to make sure that your "good" creditor experiences get on *all* the credit reports out there. Ask your lenders to report all your information to all three bureaus. If they don't, you can either try to get credit from someone who does, or you can ask the bureaus to use the information you send in to them (although there may be a fee involved).

Follow up on these tips, as well, in order to up that credit score as much as you can during the life of your bankruptcy:

✔ **Keep one or two of your older and lower-balance cards or lines open by reaffirming them.** See the preceding section for more information.

✔ **Apply for a secured credit card.** This type of account uses a deposit of yours to secure or guarantee that the payment will be made. They're reported to the credit bureaus as any other credit card would be.

✔ **Open a passbook installment loan, and then borrow against it to demonstrate that you can make those fixed payments on time every month.**

Establishing new credit

Yes, you can probably get new credit soon after you come out of bankruptcy. In fact, establishing some new lines of credit could be the first step in improving your credit score. You'll face some new challenges as you pursue new credit opportunities — you'll discover that the best loans at the most attractive terms and interest rates may not be available to you. Instead, you may discover you're being pursued by loan-shark types that make Jaws look like a guppy.

I caution you to be extra-careful about committing to new lines of credit. Not only are you a target for unscrupulous lenders who specialize in post-bankruptcy loans, but — now more than ever — you're vulnerable to slipping back into an out-of-control borrowing situation. You don't want to get trapped in debt again. New credit is okay, as long as it's part of your plan to rebuild your rating and you're 100 percent confident you can pay it off.

Moving Forward from Bankruptcy

After you have a bankruptcy on your credit report, a number of things become more complicated for you — I mention them earlier in this chapter under "Adding up the pluses and minuses." The good news though is that you have a chance to make a new start and a better life for you and your family. I strongly suggest that you begin your new life with a plan and some help. Without a plan, making the same mistakes is easier than you may think.

Coming up with a game plan

Moving forward with a plan is very different from moving forward *without* one. Although plans may not always work exactly as you want, they help you realize when you're drifting and give you direction, motivation, and the tools to achieve your financial ends.

Begin by paying close attention to the post-bankruptcy education class you must attend as the springboard for your future. Then, if you didn't get one the first time you went to the credit-counseling agency (as you were required to do before filing for bankruptcy), work with your counselor to develop a detailed spending plan complete with goals.

A credit counselor will work with you to craft a spending plan that not only fits your current needs but allows you to set aside money for emergency savings and savings for those goals you want to achieve in the future. This will tell you how much money you can comfortably spend each month and help you to make sure that you're spending only on those things that you've consciously decided to spend your money on. No impulse buying for you. That money will be allocated to other choices you make — like a college fund, a vacation fund, or a retirement account.

Enlisting the help of a financial planner

Take your spending plan to a financial planner. Armed with this plan, you can work with a certified financial planner (CFP) or chartered financial consultant (ChFC) and lay out a savings and investment plan for your future. You'll start small, but with a plan in hand and goals to guide you, in no time you'll be moving forward to a brighter future for you and your family.

Good sources for locating a planner are the friends, relatives, and co-workers. If you're an orphan and have no friends, or even if you do, the attorney you used in the bankruptcy process may be a source of a good referral for you. Planners love referrals and are more apt to be patient with an existing customer referral while you acquire a nest egg.

Healing with time

No one can predict whether new laws or economic conditions will restrict future credit standards even more. Credit availability tends to swing like a pendulum from easy to difficult and then back again. Nevertheless, you can trust that by developing good credit habits, you can recover from the devastation that bankruptcy may have dealt. As time goes on and you continue to pay your bills promptly and establish new credit, the effect of your bankruptcy will diminish. Each month, it will move a little farther into the past and count for less on your credit report.

As with *Monopoly,* you're in this game for a long time. You *can* recover from landing on Boardwalk if you build up your savings and stay in the game.

Part IV
Transforming Your Credit from Bad to Beautiful

The 5th Wave   By Rich Tennant

"You have the first case of identity theft I've ever seen where the thieves actually returned the identity because the credit was so bad."

In this part . . .

Whether your credit has suffered some setbacks or you're just beginning to build a credit history, this part can help you move from ugly or nonexistent credit to attractive credit in the shortest time possible. I concentrate on long-term solutions that work rather than short-term tricks that can come unwound when you least want them to. My advice is the difference between real beauty versus a lot of makeup for the ladies and growing real hair versus wearing a toupee for the guys! This book is packed with chapters that address building — or rebuilding — a positive credit history and score.

It includes a chapter on creating a winning spending plan (or budget), which is the foundation for real credit beauty. You discover how a simple, useful, even fun financial tool allows you to spend with confidence while saving for the goals that you've set. I show you how to plan for and control damage when one of many major life events brings the possibility to wreak havoc on your credit — including marriage, divorce, illness, unemployment, education, or death of a spouse — and I reveal the secrets to getting through them with your credit strong. Finally, I set you straight on what you can and should be doing to avoid becoming a victim of identify theft, and I tell you how to avoid the damage it can cause if left untreated.

Chapter 12

Getting Your Credit Back in Good Shape

*H*aving good credit can open up doors of opportunity whereas having bad credit can close doors or at least make it harder to get through them. Getting your credit back in good shape is, therefore, something you want to do as quickly as possible. Exercising is a way of shaping your body; improving the shape of your credit takes just as much motivation and patience. You'll be more likely to stick to it if you have specific, self-serving, and enjoyable goals in mind when working to get into better credit shape. Credit — like exercise — is a means to an end, a tool and nothing more. Building up your credit for no purpose is dull. Credit with a purpose is exciting!

Like a fitness program that transforms your body into a healthier, more attractive *you,* building or improving your credit record is a tool that helps you achieve your life goals: taking a once-in-a-lifetime or annual vacation, retiring, or sending your kids to college (or anywhere for that matter). Identifying those goals is your first step. You don't have to lay out your whole future in financial terms, but taking a peek at least five years into the future is an excellent place to start — and it's easy and fun to boot!

This chapter is dedicated to helping you improve your credit and boost your credit score. Consider it your own fiscal fitness plan, designed to help you prevent those unwanted credit negatives from adding up. Allow me to serve as your personal trainer. Time to lace up those sneakers and get to work!

Figuring Out Your Financial Goals

Some people think of credit as enabling them to spend more money for the stuff they want when they want it, which is usually right now. Well, they're right *and* they're wrong. Credit doesn't put more money in your pocket. Having a credit card with a $5,000 limit doesn't mean that you have $5,000 more to spend. It *does* mean that you can spend $5,000 you haven't earned yet (and, heaven forbid, may never earn) today with the promise that you will pay it back tomorrow. Credit is borrowing against the future or, as I'm fond of saying, "spending tomorrow's money today."

Problems often arise, however, when you spend *more* of tomorrow's money today than you will be able to repay. The government is the only entity I can think of that can get away with this, and even then I'm not sure it's a great idea. But in your case, spending *some* of tomorrow's money today can actually help you lead a better life now — as long as you're spending those future dollars on things you've decided *you* want rather than things *someone else* wants to sell to you.

A good example is buying a house. If you had to wait until you saved up, say, $200,000 to purchase a house in cash, you may be ready for assisted living before you moved into your first home. Borrowing on future income to move in today makes sense and may well improve the quality of your life for years to come. On the other hand, buying a $200,000 Ferrari on borrowed money may be a mistake. Chances are you're buying the Ferrari because you were sold on the idea by some clever marketing campaign or plan.

This gets me to the concept of your goals. Everyone I know who sells a product has a plan to get you to buy it. It is because of a *plan* that milk in a convenience store is always at the opposite end of the store from the door. It is because of a *plan* that candy at the checkout counter is placed low where kids will see it and ask parents to buy it for them.

What are your financial goals? If you don't have any, then like it or not, believe it or not, you'll end up following someone else's plan and you may end up sleeping in that Ferrari you bought instead of a house — until they tow it away for nonpayment, that is.

Setting some goals is easy. Just keep these steps in mind:

1. **Do a little prep work.**

   Set aside an evening or a weekend afternoon, sit down with your partner or alone (if you're single) without distraction, and look into the future. No need to pull out the crystal ball or Ouija board. Simply sketch out what you want the future to look like. Consider the short term (generally from a few months up to a year) and the long term (one year and beyond). Your goals may include such things as getting a car (maybe the Ferrari fits here), buying a home, having a family, saving for college or weddings, or going on a fabulous vacation. In no time, you'll be having a ball as you imagine doing all those things you've always wanted to do.

2. **As you identify your goals, write them down.**

   Documenting your dreams is important because it makes them more real. Better yet, cut out pictures from magazines or newspapers that illustrate your goals. Maybe a picture of a big cruise ship or a tropical island surrounded by blue waters or, yes, that Ferrari.

Now you've taken the first critical step toward creating a successful plan for yourself: You've established a reason to save some portion of your income. If you have a partner, you have some shared goals to work toward. And you have the motivation to get your credit standing back on track to help achieve those goals. Believe it or not, achieving your goal is generally not the problem. Knowing where you want to go — and, for couples, agreeing on a mutual goal — is the trickiest part.

 Take the list you made to create your plan and keep it for reference when things get a little rocky. It'll be a big help in getting through difficult periods (for example, when something *not* on your list of goals is calling your name).

Selecting the Best Tools for Cleaning Up Your Credit

Now that you've established where you're going, the next step is to open up the big chest of credit tools and select which ones will best work for you to build your financial goals. This section focuses on the following three credit tools you'll want to become very familiar with:

- ✔ A plan for spending, saving, and credit building
- ✔ Copies of your credit reports
- ✔ Your FICO score

Crafting your spending plan

Unless you're independently wealthy or you make a huge amount of money and just can't seem to spend it all, you need a spending plan. A spending plan, which will help you take care of today's responsibilities and tomorrow's goals, has three components:

✔ **Living expenses:** Your daily, weekly, and monthly financial commitments — from groceries and lunch money to rent or mortgage. Also consider those nonessential frivolities that crop up — your daily dose of designer coffee or the occasional shopping spree.

✔ **Savings for financial goals:** This is where you account for the vacation, the college education, the dream house — or the Ferrari.

✔ **Emergency fund:** An emergency fund covers those unexpected (and usually unpleasant) life events, such as a medical expense or job loss. Saving for that unexpected emergency is as critical as saving for a desired goal. If you don't have an emergency fund — between three and six months of living expenses — when the emergency comes along, the money will come from one of two sources: the future (as in spending tomorrow's money today) or your savings (as in the money you were setting aside for that Ferrari).

Adding up your income

Here's how a spending plan works: You identify all your household income — that's the money coming into the house from salaries, tips, overtime, bonuses, royalties, all that stuff. Be sure to consider your payroll deductions (such as money you're putting into a retirement plan) as income.

Saving in your company retirement account makes sense, especially if your employer is contributing a matching amount to the fund. Plus, saving for retirement probably ties into one of your goals (unless you plan to die at your desk).

Tallying your expenses

After you have the income part down on paper or in your computer, do the same with your expenses — making sure to include a savings category as an expense for each of the financial goals you listed earlier. The best way to manage this goal-based savings is to estimate how far in the future the goal is, what the goal will cost, and what you'll have to put aside each month to cover the expense in time.

For example, say you want to take a cruise on your wedding anniversary three years from now. The cost is $3,600 for the two of you. That's 36 months at $100 a month. If you can't afford the $100 a month, postpone the cruise for a year and save $75 a month — or take a cheaper cruise and still go in three years. The next time you find yourself standing before the flat-screen HDTV at the mall, your picture of the future will be in clear focus: the cruise or the TV — but not both.

Taking into account your existing debts

Don't forget to set aside money to pay your existing debts, such as credit cards and car loans. You may need to tweak your plan a time or two so the numbers and time frame for your goals reconcile. But you're now more firmly in control of your financial future. From here on, you make the decisions about what money goes to what categories — not those marketing guys.

On the CD included with this book are forms that help with setting up a spending plan. In Chapter 13, I get into more detail on budgeting for your future.

Paying attention to your credit report and credit score

Credit is an essential tool in achieving your future goals. If your credit isn't in decent shape, you'll be paying more for everything you plan to finance. And that difference could be tens or hundreds of thousands of dollars.

Order a copy of your credit report from each of the three credit-reporting bureaus. The Fair and Accurate Credit Transactions Act (also known as the FACT Act or FACTA) now requires the three major credit bureaus to provide you with a free copy of your credit report once each year. Get a copy of your report from *each* of the three bureaus — they often contain differing information. (See Chapter 5 for information on how to get your reports.)

When you get your credit reports, read them over and make sure that the information is accurate and complete and that there are no expired items that should be taken off. Chapter 7 provides information on how to scrutinize your credit report and fix any errors that you find.

Steve Bucci's theory of good-enough credit

I often advocate the concept of *good-enough credit* as opposed to *perfect credit*. Your credit standing, which is represented by your credit score, is a reflection of your life in financial terms. Lose your job, get a divorce, suffer an illness — the fallout from all these life events shows up on your credit report and affects your credit score one way or another. Late payments and too much borrowing activity are some of the symptoms that may appear in your credit data. Although these events may lower your score to a degree, you shouldn't be driven to aspire to a perfect 850 (or 990 if you're using VantageScore). Your life isn't perfect (just ask your mother-in-law), so don't expect your credit history to be perfect either. Again, credit is a means to an end. As long as your credit score remains good enough to get what you need and want, you're in good stead to pursue your financial goals. No need to stay up nights worrying if your credit score has dropped from 745 to 744.

A bad credit score can cost a lot in extra payments. For example, say you bought a house for $300,000 at a 30-year fixed rate with a down payment of 20 percent. If your credit score was 579 instead of 760, you would have nearly twice the interest rate and pay $291,960 more in interest over the life of your loan. That may even be enough for that red Ferrari!

Generally, negative items stay on your credit report for seven years. The most notable exceptions are:

- ✔ Student loan defaults, which remain until they're paid
- ✔ Overdue tax debts, which stay until resolved
- ✔ Child support defaults, which stay posted until cleared up
- ✔ Bankruptcy, which remains on your report for up to ten years

Positive account information will stay on your credit report for much longer. Some positive trade lines continue to be reported for 10, 20, or even 30 years.

Using Small-Ticket Purchases to Build Credit

Because a lot of your score is based on using credit and making payments on time, I recommend using smaller purchases to get back in good standing more quickly. Why does making small purchases work so well? Because each item costs less (taking less of a bite out of your budget), and you'll have more purchases reported to the credit bureaus as well.

Major bank cards will certainly report your activity to the credit bureaus. Some store cards and credit-union cards only report to one bureau — or they may not report at all. To be sure your credit purchases are being reported and scored, call the customer-service number for your card and ask to which bureau(s) they report.

Creditors who don't report to the bureaus

Why doesn't every creditor report your history to all three of the credit bureaus? Because every time they send data on you to the bureau, they have to pay a fee. Some lenders don't think this is worth the expense. They may still order a credit report before approving your loan or credit card, but they want to save as much profit as they can. Typically, these non-reporters may include

- ✔ Credit unions
- ✔ Utilities
- ✔ Tradesmen
- ✔ Doctors
- ✔ Hospitals
- ✔ Local finance companies
- ✔ Landlords
- ✔ Insurance companies

Pick up some extra points on your credit score by following a simple plan when paying down balances. What you want to achieve for credit-score maximization is not having any cards that are above 50 percent of their credit limit. Some people suggest that you pay down balances based on interest rate to save more money on overall payments. Others say that paying off smaller accounts gives you a feeling of accomplishment and, therefore, you're more likely to achieve your overall goal. You get to make the choice about how you do this. My only advice is that *you* make the choice and don't let the first bill that shows up get the extra payment by chance.

Make a list of the smaller-balance accounts (under $200) and then a list of the larger-balance accounts (over $200). Next to each item, note the minimum payment and the credit limit. Starting with the smaller accounts, allocate available cash to the minimum payments first. Go through the entire list. Then with what money you still have available, go back to the smallest account and work on paying it down to 45 percent of the credit limit. This will get some great positive data in your credit report. As you pay down the smaller accounts, you'll work through each account toward the larger accounts. The big ones will take an extended amount of time to pay down to about 45 percent of their credit limit. This approach not only allows you to regain control of your accounts but helps you maximize your credit score, because accounts that exceed 50 percent of the limit count against you. When you're at the 45 percent limit on your cards, you may want to allocate more money to the highest-interest-rate cards.

If you don't have a major bank credit card, you may want to try a secured card. You can get one without a fee if you shop around. The secured card differs from the regular Visa or MasterCard in that you maintain a balance in a savings account equal to your credit limit (some may allow more) to guarantee your payment. Secured-card activity is reported just as any other credit-card activity is reported, and it affects your credit score in the same way — so it can be a great option if you're trying to build credit.

If you get too close to your credit max, as defined by each lender, this may not only decrease your credit score but also increase your overall risk profile. The result can be a rise in interest rates that will curl your hair! Often up to 30 percent and sometimes even more.

Generally, if you make all your payments on time for a year, you should have enough of a positive payment history to get an unsecured credit card.

Turning Big-Ticket Purchases into Good Credit History

Big-ticket creditors — those lenders who specialize in expensive products or services — typically report to the credit bureaus. The reasoning is simple;

they have a lot more to lose if they lend based on inaccurate information, so they want to see as complete and accurate a file as possible.

Making a major purchase may give your credit score a boost for two reasons:

✔ **When you make a major purchase, the lenders are more likely to extend credit in the form of a secured installment loan.** *Secured* means you have pledged collateral or the item you purchased as security for the loan. If you default on the loan, the lender repossesses the security you pledged — in other words, you don't get to keep it. Adding some secured credit to the variety of other types of credit you use, such as revolving credit, helps your credit score.

✔ **The payment will be the same each month.** When it comes to credit scoring, this equal monthly payment is an opportunity for the people who come up with your score to discover more about your creditworthiness. Your stability and ability to make a set payment at a set time every month can be measured. This scenario is different from paying on a credit card, where you can vary your payment up or down to a minimum, depending on how your month is going financially. Adhering to a regular payment schedule also indicates that you can handle what may be a higher limit than you may have on a store, gas, or credit-card account.

Examples of big-ticket items that may enhance your credit activity are

✔ A home mortgage

✔ An automobile (or boat)

✔ A student loan

✔ Furniture and appliances

This section takes a closer look at some pointers you need to consider when buying big-ticket items.

Leveraging your mortgage for good credit history

Owning a home and paying your mortgage can help build your credit in a few different ways. Credit grantors look at your credit report and credit score in order to rate your lendability, but they ultimately rely on you to be responsible for making the payments. Here is where the three Cs of credit really show up: Character, collateral, and capacity are really what credit scoring and lending are all about.

A mortgage on your report tells the reader and the scorer that you have all three of the Cs and that some lender was so sure about you that she was willing to lend you a huge amount of money. The report indicates a large installment loan with fixed payments for a long period of time. All these items favorably impact your credit score. The opposite is also true. Because of the huge amount of money involved and the seriousness of a long-term commitment, a mortgage default counts for a large negative on your credit history. A foreclosure, even more.

A mortgage is secured by the house, so if you default, the lender forecloses and takes the house back to pay off the loan. A foreclosure ends up costing the lender an average of tens of thousands of dollars when all is said and done. But don't feel too bad for the lender: *You'll* be held responsible in one way or another for any loss on the loan.

Home-equity lines of credit and home-equity loans are a popular subset of traditional mortgages. They're good ways to access money at a low interest rate. They also represent new and additional borrowing on your credit report. For example, you could have taken out a big mortgage and had only one lender report one loan to the bureaus. If you use a home-equity loan or line of credit in addition to your mortgage, you're using the same collateral (your home), and you're borrowing the same amount as you would have with a bigger mortgage, but with more than one loan. Thus, more than one item gets reported to the credit bureau each month, building more positive information in the same time period.

There is a hitch, however: As you stack more debt on your home or your home decreases in value, you may reach the point where you and your castle are *upside-down* (that is, you owe more on your home than it's worth). So, who cares? You have a 30-year mortgage and by then everything will be cool. But what if your boss offers you the general manager's job in a city too far to commute? Or what if the company lays you off and you either have to move to find work or downsize to reduce your mortgage commitment? Or what if your adjustable rate mortgage resets and you can't afford the payment anymore? You would then be in the position of needing to sell the house but not at a price that would satisfy the loans attached to your home. If you didn't have the money to make up the difference, you could face a potential foreclosure. (See Chapter 9 for more information about how to avoid a foreclosure.)

Purchasing a vehicle

Because of the very large price tags on most cars, most people require some financing in order to afford one. Such financing typically comes in the form of a two- to five-year installment loan. Anyone lending you the amount of money it takes to buy a car receives data from and reports data to the credit bureaus. When lenders go on the hook for that much money, they want to be protected if you get in a cash squeeze at your end. Most car loans are secured by the car.

Lines versus loans

What's the difference between a home-equity loan and a home-equity line of credit? Here's the scoop: A *home-equity loan* is for a specified chunk of cash — say, $10,000. When you get the home-equity loan, you get the ten big ones to put down on that car (or whatever else you want to buy) and you have an installment payment due every month usually at a set interest rate for a set amount of time. In the old days, these were called *second mortgages* and they were a sure sign you were on the path to ruin. Today, they're called *equity products* and it seems everyone has at least one. And, yes, they are still a sign that you could be on the road to ruin!

With a *home-equity line of credit,* you get a line of credit, maybe for $10,000, maybe for $20,000, depending on how much you want to have available just in case you need it. You don't have to take any money out of the line at all, unless you have a use for it. It just sits there like a wallflower at a dance, waiting for you to ask it for a tango. Generally, you have a set period of time (called a *draw period*) when you can access the line of credit and a set period before which you have to pay it back. So, until you use it all, the money is available and just sits there through the remainder of the draw period for free (or sometimes a small annual fee).

When you do draw money from the line, you generally have the option of paying it off anytime without a prepayment penalty. The loan terms often allow you to pay only the interest and not the principal (an interest-only loan); the principal is due at the end of a time set in the loan agreement. Or you can choose to pay both interest and principal until the debt is paid off. Some loans allow you to decide what you're going to pay on a month-by-month basis. Pay principal and interest one month, but only interest the next. You decide.

If you're debating using equity in your home to purchase a car, be careful. Using a home-equity loan to buy a car may offer a tax advantage (with tax-deductible interest), but if you default on that home-equity loan, your car won't be repossessed — instead, your home may be foreclosed on.

Be sure to pay off the loan you used to buy your old car before you buy your next new one! Some people keep old car loans on their home equity lines long after the cars are gone and just keep adding new balances without paying off the old ones. This can lead to an unpleasant surprise when interest rates go up or you need to sell your home.

Weighing the pluses and minuses of leases

Leasing is an increasingly popular way to get a car. Please note, I didn't say *buy* a car, because that doesn't happen in a lease arrangement. Consider a lease a long-term rental. Leases are popular because they generally require only a small down payment — or perhaps none at all. Plus, they're a tax write-off if you're a businessperson. Signing the lease commits you to a stream of payments for an extended period of time, so this activity is normally reported to the credit bureaus.

Leases are very difficult and costly to terminate. Unlike with a car loan, you can't sell the car and pay off the loan. With a lease, you owe all the payments and you can't terminate without making all the payments first.

If you're an active-duty serviceperson called away, you can get out of your car lease. Chapter 6 covers this in more detail. For the law itself, check out the Servicemembers Civil Relief Act (SCRA) on the CD.

Steering clear of upside-down loans

The term sounds as uncomfortable as it is. Basically, in an *upside-down loan,* you owe more than the item securing the loan is worth. Avoid being upside-down in a car loan — or any secured loan (upside-down house mortgages work similarly) if you can help it. Any repossession or default will show negatively on your credit report and your score will fall.

An upside-down loan can hurt you when you want or need to sell the car and stop making payments. If you owe $10,000 on a car loan, and the value of the car is $7,000, you have to come up with the $3,000 difference or you can't sell the car. If you're in a car accident and the car is totaled, the insurance company will only pay what the car was worth — you get to pay the rest.

This situation becomes worse if your financial situation changes and you can't make the payments on the car and the creditor repossesses the car (whether they get you to agree to a voluntary repossession or do it the old-fashioned way — when you aren't looking). The car is worth $7,000 — but that was a retail value. The lender will likely sell the car at auction where the creditor only gets $5,000. The fees on the repossession were $2,000 between the tow guy, the sales commission to the auctioneer, and the attorney's fees. So you get credited with $3,000 against the $10,000 you owe. Now you owe $7,000 in a lump sum to settle your account — and you have no car in the bargain.

Paying student loans to repair your credit

Because of the increasingly unaffordable price tag on higher education, more and more people have student loans. Student loans make a lot of sense to lenders: Although the person responsible for repayment may have no income at the time of the loan, the lender knows that good income is on the horizon, and the loan will soon be paid back. But what really makes these loans attractive to the lenders is that they can't lose. Almost all student loans are guaranteed by the U.S. government. The bank gets a fee for origination of the loan and for servicing it, but losses are Uncle Sam's problem.

If you have a student loan, chances are it appears on your credit report. It may also be reported more than once. Why? Each loan, be it on a semester or yearly basis, is reported as a separate loan for each enrollment period. So four years of loans add either four or eight loans to your credit report. If you make payments and/or file for benefits on time, your credit report will reflect a positive history and add to your credit score. This can be a lot of good news for your credit report.

Conversely, if you end up in default on your student loans, you'll see a lot of negative marks on your credit report and credit score from all those individual loan entries. Any missed payments are reported to the bureaus, and you'll be subject to the full range of collection activity just like you would with any other loan.

If you've consolidated your loans after graduation, they'll show up on your report as one loan. (*Consolidating* is the process of refinancing all your individual loans into a single loan. The original loans are marked "paid in full," and the interest rate is often lower and the repayment term is typically longer for the consolidated loan than for the individual loans. The net result is the convenience of a single, lower monthly payment.) With consolidated loans, you typically have a number of different repayment options, including paying the same amount each month, paying less now and more later, and payment plans that change with your income.

Student loans are not secured with collateral in the normal sense of the word. When you're in default on a student loan, you can't defer payment of the loan. In fact, you may have to pay it all at once unless you come up with an acceptable repayment scheme. Additionally, you won't be eligible for further student aid, your school may withhold your transcripts, state and federal income tax refunds may be used to offset the loan amounts, and your wages (when you get that job) may be attached or garnished. Finally, student loans are not dischargeable in a bankruptcy (see Chapter 11 for more info).

Understanding Why Some Debt Is Good

No doubt about it: Getting into debt *can* get you into trouble. And if you're reading this book, chances are you've had some experience with that sort of trouble — or you're being proactive and hoping to avert a potential credit disaster. Although debt certainly has a downside, borrowing money can also do a great deal of good for your credit record. In the following sections, I tell you how.

Achieving goals with the help of credit

Debt allows you to take advantage of those opportunities and experiences that enhance your life and create joy and fulfillment: that dream home with the white picket fence, the around-the-world cruise, the Ivy League school — yes, even that Ferrari. When you can put your sights on your life goals and develop a spending plan that allows you to get there in the time frame you've set, you've found the secret to the true value of credit.

Sending a message to potential lenders

If you had no debt — ever — then you'd never have used credit and wouldn't have a credit report or credit score. Let's face it: In today's world, it's hard to live without credit. Most people need credit to buy those big-ticket items — vehicles, homes, higher education — not to mention rely on it in the case of life's emergencies. Creating a positive credit history — a credit reputation, of sorts — says to prospective lenders that you're a good credit risk. Showing that you can handle debt puts you in a position to attract creditors who offer favorable rates and terms.

Not only is using credit wisely a good thing for your lifestyle, it gives prospective creditors the opportunity to show you the respect you deserve based on your past performance. Lenders prefer to loan money to individuals who've borrowed before, who can show that they understand the commitment of credit, and who have a history of prompt payment and reliable follow-through. In fact, given the choice between lending to someone who's *never* borrowed before and an individual with a history of debt — even with a couple of blips on the report — my guess is most creditors will go for the credit veteran over the rookie.

Think of it this way: Say your two 20-year-old nephews ask to borrow your car. One has never driven before, the other has a four-year history, but with a parking ticket last year. Who would you pick?

Giving people a sense of how you handle responsibility

If you've had no debt, and therefore have no credit history, you may find yourself disadvantaged in other ways. If a prospective employer checks your record and comes up empty, they'll probably see this as strange — and they won't be able to use your credit history as a positive factor when trying to decide whether to hire you. Without that credit record, they miss one additional tool in comparing your application to those of their other applicants.

The same holds true when it comes to renting an apartment, applying for insurance, and so on. When you have no track record, you represent an unknown risk.

To Use a Cosigner or Not? That's the Question

Getting a loan by having someone cosign for you is very much a triple-edged sword. *Cosigning* means having another party (usually with better credit) sign along side you to guarantee future payments if you default, drop dead, or are abducted by aliens. As long as your lender reports to the bureaus, each time you make a payment on time and for the right amount, you'll both accumulate more positive items. As time goes by, this will help offset earlier negative items on your report. Like snow falling on the ground, the good stuff will cover all the murk underneath.

Although a cosigned loan can help you get positive info on your credit report, I consider it a triple-edged sword. The following are my reservations:

- ✔ **Edge #1: You may borrow when you shouldn't.** If a professional lender is reluctant to give you a loan, there may be good reason. So now the cosigner, who is not a professional and who likely has emotional ties clouding their judgment, decides to guarantee your loan.

- ✔ **Edge #2: The cosigner is at risk if you default.** The cosigner is fully responsible for the payment. If it takes 60 days for the cosigner to be informed that you haven't paid on time, the cosigner's credit gets dinged, as does yours.

- ✔ **Edge #3: A default could destroy a relationship.** If your ability to pay off the loan is compromised and you incur late fees or penalties, or you default on the loan, your cosigner is fully liable and her credit score may be damaged. Plus, she'll have to assume liability for the loan. This — no surprise — just may be the end of your relationship . . . but not the loan obligation.

My advice: If you're going to ask a friend or relative to cosign a loan, make sure the life of the loan is for a short period of time. Also, put your agreement in writing to make it official and to make sure you both understand what you are agreeing to.

A final word of caution to the *good*-credit partner: There is probably a good reason that a lender doesn't want to give your other half a loan. You need to understand that reason and then decide if you want to guarantee the debt. The worst of all possibilities: You end up on the loan, but not as a co-owner of the property. In my counseling days, I had a client who had cosigned on a car loan for his sweetie. After she got the wheels, she hit the road, and the collectors were all over him for payment. ***Remember:*** Love may be blind, but it doesn't have to be stupid.

Community-property states: Till debt do us part?

Currently 9³/₄ states are community property states: Arizona, California, Idaho, Louisiana, Nevada, New Mexico, Texas, Washington, and Wisconsin. In these states, each spouse is liable for the debts accumulated by the other during the marriage, even if they don't know about them. So particularly in these states, using your spouse as a cosigner or joint borrower is not a big issue. The one-half state is, of course, the ever-unique Alaska. In 1998, Alaska enacted The Alaska Community Property Act.

Couples must "elect in," partially or completely. For example, a couple may elect to have only certain assets characterized as Alaska community property. I recently visited Alaska and found the state to be refreshingly different. In fact, they have a saying that addresses the larger numbers of men than women. They say that the "odds are good, but the goods are odd." Enough said. My quarter state is the Territory of Puerto Rico, as American as chicken and rice, but not actually a state — yet.

Chapter 13

Budgeting for Your Future

- -

- -

*O*f all the topics in this book — or any other book that deals with the ins and outs of personal finance and its effect on credit — no subject is more basic and nothing is more important to the ultimate fate of your credit report and credit score than budgeting. Based on the lack of attention that this topic gets from lenders, financial planners, and even schools, you might conclude that all Americans are born with a financial gene that innately allows them to sense when they're overspending or under-saving.

Unfortunately, nothing could be further from the truth. The popular American misconception seems to be that credit can take the place of savings. The fact is that you may use credit in place of savings, but only for a limited period of time — and at a cost. When I say *cost,* I'm not just talking about the cost of interest or the fees involved in using credit. The largest cost comes when you can't attain a dream because the money you need is already committed to paying a loan.

In this chapter, I show you how budgeting can be a valuable tool that allows you to spend your income the way you want, save enough to be able to afford the goals that you set for yourself and your family, protect and build your credit, and sleep peacefully at night. I walk you through the process of determining how much you spend and where the money is going now, and how you would like to spend your income in the future. You accomplish this task by allocating funds for particular areas of spending that you choose. I help you understand how budgeting and planning can help you get your credit back on track and keep it there. So sharpen your pencil and get out those checkbooks and credit-card records. You have some budgeting to do!

Budgeting: Crafting Your Financial Future

A *budget* (also known as a *spending plan*) is a money-management tool that puts you in control of your spending and keeps you out of credit trouble. It's your personal plan for spending the income you have, building savings, and using credit wisely. A budget can be as detailed or as general as you want. In order to create a budget, you need to know your income and expenses, plus have a general idea of your financial goals over a set period of time. A budget can help you get your financial life back into shape, as well as plan and save successfully for the future.

Many people incorrectly think that budgeting is like dieting, where you don't get to do what you want and have to suffer to achieve a goal. Actually, a budget used effectively has the opposite impact. You get to do *exactly* what *you* want to do. How can this be? You discover how to stay within your income limitations and not waste money on things that aren't important to you or your family.

As I explain in Chapter 12, credit is only a tool. It doesn't give you more money to spend; it simply helps you leverage the money you anticipate having in the future. If you're borrowing to cover emergencies or big-ticket items, you're spending money today that you won't earn until tomorrow.

So, what happens when you get to tomorrow and find that you spent all the money that was supposed to be there yesterday? Nothing pleasant, I can assure you. Many people use credit to extend their incomes and never give a thought to whether they'll be able to pay all their bills when an unexpected expense comes along. Why? Primarily because no one ever told them that another way exists. One that allows you to set and achieve important goals. One that results in reducing debt — not adding to it. One that allows you to provide for family or loved ones without an elevated level of stress. And, yes, one that can significantly improve your credit report and your credit score. The way to achieve all this and more is to design and implement a budget.

Look at this another way: If you couldn't see the speedometer on your car, what would the result be? You might go too slowly — but if you're like most people, you'd go way too fast. You wouldn't think you were speeding, of course, because you wouldn't have any reference points to tell you so. As a result, you could get in a destructive crash — or at least land yourself a speeding ticket.

You may have let your spending get out of control — but a budget serves as your own personal *spendometer,* putting you back in the driver's seat, controlling the direction of your financial future. It allows *you,* not out-of-control spending, to determine the route to your personal financial goals.

Here's a short list of things that a budget can help you do:

- **Reach your financial goals:** Your budget is a compass that keeps you on course, helping you to put aside money to reach your goals. Whether your goals include an exotic vacation, an addition to your home, or a new car, a budget helps you get there.

- **Control your money:** Allocating money for every aspect of your daily life allows you to decide how your money is used and helps you pay your bills on time (35 percent of your FICO Score and 32 percent of your VantageScore). Without a budget, it's easy to spend on things you don't need and that can put you into a position where you must use credit for those things you really *do* need.

- **Live within your means:** You may notice when you begin the budgeting process that your expenses often equal or exceed your income, particularly if you have easy access to credit cards. Bringing spending in line with income is a great way to ensure you keep your balances reasonable and don't accumulate unmanageable debt and damage your credit.

One of the best ways to live within your means is to keep each of your credit card balances below 50 percent of the card's limit to avoid credit score damage. When the balances go above the 50 percent level, it becomes a negative factor in your FICO score.

- **Free up cash:** The best bonus of budgeting is that you get to decide how to spend. Instead of spending all your money on things you don't remember buying or didn't really want or need, a budget gives you the power to make better decisions regarding how your extra money is spent.

- **Focus on common goals:** An effective budgeting process involves the entire family. For example, your children are much more likely to go along with skipping pizza night for several months if they understand that doing so will allow them to go to Disney World! The same is true of your sweetie: If the two of you decide that an addition to your home is your top financial priority, you'll both be on the same page when it comes to making necessary financial adjustments.

- **Prepare for the unexpected:** As part of your budget, you put aside money each month in an emergency savings account. This account covers expenses such as major car repairs, large appliances that need replacing, or unexpected medical bills.

- **Get and stay out of debt:** Because budgeting helps you bring your expenses in line with your income, you stop adding to your debt. In fact, you *decrease* your balances with regular payments.

✔ **Build your credit:** Paying down your debt improves your credit and builds your credit score. Amounts owed including number of accounts with balances, proportion of credit used, and the amount owed on specific types of accounts make up 30 percent of your FICO score and 38 percent of your Vantage credit score.

✔ **Save your sanity:** Gaining control of your money relieves financial stress that could be causing sleepless nights, reduced productivity at work, and even physical symptoms (like headaches or ulcers).

Setting Goals: Making Financial Dreams Come True

Focusing on your financial dreams is the fun part of building a budget, but many people overlook goal setting as a key first step. Many people stumble through life with vaguely defined goals, letting the moment carry them where it will. Well, that's all about to stop for you. The first part of getting control of your finances is to decide what you want to do and when — both long-term and short-term. Don't worry; this process doesn't involve a test, and there are no wrong answers. In fact, you can change your goals as often as you want.

Setting aside the time to plan

Set aside an hour or so — even an entire evening or afternoon — to explore your most treasured dreams. If you're sharing your life with a significant other, involving him or her in the discussion is critical. Heck, make it a date! Over a glass of wine or a steaming cappuccino, curl up on the couch and dare to dream. Or go to an inspiring place — a nearby park, the steps of a monument, a scenic overlook — and let your surroundings stimulate your aspirations.

Wherever you do your planning, use a stack of 3-x-5-inch cards or sticky notes, and write one goal on each card or note. Put a *due date* — the date by which you want to achieve this goal — next to each item. If you're in the mood, you can have some fun with this: Get out the scissors and cut out pictures from magazines, calendars, or other sources to illustrate your goals. These images can be powerful motivators. Put them up on your refrigerator or in a scrapbook that you can refer to as you make your plans.

At this point, don't limit yourself. Dream as big as you want. You've always wanted to retire and cruise around the world? Jot it down. Yearn to go back to school or launch a new career? Add it to the list. Buying a home, owning a sports car, taking a dream trip — this goal-setting stage is your opportunity to indulge yourself in *all* your financial fantasies. Getting them down on paper and discussing, assessing, and prioritizing them is an important part of the process of tailoring your budget to meet your own personal goals.

Be as specific as possible. For example, you may have written down, "Go to Disney World." But keep going: Will you stay in the park or outside? Go for a week — or two? Try to be as specific as possible. Not only does this level of detail give you a clearer target, it keeps your expectations in check.

Thinking long-term, short-term, and everything in between

To keep from being overwhelmed and to make sure you don't miss anything, I suggest that you segment your goals into categories. Some of you may tend to focus on just short- or long-term goals otherwise, depending on which is the most comfortable for you. For the best results I suggest that you use varying time frames. Goals can be divided into four general categories:

- ✔ **Short-term goals** are generally things you want to do within one year. They may include taking that vacation to Disney World, investing in your retirement plan, donating to charity, saving money in your emergency fund, moving into a bigger apartment, buying jewelry or clothes, becoming a member of a local sports club, or reducing your debt.

- ✔ **Intermediate-term goals** are things that require one to five years to accomplish. These might include saving enough money to buy a new car, beginning a family, purchasing new furniture, or paying off your debts.

- ✔ **Long-term goals** are things you don't plan to do until at least five years down the road. These might include saving for your kids' education, starting your own business, buying a home or boat, or retiring.

- ✔ **Life goals** don't have a time frame because you'll probably never *fully* achieve them. These goals aren't necessarily money-driven, but capture the imagination. For example, you might want to be happier. After all, the pursuit of happiness is an American ideal. Imagine what it would take and write it down. Have at least one goal you can pursue that may be unattainable through money. Who knows? You may find it if you look.

As you start thinking about your goals, try to determine whether each goal fits into the short-, mid- or long-term category and make stacks for each category. Pay attention to how many goals you have in each pile. Are all your goals focused on the short term? If so, spend some time thinking a little farther into the future.

Build in at least one or two goals that don't require money, if only to show the kids or your other half that you see the future in other-than-material terms. For example, camping can be almost free — and it's a great exercise in togetherness. Look for other opportunities to work "free" into your future.

Prioritizing your goals

After you've written down all your goals and put them into stacks based on when you want to accomplish them, you need to prioritize. You may not be able to achieve *all* your goals, so you need to determine which ones matter most. To start off, choose a short-term goal that you can attain fairly quickly and easily as your first priority. Doing so gives you the opportunity to see how satisfying reaching a goal can be and also gives you the incentive to keep going for those longer-term goals.

If your goals are too challenging, you may get frustrated. Break down more-difficult or long-term aspirations into stages so you can build on successes as you go along. If a goal calls for you to save a large amount of money, you may want to schedule smaller amounts per year so you don't give up. Be sure to recognize and celebrate each step as you attain it.

If your goal list is very long or requires winning the lottery to achieve, I suggest you recognize that some are more important than others and concentrate on those that you have the means, motive, and opportunity to realistically achieve. Keep the others in the incubator and if the time and conditions are ever right for them to become real, bring them out into your life again.

Any plan requires minor or major tweaking as circumstances change. Building in some checkpoints is helpful in allowing you to adjust. An un-expected bonus can move up a timeline; a layoff can set it back. Adjust your plan accordingly.

Building Your House of Dreams in Seven Steps

After you've set your goals, your next task is to find the money to make them a reality. Here's where the budget comes in. You're not creating a budget to *restrict* your spending, but rather to *channel* it in the direction you want to go. You begin by listing your current income and expenses. You can't decide how much and where to spend until you know how much there is to go around.

Step 1: Figuring out your annual income

Determining your income should be fairly easy. If you earn a salary or work a consistent number of hours every week, you're used to seeing the same figure on your paycheck payday after payday. But some situations are trickier. For example, if you work a service job — you're a waiter, for example — you may rely on tips, which may fluctuate dramatically depending on which shifts you're scheduled. Perhaps your work is seasonal (you're a landscaper or tax accountant, for example) and you bring in more income at certain times of the year. Maybe you have periodic bouts of overtime which affect your income.

Whatever your situation, do your best to gather a good year's worth of income activity. Although you may find it helpful to come up with a monthly average, you still need to be aware of the natural ebbs and flows of your earnings rhythms and alter your budget accordingly.

In addition to your paycheck stubs, don't forget to gather details on other income such as child support, alimony, overtime pay, bonuses, investment income, royalties, or rental-property income. In addition, consider other money sources. Your garage band earns a few bucks playing for weddings and occasional gigs? Your monthly yard sales keep your closets cleared and add a bit of fun money to the household income? Your reputation as a first-rate résumé writer has kept a steady stream of co-workers at your office door? Add it all to your money pot!

You can use Table 13-1 to list all the sources of income you expect each month. List your take-home, or *net,* pay rather than your *gross* pay (your salary before taxes and other deductions). You may also want to list the expenses that are deducted from your paycheck. This can be useful if you think you may be able to reduce or eliminate some. Say you have $400 in federal taxes withheld each month, but you got a $2,400 tax refund last year. You may want to use half of the refund for current expenses by reducing your withholding by $100 a month. This will still leave you a cushion with the tax man, but add some extra cash to your budget. So list any expenses and savings that are deducted directly from your gross pay that you may want to consider reallocating. Add them back into your take-home pay, and then enter the new amount of each deduction as an expense.

Table 13-1   Income Worksheet for _____

Source of Income	Planned	Actual	Difference	
Salary 1				
Salary 2				
Bonus				
Interest				
Dividends				
Child support/alimony				
Rental income				
Gifts				
Deduction changes/other				
Total income	$	$	$	

After you've established all your income sources, come up with an average monthly income. Why monthly? Because most of your major expenses are paid out on a monthly basis — utilities, mortgage or rent, phone, even many charitable contributions are portioned out in monthly increments.

Be sure to use your *take-home* pay — not your *gross* pay — to come up with your monthly income. For example, if you earn $60,000 per year, your gross income is $5,000 per month — but you're only taking home $3,600 or so after Social Security, federal and state taxes, and other deductions are made.

If the difference in gross and net income jars your senses somewhat, carefully consider your deductions. Some deductions, such as Social Security tax, are beyond your control (although if you earn enough to max out your contribution before the year is over — currently, around the $102,000-a-year mark — be sure to account for the extra income you take home after you go over that number). Other deductions, such as your withholdings for federal and state taxes, are worth review. My advice: Don't use tax withholdings as a forced savings plan — you lose out this way. After all, is the government paying you any interest for holding your cash for the year? You can do much better if you allow yourself a $600 to $1,000 annual cushion and adjust your withholding accordingly.

Look at last year's taxes: If your income and deductions are relatively stable, and you got back more than $600 to $1,000, increase your deductions. If you owed money, decrease your deductions to bring your refund into the $600 range. This strategy may improve your cash flow, while avoiding an unpleasant surprise in April.

Step 2: Identifying your annual expenses

After you know your annual income or what's coming in, you need to look at your annual expenses or what's going out — and where it's going. Using your checking- and savings-account statements, credit-card statements, and/or a financial planning program (such as Quicken), write down all the expenses you can identify to figure out what you spend each month.

Determining your monthly spending isn't difficult — though, as with gathering your income information, it may require some scrutiny. Many of your major expenses — mortgage, credit-card bills, utilities, car loans — hit monthly. If you have an expense that occurs other than monthly, prorate it to a monthly amount. For example, a $1,000 homeowner's insurance bill due once a year is $83.33 a month. For frequent yet varying expenses, such as electricity and entertainment, gather several months of history and then determine a monthly average.

Table 13-2 helps you get started. Begin by collecting checkbook registers, receipts, credit-card bills, online statements, and any other financial records you may have. This helps you get the most accurate information. If you don't have complete financial records, use your best estimates to fill in the blanks.

Table 13-2 Expenses Worksheet for _____

Expense	Planned	Actual	Difference
Rent/mortgage			
Property tax			
Renter's/homeowner's insurance			
Home maintenance			
Water			
Sewer			
Garbage			
Gas/oil for heating			
Electric			
Telephone			
Car payment			
Car insurance			
Gasoline			
Car repairs/maintenance			
Clothing			
Groceries/household supplies			
Doctor/dentist			
Prescriptions			
Health insurance			
Life/disability insurance			
Childcare			
Tuition/school expenses			
Child support/alimony			
Personal allowance			
Entertainment			
Eating out/vending			
Cigarettes/alcohol			
Newspapers/magazines			

(continued)

Table 13-2 (continued)

Hobbies/clubs/sports			
Gifts			
Donations			
Work expenses			
Cable/satellite			
Internet connections			
Cell phone			
Student loan			
Other:			
Other:			
Other:			
Total Expenses	$	$	$

If you're like most people, you know where between 80 and 90 percent of your money is spent. But you're likely to find that some fraction of your income inexplicably disappears on unknown items. I call these items "money gobblers" — the small cash expenses you make that never seem to register in your memory, let alone make it to the check register or any account ledger. I've assembled a list of some of these expenses (you may be able to add to this list, and not every item will apply to your life). These are all areas where your money may be flowing out — and each item is something you can save on if you're willing to get creative:

✔ **Allowances:** Your kids will hate me for this, but you don't have to give them set allowances, especially if your own financial situation is tenuous.

✔ **Baby pictures:** You'll be surprised at what great pictures you can snap with your own digital camera. Dress your little one the same way you would if you were going to a fancy studio, drape a pastel-colored bed sheet behind her, and snap away. The shots you get will be even more special because of the time you spent together.

✔ **Babysitting:** See if you can work out a deal with one of your friends or neighbors and watch their kids one day in exchange for them watching yours the next. Or take shameless advantage of the grandparents — most are only too happy to volunteer their services.

✔ **Salon:** Instead of going to a high-priced salon, look in the Yellow Pages for a beauty school in your area. You may be able to get your hair done for free (or for a very small charge), and the attention to detail you get is phenomenal — the students are supervised by teachers and they're working to impress.

✔ **Beer and soda:** For some people, the thought of giving up brewskies or soft drinks may be akin to torture. But when you add up how much money you're spending, the motivation to get your calories elsewhere is great. At the very least, try to reduce your intake of these nonessentials, and when you do drink them, do it at home instead of at high-priced bars and restaurants.

✓ **Fast food and vending machines:** The stuff is bad not only for your body, but also for your wallet. Shop at the grocery store instead; use coupons for amazing savings.

✓ **Books, magazines, newspapers, CDs, and movies:** One of the greatest resources at your disposal is your public library. You can get all the books, magazines, and newspapers you want — free of charge. Most libraries also lend out audio books, music CDs, and movies for free.

✓ **Car washes:** Now, I'm not suggesting that you never wash your car. I'm just suggesting that, when you need to do it, you do it yourself or toss a sponge, some soap, and the hose at your kids and set them loose. They have fun, your car gets a little cleaner (if not flawless), and you save significant dough.

✓ **Cards, gambling, and lottery tickets:** A dollar in the bank (or put toward your credit-card bill) is much more valuable than a dollar spent gambling. End of story.

✓ **Charities:** I'm not suggesting you change your name to Scrooge, but if your own finances are stretched, you need to take care of yourself first. Then, when you're back on your feet, you can think about lending a hand to others. In the meantime, you can give to charities by donating your time. That's just as valuable as a check.

✓ **School fundraisers:** When your neighbor kids come a-knockin', just say no. This falls into the same category as the preceding bullet. If you want to be of help to your local school, you can volunteer at the library, coach a sports team, or lead a scouting troop.

✓ **Cosmetics:** Spending big bucks on makeup when you can't pay the bills doesn't make much sense. You can find inexpensive cosmetics if you look for them. If you have to, splurge on one higher-priced item and make it last.

✓ **Dry cleaning and laundry:** Dry cleaning is a money-eater if ever there was one. Until you're in a better financial situation, stick to clothes you can wash at home. And launder your own shirts instead of sending them out. Your iron will wonder where you've been all these months.

✓ **Entertainment (concerts, movies, sporting events, and so on):** Look for ways to entertain yourself and your family free of charge. Instead of going to a professional baseball game, go out in the yard or to the park and toss a ball around with your kids or your friends. Instead of going to a movie, check out a DVD from the library.

✓ **Film developing:** You can spend a lot of money getting film developed. Save the camera for special occasions, or if you have a digital camera, use that instead and wait to get prints until you have money to spare.

✔ **Health foods:** Eating healthy is important, but health foods can be pricey. Shop the produce department of your grocery store, stick to whole grains and lean meats, and you'll be fine. Go granola when you've paid down your debts.

✔ **Hobbies:** Most hobbies cost money, and although they're fun, so is paying off your debts. Make *that* your new hobby.

✔ **Eating out:** Even if you're eating at fast-food restaurants, eating out costs a lot. You can save big money by preparing your food at home.

✔ **Pets:** If you're in financial trouble, getting a new pet isn't a good idea. (Let me tell you about my free cat!) Even healthy pets cost money, and if your pet gets sick, you're in for even more expense. If you already have pets, stick to the necessities (food, vaccinations, hugs) and avoid the store-bought toys. You can make a rope bone out of old T-shirts or throw a tennis ball around in the yard — all your pet cares about is that you're spending time together.

✔ **Tobacco:** You already know you shouldn't be smoking. Add up the financial costs, and you can see the damage it's doing *beyond* the damage to your health.

✔ **Yard sales:** If your idea of a fun Saturday morning is going from one yard sale to the next looking for bargains, wash the car instead. Most people think they're getting bargains, but they usually end up buying things they don't really need.

You don't have to cut all the preceding items out of your life. Just be aware that you're spending discretionary money and cut the ones that aren't top priorities for you. For example, you may not be willing to scrimp when it comes to Fido's organic, super-premium dog food — if that's the case, just make sure to budget for it every month.

To get to the point where you're able to identify that last 10 to 20 percent of expenses, track your daily expenses. Record all those cash expenses that are such a part of your routine that you hardly notice them — items such as the morning coffee, newspaper, snack, kids' allowances. Again, I'm not saying you shouldn't *have* them — the goal is just to be aware of where your money is going so you can decide if that's the best use of your funds.

Was eating breakfast at the coffee shop every morning on your short-term goals list? I bet not. Did you know that if you took the $9 a day that breakfast costs and multiplied that times 260 business days in a year, you'd get $2,340 — which might translate to a five-night Caribbean cruise for two? You get to make the choices here.

The really good news about this tracking is that you only need to do it for two months to catch most everything. Now that's not so bad. After that you'll have a good handle on what's gobbling up your free cash — and you can either plug the hole or include it as an expense in your budget.

And now, a word from the Bureau of Labor Statistics: Are you an average spender?

You may be looking for some guidelines to tell you if your spending is in line with that of others. Look no farther. The nice people at the Bureau of Labor Statistics have been hard at work adding up grocery-store tapes and watching what you bought the last time you went to a liquor store. Their report is available for all to see at `www.bls.gov/cex/home.htm`. I'm only kidding about them watching you at the liquor store — but they do have their ways of getting the stats on what Americans are spending and for what. The latest data is a year or so old but probably still fine for your purposes. Here's the scoop:

- **Housing:** 32.7 percent

- **Transportation:** 18 percent (vehicles: 7.6 percent; gasoline and motor oil: 4.3 percent; other transportation: 6.1 percent)

- **Food:** 12.8 percent (at home: 7.1 percent; away from home: 5.7 percent)

- **Personal insurance and pensions:** 11.2 percent (premiums for whole life and term insurance; endowments; income and other life insurance; mortgage guarantee insurance; mortgage life insurance; premiums for personal liability, accident and disability, and other non-health insurance other than for homes and vehicles: 0.8 percent; pensions and Social Security: 10.4 percent)

- **Healthcare:** 5.7 percent

- **Entertainment:** 5.1 percent

- **Apparel and services:** 4.1 percent

- **Cash contributions:** 3.6 percent

- **Education:** 2 percent

- **Personal-care products and services:** 1.2 percent

- **Alcoholic beverages:** 0.9 percent

- **Tobacco and smoking supplies:** 0.7 percent

- **Reading:** 0.3 percent

- **Miscellaneous:** 1.7 percent

The percentages were arrived at by taking an average expense as a percentage of an average income. So if you have $3,000 a month coming in and you spend $1,000 on housing, you're spending 33 percent. All the numbers work off take-home pay. (The government always allows for taxes!)

I'm not suggesting that you budget according to these percentages. Just use them to see if you're way out in left field on your estimates. For example, my family may choose to spend 40 percent of our income on housing and less on clothing and transportation, and yours may spend more on matching Corvettes or that infamous Ferrari and less on the old homestead. **Remember:** You get to decide.

Step 3: Making your savings goals a part of your budget

Most people don't budget for savings, but I recommend that you do. Include in your budget a line item for savings. Add up what you need to save in a year to reach your prioritized financial goals and divide by twelve. That is the monthly amount you need to save and include in your budget. If you don't have that much to allot for savings, you have a decision to make — spend less in another budgeted area(s) or rearrange your goals.

The old saying "Pay yourself first" is a wise one, indeed. If you only save what drifts to the bottom line, you're significantly shortchanging yourself and losing out on a great way to protect your credit — an emergency savings cushion.

Ideally, savings should go directly from your paycheck into a savings or checking account. When you get into the habit, you won't even notice the cut to your spending money — and you won't think to spend it if you can't see it. I do this myself and have found it to be painless.

Have your paycheck set up so that the amount of money you need to run your household (your monthly budget minus savings) goes into your checking account every pay period. Any pay raise, bonus, or leftover money goes directly into your savings. You never see it and never spend it — unless, of course, you want to. If you feel this is too extreme, at least consider directing half of all raises and bonuses into your savings account until you see how this strategy works for you.

Your savings plan is really two-pronged: You're saving to achieve the goals you've set for yourself, and you're saving so that you have money in case of an emergency. I cover both in the following sections.

Saving for a particular goal

At this point you've established your goals, calculated your income, and tracked your expenses. The next task is to revisit those goals that you're looking forward to attaining. If you break down a goal into bite-size pieces, it becomes more easily attainable. If you can do this with *all* your goals, you'll be closer to a plan that works for you.

Take an intermediate-term goal as an example: If you want to take a vacation, first you have to estimate the cost. Say the cost is $1,200. If your goal is to go in 18 months, you divide the $1,200 by the 18 months. The result — $66.67 — is what you must put aside each month in order to pay for the trip by the time you're zipping up your suitcase and canceling the newspaper delivery.

But where will the money come from if your budget has little to nothing left after expenses? You need to either increase income or reduce expenses by the amount needed. Again, taking the vacation example, if you can get overtime at, say, $15 an hour, you'll need one hour a week, or 4.4 hours a month ($15 × 4.4 hours × 18 months) to swing it. On the expense side, you'll be looking to redirect $3.07 per workday ($3.07 × 390 days) or $2.19 per day ($2.19 × 548 days). Maybe your trip really is as easy as passing up that latte and brewing your coffee at home.

Saving strategies: The grown-up's version of the piggy bank

A technique that helps me make the most of my spare pennies is to roll change. No, I don't mean act like someone else or switch from Parker House rolls to crescent rolls. At the end of the day, I place my loose pocket change into those cute little tubes you can get (for free) at the bank. For guys, this is easy, as the coins usually fall out onto the floor when you hang up your trousers. For the ladies, not only will you be saving money, you'll save the strain on your shoulder from lugging around a pocketbook weighted down with coins. So stop giving exact change at the checkout register, and start collecting your pennies, nickels, dimes, and quarters for your change rolls. My experience is that this strategy will yield about $200 a year per person.

Use cash more. Not only will this retrain your fingers from reaching for the plastic every time you buy something, it may help establish a link between paying, earning, and the value you're getting. Buying a $100 item is easy with a swipe of your favorite, mileage-accruing credit card. If you have to peel off ten $10 bills, the experience is different. It's real money — and a lot of it! Plus, when the stash of cash is nearly gone, you really have to think about a purchase.

You can also save money by packing your lunch. Going out to lunch adds up to some real money: 260 business days in a year, $15 per lunch (including tax, tip, and gas, if you drive) equals $3,900 a year. If you pay 25 percent federal tax, 7 percent state tax, and 7 percent Social Security, your brown-bagging it will be the equivalent of nearly a $6,400 raise ($6,400 – $1,600 (.25 percent of 6,400) – $448 (.07 percent of 6,400) – $448 = $3,904 take home). Think of the vacation you can go on with that money instead!

Finally, get a Sunday paper and cut coupons. Now that's real news. If you can put in a half-hour and come up with $20 in savings every week, you've made a great trade. How much? How about the equivalent of a $1,700 raise!

With some of your longer-term plans, it's fair to apply income that you're pretty sure will show up but hasn't yet. Say you expect a 4 percent raise in six months. You may want to count that raise in your figuring.

Saving for emergencies

As an ultimate goal, you should have between 6 and 12 months of living expenses in an emergency account for the unforeseen financial emergency. A number that big can seem impossible to achieve. But, realize this: You're aiming to cover *expenses,* not income. You don't have to replace that annual salary, but rather the expenses you'd have during, say, a lengthy period when you might not be working. You now know what your expenses are — thanks to your budget — so the number is at least a real one and not just some huge, unknown amount.

Avoiding budgeting backslides

For all your good intentions, there are five major causes of backsliding to be avoided in getting your plans in high gear. They are

✔ **Using credit cards outside of your budget:** If the expense is in your budget, how you pay for it is up to you. But if the expense isn't something you've budgeted for, putting it on a credit card is not a good idea.

✔ **Premature spending:** No, I'm not talking about a new medical problem. I'm talking about this situation: An item is in the budget to be purchased in the future, but you buy it early, before you have the cash for it. Instead, set dates and stick to them.

✔ **Lacking flexibility:** As situations change and opportunities appear, your budget needs to change accordingly. If it doesn't, it won't last. Remember who's in charge. Just don't charge like you're in charge.

✔ **Holidays:** They only last 24 hours, but the damage they can do to a budget is legendary. As gift-giving holidays approach, set a limit and use a list. Your family and friends love you and won't notice you didn't overspend — but they will notice how relaxed you are and that your smile is genuine.

✔ **Summer vacation:** Immortalized in Chevy Chase's assault on Wally World, the summer vacation — any vacation, really — can become a frenzy. Vacations are supposed to be relaxing rather than expensive — not just while you're on them, but after you return, too. You can't make up lost time with your family by spending more money. Make this discovery and see how a budget can really set you free.

Some people may try to tell you that a line of credit is as good as an emergency savings fund. Not so. Using credit to pay for an emergency can leave you much worse off if the emergency (such as a layoff) lasts longer than your credit does. Use up your savings and you're back to square one. Use up all your credit and have no savings, and you're at the bottom of a deep hole.

To start, shoot for just six months — or even *one* month or one *week*. All you need to do is start building today. Having one week of expenses saved can be a world of difference from having none. Two weeks is divine. And a month — you're ahead of most people. So relax, get started, start small, and keep at it.

Put aside money for emergencies while you're saving for other things. But if you're saving for three things at once, won't it take three times as long? No! Because if you're saving for three things at once and at least two of them are things that have a personal payoff to you — like that vacation — you're more likely to stick with it. And that will get you there much faster. When you have that cash socked away for an emergency, turn those incoming dollars toward achieving one of your other planned goals.

I mention this strategy earlier but it bears repeating: Automate your savings plan. Arrange to automatically deposit part of your pay into different savings, checking, or investment accounts. If you never see the money in your check, you won't miss it. As you get those raises or bonuses, put at least half into your savings account. Tax refunds get the same treatment. Make it easy and automatic, and your savings will grow before your eyes.

Step 4: Using credit and loans to your benefit

Yes, even credit and loans have a place in your budget. Credit is a tool to be used — as long as the tool fits the job. In fact, credit can make things easier. It can allow you to defer a payment to a more convenient time or to make a payment in such a way that it benefits you more than paying cash. However, credit cards should only be used to enable you to spend money you already have or know you'll have soon.

What I'm talking about here is consumer credit. A number of different incarnations of consumer credit are out there, and you can use each type to your advantage:

✔ **Non-installment credit:** This is the type of credit I grew up with. My dad had a charge account at the local gas station. I gassed up the family car, and he stopped by the station and paid the bill at the end of the month. With non-installment credit, you pay in full each month and don't carry a balance. This type of credit is used in some retail stores, country clubs, and the like. It is credit in its simplest form, available as a convenience to you — and a benefit to the merchant: You're not deterred from spending simply because you don't have the cash at the moment. You get what you want, the merchant makes money, and everybody's happy — which is the essence of using credit properly.

You can use this type of credit in your budget to handle expenses for local services like trash removal, gardening, or lawn care. An extra benefit here is that you get the service first and, if it's faulty, you're more likely to get it fixed — and get your money's worth — if you haven't handed over the dough already.

✔ **Installment, closed-end credit:** Frequently used by department or furniture stores, in this type of credit, an amount equal to the amount of a specific purchase is lent to you.

Here's an example of how you can use this type of credit: I bought a new bedroom set at a local furniture store, and they offered me installment credit allowing me 18 months to pay for the furniture in full. Normally, interest is associated with this type of loan, but the Cardi boys were having a special sale — no payments for six months, and no interest for the next year. A sweet deal from my perspective, and a sweet sale from theirs.

If you use this type of credit and don't want or can't afford to pay interest, make sure you pay off the entire amount before the end date or you will be charged interest from the date of purchase.

✔ **Revolving, open-end credit:** This is how most credit cards work. With your card, you're granted an amount of credit — with a limit, say, of $5,000 — to be used as you want. You can choose how much of the limit you use at any point in time. As you use the card, you must make periodic payments, subject to a minimum-payment requirement. As you repay the credit line, you in essence recharge the line. You can pay off the entire amount, which restores the credit line to its original and full size, or just make a smaller payment — or even make only a minimum payment. You get to decide.

An example of using this type of credit in your budget is to help spread the cost of airline tickets. You would need to have a set time frame for paying off the purchase (90 days or less preferably) and make sure the needed monthly amount fits in your budget before making the purchase. Don't forget to include the interest that's charged for carrying the balance when you come up with your monthly budget amount.

You're supposed to benefit from the use of credit — you aren't supposed to get hosed. Choose credit cards as a tool when they fit the job at hand. For example, I could have used my credit card to finance the bedroom set, but I would have paid 18 percent interest and I would have had to make payments right away. Clearly, the installment, closed-end type fit the job better.

Step 5: Planning for taxes

Books have been written on the subject of tax planning. Big books. Don't worry, though; I'm not going to get into tedious detail about deductions or schemes that can save you money, or how you can defer taxes until the cows come home. I want to look at the issue as an important component of budget planning. What do taxes have to do with budgeting? A lot if you owe tax money, if you're counting on your tax refund to bail out your budget, or if you're considering bankruptcy.

Typically, your employer deducts or withholds income taxes from your paychecks based on the number of your deductions. The deductions reflect an *estimate* of what you'll owe — but most people end up either paying something more to the IRS on April 15 or getting a tax refund.

You may have income *not* subject to withholding, such as dividends, interest, income from side businesses, tips, stock gains, gambling winnings, money paid to you as an independent contractor, small-business income, forgiven debts, hobby income, rents, and gifts above a certain dollar level. Because you haven't paid out taxes from these streams of income, be sure that you prepare yourself for that inevitability.

As you do your planning, you can choose one of three approaches to what I very generally call tax planning:

- ✔ Overpay
- ✔ Underpay
- ✔ Strive to pay just the right amount

You can probably already guess which strategy is the right one, but just in case, I cover them all in the following sections.

Overpaying your withholdings

Many people tell me they deliberately overpay their taxes as a budgeting strategy: "I don't want to owe any money" or "I use my refund to pay down my cards after holiday shopping."

The problem with overpaying is that, at a minimum, you're giving the government an interest-free loan of your money — money that you could be using to pay down debt, build up savings, or achieve any of a zillion good purposes. If you've overpaid all year and an emergency comes along in November, you can't ask the government for an advance of your refund to cover it. But you could use that money if you had it in a savings account, or even in a cookie jar.

If you're consistently getting a refund check, talk to a qualified tax preparer and go over your situation. You're likely to find a way to cover your taxes (and not owe something on April 15) without overpaying along the way.

Underpaying your withholdings

If you don't have a plan for your spending and savings, you may convince yourself that under-withholding your taxes provides the equivalent of an interest-free loan from the IRS. You tell yourself you'll figure out the tax issue when it comes up, which is a really long time from now. Besides, you have pressing needs for the money, and they have to be taken care of immediately. The backup plan: If you owe money April 15, you can always pay it with your credit card, right?

If you underpay your withholdings and owe a big tax bill in April, you'll find that your credit cards will be absorbing more unplanned items than just taxes, but tax penalties and interest as well as a fat convenience fee. How inconvenient! Plus your card may well be full already. A further caution about taxes of all kinds is that under current bankruptcy rules, local, state, and federal taxes usually cannot be discharged in a bankruptcy, nor can credit-card debt incurred from paying your taxes.

Paying the right amount of withholdings

Adjusting your withholdings so they jibe with what you owe at the end of the year is not as difficult as it may first seem. You may be surprised to discover that you can have more deductions than you have people in your household. It's true. I don't recommend adding the cat as a dependent, but a deductible mortgage payment can count as one or two additional deductions. I suggest that you at least consult with a tax preparer to get a good forecast of your tax commitments for the year. You may get an early budget bonus if you find you're over-withholding and can decrease your deductions — which may allow you to fund some of those short-term goals you've been saving for.

Conversely, if some shortfall is in your future, you're much better off knowing about it in advance so you can do something before it shows up on your doorstep like a big, wet, shaggy dog that just rolled in some very smelly stuff. Got the picture?

The right amount isn't a precise number. Until all the figures are in, there's no way to know what your tax bill is going to be. I like to shoot for a safeguard of $600 to $1,000 in excess of what you anticipate owing. This cushion doesn't make a big difference to your monthly budget, and as long as your income is relatively stable and your deductions from last year haven't changed a lot, you should be in the ballpark.

Step 6: Planning for retirement

Retirement isn't what it used to be. If you expect me to wax eloquent about how good my father had it with three pensions, forget it. When I said it isn't what it used to be, I mean it is much longer, better, healthier, and just plain different. No gold watch, no rocking chair — just the good stuff that you always wanted to do.

Retirement is a topic that warrants a book of its own. From the budgeting and credit perspective, I suggest that you find either a Certified Financial Planner (CFP), a Chartered Financial Consultant (ChFC), or, if you're in the heavy-duty-investment end of things, a Chartered Financial Analyst (CFA) to help you set up a plan that will meet your retirement goals. Armed with a workable budget and goals, you'll be light-years ahead of most people who walk through a planner's door looking for assistance. If you tend to be more of a do-it-yourself person, you can find good resources on this topic at both Charles Schwab (`www.schwab.com`) and Fidelity (`www.fidelity.com`).

Whichever approach you take, you need to make some calculations to help you determine how much you're going to have to start putting away to achieve your goals. Here are some simple tips for the budgeter looking down that long (or short) road:

- ✔ **Figure your life expectancy.** Chances are it's longer than that of your parents. Just don't guess too short. The Centers for Disease Control (CDC) estimate that 75 is the life expectancy for men and 80 for women. Those of you, like me, who weren't born yesterday and who are still in reasonably good health are looking at more than that. You can check out the good news at `www.cdc.gov/nchs/fastats/lifexpec.htm`.

- ✔ **Determine when you want to retire.** The difference between the age at which you want to retire and the age at which you think you might check out is what you have to budget for.

- ✔ **Consider inflation.** If you know you won't want to live on less than $40,000 a year in retirement, realize that you have to increase that number for the future because of inflation — the further out your retirement, the more you need to increase it. A number of good Web sites or financial planning programs adjust for inflation and investment experience (how much your investments will earn). Check out "Using Cool Budgeting Tools," later in this chapter, for some suggestions.

- ✔ **Don't underestimate medical expenses.** The good news is that you're likely to live longer than earlier generations. The not-so-good news is that you'll likely require more medical assistance to live a quality life in your later years. Because medical costs have risen and show no signs of abating, getting your medical expenses and insurance coverage budgeted in your retirement planning is very important.

- ✔ **Remember that time may be money.** If you end up with too little money and too much retirement, three courses of action are available: Save more, save longer, or cut the retirement budget. You can increase your current savings by earning more or spending less. You can just keep pushing out the retirement date until the surplus you've accumulated or an increased retirement benefit makes your numbers work. Or you can do with less later. The choice is up to you.

The miracle of compound interest: Investing for the future

One of the key components of successfully budgeting for your future is having your limited money in savings contribute as much as possible to your future needs, taking some of the pressure off you to earn everything, forever. We've all seen the charts that loudly proclaim that if you had only saved *X*-amount a year from the time you were 10 years old until you retired, you'd have a zillion dollars.

Well, behind all the hype and improbability of 10-year-olds investing their birthday money from Aunt Sophie in municipal bonds is a grain of truth. Investing is important. However, you have the right to feel comfortable with the process. So, if you haven't started, don't beat yourself up. Check out some of the resources in this chapter and start at your own speed and with your own goals in mind.

Whether you do it on your own or with a paid professional doesn't matter. The compounding of interest and tax advantages available today from some types of investments makes investing too great an opportunity to miss.

Step 7: Looking at your insurance options

Insurance isn't the sexiest topic, and for that I'm glad. It is, however, an essential part of budgeting for your future. Catastrophic illness or loss of property can derail the best-conceived plans. I don't advocate insurance for every little thing that comes up — which insurance you buy is a personal decision. To some degree, it depends on your resources and willingness to absorb the cost of some lower-level exposures in your life, such as car-insurance deductibles.

But you should be concerned about the major life events and expenses that could dramatically affect your finances at all stages of your life — from the death of a spouse to a major medical disability that prevents a wage-earner from working, to losing your home.

Here are a few critical coverage areas you want to consider as you pull together your budget for the future:

- ✔ **Life insurance:** If you have someone who will miss your income if you die, you need life-insurance coverage. You can get cheap *term life insurance.* Term life insurance covers you for a specified term or time frame, but it can usually be renewed at an increasing expense as you age. It has no cash or investment value — you get paid when you die, not before. Make sure you have enough coverage to bridge the gap your death will cause to the household budget. A little bit of thought should identify the shortfall from your premature downfall. And, of course, you want to have appropriate coverage on your partner as well. *Note:* Bad credit can increase your life insurance costs.

✔ **Disability insurance:** If you're unable to work for a period of time, disability insurance helps cover your expenses. It is available to cover both long- and short-term problems. Be good to yourself and your loved ones, and be sure that you get this.

✔ **Homeowner's insurance:** One of your biggest assets and one of your biggest liabilities is your home. As an asset, you'd have a tough time replacing it if an uninsured accident took part or all of your home. Keep up with building-code changes that affect your replacement costs and add insurance that covers the unlikely stuff. If it happens, you'll be glad you did. Some examples of the types of insurance you should have include flood insurance, earthquake insurance, and umbrella coverage on top of your limits (to insure you for personal and medical liability if someone falls down your front stairs and you get to become the long-term disability insurer by default). Be sure to deduct the value of your lot from your insured value.

Building your future into your budget

Depending on your stage of life, your primary budget needs vary. The basic tools remain the same, but the emphasis shifts. Your priorities are different in each stage:

✔ **In your first job:** Chances are you have big ideas and little money. At this stage, just establishing habits such as developing a spending plan and beginning a small savings program is most important. Be sure to keep current on student loan payments or getting deferrals if needed.

✔ **As a couple:** Your focus may be paying off old debts, finding out how to communicate about money, agreeing on financial goals and a spending plan, establishing joint and separate credit and savings, setting up a household account, and preparing for a family.

✔ **With a growing family:** Adjusting to a stay-at-home spouse or childcare expenses, paying for your kids' sports programs and braces, expanding living expenses, and saving for education and weddings are just some of the issues a family faces.

✔ **Going solo:** Whether you never marry or you go through a split-up, you're likely to confront situations such as living and saving on one income, taking care of children solo, and perhaps paying off divorce expenses and dealing with alimony and child support.

✔ **In an empty nest:** As the kids fly the coop, it's time to confirm your vision for the future and recast your budget for a new lifestyle. This may include retirement, exploring estate planning, considering Social Security and Medicare issues, and having some fun with your savings.

I favor high limits and as high a deductible as you can be comfortable with. The best use of insurance is not to reimburse you for everything that may go wrong — just the big things that you can't handle on your own. So, can you handle a $1,500 or even a $3,000 surprise, using your emergency fund? If so, set your deductible that high and in a few years you'll have saved enough in lower premiums to cover the deductible. After that, you get to keep it all.

✔ **Car insurance:** Insuring yourself against being sued for running someone over, medical payments, and uninsured motorists is actually more important than having coverage to replace or repair your damaged car. Many states require certain levels of insurance to drive. Your insurance rep can help you choose a policy that meets your needs. *Note:* In a number of states, bad credit can increase your auto premiums.

For much more information on insurance policies, check out *Insurance For Dummies* by Jack Hungelmann (Wiley).

Keeping Detailed Records the Fun Way

Okay, you caught me. I lied. Record keeping may be one of the duller ways to spend a rainy Saturday, but it really pays big dividends when you need quick access to important financial information. In fact, record keeping is so important that you'll have a difficult time knowing what to estimate for expenses or income if you don't keep some records.

I'm pleased to be able to say that I can find the receipt for any purchase — no matter how small — for the last year and bigger ones for much longer. I may not be cool, but I *am* organized. Having a good system that works for you for keeping records such as policies, receipts, and such can save time, money, and frustration.

You know you're not doing as good a job as you should in record keeping if:

✔ You can't find your last three years of income-tax returns.

✔ You don't know where your original Social Security card is.

✔ You don't remember where or when you last saw your auto/homeowner's/umbrella insurance policy.

✔ You haven't made photocopies of all your credit cards, front and back, and the emergency numbers.

✔ You don't have a notebook or other single source of information to help your loved ones find all your bank accounts/insurance policies/investment accounts when (not if) you die.

✔ You couldn't tell your insurance agent, after you found the lost policy, what was in your house before it burned to the ground.

✔ You don't even remember who your insurance agent is.

How can you accomplish the feat of having a good record-keeping system? A number of perfectly good record-keeping methods and products are available, so pick one you like — or choose parts of various ones and put them together. I have a few guidelines to offer, of course:

✔ Keep all your stuff in the same place or general area, such as a desk, cabinet, or closet.

✔ Have some way of breaking down the information by subject: bank statements separate from investment statements, credit-card statements, and so on.

✔ If you have a spouse or partner, decide who is responsible for keeping records. It's okay if you each want to do your own. But someone has to assume responsibility — or it will be left to the budget elves, who aren't too reliable.

✔ Try to establish a routine to update things — once a week, once a month — the timing matters less than having a routine and sticking to it.

✔ Get a safe-deposit box for your irreplaceable papers. It doesn't cost a lot of money and the expense is tax-deductible if you itemize your deductions on your tax return. A fireproof safe may do just fine. Include documents such as car/motorcycle titles; marriage, divorce, and birth certificates; wills; savings bonds; and so on.

✔ Once a year or so, clear out old or outdated information like old policies or tax returns more than seven years old. Keep anything that relates to an item with an extended life (like a TV), including the receipt, warranty, and owner's manual.

Check out the next section to find out about different tools you can utilize to help you with your record keeping.

Using Cool Budgeting Tools

What with the advent of the computer, the world of home budgeting can be as slick an operation as a NASA command center. From high-tech pocket calculators to sophisticated software packages, tools to help you develop a spending plan — and stick to it — fill the shelves of most office-supply outlets.

But not all budgeting tools have to be electronic to be cool or even useful. If you want a less technological approach to budgeting, here are some suggested tools to add to your budgeting kit:

- ✔ **Pencil:** Lead, not ink, is the tool to use when developing a plan that you'll be changing throughout the process.

- ✔ **Sticky notes:** An easy way to supplement your planning ideas. They can be moved around to different places on a planning board or form as you make changes.

- ✔ **Envelopes:** They're handy for keeping dollars to be spent or receipts for what was spent, by category. You may consider one envelope for tax-deductible receipts, for example. Filing by expense categories or pay periods can be helpful, and envelopes can help you do that.

- ✔ **Accordion files:** They work similarly to envelopes, but they're more portable — and you're less likely to misplace them.

This section takes a closer look at different tools you can use when keeping good budgeting records.

Web-based financial calculators

Web-based financial calculators help you figure out where you stand and what it will take to get to where you want to be. They're a great tool to help manage your money because they give you the information you need to make informed choices about what a course of action or purchase will actually cost you and for how long.

You can find calculators to help you figure out your mortgage payments at different interest rates, calculators to tell you the true cost of a loan and its impact on your budget, and even calculators that tell how much you need to budget for how long to get those credit cards paid off.

If you need a Web-based calculator, check out the following:

- ✔ **www.finance.cch.com:** Among the best in this class are the seemingly endless variety of calculators found at CCH, the tax and business information people who've published big books that accountants have used for years. Their Financial Planning Tool Kit is at `www.finance.cch.com/tools/calcs.asp`.

- ✔ **www.myfico.com:** For determining what effect differing credit scores have on loan interest rates and the total costs to you, go to this site.

- ✔ **www.bankrate.com:** General calculators for many financial functions are available at the home of the Debt Advisor, yours truly, at the financial megasite, Bankrate.com.

Budgeting Web sites

You can find some easy-to-use, basic budgeting advice and tools online. The following are a few of my favorites:

- ✔ **www.moneymanagement.org/FinancialTools:** Money Management International's Web site is a good start.

- ✔ **www.consumerlaw.org:** The National Consumer Law Center site has a large amount of consumer-oriented material that you may find helpful in sifting through the competing claims of those who want to help you deal with financial issues.

- ✔ **www.militaryonesource.com:** This is a good site for military personnel. Military OneSource is provided at no cost by the Department of Defense to all active duty, Guard, Reserve members, and their families. The 24/7 service provides information and referrals plus private, local face-to-face counseling. Call 800-342-9647. They have good tips and online budgeting tools that are tailored to service personnel plus a lot more — just look under the Budgeting and Basic Money Management tab.

Budget-counseling information sources

There's no shortage of places you can go to get support in putting together a budget that will work for you. In fact, one of the problems is sifting through those who are trying to sell you something or scam you. Here are three great places to start:

- ✔ **www.moneymanagement.org:** Money Management International is the largest and oldest full service national financial counseling and education nonprofit in the United States. They have been doing budgets for more than 50 years. And it's free as well as confidential.

- ✔ **www.debtadvice.org:** The National Foundation for Credit Counseling has good advice and referrals along with a good, high-level budgeting calculator that plots your spending, based on income, against national averages to let you know if you're in the ballpark of your peers. Their member-agency network offers budgeting assistance as well as debt-management solutions.

- ✔ **www.aiccca.org:** The Association of Independent Consumer Credit Counseling Agencies has a listing of member agencies, many of which can help you with budgeting issues, but all of which have debt-management products.

Chapter 14

Minimizing the Effect Life Events May Have on Your Credit

*J*ohn Lennon said, "Life is what happens to you while you're making other plans." My take on this quote is, "A good plan can help you make the most of life's unplanned events." Your credit report typically reflects what's going on in your life: If your personal life crashes into a divorce, you may see a drop in your credit score as well. If you lose your job, you may soon discover that your access to credit has been reduced.

Unemployment, marriage, divorce, illness, the death of a loved one —all these significant life events, whether of your choosing (like marriage) or beyond your control (like illness or death), can have a major impact on your emotions, stress levels, and health. They can affect your credit status, too. The life situations themselves don't hurt or help your credit report and score directly — you don't lose points simply because you lose your job. No one's going to pull your credit report and stamp it divorced. You don't get placed in a lesser category if you become widowed. The events themselves have no impact on your report and score — but indirectly, they can pack a punch. To the extent that these events have a financial impact on your life, they impact your credit accordingly.

In this chapter, I present some of life's unplanned events and offer strategies to help you make the most of these credit-challenging situations. I show you ways to shelter your credit status from the financial curveballs that life throws your way.

For Better or Worse: Building Good Credit as a Couple

Congratulations! Two separate credit identities have come together. Keeping your credit in its best shape can be tricky enough when you're only making financial decisions for yourself. Add another person to the mix, and the process becomes more challenging. On the other hand, marriage can also pose opportunities for at least one of the partners to improve his or her credit standing. A recent study at a nationally recognized university found that couples do better than single people at solving debt problems. Score one for the till-death-do-us-part group! In the following sections, I lay all the cards on the table.

Talking about credit compatibility

When my wife, Barbara, and I go out to dinner, she always looks at the dessert menu first. In the beginning of our courtship, this behavior baffled me. As a typical linear-thinking man, I approached my meal choices in the order I planned to consume them — starter, salad, entrée. In fact, I typically wouldn't even think about dessert until I was sopping up the last of the marinara sauce from my plate.

Finally, I got up the nerve to ask her about this display of, in my view, backward behavior. She explained that dessert, for her, was the most important part of the meal and she wanted to plan ahead to accommodate for her priority. If she saw tiramisu (her favorite) on the menu, she'd go for a light entrée or salad and skip the bread. If the dessert choices were fairly pedestrian, she'd order a heartier main course and perhaps settle for some tea.

I share this slice of our domestic life to illustrate two points:

- ✔ My wife's logic, as always, is unassailable and, what's more, her approach to dining out is a superb metaphor for household budgeting — one that has served our relationship well. (I get to that later.)

- ✔ Understanding and communicating with each other is a critical component, not just when it comes to ordering dinner, but in all aspects of married life — especially when it comes to financial issues.

Exploring all money issues

I advise all engaged couples to spend at least as much time discussing and exploring financial compatibilities, strategies, approaches, and goals as they do in choosing a honeymoon spot. After all, the goal is to continue the honeymoon as long as possible and arguing over finances does nothing to achieve that goal.

If you're soon to be married (or even if you're already married and haven't yet talked money), you need to openly discuss a range of money issues, including your current financial status. If you could live on love, the conversation would be unnecessary — but if you two are pooling your resources, you need to determine together how you will use your money in your lives as a married couple.

Here's a list of ten things you need to do with your betrothed before the wedding day. If you're already married and you haven't yet discussed these issues, the sooner you do so, the better:

- ✔ **Show each other your credit reports and credit scores.**

- ✔ **Discuss your current annual income or salary and your income hopes for the future.**

- ✔ **Determine your financial style — are you a saver or a spender?** Find out the same about your spouse.

- ✔ **Talk about any of your debts and how you plan to handle them.** Will you each pay your own debts? Will you pool them together and split them 50-50? Or will the bigger earner pay more?

- ✔ **Tell each other about any bankruptcies or other major financial events in your past.** In some second marriages, a bankruptcy will be around longer than the kids, and you wouldn't forget to talk about *them*.

- ✔ **Discuss your spending and budgeting habits (whether you're frugal, indulgent, or even know how to budget).**

- ✔ **Talk about whether you've cosigned any loans.**

- ✔ **Discuss your personal budgeting approaches.** Will you count every penny, or go for estimates instead? Yes, you need a budget!

- ✔ **Discuss your financial goals for the next five years.**

- ✔ **Talk about your long-term financial goals and how you will fund them.** Will you retire at 50? Sail around the world? Give all your worldly possessions to charity?

I strongly advise that you each get copies of your credit report. These days, many newly dating couples request HIV blood tests and background checks. Credit is a critical relationship factor, too. You may have bared your heart and soul to your sweetie, but until you bare your credit, the job's not done.

Customizing a budget for two

I strongly recommend that you and your partner sit down and make out a budget for your new household. Budgeting is among the most important first steps you can take together to strengthen your marriage and reduce the risk of divorce because of financial stress and spending incompatibility.

Explore together and agree on what you want to save for — a family, a house, early retirement. This discussion whets your appetite for all the spending steps you'll want to establish in order to get there. You'll also need to budget for the mundane everyday stuff like utilities, transportation, food, housing, and so forth. If you find that you just aren't able to get the numbers to add up, you can always refer to Chapter 3 for a second helping of advice, or consider a credit counselor. The good ones aren't just for credit, debts, or problems — they can help you before disaster strikes.

Chapter 13 of this book includes suggestions on how to budget. You'll find a number of resources on the CD that can get you going, too.

As my wife would advise, when working with your budget, always start with dessert — that would be the fun part: your future goals. What could be more fun than describing all the things you're going to do and the adventures you'll share together over the years? For example, my wife and I plan an extended road trip looking for the perfect piece of blueberry pie.

Over the years, I've adjusted to my wife's ordering style in restaurants. I'm no longer a bemused bystander but often an active participant. If, for example, she's saving up for that decadent chocolate cheesecake but is tempted by the filling featured entrée, I'll offer to order the fat main course and give her a few bites, and she'll settle for a salad. But, of course, she has to share her dessert!

Through a commitment to communication, establishing common goals, and working together for mutual benefit, couples can achieve financial bliss. A perfect example of having your cake and eating it, too.

Considering the implications of joint accounts

If your spouse has a less-than-glowing credit history, it will affect *you* as soon as you apply for credit together and open joint accounts, because both your credit histories will be reviewed. You each keep your own original histories but, in addition, your new joint accounts appear on both of your credit reports. So if you're concerned that your spouse may not be as diligent as you are in paying bills on time, paying the bills yourself is a good idea.

Many newlyweds decide to merge their financial accounts because consolidated accounts often make for easier record keeping and enhance that feeling of "togetherness." But beware: Both of you are responsible for all debt incurred in any joint credit accounts. Regardless of which one of you takes the credit card out for a joy ride, if you miss a payment on a joint account, that missed payment will negatively affect both of your credit records. Also, if you miss a payment on an individual account, that missed payment may affect your ability to open joint accounts because both credit histories will be considered.

In those states with community-property laws, you may be responsible for your spouse's debts even if you aren't on the account. Currently nine states fall into this category: Arizona, California, Idaho, Louisiana, Nevada, New Mexico, Texas, Washington, and Wisconsin. Alaska can be either.

Even if you decide to consolidate your accounts with your spouse, always keep at least one credit account in your own name as a safeguard in the event of an emergency. Keeping an individual account can also be a good thing in the event of divorce or the untimely death of a spouse — having your own account can help you reestablish an individual credit history.

Keeping separate accounts

One alternative for those with a credit-challenged spouse or for those cautious couples who want to take the credit-sharing slowly, is to keep separate accounts and allow one another to be authorized users on your accounts. Both of you can charge on the account, both of you get the credit history reported on your credit reports (although you no longer get the credit scoring benefit), but only one of you pays and is responsible for the bill.

Although this strategy can safeguard your credit score from a late payment, it also exposes you to the *potential* of at least one bigger-than-expected bill (if your spouse is a dangerous shopaholic, this setup won't protect you from his or her spending). But if you can trust your spouse not to go crazy with the credit card, this method allows your spouse to add additional credit history, while you keep responsibility and overall control for the account in your hands. (And, of course, if your spouse gets out of control with the credit card, you can always remove him or her from the account.)

Separate accounts (for those not in community-property states) make sense to some people, especially those who come together later in life with substantial assets of their own. As long as you both agree, this sort of financial independence can keep you looking attractive to your sweetie long after your personal charms have become less charming. It can help each of you to feel that youthful independence and financial vigor that only money of your own can provide. For my recent birthday, my sweet Barbara took me, at her exclusive expense, to Walt Disney World. If we had merged all our finances, she couldn't have done this without spending at least some of my money. Happy Birthday to me!

When money is the cause of conflict

The moose on the table. The elephant in the room. These are euphemisms I've heard to describe those huge, looming issues that couples or families pretend don't exist. But ignoring credit and money conflicts is done at great peril to a marriage. As in the case of the elephant, you can pretend it's not there — but it will still wreck your home.

Too often, couples convinced they're compatible on all fronts discover that they're polar opposites when it comes to spending, borrowing, and saving. Couples who thought they were in perfect — though unspoken or assumed — agreement find out after the nuptials that they're opposites financially.

Of course, if you talk about your finances, you shouldn't run into credit conflicts — certainly not any that destroy your marriage. But money seems to be a taboo topic, even among married couples. Not until that bounced check, late-payment notice, or mammoth-sized credit-card balance shows up are money conflicts discovered — and by then, the discussion may not be pretty.

Lack of careful and constant communication about money can lead to irreconcilable differences that result in divorce. When divorce is on the horizon, I think you can see how the fighting can escalate. Here are some of the pitfalls I hope you can avoid:

- ✔ **Not being open with each other about how you see and value savings, money, and credit:** Silence is your enemy.

- ✔ **Pooling all your funds, earnings, and credit:** Keeping some credit in your own name is important. The same goes for money.

- ✔ **Surprising your partner with a big expenditure (a car, boat, home theater, designer shoes, large donation to the cat-rescue fund):** Spending joint money without consulting your spouse is a big no-no. Determine together an amount over which you need consultation to purchase an item, such as more than $100. You'll both be looking at any household purchases for a long time, so before you buy that great moose head to hang over the bed, talk about it.

- ✔ **Criticizing your partner's money style in front of others:** No one wants to be ridiculed — even in good humor — in front of others. If you're uncomfortable with your mate's spending behavior, talk about it when the two of you are alone.

- ✔ **Failing to set mutual goals:** Discuss them and agree on a plan for achieving them.

> ✓ **Not meeting your financial obligations:** If you're unable to pay something that is your responsibility, let your spouse know as soon as possible.
>
> ✓ **Letting kids set the rules:** If you have kids (or monkeys for that matter), they'll learn how to play one of you against the other to get what they want. This time-tested kid strategy can lead to discipline issues and fights between mom and dad. If you have a blended household (kids from different marriages), establishing the rules and standing together as a united front is especially important.

Protecting Your Finances in a Divorce

Marriage has its challenges, and, too often, financial issues are the trigger that can set off a divorce. If your financial and credit life was challenging as a married couple sharing a common future, in divorce it will become much more complicated. Plus, some of your expenses may be even greater as you separate into two households (you'll have two mortgage or rent payments every month, for example). Toss in one of the most emotionally stressful life experiences, and anticipating what may happen to your credit during a divorce is easy.

The financial fallout from divorce may include difficulties in opening new accounts and obtaining new loans in your name. Given that half of marriages end in divorce, you can do some of the following "what-if" planning ideas to protect and, if need be, restore your good credit.

Taking action if a split is a possibility

If you suspect that divorce may be a possibility in your future, I suggest the following. Even if you're sure you're married 'til death do you part, these strategies are good to follow.

✓ **Keep good credit in your own name.** One or two accounts chosen from a few different types — such as revolving (credit card), installment (car loan), and retail (department-store card) — should be sufficient. Be sure you handle the accounts wisely.

✓ **Build your own credit while you're married.** Remember that your credit score is made up of five main components: paying on time, the amount and type of your debt, the length of time you've held credit, the variety of accounts you have, and the number and type of new accounts you have.

✓ **Open your own bank account with checking and savings features.**

✔ **Get overdraft protection on your checking account.** This benefits you in two ways: by making sure checks don't bounce and by exhibiting responsible use of another type of credit.

✔ **Keep track of your joint credit by checking your credit report frequently or by enrolling in a credit monitoring service.** This may provide an early warning that your partner is having some issues. At a minimum, check one of your three credit reports every four months.

Preparing for divorce

If the possibility of divorce becomes a reality, you'll want to ratchet up your credit-protection action. At this point, separating your financial selves to your best ability is important. Here's how:

✔ **After informing your other half that you will be closing joint accounts, send a letter to each joint creditor asking that the account be closed to any new activity.** Closing the accounts protects you. Telling the other person in advance allows them to make other plans and is the decent thing to do. Just don't wait too long to send the letter.

✔ **Attempt to come to an agreement about how accounts will be paid and who will be responsible for making the payments.** If you can't reach an agreement, make the minimum payments yourself rather than let your credit deteriorate. You can always recoup the money in a reconciliation or divorce settlement — just keep track of what you're paying.

✔ **If possible, transfer the balances on closed joint accounts to individual accounts.** Consider including this as a stipulation in your divorce decree with specific amounts assigned to each person.

✔ **Establish credit independently as soon as possible.** Start small and build up gradually if you have to. If your credit is damaged already, start with a credit card that has a small credit limit, perhaps from a local department store, gas station, or credit union. After paying your bills on time for six months or so, apply for another card and continue paying bills consistently. Remember that you can dilute negative credit information by adding positive experience to your history. (Check out the "Getting new credit in your own name" section for more info.)

✔ **Check your credit more frequently than normal.** Consider subscribing to a credit monitoring service offered by the credit bureaus in order to be notified immediately of key changes in your credit report, such as late payments or new accounts being added.

Even if your prospective ex is uncooperative, keep paying all bills on remaining joint accounts on time. Don't listen to uninformed but well-meaning friends and relatives who may tell you to ignore making payments or to run up debts to spite your ex. During the divorce process and as long as you still have joint accounts, be sure that at least the minimum payments are made, on time. Missed payments will stay on your credit profile for seven years, making it hard or more costly to obtain new credit (and maybe a new spouse) on your own.

If you change your name, be sure to write to all your creditors and the three bureaus to let them know. Doing so helps keep errors based on name mix-ups from affecting your credit history.

Considering joint credit history: It may outlast your marriage

From the time you open your first joint account, you and your mate are linking your credit futures together. Your credit history and credit score will now be influenced by the behavior of your spouse. A blemish on your spouse's part is a blemish on yours, too.

How long will you have to suffer from your ex's joint-account misdeeds? Conventional wisdom says seven years. But what if I told you it could be longer? Maybe *much* longer. Just look at the numbers: Negative credit items are reported for seven years in most cases. Your ex's credit may be part of your credit report for seven years from whichever event happened last:

✔ Seven years from when your honey first forgot to pay the credit card

✔ Seven years from when you got that notice saying your ex was 60 days late

✔ Seven years from the date your ex's loan charged off after going six months past due

  If, however, after the six months of charging off, the bill goes to court and, if, after another six months of insincere attention on your ex's part, the creditor goes for a wage garnishment, which precipitates a bankruptcy filing, the original account is reported for seven years, as is the public record of the court action. The bankruptcy overlaying that, however, is reported for up to ten years.

It can get even worse in certain situations, but I think the point is made. 'Til debt do you part — but your spouse's debts may be with you for a long, long time after you go your separate ways.

Getting new credit in your own name

The first step in successfully getting credit in your own name is to find out where your credit stands. Begin by obtaining your credit report and your FICO score from myFICO.com. FICO tells me that a "good" score is between 660 and 725. If you are at 760 or above, you're a *FICO High Achiever!*

A Good FICO score (660 – 725)

After determining your credit score (check out Chapter 6 for more info), if you're in the 660 to 725 range or above, you probably have a good chance of getting new credit in a normal credit environment. Remember, credit tightens or loosens from time to time. In loose credit times, a good score will get the job done. If you are in a tight credit environment, a good score may not be enough to get the terms or even the credit you want. I suggest you apply for the following in your own name:

✔ Checking account

✔ Savings account

✔ Small installment loan (use the savings account for collateral, if you must)

✔ Retail-store credit card

✔ Major bank credit card

✔ Library card (because it'll save you money on books and videos)

This diversity of credit will help you respond to most financial situations that may arise and help build your credit score with on-time payments.

FICO score below 660

If your score is around 660 or less, your journey toward establishing credit in your own name may be a bit slower. (If you have a sympathetic parent or relative with decent credit, you may be able to move things along faster by having your parent cosign for you but I don't recommend it. Too often this fails and relationships are damaged along with credit.) Reestablish credit on your own, if at all possible — you'll feel better and so will your family. Begin with the following:

✔ Checking account

✔ Savings account

✔ Passbook loan (secured by your savings account)

✔ Major bank credit card (if you qualify)

✔ Secured credit card (if you don't qualify for a credit card). Secured cards give you a line of credit based on a savings deposit to secure the credit line. These show up on your credit report just like an unsecured card — no one but you and the issuing bank will know!

✔ Retail-store credit card (you're likely to qualify if you qualified for the bank credit card)

✔ Library card

If you apply for a credit card from your credit union or bank and you aren't sure whether you'll qualify, bring your credit report into a branch and have them look at it rather than have them pull one themselves. Why? If they decline you, a credit report inquiry won't show up on your credit report and lower your credit score unnecessarily (see Chapter 5 for more information).

Protecting your credit in a divorce decree

When the judge rules in your divorce decree, be sure that all joint debts are clearly and specifically assigned and that both you and your ex understand that these debts must be paid on time. Close all remaining joint accounts by the date on which the divorce is granted. In the case of joint real estate that will eventually be disposed of, the party living in the property has the most interest in making sure that the payments are made and should ask the judge to rule that the person in the house will send in the payments, even if the money to make the payment has to come from the other party.

A divorce decree does not end either party's responsibility for joint debts incurred while married. This generally includes individual debts in community-property states. After all, you both promised the lender that you'd repay the loan. The fact that the judge says that only one of you has to make the payment from now on does not change your contract with your lender. Each person is fully responsible for the entire balance of joint accounts, from credit cards and car loans to home mortgages.

A default on a joint account by your ex will show up on your credit report and lower your score. For this reason, checking your credit report regularly — once a year at least or one report every few months— after a divorce is a good idea. If your ex doesn't pay at all, you'll probably be subject to collection activity and have to pay, or you may end up in a different court. If this seems unfair to you, the rationale is that a creditor shouldn't be made to suffer (poor baby) because your marriage failed.

Overcoming your ex's defaults on your joint accounts

Given the stress associated with divorce, the fact that your ex may miss a payment or two is almost understandable. I said *almost*. Although you may be understanding of such a mishap, keeping your credit record as clean as possible is critical in order to rebuild a positive credit history as a single person.

Because you want to address any missed payments as soon as possible, you need to stay up-to-the-minute on payment status. You may find out about a delinquency in a number of ways: a letter, a phone call, a Web site visit, a credit-monitoring service, and so on. As soon as you know that a payment was not made, take action.

Consider taking the following actions:

- **If your relationship allows, contact your ex to find out if the bill has been paid.** If trust is a concern or if your relationship precludes such direct communication, let the lawyers handle it. Instruct your attorney to notify your ex's attorney that the court order has been violated, and ask for a response.

- **If the situation isn't resolved, you can always go back to court.** You can ask the judge to reorder your ex to pay as agreed or face the not-so-pleasant legal consequences of contempt of court which can include spending some time in jail. Returning to court to enforce paying of assigned accounts is a lengthy and expensive course of action, so you may consider making the payments yourself if you think the issue can be resolved between the two of you. Making the payments will cost you money, but perhaps less than bad credit (not to mention attorney fees) will cost you.

By now you've probably figured out two things: Life isn't fair, and paying a bill yourself may be a lot easier than having to deal with your ex and can be beneficial to you in the long run.

Controlling the damages

Credit damage from divorce or its aftermath is not unusual, but you can take steps to lessen the negative impact to your credit record and score:

- **Pay your bills on time.** Paying on time adds positive credit history on top of any negative history. Over time, your score will count a large number of new and positive reports with more weight than older negatives. As your credit report ages, older items count for less, so make the most of new credit going forward.

- **Add a 100-word statement to your credit report.** You can explain mitigating circumstances that a prospective lender or employer may not know about in considering your application.

Be careful not to leave this statement on your report longer than you need to, because it may draw attention to a past problem that is no longer a factor in your credit score.

> ✔ **Review your credit report frequently.** Getting copies of your credit reports may be a good investment in controlling unexpected negatives, especially if your ex is still paying off joint or community-property debts. You can pay for monitoring services that alert you to any negative credit-reporting entries as soon as they occur, allowing you to take action to reduce your credit damage.

Keeping Credit under Control while Unemployed

On the predictability scale, finding yourself out of work, laid off, downsized, or just plain unemployed is something you'll probably encounter at least once in your life. Although you don't expect to work for the same company for your entire career, you probably expect to make a job change of your own volition and for good reasons (getting a new job at higher pay, for example).

But considering today's uncertain and volatile job market, the likelihood is that your *employer* will make the decision to say farewell at least once in your career. I can tell you from experience that the event will arrive at the least advantageous time possible. In the following sections, I help you through this almost inevitable fact of modern-day life.

Employment information is not regularly reported as part of your credit report. The bureaus are not keeping track of where you work or what you earn. As part of the loan process, a creditor may ask where you work, and that information may be reported on new loans, lines of credit, and credit cards. But unlike payment history, for example, your employment being included on your credit report happens infrequently. So unemployment won't show up on your record unless you fail to make your payments on time, go over your credit limits, or do something silly, like opening a lot of credit lines just in case you need them.

Preparing your credit for unemployment

Because the information contained in your credit report tends to follow your personal financial experience, you can do a few things in advance to protect your credit in case of unemployment.

First and foremost, if you don't have an emergency savings account, start one. Fund it regularly so it grows to somewhere between six months to a year of living expenses (not income — your expenses are supposed to be less than your income). This is a good number to work toward, because six months to a year is how long you're likely to be unemployed if you're caught by surprise.

Having more than one or two credit cards or lines of credit is also useful. You don't want to draw undue attention to your credit report if you're unemployed. So you want to make sure you continue to pay your bills on time, keep your credit-card balances at less than 50 percent of available credit if possible, and so on. (See Chapter 2 for more on what you can do to look "normal" and not raise any red flags on your credit report.)

Using credit during unemployment

If you're already unemployed, don't beat yourself up. You're in good company. It happens to many people, and it often happens more than once. Now that the unwanted and unplanned event has arrived, if you've established savings, regardless of the amount, and you have some available credit lines, you have two tools that will be a big help to you to get through this time without damaging your credit. Using a combination of credit and cash, you can put together a new plan that includes finding that new job and a budget/ spending plan that will work while you do so.

Prospective employers often pull a credit report as part of the employment process, so to maximize your chances of getting a job, you want the best credit you can realistically have.

Stay away from using cash advances on your credit cards! The cost to spend money this way is much greater than using the credit card to pay for it. Even if it seems silly, using the card to buy a $10 item is much better than using a $10 cash advance. Cash advances come with an extra fee, often have a higher interest rate, and often have a maximum lower than your credit limit.

Looking at credit differently

Now that you've shifted from spending to *conserving* your resources, your credit-use priorities have shifted. You need to recognize this upfront by looking at credit differently. Originally, you used credit to spend your income in a different way from carrying around your paycheck in your pocket. You also used it for larger purchases that you needed some time to pay off.

When you're unemployed, possibly for longer than you anticipate, you don't have those earnings coming in (you may have a severance package or unemployment benefits, but they're only temporary — and they may not last as long as your unemployment does). Now you may need to use credit for basic living and job-hunting expenses only. This is just about the opposite of what most people will tell you, but you'll do this only for a limited period of time and for a specific, worthy purpose. If it helps, think of it as borrowing money to invest in a surefire investment: yourself and your future.

Preserve your cash for as long as possible by using credit first. You want to keep your cash because you can't replace it after it's gone. This advice may be the opposite of what you've heard in the past. Conventional wisdom says to control expenses by paying cash for as much as possible. The opposite is now the case. Pay with credit *for essentials* as much as possible and save the cash. You'll keep your overall spending to essentials by closely following a budget (see the following section).

Refiguring the family budget

To keep your spending in line with your reduced resources, begin by sitting down with your family and discussing the situation and the need to temporarily reduce expenses. Don't be embarrassed in front of the kids. This situation is an important lesson in reality for them. And you can show them how adults face difficult issues and win.

The CD includes worksheets that are helpful when you're trying to put together a budget. Chapter 13 of this book focuses on budgets — whether you need to start from scratch and create a budget or revise a budget that you've already created.

As you begin to figure your income into your spending plan, if your severance is being paid out over time or you haven't yet received it, ask your employer or HR department to raise your deductions to the maximum allowed. The IRS wants a report of anyone with more than ten deductions. So, generally ask for ten (you don't want the IRS looking at you if you can avoid it). This strategy results in more cash flowing through to you for the present, when you need it.

Yes, you may owe some taxes on this money in April (though your deductible job-hunting expenses and reduced earnings for the year may offset that). You want to maximize today's income at the possible expense of tomorrow's demands.

Getting credit counseling to help

If you're overwhelmed and think you could benefit from some professional perspective or guidance, go to an accredited credit counselor. You can get more information on credit counselors and where to find them in Chapter 3.

Protecting your credit lines

The downside to using your lines of credit for your basic living expenses while unemployed (a strategy I recommend) is that you *may* do some damage to your credit. Here are some tips for protecting your status while you leverage your available credit to help you get through this challenging time:

✔ **Keep balances at less than 50 percent of your available credit.** Spread your credit use over several accounts in order to keep your balance on each credit card at less than 50 percent. For example, rather than have a $2,000 balance on one card and a $0 balance on three cards, consider spreading the amount over four cards — with each balance at $500.

✔ **Make all payments on time.** Remember that 35 percent of your credit score has to do with whether you make payments on time.

Don't try to keep your same standard of fully employed spending in place during this period of economic challenge. The more your balances grow, the more likely they are to attract the attention of someone looking at your credit report. You may need to use the credit, but not in such a way that you attract a crowd.

✔ **Pay the car loan first.** A car can get repossessed in as little as two weeks. Then how will you get to work to earn the money to pay the mortgage?

✔ **Pay your mortgage a very close second.** Not all bills are created equal, and your mortgage is among the most unequal of them all. Partial payments don't work, and falling behind 90 days begins a very difficult-to-stop foreclosure process.

The 90-day period begins when the mortgage was originally due — it does not start from the end of the grace period. For example, if your payment was due on January 1, even though you had until January 15 to make the payment, count from January 1. You're considered 90 days late, then, on April 1 (not April 15). At the 90-day mark, you may well have to pay the entire three months of mortgage plus late fees in one shot. That can be thousands of dollars. Send in less, and they'll send it back. The bottom line: Always pay your mortgage in full and on time.

Don't contact your creditors unless you *know* you're going to default. If you just *think* you may miss a payment, it's none of their business — and they may ratchet your interest rate up to cover the additional risk you now represent in their eyes (even if you end up making the payment on time). If, however, you know you're going to miss the current month's payment, telling them before it happens is important.

If you have any income, ask for a *hardship program* (a special repayment arrangement that may be offered to a good customer in need of some extra help; they tend to last for no more than three to six months). Most companies have them, but the hardship has to be real and imminent and you have to ask for it.

If the hardship program is not sufficient to bridge the gap between what you can afford to pay and what they insist you pay, send a letter stating that you can't make any payments but intend to in the future as soon as you find employment. The letter might look like what you see in Figure 14-1. (You'll find this and other letters on the CD.)

Date

Creditor Name
Creditor Address
City, State ZIP

RE: Account #:
        Name on Account:

Dear Sir or Madam:

I have been unemployed for *Insert Length of Time*. I
have exhausted my savings and unemployment benefits looking for work. For the present, I am
unable to pay the monthly amount required under
our agreement.

Due to my desperate financial situation, I
cannot promise a date by when I will be able to
resume payments, although it is my intention to do
so. I can, however, promise to inform you immediately when my financial condition improves and I
am able to resume making normal payments.

Thank you for your understanding and help.

Sincerely,

Your Name
Your Address
City, State ZIP
Your Phone

Figure 14-1:
Writing a
letter to a
creditor
when you're
unemployed
and can't
make
payments
is always a
good idea.

What to do when you run out of credit and options

If you aren't able to make any payments on maxed-out credit cards or credit lines and you still have no job on the horizon, something will have to give. There are only three sides to this triangle: income, expense, and credit. If credit isn't an option, income and expenses are the only things you can alter.

Take out that budget you prepared when your unemployment started and consider some extreme moves to cut expenses. Can you move to a smaller home? Can you move in with a friend? Can you sell things to raise some cash? On the income side, have you considered taking a job that will tide you over until something in your field opens up? The task here is to generate some income, not move a career forward. *Remember:* Given time and perseverance, you *will* come out of this stronger than you went in.

Facing Student-Loan Default

Student loans are critical to many people and their families as the preferred and, in some cases, only method for financing not only a college or technical-school education but a big part of the American dream. Studies show that about 50 percent of recent college graduates have student loans, with the average student carrying a loan debt of $10,000. The average cost of college is increasing at twice the rate of inflation, with public schools costing an average of $13,000 a year and private schools approximately $30,000 a year. Multiply times four — or, increasingly, five — years, and the result is $65,000 to $150,000 of debt.

Student loans are a powerful tool that has to be handled with care — often with more care than the people who give them out use when they explain the ins and outs of these debt instruments to the borrower. Student loans are unlike most others in their generous terms, low eligibility standards, and flexibility. They also stand out as being among a select number of bulletproof debt obligations that are inviolate under the law. What this means is that neither bankruptcy nor the passage of time will release you from your obligations to pay off this debt. In this section, I help you deal with the aftermath of a student loan and its credit implications.

Preparing for payback: When student loans come due

Even though the price of a college education may seem high, the return on investment potential has always made it worthwhile. Estimates indicate that a college graduate will earn $1 million more than a high school graduate over the course of his career. And the figures go up for those with a graduate-school education.

If you're a typical student and you left school with $10,000 of debt, your payment is probably between $75 and $100 a month, depending on interest and the length of the loan (which can run as long as 30 years). Medical students are looking at an average of between $500 and $1,000 a month.

You usually have a good idea of when you have to start paying back your student loans (generally shortly after leaving school) and at what rate well before you're out of school — the lenders are good about keeping you informed about this. So the first thing I advise is to come up with a plan for payback, even socking away some of that summer job income to create a cushion in case your first real job doesn't bring in as much as you hope. Then adjust your living expenses to accommodate the loan payment.

Although student loans do offer generous terms, the danger here is that many young people just out of school don't have much experience budgeting and living on their own. When they find themselves in a real-live, "grown-up" job with a salary, they may feel like millionaires — and they may start spending like millionaires, too. Without tools such as a spending plan, fledgling wage-earners may quickly lose control of credit and debt responsibility, and find negative notes being added to their credit reports.

Create a spending plan (see Chapter 13) so you're assured of having the money to pay your loan installments. Don't start off on the wrong foot. The majority of student loans may be guaranteed by Uncle Sam, but they're all reported to the three credit bureaus. Missing a payment is not like cutting a class. Starting off a new life with debt is one thing, but starting off with bad credit is unnecessary.

Several repayment options are available for new grads:

- ✔ **Normal repayment:** You make principal and interest payments each month.

- ✔ **Graduated repayment:** You make lower payments at the beginning, and your payments increase at specified intervals throughout the life of your loan.

- ✔ **Income-based repayment:** Your monthly payments are set based on a percentage of your monthly gross income (for Stafford, Plus, and Smart Loan) and federal consolidation loans.

- ✔ **Extended repayment:** Your repayment term is lengthened.

- ✔ **Consolidation:** Your federal loans are refinanced into a single fixed loan with a long payback period.

- ✔ **Serialization:** You consolidate only the payments into a single payment but retain the original terms and interest rates on all your loans.

Financial aid: The ultimate gamble?

Who would lend tens of thousands of dollars to a teenager with no income, no employment history, and no track record of handling money or credit? It happens every day in schools across the country. The idea is that these teens will mature into responsible, productive, self-supporting adults who will repay their debt and contribute to society with their new knowledge and skills.

The loan gamble really isn't as risky to the lender as it seems. Lenders expect that a parent will bail out an offspring if only to keep bad credit or the lack of transcripts from ruining a job hunt. And if that fails, Uncle Sam guarantees the loan for the lender.

That said, student loans are risky for the *borrower*. Instead of addressing the rising costs of education by making it more effective and efficient, our protectors in Washington have instituted a maze of loans that the government guarantees payment on. With very attractive rates, these loans allow kids to afford to be educated at increasingly inefficient colleges and universities at inflated prices.

The result: Many kids graduate with huge debt loads and have to devote scarce first-job income to repaying their student loans. And those kids who don't graduate don't get their loans forgiven. They still have to pay perhaps 80 percent of the full amount a graduate does, but with significantly reduced income prospects.

Resolving overdue payment status

Because student loans are guaranteed against default and survive even a bankruptcy, the lenders and *servicers* (the people you send your payments into and talk to if you can't) have little to lose, so no one gets excited when loans are overdue (unlike the credit-card guys whose loans directly affect their bottom line and performance evaluations — and whose loans can disappear with a bankruptcy). But the fact that the lenders and servicers won't get all worked up about it if you're late shouldn't encourage you to put off repayment.

If your payment is already past due, contact your lender and explain the situation. Ask what programs you may qualify for. All this is much better done *before* you default because more options are available to you. Student loans are one type of debt you cannot shake off. The full range of debt collection and legal options (including wage garnishment) are available to the lender — but bankruptcy relief is *not* available to *you* (if you declare bankruptcy, you still have to pay back your student loans).

Before you call or write the loan servicer (and I suggest you begin with a call and follow up in writing), organize your thoughts. Treat this as a very important job interview. Be able to explain coherently why you weren't able to pay: medical issues, job loss, pay reductions, armed-service call-up, family emergency. If you're calling to propose a payment alternative, have a number prepared and be able to justify it based on your budget.

The student-loan agencies and lenders generally accept regular monthly-payment alternatives that are both reasonable to the agency and affordable to you. Call your servicer or the U.S. Department of Education information line at 800-872-5327, but be sure to do it before you miss a payment.

Reporting your loan status to the credit bureaus

Student loans are reported unlike any other loan. They're similar in that a good payment history helps your credit and credit score, and a default hurts it. If you're delinquent on your student loans, they may be referred to outside collection agencies that may also report your delinquency to the credit bureaus. But here's where student loans are different:

- ✓ **Each semester's or year's loan may be reported as a separate loan.** So you could have four to ten credit lines reported on what you think of as a single loan. That's potentially four to ten negative items on your credit report, not just one.

- ✓ **Your tax refunds may be seized until the government gets its money back.**

- ✓ **You may be unable to get other government student aid.**

- ✓ **Your student loan stays on your credit report until you pay it off.** How long will a student-loan default stay on your credit report? Well, if you haven't paid back your loan by the time you begin to collect Social Security, they take it out of your Social Security checks (along with fees and interest). No kidding.

Managing Medical Debt

If you have a lot of medical bills and you have health-insurance coverage, your approach to maintaining your credit will be different than if you don't have insurance, at least initially. Even if you're insured, dealing with health insurance and how it covers your medical bills can be a complicated and stressful issue. Problems can arise in terms of claims handling, and unless those problems are caught early, they can grow into major financial, credit-reporting, and legal dilemmas. Not to worry though. This section discusses the relevant issues concerning medical debt and your credit report.

Understanding the Medical Information Bureau

Because the focus of this book is credit, I'd be remiss if I didn't mention the MIB. Not the Men In Black, but the even more mysterious Medical Information Bureau. Yes, there is a bureau that specializes in your medical records. The information in your file can affect the price you pay for insurance (life, health, disability) — and the MIB can make mistakes. The MIB database, packed with health-related information on more than 15 million people, is used and shared by insurance companies.

Insurance companies use the MIB information to check your history before pricing or issuing you life or disability insurance and individual health-insurance products. Generally, when you apply for insurance, the insurance company asks you to provide information about your health or have medical tests. If something noteworthy turns up, the insurer reports that information to the MIB.

The MIB is a national specialty consumer-reporting agency (see Chapter 4), subject to the federal Fair Credit Reporting Act (FCRA). If you're denied insurance based on an MIB report, you're entitled to obtain a free report and to have erroneous information corrected. If you have an MIB file — and not everyone does — you want to be sure it's correct. You can obtain a copy for free once a year by calling 866-692-6901 (866-346-3642 TTY, for the hearing impaired), visiting the company's Web site at www.mib.com/html/request_your_record.html, or writing to Medical Information Bureau, P.O. Box 105, Essex Station, Boston, MA 02112. If you decide to visit, don't forget to wear your sunglasses!

Monitoring insurance claims for errors

You may be tempted to ignore the whole medical-payment process and assume that the insurance company and the doctors are handling everything satisfactorily. But you know better — what can go wrong often does. Claims payments or treatment-authorization communication between doctors and insurance companies is in codes, and one misplaced digit can make a big difference in the medical care paid for or allowed. Catching those small errors early is important — and you, as the claimant, have the most at stake.

Between the insurance companies — which have a better day when they don't pay a lot of claims than when they do — and the underpaid help in the medical office or hospital who must code all your procedures, errors are common, and legitimate claims are sometimes rejected. If your claim is rejected, always ask for the bills to be resubmitted and ask for an explanation of why they were rejected.

You don't have to be a claims whiz to keep track of your insurance process. Familiarizing yourself with your coverage limits is worth your time. Read through your insurance contracts (sorry, it's not the most scintillating reading). Get a copy of your coverage if you don't already have one. It may be a policy, a booklet, or something called a "summary plan description." (The insurance policy itself is the best and most complete source.) The health plan description is 20 to 30 pages or more. Points to pay attention to include

✔ **Schedule of benefits:** Explains what the insurance company pays and what you pay, deductibles, percentages, co-pays, and so on.

✔ **Covered benefits:** Often separate from the schedule of benefits, a laundry list of what is covered.

✔ **Exclusions and limitations:** What is not covered, as well as items covered but with limits.

✔ **Claims procedures:** Steps for filing claims and appealing denials. You may want to read that through, as there are usually some important time limits and details.

Reviewing these key components should give you a good idea of your coverage. If keeping track of medical expenses and reimbursements after or during an illness is just too taxing, consider a *daily money manager* (DMM). Relatively new on the scene, the DMM is similar to a personal financial advisor, someone who can provide a wide range of services, depending on your needs. This individual can also keep track of medical bills and insurance forms. The best way to find a good DMM is through a referral. If you come up short here, contact the American Association of Daily Money Managers (AADMM) at www.aadmm.com or call 301-593-5462.

Dealing with denied medical claims

Most doctors and hospitals do not report payment histories to credit bureaus. They don't like to pay the fees — and some of them don't like to think they're in the credit business. However, if a debt moves from the medical provider to an outside collection agency, odds are it will hit your credit report. The message here is that you have more room to work with the medical provider — but to be sure, ask if they report your payment history to one of the credit-reporting agencies.

Keep in touch with the hospital and billing people. They assume that if the claim is denied by the insurance company, you'll pay the difference. Communicating that you don't consider the claim settled and need their help to resubmit or appeal a decision will make them a part of the process and keep their expectations in line with yours.

When your insurance doesn't cover it

If your insurance covers only a portion of a bill, and you can't afford the balance, rather than letting the bill go to collections and damage your credit, you have a couple of alternatives:

✔ **You can ask for a discount.** The big insurance companies ask for discounts all the time and the hospitals grant them. Don't be afraid to ask.

✔ **You can ask the doctor to accept the insurance payment as payment in full.** Doctors do this all the time. If you're a doctor in a network and a network member comes in for something, whatever the insurer pays is all the doctor gets. The doctor agrees to this upfront in order to be a member of the network and get referrals. You may be able to get the same deal if you ask.

Lack of communication is not a good thing in these cases. Just as you take an active role in your health care and treatment as a patient, you also have to take an active role in the payment of your medical costs.

If you have a hard time getting your bills covered and you think the insurance company is wrong, take the following steps:

1. **Complain.**

   Most insurance carriers, believe it or not, don't like complaints. Here's a list of people to complain to, starting with the lowest one on the totem pole:

   - Claims adjuster
   - Supervisor
   - Unit manager (over several supervisors by line of business)
   - Assistant manager (over unit managers, but not in all offices)
   - Claims manager or claims vice president (in charge of local office)
   - Regional claims vice president (in charge of several offices in a region)
   - Home office claims, senior vice president

2. **Maintain detailed records.**

   When dealing with insurers, keep records of conversations (times, dates, and what was said), as well as copies of any documents you receive. If you write to an adjuster, copy his supervisor and request a written response in a set time frame. Be polite and direct. Nasty complaints are easily dismissed or sent to a lawyer.

Managing expenses to avoid credit repercussions

If, when all is said and done, you're still left with medical expenses you're responsible for paying, you have some options:

✔ **Suggest a reduced repayment amount either in a lump sum (ask them to consider an ease-of-handling discount for cash) or a set payment every month.** Do this before you get billed. When a third-party biller gets hold of a debt, they're tenacious and the doctors, who consider themselves either artists, healers, or above it all, generally don't want to get in the middle. Deal with the doctor first, if you can.

✔ **Find out if your hospital is covered under the federal Hill-Burton Act, which** prohibits discrimination in providing services. In 1975, Congress amended the Hill-Burton Program, which established federal grants, loan guarantees, and interest subsidies for certain health facilities to require that they must provide uncompensated services forever. The U.S. Department of Health and Human Services at the Health Resources and Service Administration has information about where to find the 316 facilities covered under Hill-Burton. Check at www.hrsa.gov/osp/dfcr/about/aboutdiv.htm. There are no such facilities in Indiana, Nebraska, Nevada, Rhode Island, Utah, or Wyoming.

3. **File a written complaint.**

    If you reach an impasse, write to your state insurance regulatory agency. Don't go into great detail — just give the very basic issues in dispute. To find your state regulator online, go to www.naic.org. Complaining to your state regulator is likely to motivate the insurer to pay better attention to resolving your claim.

If you have no insurance, definitely let the doctor or hospital know this early on in the process and ask about discounts and payment plans. Be sure you can afford the payment plan before you agree to it. (You may want to follow the same process recommended in the "Keeping Credit under Control While Unemployed" section, earlier in this chapter, which involves resetting your spending priorities until you have the new bills under control.) Being willing to pay a reasonable bill over time is the best course of action to keep any collection activity off your credit record. Communicating with your doctor and hospital is the key.

Dealing with Debts of the Deceased

If you've lost a spouse, you're already going through one of the most emotionally draining experiences possible. Unfortunately, in the midst of the often debilitating experience of losing a loved one, numerous financial matters surface, including credit and debt issues.

Stabilizing your credit in the event of a death can be difficult, especially if your spouse held all or most of the credit in his or her name. A creditor wants a copy of the death certificate and typically asks the estate to pay the bill. As a rule, the living spouse is not personally responsible for credit held in the deceased's name alone.

Keep in mind, however, that in community-property states — Arizona, California, Idaho, Louisiana, Nevada, New Mexico, Texas, Washington, and Wisconsin — credit accounts opened during marriage are automatically joint. That means you're responsible for any debt that your deceased spouse incurred during the marriage. Alaska may be another one if you opted for community-property status when you moved there. Although Puerto Rico is an American territory and not a state, it has community property laws too. This section focuses on how to protect your credit when the debts belong to a deceased spouse.

What happens to joint credit when you're single again

By law, a creditor cannot automatically close a joint account or change the terms because of the death of one spouse. Generally, the creditor asks the survivor to file a new credit application in his or her own name. If the creditor doesn't approach you with this option, close the joint account and open a new account in your name alone. The creditor will then decide to continue to extend credit or alter the credit limit. You don't have to deal with this the next day. But waiting too long to notify them may look like you are trying to deceive the lender about the true risks of the account.

Keep in mind that, when you're applying for new credit lines, you must use your name only. Including your deceased spouse's name will result in a joint account.

Credit bureaus automatically update records with periodic reports from the Social Security Administration. When the update is made, your spouse's credit history will be flagged and his or her name will be removed from any preapproved credit-offer mailing lists. This will reduce the mail you get in your spouse's name.

Understanding your liability

If you're a joint account holder on a credit card or if you live in a community-property state — Arizona, California, Idaho, Louisiana, Nevada, New Mexico, Texas, Washington, or Wisconsin (sometimes Alaska) — you may be liable for the debts of the deceased. In a community-property state, as long as the debt was incurred during the marriage, even if the other spouse received no benefit from it or didn't even know about it, he or she is still liable.

In the non-community-property states, credit-card and other debts that are only in the name of the deceased are not passed on to surviving spouses or children. When a loved one dies, however, notifying creditors is a good idea, even if you aren't liable. They'll ask for proof of death and generally request that a certified copy of the death certificate be forwarded to them. If there are assets in the estate, they may try to collect from the estate's executor. If there isn't enough cash and the assets that can be sold are few, that will generally end the issue.

Some loved ones feel that they should pay the debts, whether out of a sense of obligation or honor or just to set the record straight. Paying the debt of your deceased spouse is not necessary — unless you're required to by law. The creditors understand risk very well. When they charge a fee or an interest rate, this is just the type of risk they're collecting a premium for. So, in that regard, they've already been paid. If the creditor tries to pressure you to pay a debt that you aren't obligated to pay, I recommend telling them to go to *<insert your choice of venues>* and ask there.

Building your credit record — on your own

If the deceased was your spouse or life partner and you shared financial matters, you'll need to reestablish yourself as an individual once again. You may have done this once before when you were much younger. But the rules have probably changed, so the following takes you through the process from the beginning.

Notifying the credit bureaus

Begin by notifying the credit bureaus — Equifax, Experian, and TransUnion (see Chapter 5 for contact information). You want the preapproved and other junk mail in your spouse's name stopped. Also, although the Social Security Administration will notify the bureaus eventually, they aren't as fast as identity thieves. Some thieves make the most of the time between a person's death and when the death is reported to the credit bureaus. They use the deceased's Social Security number and identity to open fraudulent credit accounts. Generally, the family doesn't know anything about these accounts because the criminal has the monthly statements sent to another address.

Prompt notification to the bureaus can help eliminate this crime. Some experts even suggest that you add a security alert on the deceased person's credit reports. Such a statement might say that the person is deceased, not to issue credit, and that any application for credit in this person's name is fraudulent.

Creating a new spending plan

Coming up with a budget or spending plan that covers your expenses as a single person is important. This budget will help you understand how your financial situation has changed — for better or worse. Chapter 13 offers suggestions on how to create a budget. Chapter 3 helps you figure out if you could benefit from the help of a credit counselor. I recommend a credit counselor — in stressful situations, a clear, professional perspective is an asset, especially one so reasonably priced.

After you have the income and the expense pieces in place, look at your monthly debt payments. The combination of these three categories — income minus expenses and debt — will give you a final number. If you're spending down your savings and investments as part of your retirement plan, consult your trusted financial planner or advisor to make sure you're still on track. If you aren't on track, you may want to use a professional counselor to help you find ways to make ends meet.

Budgets can be as simple or as complex as you make them. When I did my own, I used a program; when I helped my mother with this process, my mother just looked at the amount of money she had to move from checking to savings each quarter to gauge where she was. You get to pick what works for you.

Like so many things after you've suffered such a major loss, fine-tuning your budget may take several months. Be patient with yourself.

Familiarizing yourself with your credit report

When you know where you stand financially, you can begin deciding how you want to use credit. Because your credit score determines what you pay for credit and under what terms it may be available, I suggest you get your FICO score from myFICO.com, along with your credit report. The better your score, the less you'll have to pay to borrow or use credit. Chapter 6 helps you get headed in the right direction.

Don't close old accounts with positive credit histories unless you have to. The length of time an account is open counts in your favor for credit-scoring purposes. A variety of accounts also helps your score. If you have a mortgage or a car payment and you can afford to pay them off, you may want to consider keeping them open for a short while (instead of paying them off), just to keep new positive information flowing into your credit file.

Chapter 15

Safeguarding Your Identity from Theft

*W*hen someone steals your identity, he pretends to be you. Not in a way where he would have to convince people who know you that he is you, but in a much easier way. The thief uses the myriad numbers that are associated with your name to become you. Whether they steal your mail, hack into your computer, break into your home, or sift receipts and personal information from your trash can, identity thieves gain access to valuable data that allows them to tap into your existing accounts and lines of credit or to open new accounts.

With your data in hand, these thieves can take vacations, buy cars, rent apartments, order designer furniture, pay for a week at the Ritz, get a job, max out all the credit card accounts they have access to, and profit financially because the businesses they're dealing with believe they're *you*. This activity, of course, hits your credit report. But if the thief is lucky — and you aren't — you may not discover him living it up and wrecking your credit rating for months or maybe longer, sometimes much longer. You may apply for a line of credit and discover you're rejected. Or you may get a flurry of aggressive calls from collections agencies who are sure you're the one responsible for unpaid bills.

Of course, you get to defend yourself and prove otherwise, but the process can be expensive and may take a long, long time to resolve. And while you're doing it, you may be subjected to unwarranted harassment, be passed by for that new job you've applied for, be turned down for a credit card or car loan, or miss out on all kinds of other opportunities because your credit report includes negative information put there by someone else pretending to be you. In this chapter, I let you know how you can protect yourself, your identity, and your credit from these crooks. And I help you deal with ending the situation as quickly as possible if you've already been hit.

Keeping Thieves at Bay

Although your identity is most likely to be stolen by someone you don't know, many times the culprits are people victims willingly let into their lives — friends, relatives, or co-workers. So you can significantly reduce your chances of falling victim to identity theft just by making yourself more secure in your home: In short, don't leave financial documents and confidential information where they can be easily seen.

In response to the billions of dollars lost to identity theft, Congress amended the Fair Credit Reporting Act (FCRA) with the Fair and Accurate Credit Transactions Act (the FACT Act or FACTA) to help reduce the threat of identity theft and give victims new rights.

Find out more about the FACT Act in Chapter 7, on the CD, and at the FTC Web site (www.ftc.gov/os/statutes/fcrajump.shtm).

As a teenager, I vividly recall my father using the dining room table as a sort of open-shelf filing system or landfill. In the middle was a huge bowl with a great heap of letters, bills, statements, and the like. To greater or lesser degrees, the rest of his family adopted the same system. But no more. Leaving bank statements or checks on the table today is like putting them out in the middle of the street. Anything you wouldn't want in the middle of the street is something you should take care to keep out of sight in your home. Try to envision my analogy of putting an item in the middle of your street as you read on. This simple image will help you stay focused. Do you want your bank statement in the middle of the street? No? Then put it out of sight.

In the following sections, I walk you through some simple steps you can take to reduce the chances of your identity being stolen.

Taking advantage of online transactions

One of the easiest ways to protect yourself is to handle bill-paying, information transfers, and financial transactions electronically. Having bills and statements delivered to your password-protected computer is much better than having them delivered to your mailbox outside your home. Or, as I like to say, dropped off in the middle of your street. The more information you send and receive electronically, the lower the chances of identity theft.

Using a computer has other benefits as well: When you get your information online, as in the case of your bank statement, you can check up on it anytime you want. No need to wait for the end of the month. In fact, I recommend that you do a quick once-over every week or have periodic or dollar-level alerts e-mailed to you. For example, you can have transactions over $1,000 generate an e-mail automatically — that way, you can spot a problem early.

Take precautions when conducting business via the Net. You still may be at risk for identity theft. As long as you use only secure Web sites and ensure you're protected by a firewall, you're much better protected than you are with snail mail. (See the next section for info on determining whether a Web site is secure, and the section "Keeping computer data safe" for a few words on firewalls.)

Avoiding phishing scams

Phishing is when a stranger pretending to be someone you trust (for example, a representative of your bank or credit-card company) e-mails you and asks you to confirm critical information about your account (for example, by replying with your password, Social Security number, or other personal information). It can also be perpetrated via a spyware program that you download to your computer (without realizing you've done so) by clicking on a link or opening a file; the program then records any personal information you've stored on your computer and sends that information to others.

The number of phishing scams are increasing, and they're also becoming more sophisticated. Bottom line: You need to be extremely careful when giving out your personal information over the Internet. As with phone solicitation, don't give out your personal information unless you've initiated the transaction.

Here are some do's and don'ts that can help keep you and your personal info safe:

✔ **Do be suspicious of any e-mail with urgent, exciting, or upsetting requests for personal financial info.** The sender is using your emotions to stimulate an immediate, illogical response to the request.

✔ **Don't give out personal or financial info unless you're certain of the source and you confirm that the link is secure.** You can tell you're on a secure Web site if you see a padlock or key icon in the lower-right corner of your Web browser. Also, the address of the site will begin with `https://` rather than `http://`. *Note:* Your e-mails are almost *never* secure, which means you should never e-mail your credit-card number, Social Security number, or other personal info to anyone — even if you're sure it's someone you can trust.

Exceptions to this rule apply when you're communicating with a co-worker using an internal network at work or you and the person you're e-mailing both have special security software in your e-mail programs. These exceptions are pretty uncommon, so to be safe, I recommend never giving private information out via e-mail, no matter what kind of network you're on.

✔ **Don't ever respond to e-mails that aren't personalized or that have your name misspelled.** If the message has your name wrong or doesn't have your name at all, don't reply.

✔ **Don't ever click on links in e-mail messages to find out what the great offer is.** If you click on the link, you may end up downloading spyware onto your computer, and your security may be compromised.

✔ **If you suspect that you're being phished, do forward the e-mail to the Federal Trade Commission at spam@uce.gov, and file a complaint at the Internet Fraud Complaint Center (IFCC) by going to www.ic3. gov.** The IFCC is a partnership between the FBI and the National White Collar Crime Center (NW3C). The IFCC Web site not only lets you report suspected Internet fraud but provides disturbing statistics about this growing crime.

Keeping computer data safe

You need to safeguard your computer so it doesn't end up in the middle of the street, metaphorically speaking. Here are some computer-safety rules to consider:

✔ **Don't leave your laptop out where it can be picked up.** Whether at home, in a hotel, or at work, when you're not in the same room as your laptop, put it away and out of sight. Would you leave a $100 bill laying out? The same consideration applies here.

✔ **Don't walk away from your computer and leave files with personal information open — particularly if you're online.** My wife does this all the time and it drives me crazy.

✔ **Come up with a user name and personal identification number (PIN) or password that isn't obvious, and set your computer so that this information is required in order to turn your computer on.** You can also use a screensaver that has a password, so that if you walk away from your desk for a certain period of time and the screensaver comes on, you need to enter a password to get back to your desktop.

Including at least one number, capital letter, or special character in your password is good (for example, Steve@1). Don't use birth dates or Social Security numbers — they're too easy for hackers to guess.

✔ **Don't keep a list of your passwords near the computer.** That's the computer equivalent of leaving your house key in your front-door lock.

✔ **Install a firewall.** If you use a wireless network, make sure the firewall is encrypted. (You can get firewalls for your home computer at most office-supply stores like OfficeMax or Staples.)

✔ **Use antivirus and spyware protection to keep key loggers off your computer.** *Key loggers* are programs that send out any information that you type to the crook, including your credit-card numbers, user names, passwords, Social Security number, and so on.

✔ **Make sure to thoroughly delete all personal information on your computer if you decide to get rid of your computer and really put it in the middle of the street.** Your best bet is to completely reformat your hard drive, which wipes it out and gets rid of everything. (Check with your computer manufacturer to find out how to rewrite your hard drive.)

Protecting passwords

A testament to the trusting nature of Americans is the premise that if you want to know something personal or secret about them, all you have to do is ask. I can't count the number of times I've been at the office working on my computer and, when I've needed people to do something technical for me, they've said, "Steve, give me your password." That the tech-support people continue asking for this information leads me to believe that they must be getting it from other people and not getting their hands slapped for asking. Me, I slap 'em. "No thanks," I say. "Just tell me what to do and I'll do it."

Seriously, this problem is so widespread that it has a name: It's called *social engineering*. It's using social situations to get information about otherwise secure data out of the unwitting. To make sure you're not being socially engineered, follow these suggestions:

✔ **Don't give anyone your password.** If the guy in the next cube over wants to be helpful, you can enter your password for him.

✔ **If you have to give out your password, be sure you trust the source — and then change your password immediately.**

✔ **Don't share your clever password with co-workers or friends.**

✔ **Don't use your kid's or pet's name or birthday for your password.**

Avoid giving out confidential information to friends, acquaintances — even your kids. They may not be identity thieves, but they sure are great, naive sources of information.

Safeguarding your mail

Although tampering with the U.S. mail is a federal crime, your mailbox is one of the most common targets of identity thieves. The culprit removes some statements from your mailbox and, before you miss them, begins the process of changing addresses and opening new accounts. He can also easily convert that check you sent off for the heating bill into ready cash. Acid-washing the original recipient off the check and replacing the name isn't difficult for enterprising thieves.

I suggest the following tips to help you reduce your exposure to mail fraud:

- ✔ **Convert as much of your financial business to online transactions as possible.** Doing so helps you avoid delivering information to the waiting hands of the criminal scouting your unattended mailbox.

- ✔ **Explore alternatives to your unlocked, end-of-the-driveway mailbox.** Consider using a post office box or a locked mailbox that will accept mail (not unlike the old slot in the door).

- ✔ **Don't mail checks or financial information from your home mailbox.** Use your local post office mailbox or bring your mail to work with you. (Don't forget the stamps, or the boss may cancel your work identity.)

- ✔ **Ask your bank to hold new check orders and pick them up at the bank.**

- ✔ **If you're away for a day or more, have someone pick up your mail or, better, have the post office hold it until you return.** Don't let it sit in your mailbox overnight.

Maintaining financial data in your home

When you gain control of the mail flow in and out of your home, you can feel more comfortable that you've closed off some key avenues for potential identity theft. Yet, inside your sanctuary, that pile of documents must be protected and secured. Your information is still accessible to house thieves, not to mention others who may gain access to your inner sanctum through other means. The following are ways to protect yourself in your home.

Storing your confidential documents and information

Keep all financial, confidential, and legal documents and information in a secure place — a strong box or a metal filing cabinet. Not only will your valuable data be safe from prying eyes and sticky fingers, but you'll also benefit from having all critical information in one place in case you need to access it quickly.

Sometimes a simple thing can save the day. Making and securely storing a photocopy of the contents of your wallet and account numbers is one of them. If you haven't already done so, empty the contents of your wallet or purse and photocopy everything, front and back. Write the contact phone numbers next to each item and file the paper in a locked cabinet. Voilà! You're now better prepared to deal with an identity crisis.

Shredding the evidence

Your mailbox is not the only source of private information for identity thefts. Your garbage can is also ripe with potential (not to mention banana peels and dog-food cans). A determined thief won't mind sifting through your detritus if it means snagging a credit-card number from those coffee-grounds-covered receipts. A fishing expedition in the backyards and trash cans of suburbia promises a good catch.

 Purchase a good home crosscut shredder, and shred all financial mail that contains account numbers before you discard them. This includes savings, checking, and credit-card statements. Don't overlook all those preapproved offers for credit you receive.

I recently purchased a shredder, and I recommend that you get a model that has a large capacity because the shredded paper takes up a lot of space and it fills up fast. Also be sure the shredder is easy to empty — the shredded, confetti-like material tries to fly all over the place. This pleases my cat but not my wife.

Freezing your credit information

Frozen daiquiris, frozen snickers, frozen credit? The option of freezing credit to keep it from identity thieves has become available to everyone. The concept is simple: You can freeze or lock up your credit information so that anyone who is looking to extend credit has to ask you to *thaw out* (unlock) your file. Freezing your credit information seriously hampers an identity thief from opening credit in your name without your knowledge, because few lenders will extend credit without a credit report in hand.

 The main consideration surrounding to-freeze-or-not-to-freeze is whether you value access to instant credit more than you fear your personal information being compromised. Only you know the answer to that question.

But the strategy is not foolproof. Existing accounts could still be pirated, used, and abused by such tactics as simply swiping your mail, changing your address from Peoria to Las Vegas, and getting replacement cards issued. So a freeze may help protect your *information,* but it may not protect your *money.* Given the low personal level of liability on credit cards, however, your monetary losses would not be significant.

Protecting active-duty military personnel

The last thing the United States wants its active-duty servicepersons to worry about when they're safeguarding you and me is who's safeguarding *them* from identity thieves. As a credit counselor, I worked closely with many clients enlisted in the Navy. I can tell you from experience that they are as fine and trusting and *naive* a group of young idealists as I have ever met. They're often targeted for scams when they step outside of their military environments. Fortunately, just in time for what seems to be an increasingly active period of military deployments in the world, the FACT Act has created another new alert. The *active-duty alert* allows active-duty military personnel to place a notation on their credit report as a way to alert potential creditors to possible fraud.

While on duty outside the country, military personnel — as well as their families at home in the United States — may lack the time or means to monitor their credit activity. (Calling TransUnion about an error isn't exactly a high priority when you're being shot at.) It seems only fair that, while soldiers are protecting their country, their country should protect them from credit problems.

If you're in the military and away from your usual base or deployed, you can place an active-duty alert on your credit report. An active-duty alert stays on your credit report for at least one year. This alert helps minimize the risk of identity theft by requiring that a business take "reasonable" care to verify your identity before issuing you credit. However, if you're in some distant land trying to keep the peace, that may not be feasible. So to keep the creeps away from your credit, you can appoint a personal representative to place or remove an alert.

Before you leave your base or home for active duty, be sure to appoint a personal representative and provide contact information to the credit bureau. If you don't, a creditor only has to "utilize reasonable policies and procedures to form a reasonable belief" before granting credit to someone who claims to be you. This is way too *reasonable* for my comfort level. Be sure to appoint someone you trust!

An active-duty alert on a credit report requires a creditor to take extra steps to verify your identity not only before granting new credit, but also when issuing an additional credit card on an existing account or raising your limits. When you put an active-duty alert on your credit report, you receive a copy of your credit report and, as a bonus, your name is removed from preapproved-offer lists for credit cards, insurance, and loans. You can place additional alerts if your deployment lasts longer than a year.

To place or remove an active-duty alert, call any one of the three major credit-reporting bureaus. Whichever one you call will require you to provide appropriate proof of identity, which may include your Social Security number, name, address, and other personal information.

You only have to contact one of the three companies to place an alert — the companies are required to contact the other two. (If you call all three, they'll be calling each other and getting confused — and they're easily confused.)

Remember: If your contact information changes before your alert expires, update it or have your representative do so.

If your information is stolen and the thief opens new lines of credit in your name, you can get all sorts of grief from collectors who are trained not to listen to excuses. "But I *swear,* I was never *in* Las Vegas and I never authorized that purchase of a $5,000 lap dance." They've heard it all before. So the bottom line of freezes is as follows:

✔ All the bureaus allow you to freeze your credit files regardless of the laws in your state.

✔ Freezing doesn't prevent abuse of existing accounts.

✔ Thawing an account takes a few days and may keep impulse or sale purchases from happening — which can be a good thing or a bad thing, depending on how you look at it.

A fraud alert is similar to a mini-freeze in that it only requires verification of identity. When you place a fraud alert on your file, it remains on your credit report for a specific amount of time after a theft has occurred.

Shielding your credit-card number

One of the easiest ways you can guard your identity is to ensure thieves don't have access to your credit-card numbers. Luckily for you, the FACT Act has made this task a tad easier for you. Electronically generated receipts for credit- and debit-card transactions may not include the card's expiration date or more than the last five digits of the card number. If you receive a receipt that has your full account number on it, bring it to the attention of the business and insist that they get with the program — now!

Note: Another FACT Act section allows consumers who request a copy of their credit file to also request that the first five digits of their Social Security number (or similar identification number) not be included in the file.

Spotting Identify Theft When It Happens

If your identity is stolen, you may not receive any obvious indication that you've been victimized — there's no broken window or missing masterpiece to serve as a clue. The evidence, unfortunately, may not make itself known until your credit has been sorely compromised and you're fighting on multiple fronts to restore your good name.

That said, by being vigilant, you can spot signs of identity theft. This crime is one that you'll probably be the first to notice, and vigilance on your part can make all the difference between a minor or a major crime. In the following sections, I give you some key signs to watch out for.

Instituting an early-warning alert

The FACT Act requires that creditors give you what may be called an *early-warning notice*. This can serve as your first sign that something is amiss with an account and give you the opportunity to halt devastating abuse of your credit in its early stages.

Anyone who extends credit to you must send you a one-time notice no later than 30 days after negative information — including late payments, missed payments, partial payments, or any other form of default — is furnished to a credit bureau. This includes collection agencies as long as they report to a credit bureau. The FACT Act doesn't dictate how *big* of a notice you get. You may have to look closely to even see it, so be sure you do your part by closely monitoring your credit reports, bank accounts, and credit-card statements.

This notice means something bad is in your account history, and if it's reported to the credit bureau, it will be negative. Whether it's reported or not, it's lurking out there. Before negative information is reported, the early-warning notice may look something like this:

> *We may report information about your account to credit bureaus. Late payments, missed payments, or other defaults on your account may be reflected in your credit report.*

After negative information has been reported, the early-warning notice may look like this:

> *We have told a credit bureau about a late payment, missed payment, or other default on your account. This information may be reflected in your credit report.*

The wording makes it sound as though the bad information may not show up. It will — and probably already has.

Receiving a collections call

The call, likely an unpleasant and adversarial one, will be one demanding a payment on an overdue account, one the collector is certain you owe. What should you do? The FACT Act, designed to address identity-theft issues, states that you need to tell the collector very clearly that you did not make the purchase and you believe that your identity may have been stolen.

When you tell the collector you think your identity may have been stolen, the collection agency is required by law to inform the creditor. You're also entitled to get a copy of all the info the collection agency or creditor has about this debt, including applications, statements, and the like, as though this really were your account or bill.

Predicting identity theft before it happens

The FACT Act demands that financial institutions establish procedures to attempt to spot identity theft *before* it occurs. To predict an identity theft before it happens may seem as far-flung as calling in a psychic on a murder case. But like our trusty weather forecasters who look to the skies for clues to tomorrow's weather, financial prognosticators are writing programs to look for specific activity in your financial records that may indicate a problem. In fact, several credit-card companies are now touting their own programs to fight identity theft.

Certain events — such as a change of address, a request for a replacement credit card, or efforts to reactivate a dormant credit-card account — may signal a potential fraud. That said, you can only do so much to protect yourself from identity theft, so even with prevention programs in place, in most cases you won't know about a problem until after the fact.

The best part is that, under the FACT Act, as soon as you notify the creditor or collector that the debt is the work of an identity thief, the debt cannot be sold or placed for collection.

Discovering unrecognized charges

In order to find charges on your statement that you didn't make, you have to actually read your statement in detail. Many people just look at the amount due and make a payment. Instead, take a minute and review your charges — you just may be surprised.

Don't rely on your memory as you review your statement. My memory isn't the greatest in the world (or so my wife says, although I can't remember why). So I make sure to keep all my credit-card receipts in a file — and I pull them out when reviewing my monthly statement. Keep all credit-card receipts in a convenient place — at least until you receive, verify, and pay your statement.

If you see any unauthorized charges on your statement, call the customer-service number and get the details. You may have to dispute the charge, but that's no big deal. Also, the representative may see some indication of an identity theft. That happened to me once — I saw a stray charge, called the credit-card company, and the customer-service rep recognized it as fraud right away. Make the call.

Being denied credit or account access

Rejection is always a painful thing — but it's especially painful when you're rejected because of something you're not responsible for. If you get rejections for credit, you may want to ask why — but your best bet is to order a copy of your credit report and look for evidence of identity theft (accounts you never opened and activity you don't recognize).

Another sign of identity theft is receiving a notice that you've been rejected for credit you never asked for. Take this seriously. Someone who shouldn't be may be applying for credit in your name.

You may try to access an ATM and get a denial message. If this happens to you, contact your bank immediately to determine whether it's the result of identity theft.

Missing account statements

Your monthly statement is really late. Hmm . . . now that you think of it, you didn't receive a statement last month, either. Yes, I know this was one of your birthday wishes, but the real reason you're not hearing from your creditors may be more sinister. It could mean an identity thief has changed your address in order to use your bank accounts, hoping you won't notice for a few months.

Create a system by which you remind yourself when statements are due and bills must be paid. This way, you're more likely to stay on top of your payment schedule and be alerted when something is amiss. If you pay bills and get statements via computer instead of snail mail, you make it harder on the thieves (and easier on yourself).

When Identity Theft Happens to You

If you discover that you're a victim of identity theft, you need to act quickly and comprehensively. Don't rely on others to resolve this mess. You have the biggest interest in getting this situation stopped, fixed, and behind you, and you need to assume all responsibility for doing so.

If your identity has been stolen or you believe it has (you don't need a smoking gun, videotapes, or a confession to act), do everything I recommend in the following sections right away. Most of these places are open 24 hours a day, so a late-night call won't wake anyone.

Contacting everyone who needs to know

You may read different advice on whom to call *first* if you discover you're a victim of identity theft. Some sources recommend calling the police, others suggest you call your creditors or the credit bureaus. My advice is to begin in one of two places, depending on your circumstances:

- ✔ If your existing accounts have been compromised, call your creditors first.
- ✔ If you're hearing about accounts you've never had, call the credit bureaus first.

Either way, don't wait long between the two calls.

Before you pick up the phone, you must do one more thing: Get a notebook and a pen and start writing down everything that happens from now on. You want names, badge numbers, phone numbers, names of supervisors, and so on. Documentation is critical because this situation may go on for a long time and require a lot of calling and writing to resolve. Don't trust your memory or count on anyone calling you back when he says he will. It happens all the time. Be responsible and get the facts.

On the CD, I include a handy worksheet, courtesy of the Federal Trade Commission, called "Chart Your Course of Action" that you may find useful. You can use it as is, or use it to generate ideas for creating a customized chart of your own.

Canceling your credit cards

If your credit or debit cards have been compromised, call the card companies, ask for the fraud department, and cancel the cards immediately. You can find the phone number on your monthly statements or in your terms-and-conditions brochure. Your card may also have a customer-service number you can call.

A small comfort: Your liability on stolen credit-card accounts is relatively low — just $50 maximum. Even so, you need to contact all your creditors as quickly as possible so that the thief doesn't continue to rack up charges in your name, creating a bigger loss for the credit-card company.

For ATM and debit cards, your maximum liability is $50 if you report the loss within 48 hours of noticing it, but $500 or even *unlimited* (including any overdraft protection) if you delay too long.

Contacting the credit bureaus

Calling one of the bureaus results in a 90 day fraud alert being placed on all three of your credit files within 24 hours. A *fraud alert* can make it more difficult for someone to get credit in your name because it tells creditors to follow certain procedures to protect you. (Refer to "Sending out a fraud alert" later in this chapter for more info.)

Consider putting a freeze on your accounts until you know how severe the damage is. You can always thaw your accounts later, and a freeze will shut off access to your information much more completely than a fraud alert will.

You can also add a *victim's statement* to your credit report. The victim's statement informs anyone getting your report that there's a problem with your file and it may not be relied upon to be completely accurate. Most creditors take strong notice of this fact and won't issue new credit in your name.

Adding a victim's statement to your report may motivate creditors to close existing accounts that weren't affected until they can determine you're safe again — which may keep you from using your accounts for a while.

After you've notified the credit bureau of your situation, you'll receive a credit report from each of the bureaus. Be sure to keep a copy of all reports (store them with those copious notes you're taking).

Contacting the Federal Trade Commission

The Federal Trade Commission (FTC) supports an entire department that handles identity-theft issues. The folks in the identity-theft clearinghouse don't follow up on specific instances, but they play an important role in looking for patterns and accumulating statistics that help everyone concerned with stopping identity thefts.

Call the FTC's ID Theft Hotline at 877-438-4338. From a purely self-serving perspective, contacting the FTC will bolster your claims regarding unauthorized credit-card charges or accounts opened by thieves in your name. Go to `https://rn.ftc.gov/pls/dod/widtpubl$.startup?Z_ORG_CODE=PU03` to fill out the Identity Theft Affidavit form. You can use a copy of this form when disputing accounts or charges with creditors, as well as when filing a police report.

Contacting the police

Call the local sheriff? Will he flip on his blue and red lights and tear around town to find the thief? Not exactly. But the FACT Act requires that you be official on your end, just as the government is required to be on its end. You have a crime on your hands, so you need to call the police and report it.

The police report is also a way for others in the process to get a straight, consistent story from a third party about what happened and when. You'll have less difficulty convincing that collector you aren't kidding about the Las Vegas lap-dance bill if you can refer him to your local police or send an official police report to bolster your story. Be sure to get a copy of the report as soon as it's available — or at least get the police-report number for reference.

Here's how the police reporting process works:

1. **Contact your police station after you discover an account and/or activity on your credit report that isn't yours, and you suspect someone is using your identity.**

   You don't need legally acceptable proof or a smoking gun — it's your identity, and your suspicion is enough to file a police report.

2. **File the report, giving them all the facts and circumstances.**

   No standard form or procedure exists; each police department has its own.

3. **Make sure you get the police-report number with the date, time, police department, location, and name of the person taking the report.**

   You're likely to have to provide this info if you deal with insurance claims or work with credit-card companies and other lenders to clear your account.

4. **Be persistent if the police seem reluctant to take your statement, but be polite.**

   Some police departments may not recognize identity theft as a crime they're responsible for handling. They may question their jurisdiction or not want to take the time to take a report. Remind them that, without a police report, credit bureaus may not block fraudulent items on your report, and law enforcement may be inadvertently helping a crook. For more tips on soliciting the police's support, see Chapter 16.

   Furnish as much documentation as you can to prove your case — debt-collection letters, credit reports, your notarized Identity Theft Affidavit (see the preceding section), and so on. The police report will also help cover you against liability in case someone assumes your identity and is arrested for criminal activity using your name and personal data.

Notifying the post office

Many identity-theft cases are the result of unauthorized and illegal access to your information via the U.S. mail. Messing with the mail is a federal crime. If you're a victim of identity theft and think your mail played a role, the post office recommends that you contact the nearest U.S. Postal Service Inspection Office and report your concerns. If you know for sure it was the mail, call to report a crime. Find the office closest to you by contacting your local post office or go online to `http://usps.com/postalinspectors/ifvictim.htm`.

Taking advantage of the FACT Act

The FACT Act has numerous provisions for businesses, credit reporters, and you. An entire book could easily be written on the topic, but in essence, the FACT Act was designed to address issues surrounding incomplete or inaccurate credit reporting, not to mention identity theft. The following list highlights the consumer-oriented provisions of the act that I think are most informative or useful:

- ✔ **You can receive at least one free credit report each year from each of the three bureaus.** Under certain circumstances, you can get more than one. Specialty reporting agencies, such as insurance and landlord reporting services, must also give you a free report if you ask. (See Chapter 5 for more info on specialty bureaus.)

- ✔ **You have the right to dispute the information in your file directly with the party furnishing the data, instead of having to go through a third party.** The credit-reporting agencies have up to 45 days to respond.

- ✔ **You can sue creditors and the bureaus for violations of the FACT Act for two years after discovery or five years after the violation took place.** Your case is especially strong if they continue to sell, transfer, or place your account for collection after you've communicated that it's because of identity theft and placed a block on the trade line.

- ✔ **Creditors and collectors cannot continue to report information based on an account that you've reported as fraudulent or that you've shown to be inaccurate or incomplete.**

- ✔ **You must be notified about any adverse credit actions, such as being offered less-than-favorable credit terms or a creditor sending a negative item to your credit report.**

- ✔ **Businesses must cooperate with you to help clear your name in the case of identity theft.** They must provide copies of records about goods or services they provided to the thief. The business may require a police report and may take up to 30 days to comply.

- ✔ **You can opt out of information-sharing between affiliates.** So, if you don't want Citibank to tell Smith Barney (their brokerage affiliate) that you're a big spender (and should be called to invest some of that money), they won't.

- ✔ **You may place a 90-day fraud alert, a 7-year extended fraud alert, and a 1-year military active-duty alert on your file.**

- ✔ **You may have fraudulent trade lines on your credit report blocked if you've reported the crime to a police department or law-enforcement agency.**

- ✔ **You may request that your Social Security number be *truncated* (shortened) on your credit report and communications in case it falls into the wrong hands.** And credit-report users can't just throw your used reports in a trash bin. They have to dispose of the report in an approved manner.

- ✔ **Businesses must truncate your credit-card number on credit-card receipts.** In other words, your restaurant receipt shouldn't show your entire credit-card number — just the last five digits.

Sending out a fraud alert

As I mention earlier in this chapter, contacting the credit bureaus is one of your first steps when you discover an identity theft. When you contact them, you have the opportunity to place a fraud alert and a victim's statement in your file. These two items indicate to anyone looking at your report that the request for credit they've received recently may not actually be from you. Generally, the creditor contacts you before approving the credit request.

If your ex-brother-in-law is pretending to be you and he's at a car dealership waiting to drive away with a new Rolls Royce, the fraud alert and victim's statement work well. The dealership has to verify who he is. The fraud alert does create a bit of an extra step or delay if you're simply trying to legitimately open a new credit card to take advantage of a 10-percent discount on items you're purchasing today at the local department store — but this may be a delay you're willing to live with because of the protection it provides.

A fraud alert is placed on your account for 90 days. Any new activity, including your own, is researched and reported to you. So if you open new credit lines during this time, you may notice a slower-than-normal process. Although inconvenient, this safeguard is in place to protect you.

If you aren't sure whether your identity has been stolen, but the information necessary to steal it has been compromised, consider an *extended alert* on your credit report. An extended alert lasts seven years. Why use an extended alert? Say you lose your wallet. A thief may not use your information right away — he may save your information for future use. The extended alert covers a long enough time period to prevent the information from being used to open an account, say, next year. Sort of like that weed killer you use to keep the little creepers from sprouting in the first place. Though a nuisance, an extended alert serves to warn you of any suspicious activity — even after you've forgotten about the original event that triggered you to establish the alert in the first place.

A small silver lining: After you put the alert on your file, you're entitled to *two* free copies of your credit report at any time during the next 12 months from all three agencies, not just the annual report now available to all consumers.

Blocking that line

"Block that line" may sound like a football cheer, but it can be a powerful tool. Be sure to request that the bureaus block any lines of credit that you believe are fraudulent. This prevents those items from being sold, transferred, or placed for collection. In addition, ask the credit bureaus to remove any inquiries on your record as a result of those fraudulent lines.

Finally, ask the credit bureaus to notify anyone who may have received reports over the last six months with the erroneous information and inquiries on them. Doing so helps alert creditors and other interested parties to the situation — and save your reputation.

Accessing Credit after Identity Theft

If you're a victim of identity theft, you're likely to feel traumatized, battered, fearful, and angry. You're likely to avoid any experience with credit and borrowing in the future.

But I encourage you to strive to overcome these feelings. After all, credit — though it certainly can be abused and exploited — also brings great benefits to responsible individuals, allowing them to achieve personal and financial goals they otherwise wouldn't realize. I strongly suggest that you adopt a strong offense and move forward with your personal goals. Whether you're planning on buying a house or you're simply buying back-to-school supplies at their lowest prices, don't be afraid to use credit to your advantage. Here are some steps you can take to get your credit going again, without putting yourself at renewed risk to identity thieves.

Closing and reopening your accounts

Whether your personal accounts were broken into, stolen, or just sniffed at, change all your PINs, passwords, user IDs, and account numbers. You'll probably have to close accounts and reopen them. A hassle, perhaps — but if you've been a victim of identity theft, you already know the real meaning of *hassle*.

Here's a list of which accounts to close and reopen:

- ✔ **Bank accounts:** When your information is compromised, you never know if or when trouble will pop up. Changing the account numbers will result in a dead end for a thief.

- ✔ **Credit-card accounts:** When you contact the card companies, you'll be asked for proper identification. (This is good — you *want* them to be suspicious!) They're used to closing accounts and reopening new ones quickly and painlessly. I suggest that you only reopen those you use. As a rule, if I haven't used a card in two years, I begin to wonder why it's taking up space in my wallet.

Be careful, however, about closing your older accounts. These accounts tend to help your credit score.

✔ **Other accounts:** Contact your Internet service provider and utility companies to alert them to your circumstances. Get new account numbers in every situation. If your long-distance calling card has been stolen or you discover fraudulent charges on your phone bill, close your old account and open a new one.

Changing your PINs and passwords

When you change those accounts at the bank, change your personal identification numbers (PINs), too. And when you access money at ATMs or in public places, make sure no one can see you enter the number. Getting close to the machine may block the sight of a camera with a telephoto lens or someone using binoculars across the street. (Yes, thieves really *do* go that far.)

Switch to a *pass-phrase* instead of a password. A pass-phrase uses a short series of words like "ElvisIs#1" instead of a single password. Pass-phrases tend to be longer and harder to crack. Include some numbers and characters in them if you can.

Changing your Social Security number and driver's license

If you can't seem to shake the damage done by the identity theft (either because new theft occurrences keep popping up or collectors keep landing on you like blue-bottle flies), you may need to take more-serious action. Contact the Social Security Administration to inquire about getting a new Social Security number.

Getting a new Social Security number is a huge pain to everyone, including you. Imagine all the places you've used your old number. Prepare to change all your records yourself — no one does this for you. For more information, visit the Social Security Web site at www.socialsecurity.gov or call 800-772-1213 (800-325-0778, TTY for the hearing impaired).

If you go this route, you won't be the first. Besides the storied federal witness-protection program, Social Security numbers are also changed for domestic-violence victims when warranted. But with all the emphasis on national security, changing your number isn't easy.

A few circumstances can prevent you from changing your Social Security number. You can't get a new Social Security number if:

- ✔ You've filed for bankruptcy.
- ✔ You intend to avoid the law or your legal responsibility.
- ✔ Your Social Security card is lost or stolen, but there is no evidence that someone is using your number.

Be sure to document everything. This dog can have a very long tail. You may need to dig up some documentation a year or two after you thought all the dust had settled. Good records, with everything in writing and names and dates, will be a godsend.

While you're at it, grab a good paperback book, go down to the Department of Motor Vehicles, and get your driver's license number changed — especially if someone is using yours as an ID.

Part V
The Part of Tens

In this part . . .

*E*veryone loves tens — the top ten songs, a rocket launch countdown, ten-dollar bills. In this part, you get my top ten suggestions in short, concise, bite-sized portions to help you tame, improve, repair, and protect your credit. I condense two times ten years of experience into a few pages for quick reference.

I provide ten useful suggestions to consider if you're concerned about falling behind on your mortgage. Look for ten tips to protect your identity or to reduce the damage if it's too late. I also have ten ways to establish or improve your credit standing. Feel free to check out the accompanying CD for another bonus Part of Tens chapter that helps you deal with financial emergencies. Whether you have ten minutes or even ten seconds, these chapters are bound to help you and your credit.

Chapter 16

Ten Tips for Avoiding Identity Theft or Reducing Its Damage

In This Chapter

▶ Minimizing the damage done

▶ Contacting the right agencies the right way

▶ Keeping tabs on your personal information

*T*he best way to dodge damage from identity theft is to avoid being a victim in the first place. (In Chapter 15, I address a number of ways to do this.) But the sad fact is this: Despite your best efforts, you may become an identity theft victim. From sophisticated Internet phishing (in which thieves posing as banks or other companies with which you do business e-mail you asking for your account number or Social Security number) to rummaging through your trash, criminals bent on stealing your identity bombard you from every direction. If you have gas, water, or electric service at your home; own a computer or telephone; put out the trash; or pick up your mail from a typical mailbox outside your home, you're vulnerable. If and when you're victimized, it's up to you to fix the problems caused by the theft.

But what if you're not certain you've been victimized? Say, you lose your wallet or leave your credit card behind at a store. My advice is this: Act anyway and act fast. By the time you have evidence of identity theft, damage will have been done. Don't wait more than two days before taking action. Why wait even one day? Because you may have only misplaced, forgotten about, or left whatever it is you're concerned about in your car, at a friend's, or at a trustworthy merchant's. Why not three days? Because after two days, your liability may increase.

What to do, when to do it, and who can help you get on with your life is what this chapter is all about. So read on — in the pages ahead, I tell you what you need to know to get through the trauma of being an unfortunate victim of identity theft with as little damage as possible.

Limiting Your Liability

If you have reason to believe any of your credit or debit cards have been used without your authorization, call the issuers and cancel them immediately. The numbers to call are included on your monthly statements, on the backs of the cards (you do have photocopies of your credit cards, right?), and/or on the Web sites of the issuing banks.

For credit cards, you're only responsible for the first $50 of any unauthorized charges that occur before you report the cards as lost or stolen. You have no liability for any losses after you report that the card has been lost or stolen; you also aren't liable for any losses resulting from someone getting ahold of your number but not using the actual card itself (say from a receipt or writing down the card number and using it later).

ATM and debit cards are a little different: Here, time is of the essence. A loss reported within two days of your noticing it carries the same maximum $50 liability as a credit card. If you report the loss more than 2 days and up to 60 days from the date your statement is mailed, your liability can be a whopping $500 maximum per card. And if you delay your report beyond 60 days, you may have unlimited responsibility for charges, including any overdraft line that may be associated with the card. Ouch!

You may be able to recover some of your loss through your homeowner's insurance. Check your policy. Most insurers offer reimbursement of the $50 fee(s), up to a limit, as part of basic forgery and fraud coverage. You can usually buy additional coverage if you have many cards and possible $50 fees to cover.

Placing or Extending a Fraud Alert

Good news: You only have to contact *one* of the big-three credit bureaus, and your theft will be communicated to all three. Each agency is bound by law to contact the other two agencies. A *fraud alert* will be placed on your account for 90 days. Any new activity will be researched and reported to you, including your own. So if you open new credit lines during this time, you may notice a slower-than-normal process. Although inconvenient, this safeguard is in place to protect you. A fraud alert is a short-term measure that is your least invasive to put in place.

What we've been seeing, especially in cases where a large amount of data is stolen, is that few, if any, of the compromised records result in an actual identity theft. So far. But nagging questions remain: Where does the data containing your social security number and date of birth go? Does the thief throw it away? Or is it saved for a rainy day or until you get tired of watching your account? No one knows yet. However, the extended alert may be just your answer. It stays in effect for seven years and serves to warn you of any suspicious activity after you've forgotten about the original event that triggered you to establish the alert.

Freeze Your Credit

Beyond the extended alert, you now have the option of freezing your credit data. There may be a small charge if you didn't file a police report. With a freeze, no new creditors or inquirers get a look at your file without your express permission. It may be a pain if you are trying to open an account or are looking for a new job. However, bureau reports may be unfrozen when you need information to be accessed for a small fee. This is the ultimate file protection. I recommend it if you are the type who worries about what may happen or if you have some inkling that your identity is being used by someone else.

Filing a Police Report

Identity theft is a crime and must be reported, even if you don't have a stolen wallet or actual documents missing. The police may be able to do little to keep your identity from being misused — but filing a police report is a very good idea. Having a police report is useful in challenging unauthorized charges on any credit or debit cards. In addition, if new, unauthorized accounts are opened in your name, the police report helps to document your experience.

If the police are reluctant to take your report, the Federal Trade Commission advises that you ask to file a "miscellaneous-incidents report," or try another jurisdiction, such as your state police. You also can check with your state attorney general's office to find out if your state law requires the police to take identity-theft reports. Look in the Blue Pages of your telephone directory for the phone number or go to www.naag.org for a list of state attorneys general.

After you file your report with the police, be sure you have the file number and the name of the officer who took your report. If you can get a copy of the report, all the better. This information will serve as evidence if you have problems with creditors because of unauthorized debt, and it'll back up any challenges you make.

Getting the Post Office in on the Act

Yes, even the Postmaster General wants to help. Not that Lance Armstrong will ride around like Paul Revere and give out the warning to every "middlesex, village, and farm." But tampering with the U.S. mail is a crime. If someone has gained access to your credit card and bank information by way of stealing or tampering with your mail, the U.S. Postal Service wants to meet them. Contact the nearest U.S. Postal Service Inspection Office and report the crime. You can find the office closest to you by contacting your local post office or going to http://usps.com/postalinspectors/ifvictim.htm.

Protecting All Your Accounts with Passwords

Not since Groucho Marx offered $100 for guessing the secret word have passwords been so important. You may not have had passwords for all your accounts in the past, but now that you've suffered the misery of identity theft, you'll be eager to protect all your accounts — online and otherwise — with a guess-proof password. See Chapters 15 for more password help.

Notifying the Social Security Administration

If you're a victim of identity theft, you want to make sure this most essential of numbers has not been compromised. The Social Security Administration will take your information and follow up on any fraud or illegal use of your Social Security number. Report the theft to the Office of the Inspector General at the Social Security Administration, P.O. Box 17768, Baltimore, MD 21235; phone 800-269-0271; fax 410-597-0118; Web www.ssa.gov/oig/hotline/.

Be sure to review your annual earnings record (everyone over 25 receives this information from the Social Security Administration) and keep doing so annually to see whether there are entries that don't look correct to you or that you can't account for. You can also get a copy of your information by contacting the Social Security guys at www.socialsecurity.gov/mystatement or calling 800-772-1213. If you're considering changing your Social Security number, see Chapter 15 for a deeper discussion of this strategy.

Checking Your Checking Accounts

If your checks or checking-account numbers have been stolen or misused, close the account(s) and ask your bank to notify the appropriate check-verification service. Unlike credit or debit cards, no federal law limits your losses if someone steals your checks and forges your signature. However, state laws *may* protect you.

Most states hold the bank responsible for losses from a forged check, but they also require that you take reasonable care of your account. For example, you may be held responsible for the forgery if you fail to notify the bank that your checkbook has been stolen or is missing. Your local bank manager may be able to help put you in touch with the right department in your state. If not, contact your state banking or consumer-protection agency for more information.

Notify all check-verification companies — or *registries,* as I call them — if you believe your checking information has been stolen. (Turn to Chapter 2 for more information.)

ChexSystems (`www.chexsystems.com`) is the most comprehensive of the check-fraud sites. You may place either a 90-day or a 5-year security alert. For the 90-day alert, call and get a password to allow you to file a report online. To place the five-year alert, you'll need to download the form, have it notarized, and send it to them.

Check, Check, and Check Again

After you've canceled your cards and protected every account you can with a password, you can relax, right? Sorry, but the answer is no. If your personal information has been compromised, chances still exist for thief using this knowledge — somewhere, sometime — for personal gain and your loss. Review your credit report frequently. Place an extended, seven-year alert or freeze on your credit report. You may want to resort to a monitoring service as well.

If your home were broken into, you wouldn't think twice about buying an alarm system. Consider these precautions your own personal alarm system to notify you and your "security service," the credit bureaus, that there's been an identity break-in.

Even if your thief is caught and prosecuted to the fullest extent of the law, continue to check your credit reports often — at least two or three times a year for the first two years. Be diligent in reporting any errors and make sure inaccuracies are corrected and errors are removed from your reports. Do the same with your annual earnings statement from the Social Security Administration. Protect your information and advise your family members to do the same.

Keep Good Records

Good record-keeping on your part is important in repairing identity theft damage. Keep contact information and follow up by snail mail or e-mail with everyone you've contacted. For snail mail, use certified mail and request a return receipt.

Set aside a file drawer or area for originals and copies of all correspondence or forms you send. Don't send originals of police reports or statements. Write down the name of anyone you talk to, what he or she tells you, and the date the conversation occurs. A good example of such a form for record-keeping is "Chart Your Course of Action," available on the CD. You can also find the form and other good suggestions at www.ftc.gov/bcp/edu/pubs/consumer/idtheft/idt04.shtm.

While you're gathering and securing documentation of theft activity, take inventory of your other valuable documents that contain information that may have led to your current identity-theft woes. Reconsider how you handle or store them. I have some suggestions:

- ✔ **Buy a shredder, and use it regularly.** Never throw away any papers with any type of identifying information without shredding them first.

- ✔ **Keep your information safely locked away.** Although I don't suggest you turn your home into Fort Knox, keeping your personal papers out in the open is not the way to keep them safe. A locking file cabinet or drawer will deter at least a casual thief from stealing your valuables.

- ✔ **Get a safe-deposit box at your local bank.** A safe-deposit box is the best bet for valuable papers, Social Security cards, birth certificates, citizenship papers, automobile titles, and the like. If you don't want to get a box, at least purchase a fireproof safe for these papers.

- ✔ **Password-protect your computer and its programs.** Most computers and software allow you to set up a password. If you keep banking or investment information on your computer, use a password or phrase.

Chapter 17

Ten Ways to Keep Your Home from Foreclosure

*B*uying a home is a major financial goal for most people. It takes hard work to save enough money for a down payment, shop for just the right house in just the right neighborhood, and finally take the plunge. Traditionally, most home-buyers have ended up with typical 30-year, fixed-rate mortgage loans. With this type of loan, you may have to sacrifice and work overtime to make your monthly payments in the beginning, but as time goes by and (hopefully) your income increases, the payments become easier to make.

However, in recent years many different mortgage products have been offered that have allowed people who otherwise wouldn't have been able to buy a home to do so. Some of these loans are complicated, high-risk, and poorly understood. As a result, a large number of homeowners are finding that they really can't afford their home and the mortgage loan that comes with it.

In this chapter, I walk you through the different avenues available to you to avoid foreclosure on your home if you're currently having difficulty making your mortgage payment or believe you will in the near future. I also help you to minimize damage to your credit report if delinquency or foreclosure is inevitable.

Deciphering Mortgage Loans and Terms

Just as you have many choices of lenders when you need a mortgage loan, you also have choices when it comes to the type and terms of the loan. Understanding the specifics of your loan's terms is important when you are seeking help to avoid foreclosure. One of the first questions you will be asked is "What type of mortgage do you have?" With that in mind, here is a list of typical mortgage products currently available:

- **Fixed-rate mortgages:** These loans have various terms as far as the length of the loan (10, 15, 20, or 30 years) and the annual interest rate. The monthly payment is a set amount each month and does not change for the life of the loan.

- **Adjustable-rate mortgages (ARMs):** These loans typically begin with a low, fixed interest rate for a defined number of years (usually less than ten) and then the interest rate adjusts based on a specific financial index plus an additional percentage. The rate is adjusted annually and your payment amount goes up or down depending on the index. Most ARMs have a capped interest rate over which the lender cannot charge.

- **Balloon mortgages:** These loans are short-term loans (five to seven years) with a fixed interest rate, but your monthly payment is based on the loan being amortized for 30 years. This means you have a low monthly payment, but the loan has to be refinanced once the balloon term ends.

Looking Ahead if You Have an ARM

You may be among the many homeowners who have an adjustable-rate mortgage. If so, at the end of your fixed-rate term, your rate will be adjusted. Most likely your interest rate will go up and so will your monthly payment. Find out now from your lender approximately what your new monthly payment will be once the loan is adjusted.

Now is the time to plan for the increase in your monthly expenses. You may need to make adjustments such as putting off replacing your furniture or making extra payments on your car loan so it is paid off before your mortgage payment increases. If you start now, you'll know whether you'll be able to make the necessary changes to avoid problems with the increased payment. If you think you'll have trouble making the increased mortgage payment, keep reading.

Knowing When You're Headed Toward Trouble

Mortgage lenders are not likely to cause much of a fuss if you're a month late paying your mortgage. Don't let the quiet lull you into a false sense of security. The bottom line is that no one is going to come after you for being late and threaten you with dire consequences if you don't pay. Instead, lenders quietly foreclose according to a procedures manual.

Therefore, you have to recognize when you may be in trouble with your mortgage. If you're consistently having trouble making payments and are not sure whether you'll have the money to make the next month's payment, you're headed for trouble and need to take action.

After your mortgage is 90 days past due (don't count your two-week grace period in the calculation), you may have to pay the entire amount due plus any late fees in one lump sum in order to satisfy the lender and avoid foreclosure. Partial payment plans are harder to come by after the 90-day point.

Tightening Your Budget to Stay in Your Home

If your financial circumstances have changed, either due to an adjustable-rate reset or some other reason, and paying your mortgage is now more difficult, you need to tighten your budget (or create one). Yes, this is basic, but this is where I suggest you start. List all your expenses and then list your income. Take a look at both sides of the equation and determine where you can make changes — by cutting expenses and/or increasing income. See Chapter 13 for details on budgeting.

After going over your budget, you should have a good idea of whether the changes you're able to make will have enough impact to ease your mortgage payment problems. Always make your mortgage payment a priority and then pay your other monthly obligations. If you need your car to get to work, keeping up on your car payment is equally important. Car repossessions can happen after weeks — not months — of missing a payment.

Communicating with Your Lender

No one likes to give bad news, but when the news *is* bad, sometimes the longer you wait to tell it, the worse it gets. Such is the case with letting your mortgage servicer know you can't make your mortgage payment. You need to communicate this as soon as possible. Even though you'll be giving them bad news, they'll want to help you.

Contrary to what many people think, your lender does not want to foreclose on your home. The lender would much rather work with you to keep you in your home and continue earning money on your mortgage loan. Lenders are not realtors; they don't want your home.

When you call your servicer, be prepared with an explanation of why you will be unable to make your payment, when they can expect payment, and what help you need moving forward to assure that you're not late again. This is where that budget you made in the preceding step becomes a huge help.

Seeking Out the Experts

If you're falling behind in your mortgage payments, turn to those people who can help you avoid foreclosure. Housing counselors are a great resource when you're facing problems paying your mortgage and you aren't sure what to do or how to do it. They're trained professionals with the ability to review your financial situation, make recommendations, and lead you to the programs and assistance that will work best for you. Expect to pay little or nothing for this great help. If the charge is large, try the next number for help.

You can get help from a HUD-certified housing counselor at Project HOPE at 1-888-995-HOPE or by visiting www.hud.gov. Beware of counselors who are not HUD-certified and nonprofit; they may be scam artists.

Requesting Short-Term Solutions

For financial problems that are short-term and not permanent, you have several options available to help you avoid foreclosure. Often it is a combination of what you can afford and what your lender can live with that leads you to an acceptable solution. Among them are:

✔ **A repayment plan:** Usually involves a period of three to six months where your lender allows you to catch up or get back on track with your mortgage. You make your regular monthly mortgage payment plus a percentage of the amount you're behind. For example: If you're behind by two monthly payments of $800, you might pay $1,067 for six months to bring your mortgage current. After the six months, you would resume making your regular $800 payment.

✔ **Forbearance:** You may be able to reduce or skip some payments that are made up at the end of the forbearance period. This may help if you have a sale pending or expect a windfall. This can keep your credit in good shape. If you have an FHA-insured loan (ask your lender) you may qualify for a Special Forbearance with partial payments for up to 18 months.

✔ **Loan modification:** Your lender may be willing to include the amount that you're behind in your loan balance and re-amortize the loan. Another option is to freeze your fixed interest rate for an ARM for a longer period of time than was originally in your loan.

Considering Refinancing Options

Refinancing your loan may be an option for you if your credit hasn't taken too big of a ding from late payments and you have some equity in your home. Start with your current lender and request a loan with better terms, lower monthly payments, or whatever you need to stay in your home.

Keep in mind that you don't want to jump out of the frying pan and into the fire. You want to avoid a loan that simply lowers your monthly payment for a short time unless you think your situation will improve. Your goal should be to refinance so that you're able to stay in your home for the long term.

Weighing Leaving

Sometimes staying in your home just isn't feasible. If so, you want to find a solution that is the least damaging to your credit. Keep these options in mind and discuss them with your housing counselor:

✔ **Selling your home:** If you can sell your home for what you owe on your mortgage or more, contact a realtor and put your home on the market.

✔ **Short sale:** When you owe more than your home is worth, your lender may be willing to accept the amount your home will sell for to satisfy the loan. It well may be a less expensive alternative for the lender than a foreclosure. This may save your credit if done early enough.

✔ **Deed-in-lieu of foreclosure:** This option is usually reserved for extreme hardship cases. The lender accepts the title to your home and you are released from your liability. Typically, you may not have a second mortgage, equity loan, or other lien against your property to qualify. Done early, this can avoid a string of delinquencies, but may be reported negatively by the lender. Ask how it will be reported before you agree to final arrangements.

The difference in the amount of your original mortgage and the short sale of your home or a deed-in-lieu of foreclosure could be reported by your lender as *discharged indebtedness income* in the form of a 1099c. This means that the amount of debt forgiven is considered income to you. Taxable income! You might, however, qualify under the Mortgage Debt Forgiveness Act of 2007, in which case your federal taxes may be forgiven. State income laws may vary and should be checked.

Filing Bankruptcy

Bankruptcy protection is available to you if none of the other suggestions in this chapter work for you. A Chapter 13 bankruptcy may help save your home from foreclosure if other remedies have failed. You will need to get the advice of an attorney and get counseled by a court-approved counseling agency (see Chapter 11 for more info). Expect to be on a tight budget for the term of the bankruptcy. In addition to credit relief, this course of action may provide some emotional relief if your relationships are being damaged by worrying about making an impossible payment.

You may be able to get credit counseling, bankruptcy counseling, and housing counseling all from the same source when you call Project HOPE at 1-888-995-HOPE.

Chapter 18

Ten Ways to Make Your Credit the Best It Can Be

"Do I have any green stuff between my teeth?" One of the joys of marriage is having my wife grin at me and ask questions like that. Sometimes looking the best you can is important, especially when you're meeting someone for the first time and they don't know you. First impressions can matter. And that applies to your credit, too. Creditors don't know you except by your credit report and score. You don't want any "green stuff" to show on your credit report if you can remove it beforehand.

In this chapter, I tell you ten things you can do to improve your credit appearance. I start with a checkup to see what needs to be tightened up. Next I discuss some simple banking and credit actions that are easy to do and can help improve your credit appearance. Then I help you take the bull by the horns and suggest some basic underlying actions you can take to make sure you don't tarnish your sterling image. So think of this chapter as your credit mirror, and be sure to smile while you read how to put a sparkle on your credit image.

Performing Periodic Checkups

You know you should go to the dentist twice a year and get an annual physical. Well, an annual peek at what others are saying about you on your credit report is financially just as important!

Review your report from each of the three major credit bureaus at least once a year. Read the reports carefully to make certain no inaccurate or outdated information is included and that none of the positive information is missing. Dispute inaccurate entries with the credit bureau and request that positive data be added to your file (see Chapter 7 for more information).

If you're checking credit reports because you think someone (for example, a lender or a prospective employer) may be looking at your report soon, check all three at once. You may not know which one will be pulled (or whether a merged copy of all three will be requested). If you're checking your report just to monitor progress, I recommend that you order a different one every four months — that way, you're able to check your credit report more often by rotating among the three. See Chapter 5 for help on getting copies of your credit report.

Getting More Credit Value from Your Local Bank

People trying to build or improve their credit sometimes fail to look right under their noses. Two simple ways to build your credit are right down the street at your local bank or credit union: Open a checking account first, and then open a passbook savings account to brighten your credit. How easy can this be?!

Especially for those new to the United States and/or those individuals whose credit is thin, opening a checking account and, more importantly, using the checks without bouncing any, is a little-known way to bulk up your credit score. A *thin file* is one with little information in it, hence the name. Thin files are harder to score, so information may be gathered from nontraditional sources to fatten them up. The reordering of checks is actually picked up by the FICO people and helps your score.

In addition to opening a checking account, I want you to borrow your own money! I know it sounds strange, but if you open a passbook account as I suggest and then use it as collateral to take out a small loan, it will be reported to the credit bureaus. Faster than you can say "good credit," you'll be adding positive history to your file and improving your score.

Check with your bank or credit union to make sure that the loan is reported to at least one, and preferably all three, of the major credit-reporting bureaus. If the loan is not reported to at least one of the major bureaus, request that the bank report it. If the bank is unwilling to do so, take your business elsewhere.

Building Credit with Secured Cards

You can spend your own money using a special type of credit card tied to your savings to help you improve your credit. A *secured credit card* is issued by banks and credit unions and looks just like any other credit card, but it has one small difference: You, the cardholder, must deposit money into an account to guarantee payment for the purchases you'll be making with the card. The account is reported to the credit bureaus as a revolving account. You make payments, just as you would with any credit card. But the creditor is guaranteed payment for your charges by your deposit, which they'll pull from if you miss any payments. That's where the "secured" part comes into play.

Here's how to get started:

1. **Contact your bank or credit union to find out if it offers secured credit cards.**

   Watch out for annual processing or maintenance fees. You can get secured credit cards free — you just have to look around for banks or credit unions that offer them or search online for secured credit cards.

2. **Deposit the funds to be used as security for the card.**

3. **Use the card for purchases, making sure that you can pay the balance each month.**

   You don't need to use the card a lot. Just make a few purchases each month.

4. **Make on-time payments every month.**

Some people may encourage you to use a cash advance on your secured card to open another secured card — and so on. Sure, this approach may allow you to open several lines of credit and chalk up more positive entries on your credit report. But it also exposes you to the risk of multiple negatives if you can't make payments — *and* it can cost you plenty in interest payments. My advice: Only get secured cards when you have the cash on hand to put down as security.

Using Retail Store Cards

Just as in strength-building at the gym, when you're looking to build your credit, it's good to start small and work up. Retail cards are your first real step out to build new credit muscle. A *retail card* is issued by a store for purchases at that store only and does not have a Visa or MasterCard logo on it.

These cards are relatively easy to get and can boost your credit appeal. Use them for purchases you would be making anyway and pay the balances on time and in full each month. The goal here is to establish accounts that will reflect that you pay as agreed — a positive mark in the credit good-looks department — not to charge up to your limit.

Make only planned purchases that you have the cash to cover. Retail cards can have high interest rates so be sure to check the fine print. In the case of furniture store deferred payment plans, be sure to put aside the money to make your payments before they are due or you may incur hefty interest charges. You don't want to add the extra weight of unnecessary fees and interest while you're working to enhance your credit.

I suggest planning to make that final deferred interest account payment a month before it is due just to be safe from an error that could add hundreds of dollars, or even more, to your account.

Dumping Some Debt

One of the fastest ways to improve the appearance of your credit is to decrease your *credit-availability-to-credit-used ratio*. Simply put, this means paying down the balances on your revolving credit accounts. The term *revolving balance* describes a balance you carry over from previous months' purchases.

For example, if you have a credit card with a credit limit of $5,000 and your balance is $3,000, your credit-used-to-credit-available ratio is 60 percent — you're using 60 percent of the credit you have at your disposal. Lenders like to see that ratio lower than 25 percent. Twenty-five percent of $5,000 is $1,250, so you'll be more attractive if you're carrying an unpaid, revolving balance of $1,250 or less.

The nice people at Fair Isaac (www.myfico.com) will ding your credit score if your ratio is above the 50 percent mark. So if you want to up your credit pizzazz, start by paying down your balances to below 50 percent, and then shoot for a ratio of less than 25 percent to look even more desirable.

Keeping Those Old Accounts Open

Like throwing out your favorite old shirt or that famous little black dress, you'll regret canceling an old account. Accounts older than ten years that have positive histories are the gold standard of good credit. Meanwhile, the credit mavens will lower your score if you close out a longstanding account.

They like stability and they spell it *o-l-d.* So keep those accounts, especially if you open a new one. The combination of closing an oldie-but-goodie and adding a new account will hurt your score twice. Two of the characteristics of people FICO calls "FICO High Achievers" (those with a score over 760) are that their oldest account is around 19 years old and the average age of their accounts is between 6 and 12 years.

Asking for Directions

If some of what I've recommended has you feeling a little bit lost or if you're just the cautious type and want to get some additional assurance that you can handle accounts, cards, and loans, you may want to look for professional help. Americans are getting better at asking for help. But they like to do it so no one knows. Ask for directions at the gas station? No way! Use a GPS? Absolutely!

Here are two confidential GPS-like sources you can tap into at different phases of your trip to great credit:

- ✔ A legitimate credit counselor can help you better manage your money and payments. Part of that plan will be to fund an emergency savings account. I only recommend credit-counseling agencies that are certified by the Council on Accreditation or ISO (see Chapter 3 for more information).

- ✔ Once you're paying all your bills on time, building new credit, and saving, a financial planner is the next stop for you. A good planner can give you the hope and incentive you need to balance today's saving with tomorrow's needs.

Taking Advantage of the 100-Word Statement

You have the right under the Fair Credit Reporting Act (FCRA) to add a 100-word statement to your credit-bureau file. You can use this statement for many different reasons, including improving your credit image.

Keep in mind that a good deal of loan underwriting is done by computers, so a consumer statement may or may not be helpful in this situation. But in the case of a prospective employer or a landlord looking at your report, the 100-word statement is of more value.

Start by assessing which aspects of your report are the most negative. You may have charged-off accounts, a medical collection account, a paid judgment, several 120-day-late accounts, or all the above. Whatever your situation, use the statement to place the most offensive listing in the most positive (or least offensive) light — much like telling folks you got that black eye by bumping into a door, as opposed to in a barroom brawl. (See Chapter 6 for more examples.)

The credit bureau will help you write the 100-word statement if you ask for help. TransUnion offers help on its Web site. The other credit bureaus require you to write the statement first, and then they'll help edit it after it appears on your credit report. *Note:* If you live in Maine, your consumer statement may be up to 200 words.

After you place the statement on your report, don't forget it's out there. A 30-day delinquency may only cost you a few points for a year, while a charge-off (usually over 180 days late) from your ex-spouse's account could hurt more and for longer. How long depends on how much positive information is on your file and the volume of new information being reported. So as your credit recovers over time, you may want to pull the statement or you'll be drawing attention to an old negative unnecessarily.

Protecting Yourself from Identity Thieves

Now that you're feeling great from a credit standpoint, I want you to exercise some care to be sure someone doesn't steal it all away from you. The last thing you want is for an identity thief to mess up what you've struggled to achieve. To help protect yourself from identity thieves, follow these tips:

- **Guard your account numbers.** Be careful with credit-card statements, bank statements, and other financial documents. Shred any documents that contain account numbers and personal information that you don't file in a safe place.

- **Be wary of phone transactions.** Never supply credit-card or Social Security numbers over the phone unless you initiated the call and you know who you're dealing with.

- **Protect your Social Security number.** Do not keep your card in your wallet or purse, where a thief could find it. Do know where your card is and keep it in a safe place.

- **Check credit reports for evidence of identity theft.** Review one of your credit reports every four months or all three at least annually. You can order a copy of each report for free once a year. And even if you have to pay (because you've ordered more than once per year), consider the expense valuable insurance.

✔ **Don't put bills in an unlocked mailbox.** Mailboxes are often the targets of identity thieves. Do not send bill payments by mail from your unsecured home mailbox; anybody driving by can reach in and get your account numbers. Drop your bill payments in a USPS pickup box or, better yet, pay bills electronically when possible. And keep track of your monthly statements to be sure that you receive all of them in the mail.

Check out Chapter 15 for more in-depth discussion about protecting your identity.

Using Your Previous Nontraditional Experience

Because lenders want to be able to offer products, services, and credit to you, they are digging into more records to be able to come up with a basis for doing so. What this means is that you have a better chance now than ever before to establish traditional credit and financial service relationships based on your previous nontraditional credit experience.

If you're new to the traditional banking world but have been paying bills such as utilities, furniture store (payment performance) agreements, or even your music club, then you're in luck. Ask your lender to use the Fair Isaac Expansion Score. This score targets the credit-underserved market. Yes, that's you! It uses alternative data sources from more than 90 commercial databases that may not make it into your credit bureau report.

If you have at least some credit history, asking your lender-to-be to use a VantageScore may help. VantageScore scores require less credit history than FICO scores to yield a score.

As you can see, the existence of these nontraditional experiences means that Big Brother is looking in more places than ever before too, so be sure you're on your best financial behavior whenever you are doing business. No matter what, make sure you pay all your bills on time, whether you think the creditor reports to the bureaus or not.

Appendix A

Glossary

account: A record of transactions between the creditor and the consumer. Account examples include a mortgage, car loan, or credit card.

account number: A number assigned to an account by the creditor to identify the particular account and the person who is financially responsible for the account.

account reviews: Consumer credit history inquiries made by creditors with whom the consumer has a current relationship. This type of inquiry is the equivalent of just peeking at your file to be sure everything is ship-shape. Because you don't initiate the inquiry, it is not included in credit reports or credit scoring.

active-duty alert: Members of the military who are away from their usual duty station may place an active-duty alert on their credit report for one year to reduce the risk of identity theft. An alert requires verification of identity before credit can be issued.

adjustable rate mortgage (ARM): A mortgage whose interest rate is periodically adjusted based on a variety of indexes.

adverse action: Any negative action — such as the denial of credit, insurance, or employment — taken by a creditor or other person or company. The reasons for an adverse action must be disclosed to the person who was affected, as required under the *Fair and Accurate Credit Transactions Act,* and the person is entitled to a free credit report from the bureau to which the adverse action was reported.

adverse information: Any information included in your credit report that a creditor or other interested party would view as reason to consider denying a loan or rejecting an applicant, such as past-due accounts.

application scoring: A statistical model used to evaluate and score credit applications and credit-bureau data. The score is used by banks and businesses to determine whether to accept or decline a credit application.

balloon payment: The final payment on a mortgage that does not fully amortize, leaving a large balance due at the end of the term or maturity.

bank card: A general purpose credit card issued through a local, regional, or national bank that is accepted by millions of merchants, unlike store or gasoline credit cards, which may be accepted only by a specific merchant or brand. Most common are Visa, MasterCard, and American Express.

bankruptcy: A civil court proceeding in a district bankruptcy court that allows consumers legal relief from all or part of their debts. Bankruptcies appear on an individual's credit report for up to ten years.

BAPCPA: The Bankruptcy Abuse Prevention and Consumer Protection Act of 2005 (pronounced bap-see-pa). Most of this law's provisions went into effect on or after October 17. Sometimes called the "new bankruptcy law," it was intended to end perceived abuses and unfairness in bankruptcies by making it more difficult for consumers to discharge debt under Chapter 7 and less pleasant to use.

business-version credit report: The business version of a credit report is an abbreviated version of a consumer's credit report that creditors see. The business version does not contain account reviews or promotional inquiries.

CCCS: *See* Consumer Credit Counseling Service.

Chapter 7 bankruptcy: A form of bankruptcy that requires consumers to pass a means test and give up some assets in order to be relieved of qualified debt. Excluded from relief is child support, alimony, taxes, debt incurred to pay taxes, and student loans. Also known as *liquidation.*

Chapter 11 bankruptcy: A form of bankruptcy, often used by corporations, that allows those who qualify to keep creditors at bay until the company or individual is able to pay their debts. This is the most well-known of the corporate bankruptcy chapters.

Chapter 12 bankruptcy: A form of bankruptcy that allows farmers to reorganize their debt and keep their farms.

Chapter 13 bankruptcy: A form of bankruptcy that allows consumers to keep most of their assets based on a means test and repay debt they can afford based on IRS allowances over a three- or five-year period of time under court supervision and protection. Chapter 13 is generally reported

for seven years but may be reported up to ten years at the discretion of the credit bureau. Often referred to as *wage-earner bankruptcy.*

charge card: A form of credit card that requires payment in full each month and does not charge interest. Examples include the traditional American Express card and Diner's Club card.

charge-off: The status of an account when it goes unpaid for, typically, more than 180 days, and the balance of the account is written off by the creditor as a bad debt (for tax purposes only). The debt is still valid and collectible, along with fees and interest.

ChexSystems: A check verification service and specialty similar to a credit bureau, but which only reports negative information about how a consumer has handled their checking and savings accounts.

COA: *See* Council on Accreditation.

collection: A past-due account that is transferred to an inside or third-party collector in an attempt to recover the balance due. Only third-party collectors (as opposed to collectors who are employees of the company you owe the debt to) are governed by the Fair Debt Collections Practices Act.

community property: Primarily found in the West as a result of previous Mexican legal tradition, a principle whereby most property acquired during a marriage (with some exceptions, such as gifts and inheritances) is automatically considered to be owned jointly by both spouses and is divided upon divorce, annulment, or death. It pertains to the following states: Arizona, California, Idaho, Louisiana, Nevada, New Mexico, Texas, Washington, and Wisconsin. Puerto Rico and Alaska allow property to be owned as community property also.

consolidation: Merging debts into a single loan or a single payment.

Consumer Credit Counseling Service (CCCS): A network of nonprofit counseling agencies that offer advice, budgeting, debt-management plans, and housing counseling. Look for accreditation by the Council on Accreditation.

consumer-version credit report: Credit report containing a consumer's credit information. Information may include your name, address, Social Security number, credit history, inquiries, collection records, and public records such as bankruptcy filings and tax liens. Creditors do not see this version of your credit report.

cosigner: An individual who signs a loan agreement in commitment to being responsible for repaying a debt if the primary borrower defaults.

Council on Accreditation (COA): The largest accreditor of nonprofit organizations, including credit-counseling agencies, in the United States.

credit: The ability to create a debt by having a loan granted to buy now and pay later under designated terms based on a consumer's promise, ability, and track record of repaying.

credit bureau: A company that accumulates credit data on individuals, provided by creditors, and compiles this data in the form of a credit report.

credit card: A form of credit that enables a consumer to purchase goods and services and pay for them with scheduled monthly payments. Interest is charged on balances that are not paid in full at the end of the month. A form of revolving credit.

credit check: A request to view a consumer's credit report to ascertain whether to extend credit to the consumer.

credit clinic: *See* credit-repair company.

credit file: *See* credit report.

credit fraud: Unauthorized use of credit by someone using fictitious personal information.

credit freeze: Prohibits the access of your credit data through a credit bureau without your express permission.

credit history: A record of a consumer's credit behaviors over an extended period of time, including credit account and payment activity. Negative information is usually reported for seven years with the exception of bankruptcy, which may be reported for up to ten years. Positive information will stay on indefinitely, sometimes for 20 years or more.

credit limit: An amount set by a lender establishing the maximum level of credit that can be extended on a particular account.

credit obligation: A legal agreement between a creditor and an individual that requires the individual to repay a debt.

credit-repair company: A business that alleges to be able to "clean up" or "erase" bad credit for clients. The abuses of such companies prompted passage of the Credit Repair Organizations Act to regulate their behavior. Also know as a *credit clinic.*

credit report: A consumer's credit history as compiled by a credit bureau, including both credit and personal information about the consumer. Also known as a *credit file.*

credit risk: A determination by a potential creditor of a consumer's likelihood of repaying a debt as agreed.

credit score: A mathematical model used to assess a consumer's likelihood of credit default. The risk level is expressed in a three-digit number. A creditor gets your information from a credit-reporting agency and may order a credit score or apply its own credit scoring model to calculate a proprietary credit score.

creditor: A business or person who extends credit or lends money to individuals or businesses.

creditworthiness: A term used to describe a person's credit behavior on which a potential creditor bases the decision regarding whether to extend that person credit. Those determined to have low creditworthiness will likely not be extended credit.

date closed: Point in time when an account or credit obligation is terminated.

date opened: Point in time when an account or credit obligation is established.

debt-management plan (DMP): A plan accepted by creditors and administered by a credit-counseling agency for repaying your debts.

debt settlement: When a creditor agrees to accept less than the amount owed to discharge a debt. Any debt forgiven may become taxable income.

debt settlement company: A business that specializes in trying to force creditors to accept a settlement.

deed-in-lieu of foreclosure: Signing a property deed over to the mortgagee to avoid the expenses of a foreclosure.

default: The failure to make a debt payment on time as agreed in the original credit agreement.

delinquent: The failure of a consumer to pay a credit account on time as agreed. A credit report lists delinquencies as 30 days, 60 days, 90 days, and 120 days late.

direct deposit: An automatic transfer of funds using the Automated Clearing House. Often used to deposit payroll funds into bank accounts or to make recurring payments on loans.

discretionary income: What's left of your income after taxes (disposable income) and what you consider to be essential or normal living expenses.

disposable income: Gross income minus taxes.

dispute: The official act of an individual challenging an item listed on his credit report; a dispute must be investigated by the credit bureau listing the item within 30 days of notification.

DMP: *See* debt-management plan.

early-warning alert: A one-time notice given to consumers by creditors under the *Fair and Accurate Credit Transactions Act* within 30 days of negative information being sent to a credit bureau.

emergency fund: A sum of money, readily available, set aside for use in an emergency. Usually up to six months of necessary living expenses.

Equifax: One of the three major credit-reporting agencies.

Experian: One of the three major credit-reporting agencies, formerly known as TRW.

Fair and Accurate Credit Transactions Act of 2003 (FACT Act or FACTA): The FACT Act added new sections to the federal *Fair Credit Reporting Act* that help consumers fight identity theft. The following are a few of the many provisions of the Act: It allows consumers to request and obtain a free *credit report* once every twelve months from each of the three national credit bureaus (*Equifax, Experian,* and *TransUnion*) from www.annualcreditreport.com, it gives individuals rights to place alerts on their credit histories if identity theft is suspected or if they are military personnel deploying overseas, and it requires secure disposal of consumer information by businesses.

Fair Credit Reporting Act (FCRA): Federal legislation enacted in 1970, assuring the accuracy, confidentiality, and proper use of information in the consumer files of every credit bureau. Parts of this law were updated by the *Fair and Accurate Credit Transactions Act* in 2003.

Fair Debt Collection Practices Act (FDCPA): A law that amends the Consumer Credit Protection Act to prohibit abusive practices by debt collectors.

FDIC: The government corporation created by the of 1933 which guarantees bank accounts in member banks from losses up to $100,000 for regular accounts and $250,000 for IRAs.

FICO High Achiever: *See* High Achiever characteristics.

FICO score: A three-digit number devised by Fair Isaac, Inc., to measure a consumer's level of credit risk based on information in the consumer's credit report.

fraud alert: A warning placed on a credit report by a consumer who believes he may have been the victim of identity theft; a fraud alert requires creditors to exercise caution when taking any action. Such an alert will prevent new credit accounts from being opened without the customer's express permission.

fraud statement: A notation placed on a credit report by a consumer that lets potential creditors know that the consumer may be a victim of identity theft or other credit fraud.

garnishment: A legal process by which a creditor obtains a judgment from a court on an outstanding debt, which authorizes permission to seize a portion of a debtor's assets — usually wages — to pay that debt.

grace period: A period of time during which a payment is accepted as "on time," thereby avoiding any additional finance charges or penalties. Credit-card accounts carrying a balance from one month to the next and delinquent mortgages do not have grace periods.

hardship program: A group of concessions offered to borrowers who are temporarily unable to fulfill the terms of a loan for a reason acceptable to a lender.

High Achiever characteristics: Statements you receive along with your FICO score that are meant to give insight into why your score is at its current level. They compare your score to the characteristics typically displayed by those with relatively high FICO scores of 760 and above. *See* reason code *and* reason statement.

home-equity line of credit: A line of credit using your house as collateral. The amount of money available in the line of credit varies depending on how much you want to have available just in case you need it. You have a set period of time (called a *draw period*) when you can access the line of credit and a set period during which you have to make repayments.

home-equity loan: A loan for a specified amount of money, using your house as collateral. In a home-equity loan, you have an installment payment due every month, usually at a set interest rate for a set amount of time.

identity: The unique traits and personal information that identify a particular consumer, including Social Security number, date of birth, address, and employer.

identity theft: Unauthorized use of credit by someone using another person's personal information, such as Social Security number, date of birth, or other identifying information.

inquiry: A request from a potential creditor, employer, landlord, or insurer to view an individual's credit report. The inquiry is listed on the credit report. Only those inquiries resulting from an application for credit are considered in the calculation of a credit score.

installment loan: A credit account that is paid in equal, periodic installments, usually monthly, of a specified amount for a specified length of time. An example of an installment loan is a car loan.

insurance bureau score: An insurance rating based on data from the major credit bureaus that helps insurers evaluate new and renewal auto and homeowner's insurance policies.

judgment: An official decision by a court relating to an action or suit. Typically, it is a ruling that a debt is valid and orders payment. A judgment is a public record and is listed on your credit report as a negative item.

late payment: A payment delivered to a creditor after the due date or time.

lien: A legal claim against real or personal property for the purposes of satisfying a debt.

line of credit: A specific amount of credit established by a lender that can be accessed by a consumer in whole or in part.

liquidation: *See* Chapter 7 bankruptcy.

loss mitigation: An action or series of actions whose aim is to reduce the severity of a loss.

manner of payment (MOP): Codes used on some credit-bureau reports that establish the payment patterns of the consumer — for example, "paid as agreed," "30 days late," and so on.

Medical Information Bureau (MIB): A specialty consumer reporting agency that comes under the *Fair and Accurate Credit Transactions Act.* Owned by over 450 insurance companies, the MIB is over 105 years old. It collects medical information to detect and deter fraud in life, health, disability, and long-term care insurance.

mortgage: A loan document that is recorded in official records and places a lien on real property until the creditor is paid in full according to the schedule and terms of the loan.

Mortgage Forgiveness Debt Relief Act of 2007: A law passed to help certain homeowners whose mortgages are foreclosed to avoid incurring federal income tax liability on the amount forgiven.

NCUA: Similar to the FDIC, but for credit unions.

open account: A credit account that is currently active, still in use, and/or being paid.

paid as agreed: A term used on credit reports indicating that the account in question is being paid according to the terms of the agreement.

payday loan: A small and initially short-term covering a borrower's expenses until his or her next payday. Loans normally range between $100 and $500, and carry APR interest rates in the range of 390 percent to 780+ percent. Also known as cash advance loans or check advance loans.

permissible purpose: Circumstances under which the *Fair and Accurate Credit Transactions Act* deems it appropriate for a consumer credit report to be viewed by a third party.

phishing: A computer term that relates to identity theft. It's an attempt to acquire personal or financial information, such as credit-card numbers or Social Security numbers, by masquerading as a person or company with whom you already do business.

Plus Score: A proprietary credit score issued by Experian. It's based on Fair Isaac models but is different from a FICO score.

predatory lending: The practice of making a deceptive loan that is knowingly unfair to the borrower.

prime rate: The benchmark rate at which banks usually lend to their most favored customers. Many other interest rates are expressed as a percentage above or below the prime rate.

promotional inquiry: A request to view a consumer's credit report for the purposes of consideration for an unsolicited promotional credit offer. Promotional inquiries are recorded only on the consumer copy of the credit report and do not count in credit scoring.

public records: Information included on a credit report such as bankruptcy court records, court judgments, tax liens, and other information available to the general public.

reason code: Up to four (of 60) codes that lenders receive along with your credit score to indicate the main reasons behind your score.

reason statement: Up to four statements based on *reason codes* that you receive along with your credit score that cryptically attempt to explain the main reasons behind your score. Similar to Fair Isaacs *High Achiever characteristics.*

refinance: To replace an existing loan with a loan bearing different (often more favorable) terms. This is commonly done with home mortgages when interest rates fall.

refund anticipation loan (RAL): A high-interest-rate, short-term loan secured by a taxpayer's expected tax refund. Similar to a *payday loan.*

repossess: To take back collateral pledged for a defaulted loan. Often referred to as a Repo, it is used extensively in car payment defaults.

retail card: A credit account that is issued by a retail company such as a department store or electronics store.

revolving-credit account: A type of credit account that makes available a predetermined amount of money that can be used at any time without additional approval.

risk-based lending: A loan made to a person with terms reflecting the level of perceived risk of loss. This may allow a person with poor credit who otherwise wouldn't qualify for a loan to get one at a higher cost.

scoring model: Formulas used to determine the likely future credit behavior of prospective borrowers and existing customers. A scoring model calculates credit scores based on data such as the information included in a consumer's credit report.

secured credit: A line of credit that is backed by real property, such as a home, auto, boat, or securities.

serialization: Consolidates only the payments of student loans into a single payment but retains the original terms and interest rates on all your student loans.

short sale: Selling a home with the mortgagee's permission for less than the value of the mortgage to avoid a foreclosure.

subprime: A loan made to a person with less than conventional credit usually for higher interest or a variable interest rate or term.

trade line: A credit-industry term for an account listed on a credit report including bank loans, credit cards, mortgages, or any number of other credit accounts.

TransUnion: One of the three major credit-reporting bureaus.

TRW: *See* Experian.

underbanked: A term used to describe an estimated 40+ million people in the United States who have little or no current relationship with a financial institution. These individuals often use alternative financial services providers, such as payday loans, check-cashing facilities, and money transfer outlets.

underwriting: A process used to assess risk and the eligibility of a customer to qualify for a product such as a loan.

universal default: A clause contained in many credit agreements allowing a current account that is paid as agreed to be converted to default status based on the default of another account or signs that the consumer is overextending and/or presenting a higher risk profile, as evidenced by information contained in the credit report.

unsecured credit: A loan or line of credit that is backed only by a promise to pay.

upside-down loan: A loan in which you owe more than the item securing the loan is worth — for example, you owe $10,000 on a car loan, but the car is only worth $7,000.

VantageScore: A three-digit credit score devised by the three credit bureaus that predicts delinquency likelihood consistently across all three credit bureau reports.

wage-earner bankruptcy: *See* Chapter 13 bankruptcy.

Appendix B

About the CD

System Requirements

Make sure your computer meets the minimum system requirements shown in the following list. Otherwise, you may have problems using the software and files on the CD. For the latest and greatest information, please refer to the ReadMe file located at the root of the CD-ROM.

- A PC with a Pentium or faster processor; or a Mac OS computer with a 68040 or faster processor

- Microsoft Windows 98 or later; or Mac OS system software 7.6.1 or later

- At least 32MB of total RAM installed on your computer; for best performance, we recommend at least 64MB

- A CD-ROM drive

- A sound card for PCs; Mac OS computers have built-in sound support

- A monitor capable of displaying at least 256 colors or grayscale

- A modem with a speed of at least 14,400 bps

If you need more information on the basics, check out these books published by Wiley: *PCs For Dummies,* 11th Edition, by Dan Gookin; *Macs For Dummies,* 9th Edition, by Edward C. Baig; or *iMac For Dummies,* 5th Edition, by Mark L. Chambers.

Using the CD

To install the items from the CD to your hard drive, follow these steps:

1. **Insert the CD into your computer's CD-ROM drive.**

   The license agreement appears.

   Note to Windows users: The interface won't launch if you have auto-run disabled. In that case, choose Start ➪ Run. In the dialog box that appears, type **D:\start.exe**. (Replace D with the proper letter if your CD-ROM drive uses a different letter. If you don't know the letter, see how your CD-ROM drive is listed under My Computer.) Click OK.

   Note to Mac Users: The CD icon will appear on your desktop; double-click the icon to open the CD, and double-click the Start icon.

2. **Read through the license agreement, and then click the Accept button if you want to use the CD. After you click Accept, the License Agreement window won't appear again.**

   The CD interface appears. The interface allows you to install the programs and run the demos with just a click of a button (or two).

What You'll Find on the CD

The following sections are arranged by category and provide a summary of the software and other goodies you'll find on the CD. If you need help with installing the items provided on the CD, refer to the installation instructions in the preceding section.

Shareware programs are fully functional, free, trial versions of copyrighted programs. If you like particular programs, register with their authors for a nominal fee and receive licenses, enhanced versions, and technical support.

Freeware programs are copyrighted games, applications, and utilities. You can copy them to as many PCs as you like — for free — but they offer no technical support.

GNU software is governed by its own license, which is included inside the folder of the GNU software. There are no restrictions on distribution of GNU software. See the GNU license at the root of the CD for more details.

Trial, demo, or *evaluation* versions of software are usually limited either by time or functionality (such as not letting you save a project after you create it).

Software

The files on the CD are in Adobe PDF, Microsoft Word, and Microsoft Excel formats. In case you don't have Adobe Reader, Microsoft Word, or Microsoft Excel on your computer, I've included the following on the CD, so that you can read all the files I've included:

- **Adobe Reader:** Adobe Reader is a freeware application for viewing files in the Adobe Portable Document Format.

- **OpenOffice.org:** OpenOffice.org is a free multi-platform office productivity suite, similar to Microsoft Office. It includes word processing, spreadsheet, presentation, and drawing applications. It supports most file formats of other office software, allowing you to view and edit files created with other office programs.

Legislation

If you're like me — a little strange — you may want to see the underlying legislation that spells out all the facts that apply to credit reports and debt collection. For all you kindred spirits, I've included my favorite laws. If you're like my wife — normal, or so she says — you'll go on to the next section.

- **FACT Act Updated.pdf:** This is the famous FACT Act. It's an update to the Fair Credit Reporting Act (see the following bullet), designed to give you tools to help prevent identity theft, improve the credit-report dispute process, improve the accuracy of your credit data, and give you better access to your credit information as well as free credit reports annually.

- **Fair Debt Collection Practices Act.pdf:** Here is the rulebook that collectors have to follow when contacting a person about a bill. What, when, and how they can do what they do is spelled out here. Your rights, what's fair, and what's not are all included in this act.

- **Mortgage Debt Forgiveness Act of 2007:** If you owe a debt and it's forgiven, the lender issues you a 1099 and the amount of debt forgiven becomes income that is taxable. This law excludes up to $2 million of 1099 income from taxes if the income comes from a discharge of mortgage indebtedness subject to certain criteria.

- **Servicemembers Civil Relief Act.pdf:** This is an update of the Soldiers and Sailors Civil Relief Act. It covers the special rights that servicepersons have that allow them to concentrate on defending the United States — rather than defending *themselves* from creditors.

Bankruptcy

The means test that determines what chapter of personal bankruptcy you may qualify for can be very confusing. The handy New Bankruptcy Code Filing Procedures Chart.pdf is a graphic representation of the process used to determine which bankruptcy chapter an individual qualifies for under the Bankruptcy Abuse Prevention and Consumer Protection Act of 2005.

Credit-report letters

Here are samples of letters to get you started communicating effectively with credit bureaus and creditors. Everyone makes mistakes, including the credit bureaus and creditors. You're just helping them to improve the quality of their records if you spot an error in your report.

- ✔ **Add 100-Word Statement to Report.doc:** This letter provides the format for adding a 100-word statement to your credit report explaining a negative item. This will not be picked up if your lender uses automated underwriting. The bureaus will assist you in writing a concise statement if you go over 100 words or (in the case of TransUnion only) if you ask them to.

- ✔ **Add Accounts to Report.doc:** If you have verifiable accounts that do not appear on your credit report, you can ask to have them added. You may be charged a fee or the bureau may refuse; however, often they'll add verifiable information to make your record more complete.

- ✔ **Annual Credit Report Request Form.pdf:** When requesting your free annual credit report, using the official form to do so is important. Use the Request Credit File.doc letter (see the next bullet) as a cover letter.

- ✔ **Request Credit File.doc:** This is a generic letter that you can use to request a free credit report for various reasons. If you're requesting a free annual credit report, attach the Annual Credit Report Request Form.pdf (see the preceding bullet).

- ✔ **Request to Remove Error.doc:** This provides the basics you need to dispute an erroneous or out-of-date item on your credit report.

- ✔ **Request for Creditor to Remove Error.doc:** This letter is helpful if your original request to a credit bureau did not remove a disputed item from your credit report. Asking the creditor directly may get you the attention you need.

Credit reports and credit scores

If you've never ordered a copy of your credit report or credit score, this section shows you what to expect. Sample credit reports from Equifax, Experian, and TransUnion are included on the CD, as well as a sample credit score from Fair Isaac, to help demystify the process.

- ✔ **ChexSystems Sample Report.pdf:** This PDF is a sample report that helps you manage and maintain your checking accounts.

- ✔ **FICO Sample Credit Report.pdf:** This PDF of a credit report order from the myFICO Web site shows you the reporting format used and what you should expect to see if you order a report with a credit score from them.

- ✔ **FICO Score Report.pdf:** A copy of what you get if you order your FICO Score, showing your relative score position and ways to improve it.

- ✔ **Equifax Sample Credit Report.pdf:** This is a PDF of what you should expect to see if you order a credit report from Equifax.

- ✔ **Experian Sample Credit Report.pdf:** This is a PDF of what you should expect to see if you order a credit report from Experian.

- ✔ **TransUnion Sample Credit Report.pdf:** This is a PDF of what you should expect to see if you order a credit report from TransUnion. It also includes the lender's report looks different from the consumer version. This example shows all the code meanings.

- ✔ **Understanding Your Credit Report.pdf:** This is a good credit report reference guide from the nonprofit agency Money Management International.

If you're interested in seeing sample reports from two of the major check-reporting bureaus (ChexSystems and SCAN), you can do so online:

- ✔ **ChexSystems:** Go to www.consumerdebit.com and, under Consumer Assistance, click Sample Consumer Report. Then, next to ChexSystems report, click View Sample.

- ✔ **SCAN:** Go to www.consumerdebit.com and, under Consumer Assistance, click Sample Consumer Report. Then, next to SCAN report, click View Sample.

Creditor letters

Communicating with your creditors can be a daunting task for many. This section has drafts of letters that can help you be precise, professional, and effective. In other words, they can help you get your way, with a minimum of fuss and worry.

Current accounts

As a valued customer, your satisfaction is a primary concern of your creditors. These letters help them help you.

- **Billing Error.doc:** A short and professional letter aimed at getting billing discrepancies resolved quickly.

- **Change Due Date.doc:** Changing your due date with some creditors allows you to spread your payments out to better match your paydays. Here's a letter to do just that.

- **Partial Payment Hardship Letter Current.doc:** This letter shows you how to communicate with your creditor if you can't make a full payment due to circumstances beyond your control.

- **Request to Lower Interest for Military Service Members.doc:** Service personnel on active duty can use the wording of this letter to reduce finance charges to the 6 percent legal limit allowed under the Servicemembers Civil Relief Act.

- **Unemployment Letter.doc:** When you can't make any payment to your creditors, telling them in advance is better than letting them guess why you didn't send in your payment. This letter helps set a professional and concerned tone for future communications with your creditors.

Delinquent accounts

This list of letters contains suggested wordings that you should feel free to modify to fit your situation and tone. Using a professional tone is always best, regardless of your level of frustration or emotion. A letter won't resolve the situation, only a payment will — but documenting your efforts at trying to work out a solution is very important if matters should escalate to a court action. If you copy (cc:) a lawyer, be sure the collector knows about it. If you ask your lawyer to send a letter, expect the collector's attorney to respond to your lawyer. And always be sure to send correspondence via certified mail with a return receipt requested to document your efforts.

- **Confirmation Letter to Creditor.doc:** Use this form to confirm a telephone conversation with a creditor regarding an agreement on an account.

- ✔ **Intend to File Bankruptcy.doc:** This is a short-and-sweet notice to your creditors that will stop any collection calls. Sending a letter stating your intention is usually easier and cleaner than trying to do this over the phone.

- ✔ **Offer to Return Secured Items.doc:** This letter puts you on record as trying to do the right thing in a difficult situation. Some items, like jewelry or hard goods, may be easier for the creditor to take back.

- ✔ **Partial Payment Delinquent.doc:** Contacting your creditors before you send in a short payment is a good idea. This letter asks that you be contacted in writing rather than by phone. They may call you at home if they have a current number, but you should not be called at work after they receive this letter.

- ✔ **Request a Settlement.doc:** Making an offer to settle an account for less than is owed is never the first choice of a creditor. Expect a push back from them unless you haven't made any payment in a long time. Also be prepared to answer the question about how you can come up with a lump-sum payment, but not an installment. (Perhaps a family member is willing to help out or you have a small windfall.)

- ✔ **Request No Future Contact from Collection Agency.doc:** If you decide to renegotiate your debts with the original creditor, use this letter to instruct the collection agency to cease all contact.

- ✔ **Request to Stop Harassment.doc:** If you're being harassed, it is important to be on record with as much detail as possible. The Federal Trade Commission won't investigate, but your letter may help them identify a trend with some collection companies, which may move them to action. If you include your lawyer's name, be sure to run the letter by your lawyer first.

- ✔ **Request to Stop Work Calls.doc:** This letter will stop calls at work, but it's important to tell the creditor where and when they *can* contact you. They have the right to contact you, but only when it is convenient. If you don't let them know when it's convenient for them to contact *you,* they'll do it when it's convenient for *them.*

Forms and worksheets

This section contains some handy tools to help you keep track of your communications with creditors and your money at home. You can use each of them individually or, if you want a soup to nuts approach, I suggest the Understanding Money and Credit.pdf, a comprehensive guide that delivers much of what you get from visiting a financial professional (minus the personalized advice).

- ✔ **Bonus Chapter – Ten Ways to Successfully Manage Financial Emergencies:** This extra Part of Tens chapter helps you know what to do when bad things happen to your finances.

- ✔ **Cutting Expenses.doc:** Tracking your efforts in writing is an important part of cutting back successfully and recognizing the progress you're making. Having a goal on paper is much more powerful than having a goal in mind.

- ✔ **Debt Repayment Tracking Sheet.xls:** A handy worksheet that helps you track your progress as you pay down debt.

- ✔ **Future Plans and Goals.xls:** This worksheet gives you the elements you want to be sure to include as you set goals and track your progress. Be sure to go back and make changes as necessary to keep your goals realistic and achievable.

- ✔ **Household Budget Plan.doc:** This worksheet is a great way to get thinking about what comes in and what goes out. You can make adjustments and see the results.

- ✔ **IRS Form 982: Avoid Debt-Relief Taxes:** The amount of debt that is "forgiven" by your lender may be viewed as income for that tax year by the IRS. If you owed $300,000 on your home and you and your lender accepted an offer for $250,000 (a short sale), the IRS would view the $50,000 difference as regular earnings in that tax year. So you would owe taxes on $50,000. This is a simplistic example, and most cases are more complex. However, the main point is that you need to be aware of the potential tax liability involved in a short sale.

- ✔ **Money Gobblers.doc:** In the normal course of your day, you probably spend money almost as naturally as you breathe. Recognizing which of these money gobblers you really want to keep versus those you don't need is an important part of controlling your spending. The objective is to use this form to track where your cash goes so you can spend money on those things that you really want, not just on whatever comes along.

- ✔ **Monthly Expense Worksheet.doc:** The essential ingredient in controlling your expenses is knowing where your money is going and deciding whether you want that to continue. This form, which can be customized to your needs, gives you a good starting point for identifying monthly expenses and beginning a livable budget.

- ✔ **Monthly Income Worksheet.doc:** The second essential ingredient in a good budget (see the preceding bullet for the first) is knowing exactly how much you have to spend. Be sure to look at deductions from your paycheck to see whether they can be reduced to increase your take-home pay. A good example is reducing withholding for taxes if you always get a big refund.

- **Outstanding Debts.doc:** Fewer people than you would expect actually know how much they owe. This form helps you get a handle on the size of your debts and gives you a reality check on which to base your solutions.

- **Out-of-Pocket Expense Tracking Form.doc:** A handy form to record your cash expenses so you can get a better handle on why your money is disappearing.

- **Telephone Conversation Tracking Log.doc:** Good records are essential in getting a dispute or other request resolved. This form helps you keep track of who you spoke with and what was agreed upon.

- **Understanding Money and Credit.pdf:** This is a great booklet that helps you assess where you are, set goals, prepare a budget, and begin to save for the future. It includes great worksheets and tips.

Identity theft

Identity theft is on everybody's radar these days. This section provides tools to use to keep the damage to a minimum if you think you've been a victim of identity theft.

- **Fraud Alert Letter to Credit-Reporting Agency.doc:** Quick and concise notification of possible identity theft is essential to limiting damage to your credit and those creditors who may be victimized as well. This letter has all the essential ingredients you need to stop identity theft from going any further and begin to recover from it.

- **Chart Your Course of Action.pdf:** This sample format gets you started on the path to organization while tracking all your contacts with credit bureaus, creditors, and law-enforcement agencies.

- **Identity Theft Letter to Institutions Directly Involved.doc:** Your identity has been stolen and so have their products or services. Quickly letting creditors know about a theft not only helps your credit report but limits both your and the creditor's losses.

- **Identity Theft Letter to Institutions Not Directly Involved.doc:** Use this letter when you suspect your identity has been compromised but before you *know* someone is using it illegally. Placing passwords and safeguards on your account can help keep your credit and your identity safe from a thief who has your personal information.

- **Letter of Complaint of Identity Theft to the FTC.doc:** Use this letter of complaint to inform the FTC about a credit bureau's failure to remove fraudulent accounts opened due to identity theft.

Troubleshooting

I tried my best to compile programs that work on most computers with the minimum system requirements. Alas, your computer may differ, and some programs may not work properly for some reason.

The two likeliest problems are that you don't have enough memory (RAM) for the programs you want to use, or you have other programs running that are affecting installation or running of a program. If you get an error message such as `Not enough memory` or `Setup cannot continue`, try one or more of the following suggestions and then try using the software again:

- **Turn off any antivirus software running on your computer.** Installation programs sometimes mimic virus activity and may make your computer incorrectly believe that it's being infected by a virus.

- **Close all running programs.** The more programs you have running, the less memory is available to other programs. Installation programs typically update files and programs; so if you keep other programs running, installation may not work properly.

- **Have your local computer store add more RAM to your computer.** This is, admittedly, a drastic and somewhat expensive step. However, adding more memory can really help the speed of your computer and allow more programs to run at the same time.

If you have trouble with the CD-ROM, please call the Wiley Product Technical Support phone number at 800-762-2974. Outside the United States, call 1-317-572-3994. You can also contact Wiley Product Technical Support at `http://support.wiley.com`. John Wiley & Sons provides technical support only for installation and other general quality-control items. For technical support on the applications themselves, consult the program's vendor or author.

To place additional orders or to request information about other Wiley products, please call 877-762-2974.

Index

overdraft protection, 118, 264
overpaying taxes to get refund, 247
owner, account, in credit report history, 99

• P •

paid-as-agreed notation on credit report, 178, 333
paid compared to unpaid charge-offs, 174–176
pass-phrase compared to password, 303
passbook loan, 22, 76, 208, 320
passwords, 288–289, 303, 310, 312
Past Due on credit report, 103
payback arrangement, negotiating, 150
paycheck-to-paycheck living, terminating, 143
payday loan, 78, 333
payment history, credit score weighting of, 38, 39. *See also* history, credit
Payment Status on credit report, 103
payroll deductions, 142, 247–248, 271
PCs For Dummies (Gookin), 335
penalty fee, 15
permissible purpose for obtaining credit report, 88, 333
personal identification information, 31, 117, 118, 265. *See also* Social Security number
personal identification number (PIN), 303
phantom help mortgage rescue scam, 167
phishing scams, 287, 333
PIN (personal identification number), 303
Plus Score, 105, 333
police report for identity theft, 23, 298–299, 309
positive cash-flow position, definition, 51
post-dated check to collector, avoiding, 145, 147
postal service (Web site), 287, 290, 299, 310
pre-foreclosure sale, 20, 170, 317, 334
predatory lending, definition, 333
prepaid cash card, 75–76
prepayment penalties, mortgage, 18
prime rate, definition, 333
pro se bankruptcy, 194

profit motive of creditors, 10, 13, 67
Project HOPE (Web site), 166, 318
promotional inquiry, definition, 333
public records. *See also* bankruptcy
child support, unpaid, 184, 185, 193, 218
in credit report, 31, 126
definition, 333
judgments, 178–181, 183–188, 332
tax liens, 126, 182

• R •

RAL (refund anticipation loan), 78, 333
rapid scorer option, 108, 118
rate shopping for better credit, 135
re-aging of debt-managed accounts, 59
reaffirmation debt, definition, 207
reason code for credit score, 110, 333
reason statement for credit score, 110–111, 333
Recent Balance Information on credit report, 102
Recent Payment on credit report, 102
record keeping
for budgeting, 252–255
for identity theft damage control, 312
refinancing, mortgage, 18, 317, 333
refund anticipation loan (RAL), 78, 333
registry, check, 41, 76, 311
relationships, personal, financial stress on, 46. *See also* marriage
reloadable cash card, 75–76
Remark section on credit report, 103
rental of housing and credit status, 88, 92, 93, 197
repair, credit. *See* credit repair
repayment plan option for foreclosure avoidance, 19, 317
repo fee, 15
Reported Since on credit report, 102
repossession of goods, 147, 223, 315, 333
reputation as basis for creditworthiness, 10, 55
Responsibility on credit report, 102, 103
retail store credit card, 321–322, 333
retirement planning, 142, 216, 248–250

BUSINESS, CAREERS & PERSONAL FINANCE

Accounting For Dummies, 4th Edition*
978-0-470-24600-9

Bookkeeping Workbook For Dummies†
978-0-470-16983-4

Commodities For Dummies
978-0-470-04928-0

Doing Business in China For Dummies
978-0-470-04929-7

E-Mail Marketing For Dummies
978-0-470-19087-6

Job Interviews For Dummies, 3rd Edition*†
978-0-470-17748-8

Personal Finance Workbook For Dummies*†
978-0-470-09933-9

Real Estate License Exams For Dummies
978-0-7645-7623-2

Six Sigma For Dummies
978-0-7645-6798-8

Small Business Kit For Dummies, 2nd Edition*†
978-0-7645-5984-6

Telephone Sales For Dummies
978-0-470-16836-3

BUSINESS PRODUCTIVITY & MICROSOFT OFFICE

Access 2007 For Dummies
978-0-470-03649-5

Excel 2007 For Dummies
978-0-470-03737-9

Office 2007 For Dummies
978-0-470-00923-9

Outlook 2007 For Dummies
978-0-470-03830-7

PowerPoint 2007 For Dummies
978-0-470-04059-1

Project 2007 For Dummies
978-0-470-03651-8

QuickBooks 2008 For Dummies
978-0-470-18470-7

Quicken 2008 For Dummies
978-0-470-17473-9

Salesforce.com For Dummies, 2nd Edition
978-0-470-04893-1

Word 2007 For Dummies
978-0-470-03658-7

EDUCATION, HISTORY, REFERENCE & TEST PREPARATION

African American History For Dummies
978-0-7645-5469-8

Algebra For Dummies
978-0-7645-5325-7

Algebra Workbook For Dummies
978-0-7645-8467-1

Art History For Dummies
978-0-470-09910-0

ASVAB For Dummies, 2nd Edition
978-0-470-10671-6

British Military History For Dummies
978-0-470-03213-8

Calculus For Dummies
978-0-7645-2498-1

Canadian History For Dummies, 2nd Edition
978-0-470-83656-9

Geometry Workbook For Dummies
978-0-471-79940-5

The SAT I For Dummies, 6th Edition
978-0-7645-7193-0

Series 7 Exam For Dummies
978-0-470-09932-2

World History For Dummies
978-0-7645-5242-7

FOOD, HOME, GARDEN, HOBBIES & HOME

Bridge For Dummies, 2nd Edition
978-0-471-92426-5

Coin Collecting For Dummies, 2nd Edition
978-0-470-22275-1

Cooking Basics For Dummies, 3rd Edition
978-0-7645-7206-7

Drawing For Dummies
978-0-7645-5476-6

Etiquette For Dummies, 2nd Edition
978-0-470-10672-3

Gardening Basics For Dummies*†
978-0-470-03749-2

Knitting Patterns For Dummies
978-0-470-04556-5

Living Gluten-Free For Dummies†
978-0-471-77383-2

Painting Do-It-Yourself For Dummies
978-0-470-17533-0

HEALTH, SELF HELP, PARENTING & PETS

Anger Management For Dummies
978-0-470-03715-7

Anxiety & Depression Workbook For Dummies
978-0-7645-9793-0

Dieting For Dummies, 2nd Edition
978-0-7645-4149-0

Dog Training For Dummies, 2nd Edition
978-0-7645-8418-3

Horseback Riding For Dummies
978-0-470-09719-9

Infertility For Dummies†
978-0-470-11518-3

Meditation For Dummies with CD-ROM, 2nd Edition
978-0-471-77774-8

Post-Traumatic Stress Disorder For Dummies
978-0-470-04922-8

Puppies For Dummies, 2nd Edition
978-0-470-03717-1

Thyroid For Dummies, 2nd Edition†
978-0-471-78755-6

Type 1 Diabetes For Dummies*†
978-0-470-17811-9

---

* Separate Canadian edition also available
† Separate U.K. edition also available

Available wherever books are sold. For more information or to order direct: U.S. customers visit www.dummies.com or call 1-877-762-2974.
U.K. customers visit www.wileyeurope.com or call (0)1243 843291. Canadian customers visit www.wiley.ca or call 1-800-567-4797.

INTERNET & DIGITAL MEDIA

AdWords For Dummies
978-0-470-15252-2

Blogging For Dummies, 2nd Edition
978-0-470-23017-6

**Digital Photography All-in-One
Desk Reference For Dummies, 3rd Edition**
978-0-470-03743-0

Digital Photography For Dummies, 5th Edition
978-0-7645-9802-9

**Digital SLR Cameras & Photography
For Dummies, 2nd Edition**
978-0-470-14927-0

**eBay Business All-in-One Desk Reference
For Dummies**
978-0-7645-8438-1

eBay For Dummies, 5th Edition*
978-0-470-04529-9

eBay Listings That Sell For Dummies
978-0-471-78912-3

Facebook For Dummies
978-0-470-26273-3

The Internet For Dummies, 11th Edition
978-0-470-12174-0

Investing Online For Dummies, 5th Edition
978-0-7645-8456-5

iPod & iTunes For Dummies, 5th Edition
978-0-470-17474-6

MySpace For Dummies
978-0-470-09529-4

Podcasting For Dummies
978-0-471-74898-4

**Search Engine Optimization
For Dummies, 2nd Edition**
978-0-471-97998-2

Second Life For Dummies
978-0-470-18025-9

**Starting an eBay Business For Dummies,
3rd Edition†**
978-0-470-14924-9

GRAPHICS, DESIGN & WEB DEVELOPMENT

**Adobe Creative Suite 3 Design Premium
All-in-One Desk Reference For Dummies**
978-0-470-11724-8

**Adobe Web Suite CS3 All-in-One Desk
Reference For Dummies**
978-0-470-12099-6

AutoCAD 2008 For Dummies
978-0-470-11650-0

**Building a Web Site For Dummies,
3rd Edition**
978-0-470-14928-7

**Creating Web Pages All-in-One Desk
Reference For Dummies, 3rd Edition**
978-0-470-09629-1

**Creating Web Pages For Dummies,
8th Edition**
978-0-470-08030-6

Dreamweaver CS3 For Dummies
978-0-470-11490-2

Flash CS3 For Dummies
978-0-470-12100-9

Google SketchUp For Dummies
978-0-470-13744-4

InDesign CS3 For Dummies
978-0-470-11865-8

**Photoshop CS3 All-in-One
Desk Reference For Dummies**
978-0-470-11195-6

Photoshop CS3 For Dummies
978-0-470-11193-2

Photoshop Elements 5 For Dummies
978-0-470-09810-3

SolidWorks For Dummies
978-0-7645-9555-4

Visio 2007 For Dummies
978-0-470-08983-5

Web Design For Dummies, 2nd Edition
978-0-471-78117-2

Web Sites Do-It-Yourself For Dummies
978-0-470-16903-2

Web Stores Do-It-Yourself For Dummies
978-0-470-17443-2

LANGUAGES, RELIGION & SPIRITUALITY

Arabic For Dummies
978-0-471-77270-5

Chinese For Dummies, Audio Set
978-0-470-12766-7

French For Dummies
978-0-7645-5193-2

German For Dummies
978-0-7645-5195-6

Hebrew For Dummies
978-0-7645-5489-6

Ingles Para Dummies
978-0-7645-5427-8

Italian For Dummies, Audio Set
978-0-470-09586-7

Italian Verbs For Dummies
978-0-471-77389-4

Japanese For Dummies
978-0-7645-5429-2

Latin For Dummies
978-0-7645-5431-5

Portuguese For Dummies
978-0-471-78738-9

Russian For Dummies
978-0-471-78001-4

Spanish Phrases For Dummies
978-0-7645-7204-3

Spanish For Dummies
978-0-7645-5194-9

Spanish For Dummies, Audio Set
978-0-470-09585-0

The Bible For Dummies
978-0-7645-5296-0

Catholicism For Dummies
978-0-7645-5391-2

The Historical Jesus For Dummies
978-0-470-16785-4

Islam For Dummies
978-0-7645-5503-9

**Spirituality For Dummies,
2nd Edition**
978-0-470-19142-2

NETWORKING AND PROGRAMMING

ASP.NET 3.5 For Dummies
978-0-470-19592-5

C# 2008 For Dummies
978-0-470-19109-5

Hacking For Dummies, 2nd Edition
978-0-470-05235-8

Home Networking For Dummies, 4th Edition
978-0-470-11806-1

Java For Dummies, 4th Edition
978-0-470-08716-9

**Microsoft® SQL Server™ 2008 All-in-One
Desk Reference For Dummies**
978-0-470-17954-3

**Networking All-in-One Desk Reference
For Dummies, 2nd Edition**
978-0-7645-9939-2

**Networking For Dummies,
8th Edition**
978-0-470-05620-2

SharePoint 2007 For Dummies
978-0-470-09941-4

**Wireless Home Networking
For Dummies, 2nd Edition**
978-0-471-74940-0